A CASE ABOUT AMY

In the series
Health, Society, and Policy,
edited by Sheryl Ruzek and Irving Kenneth Zola

A CASE ABOUT AMY

R. C. SMITH

FOREWORD BY FRANK G. BOWE

TEMPLE UNIVERSITY PRESS

PHILADELPHIA

Temple University Press
Philadelphia 19122
Copyright © 1996 by R. C. Smith
ALL RIGHTS RESERVED
Published 1996
Printed in the United States of America

∞ The paper used in this book meets the
requirements of the American National Standard for
Information Sciences—Permanence of Paper for Printed Library
Materials, ANSI Z39.48-1984

TEXT DESIGN BY WILL BOEHM

Library of Congress Cataloging-in-Publication Data

Smith, R. C., 1927–
    A case about Amy / R. C. Smith ; foreword by Frank G. Bowe.
    p.   cm. — (Health, society, and policy)
    Includes bibliographical references and index.
    ISBN 1-56639-411-2 (alk. paper). — ISBN 1-56639-412-0 (pbk. : alk. paper)
    1. Rowley, Amy—Trials, litigation, etc.   2. Deaf—Education—Law and
legislation—United States.   3. Handicapped children—Education—Law and
legislation—United States.   I. Title.   II. Series.
KF228.R63S45   1996
371.91′23—dc20   95-34376

The poem by Wanda Barbara on page 311 was originally published by
Atlantis/ADAPT in *Incitement* (January–February 1993): 6. Reprinted by permission
of Wanda Barbara.

To the parents
of children with disabilities,
specifically to the numerous parents
whose names are herein,
but in a general way to all,
for being there daily and nightly
for their kids

CONTENTS

Contents

4

Vindication by Trial / 63

5

A Case about Amy / 92

6

A "Voice" in the Classroom / 114

7

"Full Potential" in the Court / 126

8

Maybe It Wouldn't Happen Today / 168

9

What Amy Hears / 182

10

A Matter of Growth / 198

11

Amy in Oz / 220

Contents

FOREWORD

FRANK G. BOWE

Since the passage in 1975 of what is now the Individuals with Disabilities Education Act (IDEA), a number of important judicial interpretations of this landmark special education law have been issued. The first case to reach the United States Supreme Court, and the most important one, was the 1982 *Board of Education, Hendrick Hudson Central School District v. Rowley* case (458 U.S. 176, 181). The *Rowley* case remains the Court's definitive answer to the most central question raised by the law: What, exactly, is an "appropriate" education for children with disabilities?

This is the decision about which R. C. Smith writes in *A Case about Amy.* The case's prominence alone makes this book important. What makes it enjoyable reading is the way Smith tells the story—setting the stage, explaining the background, elucidating the issues involved, and introducing the main characters in the case. The reader sees all sides of the story as the case winds its way to the Supreme Court.

Along the way, Smith introduces the reader to the disability of deafness, to the deaf culture into which Amy was born, and to the problems she encountered as she began her schooling in her neighborhood public school, problems that gave rise to the court action. For Amy, and for her parents, Furnace Woods Elementary School was a "hearing" school—in many ways, a foreign place. By the time the reader gets to the Supreme Court's decision in *Rowley,* the story no longer is merely a case; it is real people confronting daunting challenges. That is why *A Case about Amy* is such a rewarding read: Smith has the writing ability to teach us public policy through one child's story—and to make that story interesting.

I first learned of *A Case about Amy* when Nancy and Clifford Rowley called me to discuss the project, then in the early planning stages. They told me they had been approached by North Carolina writer R. C. Smith and, knowing that I knew Smith, sought my advice on how to respond to his request to write a book about the case. The deaf community in the United States is quite closely knit; I had known the Rowleys for several years and understood their concerns. I encouraged them to cooperate, because their story was, and is, an important one, and because I knew Smith would do it justice. I am pleased, now that the project has been completed, that everything worked out so well.

The *Rowley* decision stands for the proposition that in what is now the IDEA, Congress limited the amount and quality of services to which children with disabilities are entitled to those that are necessary so that the children receive an education that is good enough to enable them to make passing grades, that is, to "benefit" from their education. This is a lower standard than many advocates wish had been set. However, Congress has had several opportunities over the years to reverse the Supreme Court's decision in *Rowley*—and never has done so. That is why *A Case about Amy* is and will remain a timely contribution to the literature on special education case law.

ACKNOWLEDGMENTS

I owe a debt to Robert Taggart, head of the Office of Youth Programs for the U.S. Department of Labor in 1979 for first exposing me to problems of individuals with disabilities by persuading me in 1979 to write the monograph that became *Seven Special Kids.*

I probably would not have taken up work on this book in 1984 without a $15,000 start-up expense grant from Gordon Berlin, then a program officer at the Ford Foundation. In 1989 and 1991 I received another $5,000 in grants from the Mary Biddle Duke Foundation in Durham, North Carolina. These grants provided psychological and economic boosts during a difficult period in the project. My deep gratitude for this assistance goes to Doug Zinn and Jim and Mary Semans.

Others deserve thanks for help provided during the preparation of the manuscript. I am most indebted to Bob Wilson and Bill Finger, two fine writers whose editorial suggestions and support were always helpful. Doris Betts provided valuable motivational support and sound editorial advice. Frank Bowe supported the project energetically from the very beginning. Andi Reynolds, Dr. Paula Burger, David Dodson, Lou Ann Walker, John Justice, Sarah Geer, Paul Hippolitus, Phil Calkins, Beth Waterfall, and Larry Queen provided suggestions, contacts, and morale maintenance. I owe a special debt of gratitude to George Autry, president of MDC, Inc. in Chapel Hill, North Carolina, who supported the project by allowing me to take leaves of absence to pursue the work while I was in his employ.

I am grateful to all of the individuals whose stories appear in this volume for their willingness to testify in print and to have their names acknowledged. I appreciate editorial suggestions made by Michael Ames, editor-in-chief at Temple University Press, which helped significantly to sharpen the focus of the book. I take full responsibility for any errors of fact or judgment that remain herein.

Last, and most important, I owe a debt of gratitude to my wife Kathryn for her invaluable help in interviewing, transcribing notes, and assisting with computer editing and printouts, and for the sacrifices she made and the loving support she gave during the years of work on this project.

When not otherwise indicated in footnotes or in the text, quotations used in this book come from a variety of sources. First, I had access to the extensive files kept over the years by the Rowley family before, during, and after Amy's public schooling. Second, I had access to records, letters, and memoranda from the official files kept in the Hendrick Hudson Central School District office during the years of her schooling there. Additionally, I conducted numerous interviews, many of them on tape, with members of the Rowley family and with individuals on both sides of the long legal dispute. I have drawn also from letters written to me by some of these players.

LEGAL CHRONOLOGY

April 1977 Parents of Amy Rowley file complaint with the Civil Rights Division of the Department of Health, Education and Welfare charging discrimination on the part of the Hendrick Hudson Central School District against their deaf daughter, Amy, under Section 504 of the Rehabilitation Act of 1973. The Rowleys seek a sign language interpreter for Amy's kindergarten classes with hearing students beginning the following September.

May 1978 Office for Civil Rights, Department of Health, Education and Welfare, finds Hendrick Hudson Central School District in compliance with Section 504 of the Rehabilitation Act of 1973.

December 1978 Impartial hearing by the Hendrick Hudson Central School District is held to determine whether the district is in compliance with the Education for All Handicapped Children Act of 1975.

January 1979 Impartial hearing examiner rules that Amy is receiving an "appropriate" education under terms of the Education for All Handicapped Children Act. Rowleys appeal to the New York State Commissioner of Education.

April 1979 State commissioner of education denies the appeal, affirming the impartial hearing examiner's decision.

September–October 1979 Hearings are held before a judge in United States District Court for the Second District of New York on the question of whether Amy Rowley is receiving an appropriate education from the Hendrick Hudson Central School District.

December 1979 Judge rules that Amy's education is not appropriate and orders a sign language interpreter for all school periods in which academic subjects are taught. Judge's full opinion, delivered in January 1980, calls for the district to supply Amy with an education providing the opportunity to reach her full potential commensurate with the opportunity provided other students. Hendrick Hudson Central School District appeals to Second Circuit Court of Appeals of New York.

May 1980 Hendrick Hudson District's appeal is heard by the three-judge Second Circuit Court of Appeals.

July 1980 Second Circuit Court upholds Judge Broderick's decision by a 2 to 1 vote, ruling that a sign language interpreter is necessary for Amy to have an opportunity to learn equal to that of hearing students.

December 1980 Hendrick Hudson Central School District petitions the Supreme Court of the United States to review the *Rowley* case.

November 1981 The Supreme Court announces it will accept the *Rowley* case for review.

March 1982 The Supreme Court hears *Hendrick Hudson Central School District v. Rowley.*

June 1982 The Supreme Court rules 6 to 3, overturning the lower courts' decisions and declaring that Amy is receiving an appropriate education without the sign language interpreter. Majority decision holds that children with disabilities who are making progress in school grade by grade are receiving an appropriate education.

Note: Other legal efforts were made on behalf of Amy Rowley following the Supreme Court decision. None was successful in bringing about a ruling restoring the sign language interpreter. Further impartial hearings were held in December 1982 and August 1983, the first on the Rowleys' contention that the Supreme Court order had dealt with four-year-old evidence and that Amy's need for an interpreter had since increased, and the second based on procedural matters not taken up in the district court hearing. In both parts, the hearing examiner ruled in favor of the school district. To this day, the *Rowley* case remains the sole substantive ruling by the Supreme Court on the Education for All Handicapped Children Act, since renamed the Individuals with Disabilities Education Act (IDEA).

A CASE ABOUT AMY

1

Time Tears Us Apart

Amy thought Ashokan was the most beautiful place she had ever seen. The woods were deep and secret and the hills were for climbing. Morning and afternoon, the campers followed the trails to blacksmithing and broom-making and to the pond, where they found insects in leaflike homes, baby dragonflies, and newts. They went fishing with live worms for bait, using poles they had made themselves.

Amy's mother, Nancy Rowley, had arranged for a woman who had a mentally retarded son in the student visiting group to keep an eye on Amy. Such a woman would understand the needs of a child with a disability, Nancy reasoned. But Amy stopped being scared almost as soon as she got to Ashokan. The outdoors were for the eyes, anyway, and Amy dashed about, gulping down the sights. The gorge made them all gasp with pleasure. And then they got to feed the animals. Amy liked that. She had animals of her own at home—a cat, a rabbit, a bird, a turtle, and three fish.

She had other interests as well. She loved libraries with their bulging stock of adventure. She burrowed inside and read Nancy Drew mysteries. As a Girl Scout, she made up a script for a play. A week with her classmates in a camp in the Catskills was made to order for her. At Ashokan she sensed a freedom that was different and more important for her than for her classmates. They were simply out of school. She was out of a world of hassle, a world of constantly being observed and discussed. That world was transformed in the woods. She could run to her heart's content.

She was free—or almost so. Someone had been going through her clothes. Later on, she learned that adults in charge of the school-sponsored camping trip were looking for her hearing aids. She had not brought them with her. The school's "trainer"—a wireless receiver used in the classroom to amplify sound directly to her—was on the blink again. And what good would it do out here, anyway? When it was working, it helped only in direct conversation with the teacher and then only if no other student asked a question. She had decided to make Ashokan a visual, private experience once she learned that she would not have an interpreter with her.

No interpreter out here, no interpreter now in class. And for all of her parents' long fight in court, Amy realized that she had never known how important an interpreter would be until she lost the one she had had the previous two years. This sense of loss had arisen sharply in her over the last few weeks as the class talked about the field trip to Ashokan. She could make little out of this free-form, classroomwide, question-and-answer session, with students sounding off from around the room, as it was impossible to lip-read such quick exchanges. Fortunately, there were handouts. Studying these afterward, she got an idea of where they would be going and what they would be doing.

She vowed to live within her fully functioning senses of sight, smell, and touch, but it was a vow difficult to keep. Once, on a long hike to the gorge, the guide up front had stopped the straggling line of children to make a little speech. Halfway back in the column, Amy could make nothing of it. She grabbed Mr. Brett, her teacher, who was walking nearby, and he repeated what had been said in his Australian–English accent, which she had always had to struggle to lip-read. She shook her head: she could not understand. Finally, Mr. Brett stripped some white bark off a tree and carved the words the guide had used on it for her. She thought it was a nice thing for him to have done.

She liked Mr. Brett because he did try hard, but the incident with the tree bark also had the effect of reminding her that she would be back in class soon and depending heavily on her friend, Marjorie, for help in understanding what was said. All the same, she kept the white piece of bark by her bedside for years, to remind her of Ashokan, her first real love affair with nature. And the words lingered in her mind long after the bark had darkened, making the carving difficult to read: *conifers—evergreen trees/deciduous—trees that shed leaves.*

Nancy Rowley had come so close to forbidding Amy to go to Ashokan with her class. Amy's teacher of the deaf, the woman who spent an hour every day with her out of class, could not go along. That meant that nobody could sign with Amy, nobody could communicate quickly information Amy might vitally need, with a high chance of being understood. After all the years of battling in the courts, Nancy had numbly accepted that the school would never voluntarily provide a classroom sign interpreter for Amy. But she thought that in the case of the Ashokan trip, she had a solution. She and her husband, Clifford, would pay for an interpreter to go along with Amy.

They put the idea to the school district through the district's attorneys. Both deaf themselves, the Rowleys were sure Amy could not experience what the other children would at Ashokan without interpretive help. Not only would they pay for Amy's interpreter; they would do anything else the district might require to assure the courts that the district had acted without prejudice to its case. The district's case was and had always been that Amy did not need a sign language interpreter. A few days before Amy was to leave with her classmates for Ashokan, the Rowleys learned that the school district was adamant: no interpreter, no matter who paid.

In the spring of 1983, the Rowley family was near the end of its rope. To have had an interpreter in Amy's classroom for two years and then to have lost that service to a decision by the Supreme Court seemed cruel and final. The case had been remanded to the district court where it had begun, but to the Rowleys that sounded like starting all over again. And problems with their children were mounting. Tearful and angry one day, Amy had simply refused to go to school. That was not like her. Then John, two years older and the only hearing member of the family, had been asked not to return to his parochial school. That was a kind of last stop for him. His parents had taken him out of his sister's school, Furnace Woods, where he had been the object of taunts over her court case. He had been in fights with other boys in school and was considered a "behavior problem." Given the circumstances, the Rowleys were seriously worried about him.

They began casting about for alternatives. A friend had a child in the school system in Mountain Lakes, New Jersey. The system was described as an excellent one, and it maintained one school for the deaf from which students were mainstreamed into the regular school part-time or fully. There would be no problem getting sign language interpretation in the classroom, the Rowleys were told, if Amy needed it. In February, the Rowleys had gone house hunting in Mountain Lakes. By March, when the effort to get an interpreter for Amy at Ashokan failed, Nancy was ready to leave. "Honey," she messaged Clifford in his office on the TTY, a telephone–typewriter device, "I'm really sick of the whole thing and am ready to move to Mountain Lakes."

In April 1983, federal judge Vincent L. Broderick, who had ruled originally in favor of the family at the district court level, maintained that he had no further jurisdiction to hear the Rowleys' final pleas. To Nancy, that was the last blow. "It looks to me that this can be an ongoing thing without ever getting things or Amy's needs accomplished, that's my feeling," she told the attorney who presented her with the bad news. "Time tears us apart."

The Rowleys' legal efforts on behalf of their daughter, which by then had extended over to seven years—more than half of Amy's lifetime—ended as they had begun, with the family losing another hearing before a school-appointed judge. Even as this decision was being announced in September 1983, a moving van was backing up to the Rowleys' house for their move to Mountain Lakes.

In December the family learned that they would have to pay $4,600 in costs for the Supreme Court action. To secure this payment, the school district had a lien placed on their house in Peekskill, which they had put up for sale.

I wrote to the Rowleys about the possibility of a book on the case that December and found myself, one spring day in 1984, at the Rowleys' being entertained by Amy herself. She had scampered out from behind her parents, leaving an image of ballet in my mind from first sight. It was not just her body and legs but her entire face and gesticulating hands that were set to dancing by the act of motion or speech. Her whole routine might have seemed a bit theatrical, even for a twelve-year-old, if not for her smile, which was fresh and full of sparkle.

As we spoke, she responded readily to my questions, lipreading me skillfully, tilting her head teasingly from side to side as though contemplating the ideal response to the question. Nancy had said that we were going to a seafood restaurant for dinner. Amy asked me if I liked seafood. It was a rhetorical question. My easy nod and too-vigorously lip-shaped "yes" were merely stage business to introduce Amy's monologue. "Yuck," she said, rolling her eyes. She then proceeded into an elaborately staged skit in which she prepared and then proceeded to eat an entire seafood dinner. She put on the tartar sauce first ("I like tartar sauce"), poured over it what might have been as much as a half-bottle of red seafood sauce, and then squeezed, very particularly, three sliced lemon halves over the whole business. "Then," she said, lifting a finger, "I can eat it." She proceeded to pantomime the eating and although her hands were busy with this process, she conveyed somehow the particular impression of holding her nose all the while.

I found myself wondering how much of this expressiveness was simply gifted mimicry and how much was the result of her deafness, a way of communicating visually to a world filled with soundless words. I had been surprised by the ease with which she lip-read me, but even more by the natural sound of her voice. The few deaf people I had met spoke a little like blind people doing semaphore signals by memorized positions: what they were doing was second-hand, operating on their faith and the tolerance of those with whom they were communicating. Clifford spoke fairly well, Nancy even better. Amy's speech was identified as coming from a deaf person only by the slightest monotone, and I asked myself, if I had not known she was deaf, would I have noticed even that?

I wanted to know what Amy thought about the matter so long at issue between her parents and the Hendrick Hudson School District now that she was in a school in Mountain Lakes that provided a sign language interpreter in her classroom. She listened, taking in the question, and the light of play faded from her face. I should talk with her mother about that. Taking a different tack, I asked about her best friends in Mountain Lakes. Her face brightened and she began to toll off the names of her schoolgirl friends. Her eyes glistened with delight. She was not merely telling me their names, she was presenting these hearing girls who were her classmates to me formally, one by one.

Nancy appeared with a piece of writing Amy had done. "She thinks she wants to be a writer," Nancy said, looking down at her daughter with amused pride. Amy had written about the author at the end of her children's story: "Amy Rowley lives in Malibu Beach with her husband and six kids. She wrote this book when she was ten years old. It has won 275 awards." Amy had sneaked up to look over my shoulder. "It's actually 276," she said. "I made a mistake."

About this time I noticed that John had disappeared. He had other things to do, Nancy said, and could not come to dinner with us. She had noted in her letter accepting my offer to write about the case that John had been the most miserable one during the troubled times. "Poor Johnny," she said, "we love him so. He's a sensitive boy and all this was very hard on him." If Amy was unwilling to look back at what happened, Johnny was unwilling to participate at all. He had been polite and then he was gone.

Nancy gestured for me to follow her into the hallway beyond the kitchen. She and Clifford were taking me downstairs to the recreation room. There, piled on the floor, were the "personal records of the case" that Nancy had alluded to in her letter. My mouth must have gaped, for they both laughed. The records were a four-drawer, stand-up file's worth: court documents, letters, stacks of press clippings rubber-banded together. In two separate grocery cartons on the floor were stacks of 8-by-11 printouts, filled with alternately red and black typing. Following my eyes, Clifford said, "TTY tapes." "Every talk we had with anyone about the case, going back to 1978, maybe 1977," Nancy added.

She obviously wanted to talk about how I planned to write the book. I realized that this was the moment of truth for my fears of communication. I found that even as we sat, looking directly at each other, I had to repeat words occasionally. Still, all went reasonably well until I mentioned the hope that I could find an agent to sell the book. I had trouble getting across the concept of a literary agent, especially to Nancy, who was having difficulty with my articulation. I tried to simplify. When words were not being understood, I fell into an exaggerated movement of the lips, an action I have since learned makes lipreading even more difficult. I even found myself talking louder and, realizing that, felt at once ridiculous and glad that Clifford and Nancy couldn't know. I repeated phrases, invented variations, sweated, and repeated again. Clifford helped Nancy with my words and we got past the literary agent. But I had written something else in my letter that bothered Nancy, "Of course, if you got an offer from James Michener to write this book, you would be free to take it and ought to take it." It was a trivial, probably stupid thing to say, but I was trying to convey that I felt privileged to have this opportunity and that they would have a better chance of widespread notice of the book with a well-known author. Nancy seemed baffled by the words, which she read back to me from the letter. It crossed my mind that she might not recognize the name Michener and so find my little half-joke mystifying. Then I thought she might very well know Michener by name and wonder seriously if he had some interest in the project. Finally, she might have wondered, with some justification, why I would bring up something like this.

For long moments, I felt as though I had fallen into a void. Communication had broken down. How long might it take to clear up such a misunderstanding? These nice, bright people had a level I could not reach on which they communicated with each other with signs and speech. I had a communication style limited to words—I had never thought of this as a "limitation" before—that might prove insufficient to them without visual support. Clearly, deafness involved more than merely a loss of the sense we call hearing; it had to do with how language develops, with how we communicate, and, most deeply, how we understand.

In any event, this moment of crisis passed. Nancy took my arm and said: "I want you to meet the cat." We went back upstairs to where an unremarkable-looking animal was stretched out in feline indifference. Nancy explained to me that while the cat still meowed at John for attention, it had learned to put its paws on the other members of the family. I thought, Well, if the cat can figure out how to communicate with deaf people, maybe even I can do it. As I glanced at Nancy, I thought that might have been the intended lesson. In effect, without saying it, she was saying, Be patient. If I was right, we were communicating better already.

I got another lesson before we left the house for dinner. Amy and Nancy were changing their clothes and Clifford was out on the deck when the phone rang and lights in the kitchen began blinking. I gestured for Clifford to come in, and he quickly ascertained that it was not a TTY call. I took the phone and a man's voice asked if I was Clifford Rowley. No, I said, but he is here. Do you have a TTY? There was a significant pause, long enough so that I knew the answer even before the puzzled "what?" response. I explained about the TTY. Mr. Rowley is deaf, I said. The caller turned out to be an electrician who had been asked to change an electrical meter. He had talked with John and either had not gotten or had not absorbed the information that John's parents were deaf. Now the electrician wanted a time to come by. Give me a time, I suggested, and I will try it on Mr. Rowley.

Clifford was standing by me all this time, aware that the call related to him in some way. The electrician suggested next Tuesday night at 6:30. I explained the situation to Clifford, who remembered asking Johnny to call the electrician, and the time was readily agreed upon. I relayed this message. There was another significant pause at the other end of the line. What do I do, the electrician wanted to know in a tone that suggested that he wished he could send someone else. It will be all right—here I was reassuring someone already—if you just ring the doorbell, they will see a light flash and let you in. The silence on the other end now spoke volumes. You won't have any trouble communicating with them, I found myself telling the electrician. They read lips very well.

The electrician would enter what might seem to him to be the walled city of the deaf for a little while, apprehensive, worried about his own ignorance of their ways, afraid of embarrassing himself. He would do the little job that brought him there and then go away. He would tell the story later, omitting the part about his fears. He would talk about it as though it were a visit to a foreign country, not so difficult a passage as he had feared, but one he had no intention of ever making again.

At La Guardia Airport and on the flight back home to Raleigh-Durham, I read federal district court and appellate court decisions, both of which had favored the Rowleys. Then I read the Supreme Court decision in what was styled *Hendrick Hudson Board of Education v. Rowley* from June 1982, which had upheld the school district's position that a sign language interpreter was not necessary for Amy, thus overturning the lower courts' decisions. The next morning I went through the process again, this time concentrating harder on the dissents. The first was by Walter R. Mansfield, a judge on the Second Circuit Court of Appeals in New York City, who had dissented in that appellate court's two-to-one upholding of the Rowley victory in district court. The second was by the three-justice minority in the Supreme Court, Justices Byron R. White, William J. Brennan, Jr., and Thurgood Marshall, who found that the Rowleys were right. Looking at these dissents, I found myself hard pressed to grasp that the documents referred to the same case.

To Judge Mansfield, the education of Amy Rowley up to the time her case was considered by the district court was a total success. She had made remarkable progress, thanks to the school's "Herculean" efforts. She had indeed far outstripped, in that progress, Congress' purpose in passing the Education for All Handicapped Children Act, which Judge Mansfield construed as an educational level "that would enable the child [with a disability] to be as free as reasonably possible from dependency on others."*

---

* United States Court of Appeals, Second Circuit, Amy Rowley by her parents v. Board of Education of Hendrick Hudson Central School District and Commissioner of Education of State of New York, July 17, 1980, pp. 4, 11.

To the Supreme Court dissenters, on the other hand, the evidence was that Amy understood scarcely more than half of what was being said in the classroom. This, said the minority, was in direct contradiction to Congress' intent, which was to provide public school students with disabilities "an equal chance to learn if reasonably possible." On the issue of what Congress had intended, Justice Harry A. Blackmun sided with the minority, concluding that "equal opportunity" was the standard. But Blackmun separately concurred with the Supreme Court majority, finding that Amy had received an equal opportunity through her education.

Based on the language of the dissents, then, Amy was getting either much less or much more out of her educational opportunity than Congress had required. And Congress either had required only that she become as free as possible from dependence or that she have an opportunity to learn as much as she could. How could two readings of the same legislative history and two scrutinies of the same lower court records have left learned jurists so far apart? Judge Mansfield's language brought me up short. Who would consider a child such as the alert, intelligent one I had just met as likely to be dependent on anyone when she became an adult? And could the Congress of the United States really have passed legislation that was *not* intended to provide an equal opportunity for education to an entire category of American children?

The boxes of rubber-banded, dated records I had asked the Rowleys to ship me by air express would provide answers to some of these questions. The metal files devoted to the case in the school district's office would also be accessible to me, with the Rowleys' permission to examine them. Through clerks' offices or from Michael Chatoff, the Rowleys' attorney during most of the court proceedings, I could get other court records, including an official transcript of the evidentiary hearings in district court.

At a rudimentary level, I had some little experience qualifying me to undertake this work. Since 1968, when I left the newspaper business, I had been employed by a nonprofit organization in Chapel Hill, N.C., known as MDC (originally the North Carolina Manpower Development Corporation). With a mixture of public and private funding, MDC's task had been to seek ways of assisting disadvantaged Americans. This had led me to an interest in those young Americans most likely to have extreme difficulties in finding employment—those with disabilities. I had written a book-length monograph (*Seven Special Kids*, 1983) on this subject for the Office of Youth Programs of the United States Department of Labor.

And yet, I had concerns, not all of which I was sure I understood. My friends in the disability movement had urged me to choose a different youthful subject to write about. They saw Amy Rowley as a privileged, middle-class youth for whom at least some efforts at accommodation had been mounted by the school district. They urged me to choose a more severely handicapped child, a minority child preferably, in a situation in which nothing had been done for him or her. I thought the historical importance of the *Rowley* case—the only one that had reached the Supreme Court under the Education for All Handicapped Children Act—overrode this argument, but I had other qualms.

My friends had asked me to consider whether the *Rowley* case was the right one for me; I found myself wondering whether I was the right person for a book about the *Rowley* case. I knew next to nothing about deafness. What I had learned about disability generally from two years' work on *Seven Special Kids* seemed to me only what any visitor from another planet would learn on a guided tour led by knowledgeable people from this planet. I had no friends who themselves had disabilities. I had nagging suspicions about myself on this score that I had never faced.

In short, I went into the business of writing this book full of doubts. For all that, I knew it was too late to turn back. The little lever that operates a reporter's mind had clicked on the "why?" button. I could not understand from what I had read why a *Rowley* case had occurred at all and why it had produced the outcome I had been reading about. I knew I would not be satisfied until I had answers to these questions. I had a mystery story on my hands.

2

The Battle Joined

Nancy Rowley first approached Furnace Woods Elementary School Principal Joseph Zavarella in the spring of 1976, almost eighteen months before Amy would be ready to enroll in kindergarten. In a letter to Assistant Superintendent of Schools Charles Eible, dated April 26, she described Zavarella as being cooperative, understanding, and willing to help.

What she wanted of Eible, who was later to become superintendent of schools, she made very clear. Amy was presently enrolled in Croton Nursery School. Nancy wanted to enroll her in Furnace Woods in September 1977, integrating her in a hearing setting with the help of an "interpreter-tutor" in the classroom. She had left Zavarella some literature and asked him to pass it along to Eible before the three of them sat down to talk.

A certified teacher of the deaf, Nancy had kept up with advances in deaf education and had worked extensively with deaf children. The literature she had left Zavarella dealt with the concept of "mainstreaming" by which children with handicaps are placed in classes with other children. This concept had been enacted into national legislation in 1975, with the Education for All Handicapped Children Act (P.L. 94-142), which called for providing all children with disabilities a "free and appropriate education" in "the least restrictive environment."

While the act was new, the concept of mainstreaming was not. The literature Nancy had left with Zavarella included an article by McKay Vernon and Hugh Prickett, Jr., of Western Maryland College, who noted that mainstreaming had been practiced, after a fashion, for twenty-five years and, they contended, had "failed miserably for the overwhelming number of deaf children." They came down particularly heavily against the practice of putting deaf children in classes with hearing children, arming them with only a hearing aid and out-of-class resource help.*

"If he is a good lip reader," the article claimed, "he may get from 5 to 20 percent of what the teacher says when the teacher's lips can be seen. . . . When student discussion takes place, the situation is even more impossible. By the time the deaf youngster locates the student who is speaking, someone else has started to talk. Thus the deaf individual misses out completely" (p. 6).

Mainstreaming could succeed, the authors observed, when an "interpreter–tutor" was present in the classroom to interpret into sign language what the regular classroom teacher said. This individual could help not only the deaf students but also the hearing ones, many of whom needed tutoring. And the hearing students would be helped to learn sign language, which fascinated many of them. In effect—the article continued, the deaf child or children contributed to the education of the class, while all class members profited from the presence of the person serving as a skilled teacher's assistant.

Nancy knew that this method was not just a pipe dream of two scholars but was being practiced daily in a number of school districts across the country. The authors' description of the failure of "mainstreaming" comported exactly with Nancy's experience as a teacher of deaf children. Moreover, the interpreter–tutor approach seemed to her perfect for Amy, who had been brought up with total communication—sign language as well as lipreading and amplification of her residual hearing.

Amy had no business being deaf. Neither Nancy nor Clifford had a history of deafness in their families and each of them had become deaf as a result of childhood disease. Their son John was born with normal hearing. Amy came into the world with every likelihood of being a hearing person.

However, on August 11, 1973, when she was seventeen months old, Amy ran a fever of 103 degrees. Clifford and Nancy were in the Adirondacks with friends at the time and were sufficiently worried to rush her home to a Tar-

---

* "Mainstreaming: Issues and a Model Plan," *Audiology, Hearing, and Education* (February–March 1976): 10.

rytown hospital where a doctor examined her, ordered a medication, and said that everything would be all right. The Rowleys were skeptical. Along with many deaf people, they believed that doctors knew very little about deafness. They had been worried for some time, noting that their daughter's speech had not progressed as John's had at a comparable age.

When Amy was three, Clifford and Nancy, both excellent swimmers, were invited to Lake Placid for the Deaf Olympics. Clifford's hearing parents, Elmer and Thelma ("Bunny") Rowley, knew how important the opportunity was for them and offered to keep Amy and John for the weekend. Both remember it as being one of the longest weekends of their lives, with Amy screaming for her mother each time they approached her. After they finally got their granddaughter to bed and had collapsed on a couch to watch television, Elmer, noting that Amy had walked away from him once when he was talking to her, told his wife that he didn't think Amy heard him. When Clifford and Nancy came home, he passed on the message.

A hearing test at Columbia University in a free program provided for children of deaf parents resulted in a referral to Westchester County Medical Center (familiarly called "Grasslands") where Dr. Barbara Kligerman, chief of the speech and hearing center, tested Amy. Kligerman found that Amy had some hearing at the lower frequencies, where gross vowel sounds are found, but as the frequencies went higher into the area where consonant sounds occur, along with the ability to discriminate and understand speech, she was deficient. Her speech and language development already had been delayed. She was seriously hearing impaired; more tests would be needed to determine how seriously. The audiologist was impressed with the Rowleys' calmness when she gave them the news, but she was used to dealing with deaf children of hearing parents—the great majority of deaf children—to whom the news of their child's deafness is often devastating. To Clifford and Nancy, deafness was not something to tear their hair over, but to get to work on.

So, while Bunny Rowley, had difficulty accepting the news at first, remembering how difficult Clifford's childhood had been for him, he and his wife were ready to accept Amy's deafness. As Amy grew, her residual hearing decreased. Privately, Kligerman speculated that the child might well have had more hearing before she had examined her. While Amy was classified as hearing impaired in 1974, by 1976—when she was four and one-half years old—she was classified through continuous testing as deaf. But by this time, Amy's parents had taught her signed English, a sign language that they thought would make it easier for Amy to follow an interpreter in the classroom and to learn to write English. She could always learn American Sign Language, the richer, more complex language most deaf adults, including the Rowleys, used later on. They thought the best way for Amy to compete and succeed in the hearing world lay in using all available communications skills. The Rowleys were determined that their daughter continue to learn in that way during her public schooling years.

Nancy Rowley saw no reason Amy would not be welcomed into a school in which the other children were hearing. She, herself, had grown up in an atmosphere of support from family and friends and assumed that other hearing people would be receptive. She believed that their lack of knowledge of the real issues of deafness was all that kept them from being more understanding. She was shocked at her own first overt experience with discrimination, from a woman staff member at the local community college who walked ahead of her (making lipreading impossible) and finally told her that she had no interest in opening channels of communication with the deaf and that a sign language course at the college was out of the question.

The incident was upsetting but not nearly so much as the silence from school officials about enrollment of Amy in Furnace Woods Elementary School with a sign language interpreter. When a full year had passed since Nancy's first communication with Eible, she and Cliff talked about it and shared their concerns. On March 15, 1977, six months before they hoped that Amy would be entering kindergarten, Nancy wrote a letter to Thomas Jenkins, then superintendent of schools for the district, reminding him of the contact and conversations about Amy. "Now what I want specifically from you," she wrote, "is to provide an interpreter for Amy when she enters Furnace Woods school." At the bottom of the page, she indicated that she had sent a copy of the letter to Seymour "Sy" Dubow, chief counsel for the National Center for Law and the Deaf.

Nancy had met Dubow at a Gallaudet University workshop on the Education for All Handicapped Children Act. She was attending as a representative of the Westchester Community Services for the Hearing Impaired, a group she had founded. The workshop outlined the responsibility of the school to involve parents significantly in determining services needed for a handicapped child. It outlined processes by which the parent could challenge the decision of a school district. A role-playing script for parents stressed the need for compromise but also established the courts as the last recourse in the event agreement was impossible.

In view of what subsequently happened, Jenkins' response to Nancy's letter is interesting. "Your letter of March 15, 1977, has been forwarded to Raymond Kuntz, attorney for the Hendrick Hudson School District, for a legal interpretation of the district's obligation under state and/or federal law," he responded. "Following the receipt of this information and the registration and screening of all potential kindergartners, a review of Amy's placement and our obligations will be made." The Rowleys did not miss the use of the word "obligations" twice or of the word "placement." Did it mean, Nancy and Cliff wondered, that there was a question about whether Amy would be enrolled in Furnace Woods?

Their deepest fear was that the district would try to put Amy in the New York School for the Deaf in White Plains, an institution known as "Fanwood" after the neighborhood in which it stood. Clifford had gone to school there, Nancy had taught there. It was a place vital to the educational growth of the average deaf child, whose language lagged far behind hearing children by the time schooling began. But Amy was light-years ahead of the average deaf child. She was already reading a little. Some of the children at Fanwood would be years getting that far along. The Rowleys felt sure Amy belonged in Furnace Woods with other children of her age and accomplishment.

Again, they did not hear from the school district immediately, but they did get a response they credited. Nancy wrote Sy Dubow on April 22: "I think there is nothing more Cliff and I can do right now unless you have a better suggestion than to sue the school as a last resort. Dr. Zavarella, principal of Furnace Woods school, told me this week that the school cannot provide an interpreter for Amy because there is no money to pay for one. . . . Dr. Zavarella and I are on very good terms and he understands Amy's needs very well. He has visited other schools for the hearing impaired nearby and agrees the classes are not very impressive. It is beyond his power to do more than express his knowledge and understanding to his colleagues. If there is no other way of getting an interpreter for Amy other than court action, we only hope that it won't take years before she gets one. Do you think we should take action now rather than waiting until September to do something?"

Dubow didn't know much about the situation, beyond that the Rowleys were respected members of the deaf community in New York. The

Education for All Handicapped Children Act was new, and the state was still processing regulations for implementing it. In April 1977, Dubow had reason to think of another piece of legislation, the Rehabilitation Act of 1973, Section 504 of which forbade discrimination against handicapped individuals in any program receiving federal money.

Lobbied zealously, Congress had passed the Rehabilitation Act and followed it two years later with the Education for All Handicapped Children Act. But while President Gerald Ford reluctantly signed the latter act, observing that Congress would never fund it at the promised levels, his administration simply failed to come up with regulations for Section 504 of the Rehabilitation Act. President Jimmy Carter had campaigned in part on the principle of nondiscrimination against individuals with disabilities, and after four years of fruitless wrangling, advocates were thirsting for action. Secretary of Health Education and Welfare Joseph Califano was accused of "stalling" in April 1977, only three months after the Carter administration had taken office.

Individuals with disabilities marched on the regional HEW offices in San Francisco and Denver, some carrying placards reading: "Califano, What's the Score/We Demand 504." In Washington, protesters sang "We Want 504" to the tune of "We Shall Overcome," the pulsating protest song of the 1960s African American civil rights movement. One evening, Washington protesters rolled wheelchairs onto Secretary Califano's front lawn in an effort to gain his attention. On April 28, Califano signed the regulations, which he maintained would open a "new world of equal opportunity to more than 35 million handicapped Americans." *

Section 504 forbade discrimination against any otherwise qualified handicapped individual under any program or activity receiving federal assistance. With the just-passed regulations on his mind, Dubow wrote the Rowleys, almost one year from the day Nancy had written her first letter to Eible, saying that he was drawing up a Section 504 complaint against the school district to the Office for Civil Rights of HEW.

If both sides were talking to lawyers at this early stage, the scene at the school building level was more encouraging. Early relationships between the Rowleys and Principal Joseph Zavarella were cordial. In May, Nancy Rowley wrote the principal requesting a sign language interpreter for the

* United States Department of Health, Education and Welfare, Press Release from Secretary Joseph A. Califano, Jr., April 29, 1977.

annual kindergarten orientation meeting at which parents meet the kindergarten teacher and principal. The request was granted, and Cliff and Nancy wrote a thank-you note afterward. "The interpreter was a big help to bridge the communications gap," they wrote, "and we realized how much we've missed from the first kindergarten orientation program when our son, John, entered kindergarten." They secretly hoped that the meeting might demonstrate to the school staff how vital a sign language interpreter was even for deaf people with excellent lipreading skills. If *they* needed an interpreter for a semisocial meeting, how much more important that their six-year-old daughter have one for classes in school—that was the message they hoped would sink in.

Joe Zavarella was proud of Furnace Woods Elementary School. He considered that its reputation as one of the most progressive schools in the area was well deserved. It was a school that focused on doing what was best for the individual child. His initial impression of Nancy Rowley had been a favorable one. He considered her a kind of "Joan of Arc" figure, a mother determined to help her child overcome a severe handicap. As an educator, he welcomed the opportunity to teach a deaf child. On the other hand, as time went by, he could feel the resistance in the administration above him, and he feared being caught in a conflict between this strong mother and his superiors.

For their part, Nancy and Clifford Rowley kept the pressure on the school district. Nancy wrote Adelaide G. Waldron, chairman of the District Committee on the Handicapped, in May about the interpreter. She was told that a decision would be forthcoming by the end of June. When no word had come to them by June 21, Nancy wrote Waldron again. . . . "My husband and I are very concerned about Amy's education this fall. We want to know specifically whether you will provide a sign language interpreter."

Nancy believed that Zavarella was doing everything he could, but he had communicated his own sense of the depth of the resistance. As a deaf person in touch with other deaf people, she knew how deep that resistance could run when sign language was the issue. She had met an attractive, young hearing couple, Tim and Mary Sheie, who were themselves involved in deaf education, and she knew from them and from the local press how this issue was heating up in Westchester County at that time.

Mary Sheie grew up in Sheboygan, Wisconsin, the middle child of seven of a medical facility administrator and a homemaker. Her first real contact with deaf people was in high school summer camp, where she also met counselors from St. Olaf's, a school in Northfield, Minnesota. She decided to attend St. Olaf's and major in speech communications with related studies in deafness. Later she decided to become a sign language interpreter and met her husband-to-be at St. Paul Technical Vocational School. Both enrolled at Western Maryland College in Westminster. In the fall of 1974, Tim Sheie got a job running a Board of Cooperative Education Services (BOCES) program (state-funded vocational rehabilitation) in Goshen, New York, about an hour's drive from Peekskill. With the birth of their first child in 1976, Mary was content to teach sign language at night and to interpret locally. At about that time, the couple met the Rowleys.

The Sheies found the atmosphere for teaching deaf students in Orange County stifling after their Western Maryland College experience. The children Tim Sheie taught were considered "oral failures" (deaf children who could not learn to speak well) by educators in Goshen. To these people, total communications, which the Sheies considered by far the best way to teach deaf children to learn language, was a last resort. When a local reporter quoted a former member of the National Theater of the Deaf, speaking in Tim Sheie's class, that to open one's world to the deaf one had to learn sign language, the mother of a four-year-old hearing-impaired child took exception. In a letter to the editor, she wrote: "I feel that by manualism, I would not be opening the door to communication, but would be leaving it more than half-way closed. For if my child was to sign, with whom would he sign?" *

Later Tim touched off a flurry of letters by appearing on a high school program with two deaf students to "debunk" some myths. He told the audience that a good lip-reader could understand only about 30 percent of what was said and, later on, made a comment that a reporter present construed as favoring communication with a deaf person through signs rather than speaking. A horrified hearing couple with three hearing-impaired children wrote the editor. Another hearing couple with two profoundly deaf children was horrified by the first letter writer's scorn of signing. "Most children who only have speech taught to them eventually learn signs," they observed. But most of the letters clearly opposed teaching sign language in any form.[†]

* *Times Herald-Record* (Middletown, N.Y.), December 16, 1978.
† *Times Herald-Record* (Middletown, N.Y.), December 29, 1978.

Mary Sheie wondered what made sign language such an anathema in this area of the country. She speculated that it might be its location below and above the sites of two hard-line oral schools where sign language was forbidden. The Lexington School for the Deaf in New York City lay to the south and Clarke School in Northampton, Massachusetts, to the north. A few years later, the Sheies had the satisfaction of reading a letter to the editor of the same newspaper from the woman who had asked with whom her son would sign. She had given up exclusive oralism after years of frustration and had found that her son had blossomed linguistically with total communication, as Mary told me. But by then the Sheies had moved back to Minnesota where the weather was colder, but the climate for their work, they felt, was, relatively speaking, balmy.

The Rowleys were well aware of this negative climate for the use of sign language operating locally. It worried them by underscoring the threat that Amy might be placed inappropriately. At least two members of the District Committee on the Handicapped were quoted publicly indicating that Amy's placement in this vocational training center would be appropriate.

The district committee actually investigated three options for Amy. She could be placed in one of the BOCES classes, she could be sent to the New York School for the Deaf, or she could be mainstreamed in Furnace Woods "with supplementary services and/or aids." In a letter to Superintendent Jenkins, Zavarella reported that BOCES had been ruled out because the school psychologist had tested Amy's I.Q. at 122 and considered her in the "superior" range of students—BOCES students included a number of mentally retarded children and covered a wide range of ages. The New York School for the Deaf was ruled out despite a considerable array of services, including sign language interpreters, because its academic program was inadequate to Amy's needs. The committee recommended that Amy be placed in kindergarten at Furnace Woods.

But the issue of the sign language interpreter remained unresolved. "The matter of the interpreter," Zavarella wrote, "is still a question among members of the committee. That is, the interpreter would be essential in a large group instruction setting where Amy's attention may be focused on the speaker, but the variety of activities in a kindergarten might produce a problem for the interpreter and Amy." The principal recommended that various approaches be tried. He wrote the Rowleys that these would include an FM wireless hearing aid system—one that would link the student directly with the teacher—and a sign language interpreter.

The Rowleys would have been better pleased with this result were it not for Zavarella's having raised the issue of the cost of interpretive service with them. Nevertheless, both felt that any fair test of a sign language interpreter would illustrate Amy's need and end the matter. After Amy was duly enrolled in Furnace Woods that September, Nancy thought it would be a good idea for her to attend a class and visit with Sue Power, Amy's teacher. Surely, she thought, Power would be happy to have as an advisor someone who had taught deaf children and was herself deaf. She was shocked to receive a note from Zavarella to the effect that her timing might have been bad, "Coming at this time, before a full week of school has elapsed, it appears more in line with your thought that she might not be doing as good a job as you think she should be doing."

As a deaf person, Nancy was keenly aware that sometimes nuances of meaning were lost in communication between deaf and hearing persons. She also felt strongly that she should be careful not to overdo her presence in Amy's classes. But she felt rebuked here, at the very beginning, unwelcome to come to school to assist her daughter's teacher. Worse, she felt as though she had been told that she had nothing to offer as an educator.

At the same time, the school was making efforts on Amy's behalf and Zavarella was at pains to record them in letters to the Rowleys. The principal wrote Nancy that the school was "thrilled by the daily challenges presented to us in our work" in creation of a new program of instruction for a deaf child. He planned to get a TTY he could use in school to communicate with the Rowleys at home. He told Nancy that members of the school staff were to take a sign language course to assist them in teaching Amy. A new FM wireless system was to be tested the next week. Later, a sign language "interpreter–tutor" would be tested out in the same fashion. From all this, an Individualized Education Program (IEP) would be developed for Amy with input from the Rowleys.

Less than a week later, an investigator for the Department of Health, Education and Welfare, Office for Civil Rights, named Frank Cedo telephoned Zavarella and, on invitation, dropped by. Zavarella summed up the visit in a memo to Jenkins, "Out of all this activity surrounding this rather small five-year-old, we recently learned that a complaint has been filed with the HEW, Office for Civil Rights, citing us as the 'bad guys.' Apparently,

Mr. and Mrs. Rowley, represented by the National Center for Law and the Deaf in the person of one Sy Dubow, filed a complaint against the district for violating Amy's civil rights by not providing her with a sign language interpreter. The complaint was filed last Spring before Amy was enrolled in our school system."

The suit against the school district convinced a number of key actors at the district level that they were opposing a national effort on the part of individuals with disabilities. Jenkins, as superintendent of schools, noted in a letter to an HEW official several weeks later that Cedo had visited three times. Jenkins again raised the option of placing Amy either in the BOCES program or the New York School for the Deaf and termed the civil rights action "totally inappropriate and certainly untimely." Zavarella got a telephone inquiry for information from Dubow and was certain that this meant that the district was the target of a national effort to create a test case. Why else, he reasoned, would a big-shot Washington lawyer like Dubow call up a principal in a little school in Westchester County?

Actually, Dubow was far from enthusiastic about the possibility of the *Rowley* case eventually serving as a test. He could find districts where absolutely nothing was being done for mainstreamed deaf children. He could find deaf children infinitely more disadvantaged than Amy Rowley. To himself, he could observe that it was not entirely fortunate that the brightest and most aggressive parents were the ones who usually pushed for advantages for their children. The squeaky wheel getting the grease might produce parental involvement, but it didn't always make for the best test at law.

Another result of the civil rights action was to put Raymond Kuntz, the school district's attorney, in a position to advise the Hendrick Hudson Board of Education on the case. Kuntz had been attorney for the school board for twelve years and had taken on a similar position with several other mid-Hudson school districts. He was fully aware of the kinds of problems that arose between a school district and parents of its children. He had a lawyer's keen nose for contention and he smelled a big case in the making in the Rowley matter. Based on his assessment of the Rowleys, he judged the issue could go just about as far as the school district was willing to go. And, with the institution of the civil rights suit by the Rowleys, he could sense backs stiffening on the school side.

On October 26, barely a month after Amy had been enrolled in kindergarten, the Hendrick Hudson Board of Education held a strategy meeting to discuss, among other things, what to do about the trial of the sign language interpreter. According to the minutes, Kuntz told the board members that the ultimate decision on what would be required for Amy Rowley would not rest with the school or the board of education but with the judicial process. He said that in Amy's case an independent hearing officer would have the authority to determine what was the "least restrictive environment." From a legal standpoint, he described himself as comfortable with placing an interpreter in Amy's classroom on a trial basis and noted that Nancy Rowley would insist on it at a formal hearing, anyway. Concerns raised at the meeting over use of a sign language interpreter included "distraction to other children," "the implications to other handicapped children in the district," and "an influx of handicapped children to take advantage of the services."

Near the close of this "confidential" memo, the anonymous note-taker slipped into the first person plural: "We can show our efforts to assess the classroom setting with an interpreter. . . . There is an element of risk either way, but the trial use of an interpreter could strengthen our hand."

The Rowleys did not see this memorandum. If they had, their growing sense of apprehension over the school district's position would have deepened. The only faintly hopeful note in the document was a reference to Zavarella's remark that it should not be presumed that Furnace Woods staff had decided what the program for Amy should be, and that the trial period with the sign language interpreter was important from that standpoint.

Meanwhile, Amy was getting her first taste of school and not liking it much. She was constantly being "observed." She hated that. Her principal, Joe Zavarella, hovered over her for several days, taking notes. On September 8, the first day of school, he noted that her teacher, Sue Power, declared that Amy was "doing beautifully." But by the third day, Zavarella was observing that Amy remained silent while the other children were chattering away.

Amy's confusion over all this may have been reflected in her behavior. Zavarella noted that she came across as overly assertive with other children. Amy felt that she could dominate and win over children and, with this new knowledge of her specialness, she wondered how far she could push adults. Sue Power had instructed the children not to use the seesaws one day, and Amy disobeyed. Power was sure that Amy had understood her and when she confronted Amy with the instructions, the child laughed. Power was convinced she was being tested. Nancy agreed. In a note to Power, she tried to convey her encouragement: "Dear Miss Power," she wrote." How are things going between you and Amy lately? Is she still disobeying you?"

Based on everything she had heard, Nancy thought Sue Power was an excellent teacher. Power worked hard at communicating with Amy, occasionally using a few signs. She made a point of looking straight at Amy whenever she spoke and she had what deaf people call a "good mouth," which is to say, even teeth and a manner of clear articulation that made lipreading less difficult. But with sick leave and teacher conferences, she did miss some schooldays, and Nancy noted to Zavarella that the other teachers were not so good at communicating. Amy told her mother that she sometimes relied on her classmates when she missed information. All this served to strengthen Nancy's intimations of Amy's having less success in the future without an interpreter and with teachers less skilled than Power.

The FM wireless was another source of discontent. It was a contraption composed of a receiver hung in a harness, with visible clips and wires, and with a microphone hung around the neck. The idea was to provide direct communication between teacher and pupil and to block out other noises that a hearing aid might pick up. Amy hated the wireless for its bulk, its tendency to malfunction, and its precluding her from hearing what her classmates were saying.

While Amy fretted and her parents waited apprehensively, the school pushed ahead to get an Individualized Education Program (IEP) in place for Amy. Under the terms of the Education for All Handicapped Children Act, the IEP establishes goals and objectives for children in special education, explains what will be done to achieve those goals, and sets up procedures for periodic checks on progress. The parents must be involved in developing the IEP and must sign off on it. A meeting of the pupil personnel services team, which included Amy's principal, teacher, speech therapist, and other staff, was set for January 18, 1978, and the Rowleys were invited to attend.

The meeting went more smoothly than any held before and, certainly, any that were to come. Nancy told the group that the Department of Health, Education and Welfare had decided to wait on the complaint that had been filed against the district. In an up-beat mood, Zavarella noted later for the record, "It was clear that these parents were well aware of the efforts put forth by Furnace Woods staff to meet the needs of their daughter." Afterward, Clifford and Nancy signed the legal form attached to the IEP, which described what was being done for Amy currently, stated the school's commitment to a trial of a sign language interpreter, and noted that another assessment of Amy's needs would be undertaken toward the end of the school year.

The Rowleys signed the IEP because they had faith that the tryout of the sign language interpreter would be successful. To them, it had to be apparent, even to hearing people not disposed to agree, that a deaf child used to total communication would fare better in a classroom with total communication. They could not imagine an interpreter so poor or a situation so chaotic that Amy would not profit, and they felt sure this would be evident to all.

But the test of the interpreter that had originally been discussed as of four weeks' duration was now down to two or three weeks. The interpreter Zavarella finally located was a young man named S. J. "Jack" Janik. Tall, gangly, long-armed and long-haired, Janik was described by one person who met him as a kind of modern Ichabod Crane. And while Zavarella arranged an orientation session for Amy, no serious effort was made to bring the interpreter into the kindergarten class setting beforehand to give the children a chance to get used to his being there.

Amy did not know, any more than her fascinated classmates knew, what to make of Janik. She was used to looking at Power as though her very life depended on it. Now she was supposed to look at this strange man instead. She ended up doing a little of both. Nancy, who had made a special point of not showing up in the classroom before, felt she had to see how Amy functioned with a classroom interpreter. She came to school one day and went home not displeased. She wrote Frank Cedo, the investigator for the Office for Civil Rights of HEW: "Everyone seemed to be pleased and the whole situation was a positive one. I would like to see the final report or evaluation sheet before saying anything. One thing the interpreter (to be kept confidential for the interpreter's sake) told me that the Board of Education would like to see Amy at the New York School for the Deaf in order to save money for expenses of paying the interpreter next year."

The test of the interpreter lasted two weeks, rather than the four originally discussed. Janik was sick one day and actually worked only nine days. As usual, Zavarella was on hand to record his impressions for the record, this time in a memorandum to Assistant School Superintendent Charles Eible. "In this case the one child needing the service was reluctant to divert her attention away from the person speaking to the hands and lips of the interpreter. On the other hand, the children in the group having 'normal' hearing were somewhat captivated by the interpreter's signing ability." The principal did find the story reading part of the class "very effective," however, and while he mentioned distraction of the other children, he noted that more study would be required to determine whether that would diminish with time, adding that the interpreter had helped all the children in serving as a kind of teacher's aide. But he concluded that Amy functioned well without the interpreter and that an interpreter might hinder her social development in class.

The experiment was deemed a failure based on a statement the school got from Janik himself. The interpreter's report to the school read, in part: "In general, interpreting was resisted by Amy almost constantly except during the story-telling time, which was approximately twenty minutes a day for three days a week. This is accountable since Amy was not used to or aware of this sudden, added attraction in her classroom. . . . Her understanding of the English language and how it works is average to above which makes for a lot easier lipreading on her part since prior understanding of the language in question is conducive to lipreading of same. As skillful as she is, however, Amy does not get everything and when she does miss something she stops the person(s) in question and has the message repeated. . . . In conclusion I would like to say that as far as interpretive services are concerned, they are not needed at this time. However, this does not rule out the fact that an interpreter will be needed at a future date when the classroom work becomes more involved and large group discussion becomes the rule."

Nancy was distraught when she heard that Janik had been let go and that the trial period had convinced the school staff that an interpreter was not needed. A person not given to emotional display, she was close to tears at the news. For perhaps the first time, she thought she could see the situation in starkly realistic terms. She and Clifford were in for a long, bitter fight they might not win. Whatever school staff members felt, she believed that others above them wanted the sign language interpreter concept to fail. Now she believed that the district would resist the provision of a sign language interpreter unless some outside force intervened on the family's behalf.

For his part, Janik later amended his report in a sworn affidavit entered into the court record. "I did not say that Amy did not need an interpreter in kindergarten," he testified. "My evaluation was limited to that particular class of Amy's and not to kindergarten classes generally. I stated that interpreter services were not needed in that particular class only because of Miss Power's concern, awareness, and consideration of Amy and because Miss Power is a very expressive and talented woman."

Then Janik added that at the end of the experiment, Principal Zavarella told him that the board of education would not have retained an interpreter whatever his findings had been because it deemed the costs excessive. Also, Janik testified, Zavarella had suggested to him that it would be in everyone's best interests for the Rowleys to take Amy out of Furnace Woods Elementary School and enroll her in the New York School for the Deaf.

The bad news for the Rowleys was not over. On May 12, 1978, the Office for Civil Rights of the Department of Health, Education and Welfare wrote to inform them that the Hendrick Hudson Central School District was in compliance with Section 504 of the Rehabilitation Act of 1973. A letter from William R. Valentine, acting director for Region II, described limitations of this act where education of handicapped children was concerned. "While you may differ with the district in its educational methods, we cannot find them to be out of compliance, because the Office for Civil Rights is not empowered to make educational or therapeutic judgments." Valentine suggested that the Rowleys not sign an IEP the following year until they were satisfied with it.

Actually, the IEP for Amy's first-grade year was already under consideration, and the Rowleys by now were in no mood to sign a document that did not call for use of a sign language interpreter in the classroom. On her copy of the school's proposal, Nancy penciled her concerns in red. She did not think Amy needed the twice-weekly sessions with the speech and auditory specialist. She thought that the (outside-the-class) tutorial sessions three to five times a week with the teacher of the deaf were provided as a way of avoiding the use of an interpreter in the classroom, where one was needed. Beside the statement, "The classroom teacher will accommodate the child by directing attention to whomever speaks at any given moment in class discussion," Nancy scrawled "impossible." As for the school supplying a teacher with "some" knowledge of sign language, she observed that to be useful to a deaf student, the signing skills of the teacher would have to be as thorough as would Spanish-speaking skills to teach an Hispanic student.

With the failure of the civil rights action and the continued adamancy of the school district, the Rowleys felt the need for more formal legal representation. Dubow agreed, not unhappy to have the case pass from his hands. Both Clifford and Nancy knew attorney Michael Chatoff slightly. He would know the issues better than most attorneys as he was, himself, deaf. Chatoff's interest was immediate and keen, and he was aware of the general outlines of their quest. Chatoff agreed to talk with the Rowleys, and they were impressed with him.

Chatoff saw the Education for All Handicapped Children Act as the way to proceed. This act specified to some degree the kind of education a handicapped child must have: a "free and appropriate education" in the "least restrictive environment," attending to the child's "unique" needs. While the law did not spell out a mandate for sign language interpreters generally, Chatoff felt that the legislative intent was their use in mainstreaming situations. The act had a means of appealing the school district's decision through an "impartial," school-level hearing, with a review at the state level. Beyond that point, lay the state and federal court systems, reaching eventually to the United States Supreme Court. That was a dizzying height and one Chatoff did not think would have to be scaled.

When Amy showed up for the first grade in September 1978, she had just been tested again at Westchester County Medical Center by Ellen Anchin, a speech and language pathologist who had been working with her for some time. Anchin's report was in essence a discharge from "Grasslands," as Amy, now a public school student, would be served there no longer. It had praise for Amy's development of language skills in all forms of communication but it also contained a warning and a recommendation: "It should be noted that when a new concept, using new vocabulary, is presented to Amy, she has great difficulty in comprehension if only oral language is used. Although her lipreading skills are well developed, it is usually necessary to present the sign, or signs, in order to accomplish full comprehension and integration into Amy's own language system." At the end of the report, Anchin underscored this: "It will continue to be necessary to present new materials in sign language as well as orally, due to the profound degree of hearing loss." Nancy made sure a copy got to the school district.

Amy also had a new classroom teacher and a teacher of the deaf who would work with her daily outside the classroom. The classroom teacher, Regina Globerman, prepared for her new pupil with some effort to learn sign language, but she became convinced early on that Amy did not need a sign language interpreter in her classroom. In a diary she kept, Globerman observed that in the two first-grade classes she was teaching, nine children could not read at all; they had no sound symbols. Another group she described as having started reading in the womb. Then, there was a bigger group in between, and she placed Amy there near the top, "high average" as she put it.

Globerman had been primarily a substitute teacher prior to the 1978–79 school year. While she had never worked with a deaf child in the classroom before, she thought the kind of socialization Amy was getting was just what the Rowleys intended her to have. To her, it was one of the main purposes of mainstreaming Amy with hearing children. She saw other students helping Amy in school and on the playground and thought that this ceased later on, when Amy got an interpreter. As for receiving information, Globerman took Amy's frequent rejection of the FM receiver and the child's unhappiness with being taken out of the classroom as signs that Amy was getting a good deal of information on her own through lipreading.

Susan Williams, Amy's new teacher of the deaf, had grown up as an Army brat with an interest in deafness that began with her sister's work with deaf children. Married to a serviceman, she was living in the Croton area, doing what she called "itinerant tutoring" of hearing-impaired children. She had met Nancy Rowley on a tennis court and had been to the Rowleys' house. She was impressed with Amy and saddened by her brother John's appearance of drifting on the outskirts of this deaf family's life. She understood this "shadow person," as she called him, because she had worked with the only hearing person in a deaf family before. The Rowleys were delighted when Williams was hired by the district as a teacher of the deaf for Amy and others.

Williams met with Principal Zavarella and other school people, all of whom seemed intensely involved in the situation with Amy. She told them that she knew the Rowleys. Zavarella told her that, although the Rowleys thought Amy needed a classroom sign language interpreter, the school's position was that she did not. She was told further that a test of a sign language interpreter in kindergarten supported the school's position. She got the feeling that she was being briefed on a strategic position that already had been taken up.

Sue Williams thought that an interpreter in the classroom would improve Amy's academics but that socialization might be as important as Zavarella and Regina Globerman thought. She felt insecure about her qualifications for working with a deaf child in these circumstances. Observing deaf parents together with a deaf child for the first time, she realized how little she knew about deafness. It was fortunate that the Rowleys were insisting that Amy learn through signed English as this was the only signing Williams knew.

Meanwhile, the battle continued at the level of the District Committee on the Handicapped. Mary Sheie, the interpreter, had begun to help the Rowleys in these meetings. She found the sessions unequal contests. The school showed up with ten to fifteen people, plus legal help, while the Rowley contingent usually numbered four or five, including Chatoff. Taras Denis, a deaf man who was a guidance counselor at the New York School for the Deaf, attended one of these meetings and later wrote a notarized letter to Chatoff stating that a school official took him aside after the meeting and told him that the whole affair with the Rowleys was a matter of money. Denis later identified that official as Zavarella.

In an October 3 meeting, at which various school officials testified to having visited a Board of Cooperative Education Services (BOCES) program in Yorktown and found a student with an I.Q. of 122 taking part, without sign language in use, the District Committee on the Handicapped (DCOH) voted to provide Amy with the same services that she had received in kindergarten. She was to have a teacher of the deaf an hour a day outside the classroom and a speech therapist three times a week. On October 12, Chatoff wrote Kuntz informing the school district's attorney of the Rowleys' displeasure with the decision of the committee and noting that they had requested a formal impartial hearing unless the committee revised its recommendations. Kuntz responded on October 26, telling the Rowleys' attorney that the board of education had approved the committee's recommendations and that the district would appoint Dr. Frank Eckelt to conduct the impartial hearing.

New York State law at that time called for school boards to choose impartial hearing officers from a list drawn up by the school districts and approved by the office of the Commissioner of Education. In practice, the school districts often picked these officers through their own attorneys. Under the circumstances, it was not surprising that hearings were decided preponderantly in favor of the school districts. Chatoff wrote the Rowleys that the "cards were stacked" against them. Then he learned that Eckelt, the man chosen by the district as the impartial hearing officer, had once been associated with Charles Eible, who had succeeded to the position of superintendent of schools in Hendrick Hudson. Kuntz responded, noting that the association complained of was in another district seven years before and that he (Kuntz) had recommended Eckelt as the most experienced hearing officer in the mid-Hudson region. Nevertheless, to avoid even an appearance of partiality, Kuntz said he would suggest appointment of another hearing officer.

One last meeting of the Pupil Placement Services Committee was held to try to reach agreement on Amy's IEP. Nancy was getting worried about Amy, who had begun to bite her clothing and show signs of stress. In their work together after school, Nancy found instances where Amy had missed important information in her lessons and told her she had not understood Globerman. Sue Williams had told Nancy that she saw no good reason to continue withdrawing Amy from class an hour a day. She was told that this procedure was required by state law. When Nancy and Clifford asked for at least another trial of a sign language interpreter in Amy's first-grade class, they were turned down.

Nancy came as close to pleading as she ever would. Stating that she and Clifford could not wait until Amy failed a subject to ask again for an interpreter, she sought a commitment from the school to help Amy. Joe Zavarella responded that the school always had Amy's best interests at heart. "We continue to observe a well-adjusted, bright, and achieving first-grader," he wrote in his summary of the meeting. "There is no reason at this time for us to consider a sign language interpreter as a necessity for Amy. However, if and when such a need arises, we've assured the Rowleys that this staff would certainly consider recommending the interpreter as an option among many to resolve the problem." The Rowleys took that bit about "an option among many" to be another reference to the New York School for the Deaf. They left the IEP unsigned.

Kuntz, meanwhile, had set about replacing Eckelt with another hearing examiner. He thought of Albert P. Roberts of Poughkeepsie and called him. Roberts, who had not previously served as an impartial hearing officer, remembers Kuntz telling him that he had a case that might go "all the way," by which Roberts understood him to mean to the Supreme Court. On December 15, the office of the clerk of the Hendrick Hudson School District wrote Chatoff to notify him that Roberts had been chosen as the hearing officer; the date for the hearing was December 20, five days away.

Chatoff hastily threw together his preparation, learning—not to his surprise—that several witnesses would be unavailable on such short notice at Christmastime. Word came to him that Roberts and Kuntz had had offices in the same building a few years earlier, but when he brought this up prior to the hearing, he was told that no request for a new hearing officer would be entertained.

The impartial hearing established that the school district had a number of witnesses who had observed Amy in the classroom and that the Rowleys had none. Kuntz made much of this point, suggesting that the contest here was between the theorizing of the Rowleys' experts and the experience of the school's front-liners. Marianne Pappas, a special education teacher and a member of DCOH, testified that Amy was getting along beautifully and that her socialization was excellent. Zavarella and Globerman testified similarly on the basis of daily observation of Amy. Williams, who had been in the classroom occasionally, testified that an interpreter was not needed in the classroom at that time, but added that she used total communications with Amy at all times and agreed with the Rowleys' expert witness on its value. Zavarella testified that he could not recommend an interpreter in the classroom for Amy.

For his part, Chatoff drew out that none of these witnesses, with the exception of Williams, had had any experience teaching deaf children. His chief witness was Mary Sheie, a qualified and degreed teacher of the deaf and an interpreter with ten years' experience working with deaf children. She testified that deaf children could not get maximum benefit from a class without a sign language interpreter. Under cross-examination, Sheie admitted that she had not observed Amy in the classroom. On January 12, 1979, Roberts ruled that Furnace Woods was supplying Amy with an appropriate education.

It was clear to school officials that the Rowleys would not let the matter rest there, and the school continued to get observations of Amy into the record. Sue Williams kept a running file of her contact for an hour a day with Amy, from January to March:

Jan. 24. Today Amy started off by remarking that she didn't want to leave the classroom. She said she didn't want to work with me next year. When we did the auditory training lesson, she did very well.

Jan. 25. Today everything was o.k. She enjoyed the auditory training lesson, and then invited Mark to play the same game as yesterday.

Feb. 2. We were observed by Nancy and another woman who was a teacher of the deaf. Amy's behavior deteriorated toward the end. She did well in the beginning but was frustrated because her mother continually interrupted me with instructions on proper signing and the lesson came to a halting screech as Amy jumped in her mother's lap.

Feb. 7. Another great day. Seems to be gaining in her ability to write and think up rhyming words.

*Feb. 15. Another visitation. Amy not happy and acting out in normal
fashion given the circumstances.*

*Feb. 16. Had a heart-to-heart with Amy, who acted as if she didn't
want to come with me. I asked her how she was feeling.*

"I feel bad," Amy said. "I don't want to come with you."

"What's wrong?"

"I don't know."

"Amy, what did you think of the man who visited yesterday?"

"I don't like those things."

"What do you mean by 'things'?"

"All the people coming."

"How does your mother feel?"

"She thinks I need an interpreter because I don't understand anything."

"Amy, you seem to understand things, not everything but most things."

"Yes."

"Do you understand Mrs. Globerman?"

"Yes, everything she says."

"Well, what don't you understand."

"I don't understand library."

"You mean the stories? You don't understand them?"

"Yes."

"You want to know what's happening, right?"

"Right."

"What about movies?"

"I don't understand them much."

*Feb. 17. I am expecting another off-the-wall day with Amy as her
anxiety level rises and falls in direct relationship with her Mom's visits.*

*March 2. My reaction to all of the above is that Amy wants to be part
of the flow of things in the classroom. Coming out with me is one more
interruption to the flow. I feel inviting classmates to work with us gives
us a wonderful opportunity to communicate actively and with Amy's
peers. It's like a microcosm of the classroom. Moreover, Amy needs an
outlet to talk. I intend to work in the classroom Monday.*

But Sue Williams knew that she would not be allowed to stay in the
classroom long. She knew the battle lines were set. The school would not
allow her to function as a sign language interpreter, even for a little while,
in the classroom. Yet all Williams' choices seemed poor to her. She felt and

understood Amy's resistance to leaving her classmates. When Amy said she understood everything, she meant it as a plea to be left in that classroom to get what she could. Ultimately, Sue belived she would fail to help Amy because she had to function outside the classroom and Amy would reject her on that account.

———

Early one cold, winter morning at about this time, Amy was alone in the house. John had gone to school. Her father and mother had gone off for a meeting, something to do with the court case. Amy was to finish her breakfast and, when the time was right, go out the front door, making sure she had locked it, and wait on the corner for the school bus. It was not a hard thing to do but Amy hated doing it. She hated the school bus and she was beginning to hate school. Most of all, she hated what all that was going on seemed to be doing to her family—her mother and father preoccupied, John sulking or angry about something that she knew related in some way to the efforts her parents were exerting for her education.

Additionally, she was not sure of the time. Unable to get the time on the radio or television she was uncertain of her clock-reading abilities. Alone and upset, she panicked, pulled on her clothes, and went out the door, locking it behind her. At about this time, she realized that the wind was more brisk than she had anticipated and that she was wearing a dress that did not cover her legs. She crammed her gloved hands into her coat pocket, scrunched herself to make as small a target for the wind as possible, and took up her post on the corner.

For a child, time can be an immense and intractable foe. Cold and gloomy, Amy realized that she had made a bad mistake. It was terribly early. Fearful of missing the bus, she had locked herself out in the cold, dark morning. She felt the anticipated wait as a sentence she had not deserved. Worst of all, there was no place to go at that hour. She had to keep herself busy, somehow, waiting for the school bus. She tried moving about, hunched over a little against the breeze, puffing steam into the winter air. She pretended she was dancing like the dancing bear in the pictures she had colored. She tried walking part of the way up the street and back, measuring her steps, but that seemed to make her even more conscious of the time and the time, consequently, move even more slowly.

She had the sense after awhile that she was colder than she had ever been before. It was an exhilarating feeling at the same time that it was a little frightening. Could someone freeze out here like this, right in front of her own house, waiting for the school bus? She wondered how early she was—an hour, more than an hour? Her feet were beginning to feel numb and she stomped them up and down to get the feeling back in them. She raised one leg and then the other and brought them down hard, harder than she had to. In a curious sort of way, the hard stomping brought her a sense of satisfaction. She was doing that when a hand touched her shoulder, startling her. She turned and saw a woman she did not know standing there in a long, heavy coat buttoned to her throat. What was she doing out there so early, the woman wanted to know. Where were her parents? Amy looked at the woman, a little afraid of her, but more afraid she would miss the bus if she left the corner. Her parents were not home, she said, turning her face away, stubbornly back into the chilly breeze. When she looked around again, the woman was walking down the block away from her.

Much, much later—Amy's face was stiff with cold by this time—she saw the school bus coming her way. The driver, a woman, was alone on the bus, but she stopped and Amy, half-frozen, got on board. What was she doing out there at this hour, the driver wanted to know. Patiently, she explained to Amy that the bus was not at the end of its run, when Amy was supposed to board, but at the beginning. Amy should go back in the house unless she wanted to ride all the way around while the driver picked up the other first-graders. Near tears, Amy told her that she had locked herself out of the house. Then she had to put up with the comments of her classmates who boarded slowly as the bus made its way along the route—it was hilarious to them that Amy was on the bus so early. Sinking inwardly, Amy told herself that the school had robbed her of her parents.

In his opinion supporting the school's position, Roberts, the hearing officer, had noted that the school had all the "on the scene" witnesses to Amy's progress in the classroom. With Chatoff's urging, Nancy vowed to put an end to that as quickly as possible. The woman who had visited Amy's class with Nancy, mentioned in Sue Williams' notes on February 2, was Mary Sheie. Nancy took her own notes. "Talking about today's date and the groundhog. When a child in front of Amy spoke out a sentence, Amy couldn't see her face to be sure what the sentence said. Children gave out answers to questions and teacher didn't repeat them for Amy. Teacher harder to lip-read than I thought. . . . Mrs. Globerman talks naturally like she does to average children (not for Amy). Big difference from last year's teacher was that Miss Power talked for Amy not what she did for average children.

"After lunch—show movie—movie itself wasn't clear (picture). No transmitter for Amy. Amy looked to me to aid her what this was about. Didn't play or communicate w/children—wanted to be around me most of the time. We wanted to observe Amy's class in Mrs. Walsh's room and Mrs. G. said it would be a distraction (she was upset)—so we respected the teacher's wishes and left at 12:15."

Regina Globerman did not in the least like what was going on in her classroom, outsiders coming in and writing down what she was doing. She did not mind the observation from school insiders but these were outsiders. Globerman thought that Nancy and Clifford were fighting for deaf children and deaf people but not considering Amy, whose needs, she felt, were being more than adequately met in her class. She was sure there were powerful forces at work in the background supporting the Rowleys in their legal action.

And she took the visits personally. She felt she was being put on trial, forced to defend her ability to teach Amy. She felt that Nancy was challenging her competence. She did observe that Amy seemed to lose information in group discussions, such as those about science, and became convinced that Amy would need an interpreter sooner or later, but that time had not yet come. As she put it, why give the medicine before the child shows the sickness or the need? She asked Joe Zavarella to come into the classroom and monitor the situation whenever she was being observed by anyone from outside the school. She regarded that as personal protection.

Another thing bothered Globerman. She had students whose parents complained that sometimes Amy's teacher of the deaf performed sign language in the classroom, where all the children could see it. Regina Globerman did not sympathize with what she considered to be a prejudice, but she did feel that there were other children in her class who needed special help and were not getting it. She had nonreaders who needed help more, in her view, than Amy, who was a good reader. She considered Sue Williams' forays into the classroom to be a distraction. Amy was teacher-oriented, and Globerman was uncomfortable teaching a student who was looking at someone else. She saw no necessity to ask Amy how she felt about an interpreter. As far as she was concerned, Amy had rejected an interpreter. That, she believed, was not Amy's issue but her mother's.

Mary Sheie felt that Globerman was reacting defensively, as many teachers did when confronted with a situation requiring special help for a child.

The school staff, in her opinion, knew nothing about deaf students' problems in mainstreaming. The school had every right to consider the education it was providing as good, Sheie believed, because to her it was a quality educational situation, but she thought that her own interest in an interpreter was taken as an implied criticism—as if she and Nancy were saying that the school was somehow blameworthy. That was too bad, she thought, because it was clear to her that an interpreter was the bare minimal tool to assure that Amy got an equitable education.

Sheie was certain that Amy was missing things, when she wasn't looking at Globerman directly. While a hearing child could put his or her head down and still get information, Amy had to pay strict attention all the time, and this was more than even the most alert first-grader could manage. The worst gaps occurred when other children spoke, Sheie noted. Amy missed out regularly there. Sheie's worst thought—one that would linger in her mind for a long time—was that Amy was cursed in being deaf *and* bright, because she would always get by and always be told she was doing fine.

After their observation, Sheie and Nancy visited Joe Zavarella in the principal's office. Nancy didn't take notes but jotted down her reactions immediately upon returning home. "Went to see Dr. Z with Mary Sheie to thank him for observing and told him re Mrs. Globerman feeling upset and distracted by our observation. He began talking softly and later more strongly at the end, saying I never thanked him for all the positive things they've done to help Amy, the TTY and the 'sign language interpreter' course for eight weeks. Naturally, these were not things we requested (my feelings are that it helps them—such as TTY and sign language—to avoid the interpreter). He spoke out saying that he was honest, and I told him that I've nothing to say, but to know him better. After leaving, Mary said his mind is closed and he needs more public relations." What Sheie did not say to Nancy was how surprised she was at how much anger there was in the classroom and in the principal's office and how calmly Nancy had taken it.

Mary Sheie wrote a letter to Globerman thanking the teacher for allowing the visit and regretting the upset it had caused. While she praised Globerman for her efforts, she noted that she was still very much convinced that Amy needed a sign language interpreter. Sheie also wrote a letter to Adelaide Waldron, chairman of the District Committee on the Handicapped, suggesting that an interpreter in the classroom is first seen by children as a novelty—"and so is a wheelchair"—but soon becomes an everyday part of the classroom scenery. While an interpreter might have to work for months to learn how to serve his or her deaf charges properly, not having an interpreter could mean academic setbacks and severe emotional problems for Amy. She appended a list of five people she thought Waldron might consider getting in touch with about this issue.

Chatoff arranged for one more visitor to attend Amy's class. He was Michael Deninger, the visitor referred to in Sue Williams' notes of February 15 and 16. A hearing person, Deninger was coordinator of the Education for All Handicapped Children Act at Gallaudet University, a teacher of the deaf with a master's degree in that area, ten years of working experience teaching deaf people, and certification as a sign language interpreter. Noting in a deposition for use in court that Amy's comprehension was negligible, even under ideal circumstances, using her hearing amplification alone, Deninger used a scale of comprehension developed by researchers. He observed periodically (usually every 30 seconds) who was controlling the conversation and whether Amy was understanding or not. The scale called for him to assume Amy was understanding unless she was clearly confused, asking irrelevant questions, or was not watching the face of the speaker.

In a small reading group led by Globerman, Deninger concluded that Amy understood approximately 25 percent as the teacher and students read aloud from their books, with the FM receiver being passed from hand to hand for each reader. While the receiver was in transit, with Amy's attention on the individual students, she could get nothing of what Globerman said. She was able to "keep her place" by taking visual cues from the other students. In an afternoon reading session, Deninger concluded that Amy understood no more than 10 percent of a section of a story read by a teacher's aide at a fast pace. In the art class that followed, he noted that the teacher talked rapidly and rarely faced Amy to allow lipreading. "Again," he wrote, "Amy was able to use visual cues to see what to do, but she understood less than 10 percent of the discussion."

Deninger concluded that in small group discussions with one or more students, Amy comprehended approximately 40 percent of what was being said, and the students with whom she spoke understood her no more than 50 percent of the time. He assumed that during special assemblies, movies, or field trips, without the aid of an interpreter, Amy was getting very little of what was being said. Sue Williams, he noted, agreed that Amy needed an interpreter for these events.

Deninger offered the opinion that Amy was in need of an interpreter in her classroom if she were to stay at Furnace Woods. "It appeared that

Amy's teacher and principal did not fully comprehend the isolation effect of a profound hearing loss or the limitations of amplification devices," he testified. "Each of Amy's teachers began sessions by asking Amy if she 'could hear.' To me this means, 'Is your trainer [Amy's FM wireless] working?' and definitely not, 'Are you understanding me?'"

The night after her mother's session in Zavarella's office with Mary Sheie, Amy came home saying that she was disappointed. She started to tell her mother about it and began crying. From her mother's lap, she sobbed that she wanted her mother there, in school. Nancy asked if this was because Amy understood her better. Amy nodded. "I want the interpreter," she said. Nancy made a note that while Amy had indicated to her before that an interpreter would help her, this was the first time she had put the request in the form of a direct demand.

In New York State, at this point in history, the commissioner of education decided appeals based on the impartial hearing, normally without taking further evidence. When the deadline for the commissioner to decide the Rowleys' appeal had passed and Chatoff had heard nothing, with the help of an associate, he telephoned Albany. They were told that the materials were still lying on the table, that they hadn't been examined. Only minutes later, the office of the Commissioner of Education called Chatoff to say that the record had been read, a decision had been reached, the appeal had been denied, and that copies of the decision would be sent to Chatoff's office. The Rowleys' attorney was amazed: the record that had been sent to the commissioner's office was more than two hundred pages long.

The commissioner's decision, dated April 10, 1979, was barely three and one-half pages long. Its wording bore similarities to that of Roberts' decision here and there, as in this commentary on an affidavit by Robert R. Davila, then an official at Gallaudet and president of the Council on Education of the Deaf. "There is no indication that he has ever met petitioner's daughter, observed her in a classroom setting, reviewed her records, or tested her for academic achievement." The wording was exactly that of the Roberts decision except for the absence of Amy's name, which had been expunged throughout the commissioner's decision, presumably in keeping with that office's rules of identification.

The commissioner's decision even repeated an error in the hearing examiner's decision. Roberts had misquoted the interpreter, Janik, as having written that "in general, interpreting was resisted by the child almost consistently." The word used in Janik's report, which was attached as part of the record, was "constantly," yet the commissioner's decision also used "consistently." Nothing in the commissioner's decision suggested that any document other than the Roberts decision had been consulted.

Chatoff shared some of this with the Rowleys in a conversation later on. "It's all right," he told them over the TTY. "We will get a fairer hearing in federal district court." Nancy and Clifford hoped so. They had begun to think that Amy's case might be more important than they had imagined. "What we are going through," Nancy wrote on the TTY, "might be what could happen to any deaf child in the country."

At the end of the first-grade year, students at Furnace Woods were routinely given two standardized tests, the Stanford and Metropolitan. Amy had been tested to death, the Rowleys thought, and they objected to the school's giving her special tests of her comprehension. As the level of trust between the family and the school plummeted, Nancy became suspicious of the intent and validity of some of these particular tests, but neither she nor Clifford objected to the school's giving Amy standardized tests along with her classmates.

The Metropolitan was given in open class to all the students including Amy, with Regina Globerman giving instructions in her normal, verbal way. For some reason, Sue Williams was asked to administer the Stanford test to Amy in a one-on-one setting using sign language. Williams liked to challenge Amy because the child responded with such delight to it. She told Amy that she wanted her to "ace" this test. She knew Amy wanted to impress her, but she was not prepared for how well Amy did on the test. She had known Amy was bright from the beginning but when this little girl was fully engaged in a task, oriented properly to it, and comfortable, she was remarkable. She was off-the-wall bright, Sue thought. The scores were great, and she was able to get Amy's sunniest smile as a reward when the testing was over.

3

Like Light Pouring Down over Me

I am trying to talk Amy into talking to me. Amy is listening, reacting or not reacting, depending on the subject. She is at least trying now, not evasive as she was on our first meeting a year and a half ago. But it does not come easily. She will answer direct, highly specific questions as best she can, but if I am not referring to a specific event that she remembers, she is vague. What does she remember about the last grade she attended in Furnace Woods? She smiles and shrugs. Does she ever hear from her old friends back in the fifth grade? She shakes her head. What she does best, always gracefully and with fun in her eyes, is to change the subject.

"What were your favorite things to do in camp?" Amy asks me.

"Goofing off," I say, wondering if this slang will register with a deaf, thirteen-year-old (or with a hearing thirteen-year-old in 1985, for that matter). "Eluding the camp authorities, hiding out."

She grins conspiratorially, message received. Amy's parents and I are getting ready to drive her from Mountain Lakes up to Pennsylvania to summer camp for a week with a hundred other deaf children. The drive is uneventful if a bit hard on my nerves. I am in the front seat so that I can lean back and talk with Amy and whichever parent is sitting in the back seat or talk directly across the front seat to the driver. The effort is to make things easier for me, but it also raises complications. If Nancy is driving and I am talking with Clifford and Amy in the back seat, Nancy is cut off from the conversation. If this seems a trivial matter, try to imagine a family chat in which you are privy only to every fourth or fifth line of dialogue—literally, try it, and you will learn how useless scattered sentences can be even when you know the words perfectly well. So when I speak to Amy and get a reply, Clifford has to communicate this exchange to Nancy, a process which requires her turning her head back to him for a few instants to read his lips and signs. We are, after all, driving along at 65 miles per hour. I find myself glancing in panic from the face of the driver, turned back to the rear, to the vanishing roadside in front and the cars ahead and speeding by. The effect is scarcely less hair-raising when I talk with Nancy, for she must study my face and lips closely and to do so she must take her eyes, however briefly, from the road. I find myself biting off my lines, keeping my questions or comments anxiously brief.

I am fascinated with the skills required here. But most of all, I am impressed with the enormous effort that is expended in what would be, for hearing people, a relaxed morning drive. Because they are left out of so much of what goes on in the hearing world, the deaf are at exacting pains to communicate with one another. Observing how much work this takes among three family members in the relatively close confines of an automobile, I get a glimmer of what it must have been like for Amy in those Furnace Woods classrooms, with children talking on all sides, from the front and behind, asking and answering questions, developing language. And for all her youthful insouciance, Amy's concentration on what is being said among us in this car is intense, both wonderfully and, at the same time, woefully adult. I have an image of her from that trip, slouched across the right rear seat, chin cupped in her hand, those luminous eyes in their eager comprehension somehow conveying the impression of hyperactivity. Later, on the trip back from camp with Clifford driving, I learn the long, restful nighttime lull of the deaf on the road, when it is impossible to read lips and too dark to read finger signs.

At the camp, it is anything but quiet. For the first time in my life, at camp headquarters in a rustic shack built to accommodate a single, large room, I am with more than three deaf people at once: fifty or more people clustered in groups, some speaking, almost all signing, many doing both. Clifford and Nancy are doing their best to keep me from feeling left out—"He's writing a book about Amy's case," they tell first one friend and then another—but they have their obligations and after a while I am adrift, alone in a strange place where everyone else seems to have someone to talk with. I walk about as though invisible. People converse, their faces alight with emotion, their expressive hands sculpting towers of language. It is far worse for me than being the only stranger at a cocktail party, for there at least the easy comfort of small talk is available. How would I begin a conversation here? How would I understand or make myself understood?

Standing there, trying not to feel foolish, it dawns on me that this must be every day in the life of a deaf person in a hearing society. I have walked through the looking glass and this is what it is like on the other side. To have common language is everything. To lack language is to be utterly alone, and the more people around, the deeper the chasm of loneliness. I experience something similar to the deaf person's envy of hearing communication, the speed and ease with which the players, motionless and effortless, transmit the words that cause merriment, or astonishment, the smiling assent of passers-by who capture meaning with scarcely a glance. But now, looking at the pageant of movement about me, I am struck with an image of a party of hearing people as a still life. The whole physical being of deaf speakers is alive with expression. Graceful gestures tumble from fingers and hands, but meanings are conveyed as well in other body movements, especially in the face, which create characters from a story, set them to debate, mediate, and resolve, to the evident delight of the listeners. It is as though I am at a convention of expert mimes. Here, I am the one who is mute, with nothing to say, nothing to do but "observe" conversations like fragile, delicate china in a crowded shop. I cannot touch them, but can only revel in their beauty.

A youngish woman approaches, her hair in a severe bun that does not go with her summer-morning smile. "So you're the writer," she says.

The shocked look on my face betrays me. She glances again and breaks into a laugh. "Oh, I can hear you all right. Or I could if there was anything to hear."

"I'm sorry. I'm not used to this . . . so many deaf people." I am literally gasping with relief at the chance to regain my lost voice. "Do you have a child here?"

"Oh, yes." She waves carelessly at the nearest window, "Out there somewhere."

"A . . . deaf child?"

"Yes, last I looked." The look on her face is one of amused patience, unsurprised, unruffled.

"I'm sorry. I didn't mean to be rude. But you're the first hearing person I have met. I thought that the big majority of deaf children were born to hearing parents."

"True, but much of the organized activity for deaf children, in my experience, comes from deaf adults. And hearing adults, like me, who can sign."

"How did you learn to sign? Was it because you had a deaf child?"

She shook her head. "No. I sign because I have deaf parents. I learned to sign early. Most hearing parents of deaf children are not interested in learning to sign. It's too bad, but it's true." She says this last slowly, as though to let me take it in a word at a time and signs the words as she says them, seeing someone else coming up toward her. He smiles and they begin signing together. As she signs to him, she speaks, not because he needs her speech but because I do. She tells the man who I am and he nods and smiles in my direction. She is at pains to see that I am included in the conversation, which is about another camp for deaf children in Minnesota, which both of their children have attended. I observe that this man does not speak at all. Once, I would have thought that was because he could not. I know now from talking with Nancy and Clifford that it is generally a matter of choice with the deaf. After some moments, the man pulls the woman away to join another group. As she leaves, she waves to me sympathetically. I feel a moment's pang. What hearing person—I am thinking to myself—would have been decent enough to include, one way or another, a deaf person in so casual a conversation as that? What hearing person would have had the language to do it?

I find later that I cannot shake the experience of being alone in that crowd of deaf people at the camp headquarters. It is unlike anything I have ever experienced. As I think of it, another scene comes into my consciousness. It is an annual Christmas party held by one of my newspaper friends years ago, when I was a cub reporter. Twenty-five or thirty people crowded into an apartment in Greensboro, North Carolina. One figure sitting quietly every year in a chair against the wall: a blind man. I remember the shock of seeing him there that first year, but that is nothing compared to the shock I am getting now as I realize that, in all those years, I never spoke to him.

Surely it shouldn't have taken me so many years to imagine how this man felt, this friend of my very bright friend, who was surely himself someone well worth knowing. And yet until this minute, reflecting on my experience standing in a "blind" man's shoes in a room full of "sighted" people, feeling as alone as if I had blundered into a forest on the darkest of nights, I had not thought of him at all.

No. That was not true. I had thought of him before. I thought of him each time I went to this party. I knew that only a few people took the trouble to come up to him and they were, over the years, generally the same few. Most of the people there did what I was doing. They avoided him. What was the origin of that avoidance? Was it simply fear of doing something stupid, or something that could be misconstrued as rudeness? Was it just plain ignorance? Or was it something else?

And again I found I was asking myself: What am I doing in the middle of this book-in-the-making? Isn't it very likely that I am exactly the wrong one to have taken on the task? Or, I thought, was it possible that my mystery story was as much about me as about the *Rowley* case?

In 1979 I had found myself writing, among other things, a weekly newspaper column for the Charlotte (N.C.) *News* and several other newspapers. In June of that year, in my weekly spasm of searching for something to fill the column, I came across an article about deaf people protesting the casting of a hearing actress, Amy Irving, as a deaf teacher of deaf children in *Voices*. The film was being picketed in San Francisco by deaf people "chanting" in sign language, and protests were lodged in other metropolises.

I conceived this as an example of the minority mind-set run amok. I had seen the film and could find nothing in it that I thought should be offensive to deaf people. Their complaint was simply that a deaf actress should have been cast in the lead part. I thought of Jane Wyman in *Johnny Belinda*, a 1948 film in which a hearing actress also played a deaf woman. As I knew no real deaf people, Jane Wyman formed my image of deaf behavior. She was, of course, mute—following the common conception that deaf people cannot speak—and she seemed childlike, helpless in the grip of her circumstances. I do not recall that she used sign language. I noted in my column that Amy Irving, thirty years later, made a far more self-reliant deaf person, one more attached to the hearing world around her than Johnny Belinda, certainly an image that the deaf should favor. Jane Wyman had won an Academy Award for *Johnny Belinda*, and Jon Voight had won another for *Coming Home* in 1978. Should the producers and director have cast a paraplegic in Jon Voight's role, I wondered in print to my readers. The deaf, I concluded, were simply taking out a considerable degree of frustration on everyone else. "It was as though," I wrote, "each of the protesters could not imagine himself as anything other than—anything more than—deaf and oppressed."

A couple of days after the column had run, the *News* printed a letter to the editor from a young deaf man observing that, with all due respect, I had it exactly wrong. It was because the deaf *could* see themselves as far more than "just deaf" that the protests had occurred. At the same time, the newspaper got a personal letter addressed to me that it forwarded to my home in Chapel Hill. The letter had a gentle, serene tone and I read it through with pleasure before I realized that I had been put perfectly and precisely in my place. She always read my columns, the letter writer said, and liked them, but it occurred to her that perhaps I did not know much about disability. In fact, she guessed, it was a subject I simply had never encountered before. If I was interested in another viewpoint—she assumed I lived in Charlotte—I might drop in and see her sometime. She signed the letter in a precise hand that nevertheless had about it a touch of elegance: Elisabeth Hudson.

I had a business trip scheduled for Charlotte, and I figured a stop-off at Elisabeth Hudson's house would be worth a sequel to my column at least. I walked up the long, concrete ramp to the front door, rang the doorbell, and was in another instant gazing down at a solid-looking woman with steel-gray hair, lively eyes, and an appraising smile, sitting in a wheelchair. She wheeled herself back out of the way and motioned me in. She had coffee and a piece of pie waiting. "If you hadn't phoned first," she said, "you probably wouldn't have caught me home." I remember being surprised at that remark, wondering vaguely for the first time how folks in wheelchairs managed to get uptown. I learned that she was widowed, a former newspaperwoman and medical secretary, that she had been married twice and had grandchildren. She was, she said, an inveterate daily correspondent who belonged to a network of people who shared their lives with each other by mail. She referred to me and others about her as "T.A.B.s," which she translated as "Temporarily Able-Bodied."

She had telephones in every room, including the bathroom. She had pictures of grandchildren standing or hanging in every possible position. Her African violets on the kitchen windowsill were enough to arouse the envy of anyone who has tried to grow these pesky beauties in not-quite-the-right-place. And she had a device she called her "sliding board," a waxed-slick oak board that she used to transfer herself from her wheelchair to her bed by slipping it under herself and dragging herself across it.

But what I remember most from that first visit is Elisabeth Hudson's cheerfulness and the inordinate amount of time we spent talking about me. Journalists who allow that to happen usually are encouraged by their editors to enter the true-confession magazine field. I remember being aware that I was not getting material for a second column, although I would have been shocked to learn that I never would write a word about her until now. At the end of our time together, I left, and it did not occur to me until later that she had not spoken to me about disability at all. She had let me see that she functioned inside the house with complete independence. She had shown me an individual with a disability who had many abilities and interests, one of which was, at the moment, figuring out the kind of person who might write the column I had written. Shortly afterward, I found myself rereading it to the same purpose.

"You're not bad or stupid," she wrote me in answer to my apologetic letter about the column after our visit. "Quite the opposite. But you are ignorant. You're as ignorant as I was before I landed in this wheelchair. This was my education and maybe I can be yours. And yes, by the way, they should have found a paraplegic to play Jon Voight's part in that movie. He would have brought insights to the part that Jon could never imagine. If you were casting for a part of someone who was down and out, wouldn't you be happy to learn that your choice himself had been there?"

Not long after this I had the opportunity, through my work with MDC, to write the monograph that came to be called *Seven Special Kids*, about the struggles of youths with disabilities and their families to receive education and employment. The first person I called with the news was Elisabeth Hudson. "This is *intended* for you," she said. "What you mean," I responded, "is that I am perfectly unqualified for it." She laughed what I can only describe as an assenting laugh. My search in Charlotte for one of these youths led me to the home of Wayne and Donna Walcott. He taught in the geography department at the University of North Carolina at Charlotte. She was a radiation-protection specialist in one of the city's hospitals. They had been foster parents and had a deaf child briefly. Donna knew sign language and taught it to Wayne and their two small sons. They wrote "use sign language" almost as an afterthought on the form they had to fill out to get another foster child and that is how I came to meet them and their new foster son, Jimmy.

Jimmy had been found by the social services people living off the street and underneath porches. He was nine years old and had never been to a school. He had virtually no language. Social services sent him to the North Carolina School for the Deaf in Morganton. When Wayne and Donna first met him there, he was thirteen and learning how to add single-digit numbers and being taught three-letter words. His social skills were nil. He had not even learned to brush his teeth. His eyes were a jaundiced yellow. After a year of visiting Jimmy when they could, taking him home for weekends, the Walcotts decided to bring him home to Charlotte and place him in an elementary school there. At least that way, they reasoned, he could live in a real home and have a family.

I went over to the Walcotts' house and we all went out to a Chinese restaurant. The conversation flowed around Jimmy, reaching him only when someone, usually Donna, stopped and signed to him. This was slow, heavy work. Donna translated some basic questions for me. Yes, Jimmy was pleased to be in a school with kids who were deaf and some who were not. Yes he was happy to be with the Walcotts and living in a real home. Yes, school was hard. Jimmy smiled but his eyes did not participate. I wondered how it would be to start from so far behind and whether a kid with as little language as Jimmy had could even express so simple a thought as that.

As I watched Jimmy eat, Donna Walcott told me that when he first came to them, he had no concept of mealtimes. He ate whenever he was hungry. He had lived like that as far back in his life as he remembered. He ate and foraged and got what he could. He did not speak. When I talked with Elisabeth Hudson about him, she smiled mysteriously. Wheeling over to a coffeepot in her kitchen, she said, over her shoulder, "the Wild Boy of Aveyron."

I didn't understand the reference. "He was discovered in a forest in France, in the nineteenth century, I believe," Elisabeth Hudson said. "Running on all fours, howling at the moon, living like an animal. They tried to civilize him."

"Was he deaf?"

"Don't think so, but he had no language. Like your Jimmy before he was sent to the school for the deaf. Famous teachers tried to teach the wild boy to speak."

"Any luck?"

"No, not even as much luck as Jimmy. He couldn't learn how to speak, and they wouldn't let him learn how to sign."

"My God, why wouldn't they?"

"I don't know. Seems to me they believed that if he learned to sign he would never learn to speak. They were trying to civilize him, understand, and that meant speaking."

The first time I received a telephone call on my TTY I spilled a drink and broke the glass. Back then, I kept the TTY in a case in a cubbyhole under the stairs leading to the second floor. Since to that point, I had always initiated the calls, I could get it out of its case at my leisure, bring it into the kitchen, place it on a counter, plug in the connector between the electrical outlet and the machine, dial the number I wanted on my telephone, hold a second to make sure the phone was ringing at the other end, ease the phone ears into the rubber cups at the top of the TTY, and wait for the familiar line to appear on my screen. "Rowley here. GA." After that, it was just a typing exercise.

But this time the phone rang at my house. Half-dressed to go out for the evening and in a mood to dispose of a frivolous call swiftly, I answered it upstairs. When I put the receiver to my ear, I heard the familiar TTY sound, an electronic beeping, and realized that someone was calling me. I had to get downstairs and set up the TTY before I could respond. Grabbing loose clothing, I stumbled down the stairs, opened the TTY case, and pulled out the machine. On the counter, I bumped a glass and turned it over. The contents spilled on the floor, followed by the glass, which shattered. All this had taken several minutes and I still had to do the remainder of the drill.

By the time I got on the line, I suspected that no one would be on the other end. But when I typed in "R.C. here. GA [Go Ahead]," Nancy Rowley came right on. I explained where I was when the call came in and what had happened. "Sounds like you panicked," she said. She was calling to make sure we had fully agreed on somewhat complicated arrangements. My wife Kathryn and I were driving up from Durham the next day with the purpose of touring Croton, where Clifford grew up, and Rochester, where Nancy grew up, with them as guides.

Since then I have learned about the TTY and conversations with the deaf. Everything is expected to move slowly. Every deaf person is more patient than any hearing person I have known. Patience is the bedrock virtue of the deaf. To rush or be rushed would be to plunge from misunderstanding to misunderstanding. For them, a calm receptivity is the modus operandi: anything less would be an invitation to chaos. For this reason, and because of the mechanical nature of the process, TTY calls tend to run long. But that is only the obvious remarkable thing about them.

You do not know until you begin to use a device like the TTY how much of your conversation is dependent on voice tone or, to put it another way, how much cuing we hearing people give each other by the tone of our voices. Are we in a hurry? The tightness of our voice and the barely perceptible increase in the pulse of our vocal delivery convey the message. Are we feeling blue? We don't have to say it—in fact we may be calling a sympathetic friend just to get a reaction to our mood, "What's wrong, what has happened?" Our excitement with good news is readily discernible before the news is out, and our barely repressed chuckle as we go through the amenities gives away our anticipation of telling a funny story. Lovers need say nothing but "hello"—the rest is deeply encoded in the wordless, warm wash of tone.

All this, and more, is missing on the TTY. Most important among what's missing are the barely audible word cues we use for encouragement or discouragement. If the other person is beginning to say what we want to hear, we punctuate that person's conversation with little pecks of encouragement—"yeah," "sure"—so soft that they serve as a complement, as an obbligato trumpet passage serves the jazz singer. Those same words, uttered in a faintly stiff way, repeated a trifle more insistently, suggest to the speaker that the purposes of the call are not being well served. It is time to move on to another subject, we are suggesting.

The TTY flattens all this out, so that on a graph of emotional involvement, it would produce nothing but a straight line. It is in this sense that I have come to think of it as a purely artificial communication, lacking both the verbal element natural to hearing communication and the visual element essential to the deaf. To watch people sign to one another is to see language come to life. The TTY is at the opposite end of the expressive spectrum. It is more than a convenience for the deaf; it is, or has been, vital. But it is inexpressive.

The signer's face, for instance, is hot with laughter as he or she tells a joke. On the TTY, the same person is reduced to typing in "ha ha" to signify humor, or at least to beg the other person not to take what has been said too seriously. But what kind of "ha ha" is it? A funny one, a sarcastic one, a derogatory or cynical one?

It is also possible to be tricked easily by the TTY. I had a conversation of thirty minutes duration once on the TTY with a person who turned out to be the hearing wife of a deaf man. Each of us had assumed the other was deaf. I remember feeling a surge of relief when I heard her voice on the phone, and I realized how infinitely more comfortable I am with verbal conversation. Sadly, that seems to effect my direct communications with deaf people face-to-face. I have found to my embarrassment that I am not an expressive speaker visually. I have a close-cropped beard that nevertheless shields my lips, uneven teeth, and, apparently, a way of speaking that yields little in the way of facial expression. I, who have always prided myself on communications skills, am what the deaf call "a bad read." And I am taking to sign language poorly. I am in a class with seven women. We meet once a week and every one of my classmates is significantly ahead of me. I do signs into the bathroom mirror sneakily, like a little boy rehearsing a scene in a school play. Nothing seems to help. I content myself with observing that women take to sign more naturally than men, using their hands to stress or convey meaning. In the end I am left with the TTY, a communication medium that seems inflectionless, like a lyric without music.

In Rochester, Nancy, my wife Kathryn, and I drove beside the river to the south of town on Plymouth Avenue, past the place where the Portuguese Athletic Club once stood and where Nancy's father, Ernest M. Mahoney, grew up. When Nancy was born in Rochester in 1938, the great "Manassa Mauler," Jack Dempsey, according to a local newspaper story, was disappointed. Dempsey's friend Mahoney had promised that if he had a son, the fighter would be the boy's godfather. Knowing Mahoney, Dempsey figured the kid would be a tiger. It may never have occurred to Dempsey or to Mahoney that a girl child might have some of the same qualities.

"King" Mahoney was a politician of the old school, a generous-spirited, loyal Irishman who had the proverbial gift of gab, organizing ability, and a sense of command. In Republican Rochester of the 1930s, one of only two heavily Democratic wards was the nineteenth, composed of the Irish with a considerable leavening of Italians. Mahoney was a power in the nineteenth because he had lived there all his life and worked for the Democratic Party from the earliest opportunity. He loved a good fight, understanding that no fight was good without a cause. He knew how to get people to dig deep for their cash and their votes.

He left grade school and went to work in a factory where he met his wife-to-be, Sarah, from Altoona, Pennsylvania, who had only a fourth-grade education, but was a passionate reader and writer of poetry. After brief service during World War I, he became manager of a clothing store on State Street. When the store went bankrupt after the stock market crash of 1929, Mahoney used his favored position in the party to open the Portuguese Athletic Club, a restaurant–bar–speakeasy. The P.A.C. provided him with the business base from which to pursue two of his main passions, boxing and helping youth.

He had put his time in himself in the ring and was a referee for years afterward. He was convinced that in crowded cities the youth with the discipline to learn self-defense had already taken a big step in the right direction away from a life of crime. He and two associates brought from Cleveland a system called "Hi-Chair" boxing, which organized youth from nine to sixteen years of age, taught them the manly art, and, in the parlance of the day, kept them off the streets. This imported system spread through Rochester's parishes.

The King's third passion was his daughter. He liked to take Nancy with him when he visited his fight haunts in New York City. In his column the boxing writer Ned Brown noted that Mahoney's knowledge of old-time fights and fighters was prodigious. The columnist also observed that little Nancy was bright enough to be one of the "Quiz Kids," a preternaturally knowledgeable group of children who answered difficult questions on a radio quiz show to the awed cooing of adults and the despair of ordinary children. "Must take after her mother," the columnist reported Mahoney as saying, with a courtly bow to his wife.*

Nancy was bright, but there was something about her that was never mentioned in these accounts of her journeys with her father: she was rapidly losing her hearing. She had had normal hearing until she was four years old, when she contracted German measles three times. She remembers a long, numbing month in bed in their white house on Genessee Street. The hearing loss was not diagnosed at first, but by the next year, Nancy was not dancing to the music. Her parents enrolled her in Nazareth Model School, a Catholic school, and got her the first of several hearing aids to use in first grade.

Mahoney was devastated by his daughter's hearing loss and would not believe it was irreversible. During her fourth-grade year, Nancy was flown to New York City by her father each month for one whole week for ear treatments. He refused to take the advice of a specialist who told him, finally, that he would take no more of the family's money for such treatments. Mahoney found a Park Avenue doctor who performed an operation intended to "widen" Nancy's Eustachian tubes, a procedure over which other patients later sued for malpractice. Nancy suffered pain and the constant realization that her father was desperate about her situation. His feelings of guilt demanded nothing less than a "cure" for her deafness. The final effort

* "Pardon My Glove," *Daily Sports Bulletin* (New York), June 24, 1948, p. 2.

was a trip he took with a lawyer friend, who had a daughter with a physical disability, to consult a Catholic faith healer in the Thousand Islands.

"He would have gone to Satan himself to find a cure," said Bob Mahoney, the orphaned son of Sarah Mahoney's brother, who was brought up in the Mahoney household as Nancy's brother. We had stopped by the Mahoney house for lunch, and Bob talked about King and Nancy. "They are a lot alike," he said of the two. "King was not belligerent but he'd never back down." The only result of Mahoney's efforts to restore his daughter's hearing was that Nancy had to repeat the fourth grade because of time missed from school for the treatments. She did this in a different school, the Academy of the Sacred Heart. It was a good school, but the principal had doubts about enrolling a pupil with a severe hearing loss. At the end of the year, the principal suggested a public school with "facilities" to help hearing-impaired children.

Public School No. 31, which Nancy attended for three years, is now the Rochester Christian Day Care/Nursery of the Rochester Christian Church Ministries, a pleasant, airy building whose rooms an unsmiling Nancy explored with us. Public School 31 was an unmitigated educational disaster for Nancy Mahoney. "It was here I made up my mind to be a teacher of the deaf," she told us as we strolled through the playrooms where once rows of chair–desks stood. She was placed in a "hearing conservancy" class, which combined hearing-impaired youths from the fifth through the seventh grades. Most of the students were behind Nancy in their academic development, but that mattered little, as academic development seemed the last thing on the school's program. Her teacher, Elizabeth Sargent, a hearing woman, was committed totally and solely to teaching the children to lip-read.

We had learned just before taking our trip that Sargent had died. Nancy was particularly sorry to hear the news, as she would have liked us to meet her former teacher. "She was very nice," Nancy said, "but it was what the school wanted that caused the problem. I was lucky to have speech, because I lost my hearing late. What I needed was subject content, not lipreading. Every deaf child learns as much of lipreading as she can by herself. And those other poor children. . . ." She made a gesture in front of her face as though to brush away a recollection, "What a waste." Nancy paused in a hallway, studying a direction, as though temporarily lost. "You know," she said, turning to us, "years later I found out the worst thing I could imagine. Mrs. Sargent could sign perfectly well and had used signing at the Western Pennsylvania School for the Deaf. She had been told by Public

52

School 31 not to use signing under any circumstances: neither teach it nor use it where the children could see it."

"Why was that?" I asked, suspecting that I knew the answer but wanting to hear exactly what Nancy would say.

"Sign language back then was associated with deaf schools. They said 'deaf and dumb.' They thought that if you let deaf children learn sign language, they would never learn to speak."

"Did deaf people believe that?"

"I don't think so. But all the teachers of the deaf seemed to be hearing people and they believed it. As for me and the other children, I don't think we knew anything like signing existed."

Nancy knew enough to be certain that she wasn't learning anything. She beseeched her father to take her out of that public school and, after the seventh grade, he did. She entered the eighth grade at St. Agnes Grammar School and credits the sisters there with helping her to make up for the three "wasted" years spent in the public school. Here, for the first time, she managed to get organized help from a classmate who would sit by her and take notes. But by this time, Nancy's hearing had deteriorated to the point where she was, legally and practically, deaf.

For himself, King Mahoney felt certain that he would not live to be an old man. He had suffered his first stroke when he was fifty-two years old; his doctor was blunt about his chances of surviving another. Mahoney was consumed with dread of what might happen to his daughter. He knew how close they were, how his death would affect her. He saw, every day, the decline of her hearing and was bitterly aware of the failure of his efforts to find help. He was, perhaps, not aware of the anxiety that his guilty feelings evoked in his daughter, who felt that she had somehow failed him. And the last thing that would have occurred to him—or to other hearing parents of deaf children of that day—was to find out how other deaf adults coped. His daughter might not hear, but he did not want her to be regarded as deaf.

At Nancy's urging, we parked at the corner of Prince and Main, not far from the St. Agnes school, where King Mahoney had parked (one day years ago) with his thirteen-year-old daughter. "I couldn't imagine what he wanted to say," Nancy recalled. "He spoke softly but he told me that he would not live more than five years. He wanted to prepare me for it. I made him repeat it. I couldn't believe it."

In that same year, 1951, Mahoney's five years as a Democratic ward leader and his long popularity in the city paid off. A commissioner of the Board of

Elections retired at the mandatory age of seventy, and Mahoney was chosen to fill out his term. Two years later, King Mahoney suffered a massive stroke, late one October afternoon, in the offices of the Board of Elections and died on his way to the hospital. They found in his suit pocket a black book that showed he was owed almost $10,000 by poor parishioners to whom he had made small "loans" for food and coal. The Rochester papers remembered him as a great force for good in the city. A boxing ring was dedicated in his name, to be used to carry on the work he had begun with youngsters. A Republican member of the Board of Elections told Sarah Mahoney that her husband was the best man he had ever met in public life.

"Mother took his death very hard," Nancy told us. "She was very good with me, very patient. She made herself very easy to lip-read. She made sure I was included in every conversation. She is why I made sure of that with Amy." Still, Nancy remembers how difficult her mother was to lip-read once she had to wear false teeth.

Nancy graduated from St. Agnes High School in 1957. Her high school yearbook makes it clear that she was popular with both the other students and the sisters. Determined to continue her education, she thought first of Nazareth College in Rochester. She was shocked when she visited that school to find that she could not in the least understand what was going on in classes. She lip-read meaningless words, saw teachers who mumbled or turned away before speaking, observed students laughing at what was said, when she understood nothing. How could she have fallen so far behind? She began to wonder if she could handle college. A neighbor had heard about a college for the deaf and wrote a friend who told her about Gallaudet University. Here was a college located right in the nation's capital, specifically created for deaf students. Thrilled that Abraham Lincoln had been involved in approval of enabling legislation for the school, Nancy wrote for application forms, took the entrance exam, and was accepted.

At Gallaudet, Nancy Rowley walked into a new world. For the first time she met other deaf adults. Everybody signed whether or not they spoke. Nancy found that the boys were more than willing to help her learn sign language and finger-spelling. In a matter of weeks she was beginning to communicate as she never had before. With this, came the realization of what she had missed, a sensation of having been closed out from the ease of conversation all her life. The experience was stunningly revealing to her, as though she had found her way through an unknown door and stumbled into a land of infinite possibility that she had never dreamed existed. "Light pouring down on me," is how she later described it.

54

In the midst of all this, a classmate of hers at Gallaudet invited her to visit with him at his parents' house and see the New York School for the Deaf, from which he had recently graduated. When they visited the library of the school, they met the librarian with two senior students who, the librarian said, would be at Gallaudet the next year. Nancy had been presented with a candy apple by the baking instructor at the school and carried it with her. She was only mildly interested in the two students, but one of them, Clifford Rowley, would remember the young woman with the candy apple perfectly.

Clifford Rowley has no memory of the sound of the human voice. He had influenza meningitis at the age of fourteen months, and his mother thought she might lose him in the spring of 1943. She was in Berkeley, California, with Clifford and his older brother, Lee. Her husband Elmer was overseas with the Marines. The doctors were not sure at first what Clifford had, or whether it was contagious. He was in the county hospital for three weeks. When his mother went to see him, he lay there, still and white. Bunny Rowley was afraid to write Elmer, unsure of what she should tell him.

Eventually Clifford got better, but he was not responding to speech. Back in the states, and based in San Francisco, Elmer reminded his wife that he himself had not spoken until he was almost five years old. They took comfort from that. When the family moved across the continent to Croton-on-Hudson, New York, and put Clifford in nursery school at the age of four, he began to have temper tantrums. For a long time, nobody could determine what the problem was. His nursery school teacher finally suggested that they have his hearing checked. In the office of a specialist in New York City, they sat and talked as the doctor went over Clifford's tests. When the doctor had finished, he turned to them and said, "Well, he's deaf and there is nothing you can do about it."

The nursery school kept Clifford for a year and then he had a year in kindergarten, after which the principal called his parents in to inform them that their son could not be admitted to the first grade and would have to go to the New York School for the Deaf. There was, the principal said, no other choice for a deaf child. Clifford was admitted and immediately put into an experimental oralist class.

"I remember the instructions very well," said Elmer Rowley, stretching back in a porch chair at the Rowleys' woodsy place in Medford, New Jersey, where we were visiting. "All these five- and six-year-olds were kept completely separate. They were supposed to use no signs whatsoever. In fact, they were really criticized if they used signs. The people in the school told us not to learn sign language and not to speak to Clifford in sign language because they would teach him to speak perfectly. Some of those deaf children came from deaf parents, and of course they signed every chance they had away from the authorities. Clifford began learning it right away. I've wished so many times that we had learned it. We always communicated easily with Clifford but with so many of his friends we can't communicate. And some of his best friends never did learn how to speak. I've always felt bad about that."

Clifford got on well at the New York School for the Deaf and soon left temper tantrums behind him. His classmates were mainly from the Bronx, where they lived in cramped, boxy tenements. Many of them did not have the advantage of supportive parents that Clifford had. Clifford saw that he could learn faster than most of his fellow students. With this, he began to take abuse from these boys. He was the equivalent of an Ivy League kid in a tough, inner-city school.

And a residential school to boot—that was the worst part of it from Clifford's standpoint. Some of the other kids might be happy to be away from their home surroundings, but he lived in a two-story, gray house trimmed in white set high above the Croton River, with a sun room view of the woods. Clifford's parents came for him every weekend, but around 3 P.M. Sunday when it was time to go back to school, Clifford developed a stomachache or a headache or disappeared mysteriously into the woods. More than one Sunday night in the early days of school, he was carried over his father's shoulder, screaming, back to school.

Croton was turning out to be a good place for Clifford's parents. Elmer was managing a chemical firm in Westchester County, and Bunny, whose interest was art, was thriving on the hilly, country landscapes. They were happy to have Clifford's friends come home with him for weekends. Once Clifford brought several classmates home, including a boy who was African American. Later Elmer asked who that particular lad was and Clifford had difficulty identifying the friend his father was asking about. Elmer decided that his son had found deafness sufficiently defining to brook no further subdivisions. His classmate was just another deaf kid, like himself.

The use of sign language by Clifford and his friends proved subversive. Girls from the area were constantly in the Rowley home, where they met boys from the school for the deaf and learned signs. When the school had dances, the Rowleys brought girls over to partner the boys. "The girls were enjoying it," Elmer recalled, "and were beginning to sign among themselves, to the point where one of the families we knew had three girls who got to signing in front of their mother. She put her foot down, 'You can't do that, I want to know what you are saying.'"

Elmer talked the manager of a golf driving range into giving Clifford a job when the boy was sixteen. The manager may have had qualms about Clifford's "handicap" but they vanished swiftly. The Rowleys were amazed one day to see their son happily waiting on customers, making change, communicating easily enough. It occurred to them, not for the first time, that they probably were more intimidated by their son's handicap than he was. After all, hadn't he been coping with it all his life? In the end, the manager developed such confidence in him that he left Clifford in charge when he went away on vacation.

Clifford's aspirations for college were not unrealistic but he had a difficult climb ahead of him. When he graduated from the New York School for the Deaf at eighteen, he had had the equivalent of about two years of high school English. He was functioning at the ninth-grade level. To be fair to the school, only a tiny minority of its students had any hope of attending college. Only one or two a year, at most, did go on, most of them to Gallaudet, which was prepared to offer one or two extra years to students who were behind academically. Clifford made a visit to Gallaudet in the spring of 1960 and set about looking up the girl with the candy apple.

Nancy had heard from the classmate who had her up for the visit to the New York School for the Deaf that Clifford was interested in her, so she was not surprised to see him again. She was surprised to learn that he was a good swimmer, and headed for the Gallaudet swimming team, while she was captain of the girls' team. When Clifford arrived at Gallaudet in the fall, they saw a lot of each other. By Clifford's junior year, they were engaged and, at the end of that year, they were married.

By this time Nancy had graduated with a bachelor's degree in economics and a master's in education. She had a job in Scranton at the Pennsylvania Oral School for the Deaf. When she inquired about "Oral" in the school's name, she was told she could communicate with students in any way she wished. Within a few years, the school had dropped "Oral" from its name, but by then Nancy was teaching at the New York School for the Deaf, and Clifford was looking for a job in the Westchester area. Prospects should have been excellent for someone with a degree in chemical engineering, but

Clifford was told by management of two chemical plants that while he was qualified, they could not hire him because their insurance would not allow it—a reason many individuals with disabilities have been given over the years.

Elmer Rowley had sold the chemical business he had built up over the years. One of the young "whiz kids," out of the Massachusetts Institute of Technology, who had bought Elmer's firm called him one day about Clifford, who had applied to him for work. Elmer told him that the only difference between him and Clifford was that Clifford didn't get quite so much out of his education as he had. But, Elmer added, "He got a satisfactory amount. He was graduated from Gallaudet. He got passing marks in every course he took. He's a chemist." Clifford got the job.

We climb a steep, sun-swept flight of concrete steps and at the top look out across a grassy quad to trees, a flagpole, hedges, and roses, all kept up to the mark and sprinkled. The buildings have an institutional orthodoxy: ivy aged on brick. Clifford brushes a strand of hair from his receding hairline and begins talking in the mildly singsong accents of the prelingually deaf. He points out places of interest: the gym back down the stairs we have climbed; the superintendent's office on our left as we face the quad; and, on our right, the closest building, Peet Hall, our goal.

The hall is dedicated to Harvey P. Peet, president of the New York School for the Deaf in the mid-nineteenth century, and its walls are lined with portraits of the movers and shakers of deaf education over the years. I ask the question and Clifford, lipreading with skill honed from working every day in a hearing world, nods, Yes, all hearing men. "Why is that?" I ask. Clifford shrugs. "As far back as I can remember," he says. I can see behind his eyes a desire to go further into the subject, but also sense that this is not the time. We have come—Clifford, my wife, and I—to meet Taras Denis, a teacher of Clifford's who has retired but is still working at the school as a kind of troubleshooter, worrying about jobs for graduates, doing psychological counseling, even visiting jails. Denis also is deaf.

In a basement office we find him behind a cluttered desk bearing the sign: "Look at this mess. Be neat. Clean your work area." He rises, beaming, when he sees Clifford and locks him in a bear hug. Clifford explains with signs and speech what we are here for, as Denis smuggles cheerfully reinforcing grins at us. When the three of us have taken seats, Denis moves several steps to the left of his desk as though to mount a podium, smiles, and says—in a voice remarkably well modulated for one who is deaf—"Tell me what I can do for you. I am all eyes."

He is short and stocky; he chews gum from which, now and then, a bubble arises precariously toward his cheek and pops ominously. This morning he is wearing a blue polo shirt sporting the world-famous alligator, green Bermuda shorts, and sneakers over bare feet. He plunges into conversation like an actor into a final rehearsal, richly gesticulative, holding us to his words by main force. After learning enough from him to understand that his good voice is the result of losing his hearing late, after language and speech development, I ask him about "Fanwood." What is its value today?

"Every penny in this school comes out beautiful. Even the slow [kids], we get them jobs. *Never* close this school, these deaf schools. It gives these slow kids a chance to get into the world." (He accompanies these last words with the gesture of reaching out with his foot, drawing it back, and then slowly extending it, as though testing the temperature of the water.) "When I graduated from college, I thought, first, what am I doing here? These kids can't even read. But I found out there were good things: when you empathize, they respond. Also humor. It warms them up, then praise them. It works. Clifford . . . " (He makes a long stern face and looks at Clifford, causing Clifford to grin as though remembering an old attention-getting trick.) "Clifford was a bright one. I taught poetry, theater—*Dr. Jekyll and Mr. Hyde* and Clifford got more than most of the others. But he needed the socialization whether he knew it or not. You know most deaf kids come from hearing parents? OK. That's a handicap. Maybe one deaf kid out of ten—less than that—has a great situation like Amy had, with language, constant language.

"Amy was different, is different. She has it all. She is one of the fortunate few, thanks to Clifford and Nancy. What that was about, Amy's case, it was all about money. The principal said it straightforward and with no holds barred, do you know how much money this could mean, how much it would cost the school? They twisted it and implied that all deaf kids are as smart as Amy is. They are not, believe me. Amy really did need an interpreter. It was a perfect time for her. So then they listened to themselves on the subject of money and they said [he makes a hush-hush movement with his lips and hands] let's don't talk about money. They didn't like the sound of that 'don't spend money' on their lips, but that was it, that was the issue all along."

Denis grew up on Delancy Street in the Lower East Side, one of five children of parents who had immigrated from the Ukraine. ("You are Ukrainians," his father told the children, "and not Russians.") Denis' father made soap for the Colgate-Palmolive Company in its Brooklyn plant and spent his nights reading and writing English. When Taras came down with spinal meningitis at eight and lost his hearing, his father stopped putting him on his lap to teach him Ukrainian. But the parents saw what had happened as an affliction visited upon them all and responded with love and their permission for Taras to roam freely, play stickball with the other kids, swim in the East River (making sure he allowed no water in his mouth), and develop as best he could.

"What do we need?" (Denis asks the question with a great, quizzical twist of his face and a pulling back of his neck, eyes wide as though in anticipation of the answer.) "We need a club for deaf kids, not a social thing but a mental health thing. These deaf kids grow up holding everything inside, without communication, and then one day they explode. Then they have to go to psychiatrists and mental hospitals, which still can't help, and it costs a lot of money. The club would socialize them and they would meet other people, learn about new products. What's a job opportunity? What's a good thing to do? This is what they need to hear. [He taps his ear and then makes a face as if not understanding at first and then, suddenly, brightening as though a light has gone on.] You normal people [The word "normal" has a light but sharp edge as he pronounces it.] turn on the radio and television set and learn even when you don't want to. Right? Did you know that? People learn the most just listening, responding, socializing. Deaf people find that difficult except among themselves."

Later in the conversation, his face darkens and he begins to speak with evident emotion. "I'm worried about deaf old people. We separate them, leave them in homes, and they are very lonely. In the midst of a thousand people, if there is no communication, you are dead. Take two eighty-year-old people in different homes and put them together and you may have something. That's where a club could come in."

Back in the motel later on, I pull out my notes to underline what seems important in Denis' conversation. When I get to the part about deaf, old people, I realize that these words have been on my mind from the instant I heard them: "We separate them, leave them in homes and they are very lonely." My mother, eighty-eight-years-old at this time, blind, deaf in one ear and hard-of-hearing in the other, is in such a home.

My wife and I had no doubts about the rightness of the decision when the time had come a few years earlier; neither, for that matter, had my mother. She had had normal eyesight most of her life until cataracts and, eventually, glaucoma, had blinded her. She could no longer live alone, even with help. She would not live with us, a family with growing children. Our only regret is that we had not persuaded her to take the step sooner, while she still had vestigial sight, so as to avoid the terrors that afflicted her the first few months in this admirable nursing home. She suffered delusions that, we became convinced, were partly the result of the medication she was being given and partly of being in an environment she had never seen. While the home had its share of hard-of-hearing, weak-sighted old people, it had never had a person as severely reduced in perception and communication skills as mother.

When we visited, mother talked about being kidnapped and taken across a river to another place where she received treatments she could not bring herself to discuss with us. A little investigation on our part turned up that she had been given a whirlpool treatment that week, which cleared up part of the mystery but would have been useless, of course, as an explanation to her. We got the nurses to persuade the doctor to change her medication. Still the delusions persisted, centering more now on things done in her room at night, people congregating to whisper plots against her when they thought she slept. If it were not for the unusual vigor of her mind on all other matters, we would have concluded that she was losing her grip on reality altogether.

She desperately wanted someone to be with her a few days a week. She had not been blind long enough to have learned all of the basic coping mechanisms, we thought, and in these so different circumstances wanted someone to help her find her way about. We were glad to find a professional practical nurse who came in for a few hours three days a week to help her dress and undress, find her way around the hall where she lived, take her for walks. For a long time during that period, I was convinced that this was why mother wanted the woman, practical nurse Maggie Ray, with her so fiercely.

It was Ray, herself, who finally convinced me otherwise. She had discovered the source of mother's delusions, or at least the kernel of actual experience that touched them off. The orderlies and other staff who came into her room were at pains not to announce their presence to her. She was, they had been told, blind and mostly deaf. Their reaction was to do what they had to do as quietly and inconspicuously as possible, "not to disturb" her, as one of them put it to Ray. And so of course they were slipping in and out of the room at night as silently as they could. Confident she was unable to hear, they sometimes turned on a portable television set in her room with the sound low, and took a break. During the day, faced with the difficulty of communicating with her, they simply did their job with no explanation, without even revealing themselves if they could manage that. They were, in effect, avoiding her, as I had avoided the blind man at my friend's parties so many years ago.

"In the midst of a thousand people" Denis had said, "if there is no communication, you are dead." As I read these words, I absorbed their full impact for the first time. The net result of the staff's treatment of my mother was utter isolation, compounded by confusion and fear of the unknown. It was this situation that she was asking for help with. She wanted someone to "interpret" what was going on and communicate with her. She wanted someone to talk with. And Ray, working with a blind and hard-of-hearing person for the first time, understood that and helped educate the others. "Speak into Mrs. Smith's left ear when you come into the room," she instructed them. "Make sure she understands what you are doing." Frowning, she told a few of those who still tended to shrink back, "She doesn't bite, you know."

What had not occurred to me until listening to Taras Denis was that my mother's problem was essentially a deaf problem, compounded by her blindness. A blind person can at least speak out and, just as important, be spoken to by those in the vicinity. Communication and understanding are available. The persons who shrank back from my mother in the nursing home feared that they would not be able to reach her with communication at all. In turn, she concluded that she had been abandoned to that most terrible of conditions, a kind of living death in a place where no word could reach. She had been left alone, at last, at the mercy of her worst fears. Poor Mother had lived long enough to get a bad bargain with both of her primary senses, but to see without understanding, I was beginning to believe, might be worse than to understand without seeing.

4

Vindication by Trial

On the morning of September 26, 1979, Ann Barbara Kligerman, chief of audiology for the Westchester County Medical Center, got up and, in accordance with a carefully thought-out decision, put on her blue cotton suit, a straight skirt and short-sleeved jacket, over a pin-striped red, white, and blue blouse—a decidedly tailored outfit. It was important to look professional and thus, as much as possible, to conceal the nervousness she felt. She had not slept well, her mind still full of the audiological test scores and definitions with which she had prepared herself. And, then, it was her first time ever as a witness in court.

She left her home in New Jersey in time to get to the United States District Court for the Southern District of New York at Foley Square in Manhattan a little early. She was mildly surprised at the crowd assembled and more surprised at the numbers of deaf people who were crammed into the back of the courtroom, with interpreters handy. Front right, she saw Nancy and Clifford Rowley and, at the attorneys' table, the man she assumed was Michael Chatoff, with whom she had talked over the TTY. On the other side of the bench, down front, was a table with two men she assumed were lawyers for the school district—one of them a slender, dapper man, impeccably groomed and looking, she thought, as though ready for television; the other, a smallish man with glasses and wispy hair. At their side were two women, smartly dressed and freshly, fashionably coifed. She wondered who they were.

How long it took to get matters under way also surprised her. The lawyers and judge involved themselves in a seemingly endless discussion over motions she was not entirely clear about. But her attention sharpened when Furnace Woods Elementary School Principal Joseph Zavarella began to testify. Zavarella told the court that Amy Rowley had scored 76 percent on a Word Intelligibility by Picture Identification (WIPI) test. Chatoff then established the principal's testimony in the impartial hearing that, in a classroom setting, Amy would probably understand "well beyond" that 76 percent. Kligerman believed that the Rowleys' attorney had put Zavarella on the stand to establish this and that her testimony would attempt to refute it.

Then, finally, her name was called out, and Barbara Kligerman was getting up a little shakily to take the witness stand. She had become even more anxious by having had to wait. It was not one of the things she did well. She remembered as a child wanting to be called on first. She had grown up in the Bronx, Ann Barbara Kane, in what she came to think of as a typical Russian American Jewish liberal home. Her father, frustrated in his efforts to go to law school by sickness in the family and poverty, had wanted a boy child to live out his dream. Still, as he walked to school with his daughter in the second and third grades, he had law school in mind for her. After graduating from high school with honors, she went to Syracuse University to study drama and switched to preparation for a general speech degree. Later, she was won over to the idea of practicing audiology, to which she devoted her master's and doctoral work at Columbia University.

Now, here she was sitting in a large, solemn courtroom, wishing she had had a little experience as being a witness. Then Chatoff was asking her the big, first question she was expecting: How did she define deafness?

"Deafness is when the hearing impairment is so severe that it precludes the use of hearing as a primary mode of communication, the primary receptive mode, with or without amplification."

"Is Amy Rowley deaf?"

"Yes, Amy is deaf." Then, after a question calling for further elaboration, she went on to testify that when Amy is asked to repeat two-syllable words, she is not able to do it in either ear until it reaches the intensity level of 85 to 90 decibels, whereas, with normal hearing, this would occur at around 15 decibels. As for speech discrimination, she said, various tests had been given and where her performance improved, it was because she had been given the same tests over and over again and had soaked up their contents.

Referring to the Gallaudet test score that Zavarella had testified to, she explained that this test consisted of identifying one out of six pictures, which were the same each time she was tested. "Therefore, I switched to a test she had never taken," she continued, "and I switched from my own speech, which Amy is very familiar with, to a tape, a commercially available, calibrated, standardized test, and with both hearing aides she scored 43 percent. . . . A normal-hearing child—a seven-year-old normal-hearing child—would understand 100 percent of those words. . . . And when we put noise into the system to try to simulate the classroom situation, her discrimination score deteriorated to 27 percent, which is no better than chance."

As she spoke, Kligerman looked first at Chatoff, who was following her testimony closely by monitoring the note-taker; at the attorneys for the other side, who seemed to be holding a whispered conference; and finally at Judge Broderick, who was listening intently. Good, she thought. What she had to say next was crucial and she was not being interrupted.

"Then we wanted to see what happened when we provided visual information—what happens to Amy's discrimination when you allow her to see your lips. So we used the Utley Lip Reading Test. She had both hearing aids on, she could see my lips, and she scored 58 percent. That means that out of 31 sentences such as 'Good morning, how are you?' and 'What's your name?'—I'm giving you examples of the kinds of things on the test—she scored 58 percent." She paused and glanced at Judge Broderick, who was still paying close attention. "When we repeated the sentence," she went on, "when we did it a second time, she was able to improve her score to 84 percent. When Mrs. Rowley was allowed to present the sentence at the same time—and this was a different sentence—with sign language, Amy scored 100 percent."

Later on, Chatoff returned to this same point, asking what effect poor lighting, background noise, group discussion, or a person with poor articulation or poor facial features would have on the 58 percent figure.

"The score would go down," Kligerman responded. "Her ability to discriminate speech comprehension definitely would go down under those adverse conditions."

Then Chatoff was back with a summational question. "The February 20, 1978, Gallaudet College test indicates that using the Word Intelligibility by Picture Identification Test, Amy understands 76 percent of spoken speech. Does it follow that Amy will understand 76 percent of what is said in a classroom?"

"No. That 76 percent was taken at Gallaudet in a soundproof room using a test which she had taken many times before."

Finally, Chatoff went to the issue of whether Amy heard better with the FM transistor or with her own hearing aids, drawing from Kligerman that on one test, Amy did better with her hearing aids. Before Chatoff could ask another question, Judge Broderick interposed, declaring a recess until the following day.

When it was apparent that the questioning was over for the day, Kligerman stood up and, to her astonishment, was greeted with a solid wave of applause from the deaf people in the courtroom. She stood still for an instant, shocked, unable to move. The applause continued, increasing in volume. As she realized she was receiving loud appreciation from the deaf community, Kligerman felt, along with the shock, a flushed warmth, as though she were blushing from embarrassment and pleasure. As a hearing person working mainly with deaf people, she had always wondered to what degree she was accepted by her deaf clients. It seemed now that she was accepted so warmly here for doing nothing more than testifying truthfully. At the same time, she felt apprehension. She expected that the school's attorneys would do their homework overnight and that she would be in for an attack the next day. She had seen how this was done on film and television. It did not look like fun from the point of view of an expert witness.

Long before Barbara Kligerman began her testimony, Nancy Rowley had gotten over her initial shock, but she still found herself unable to rationalize seeing Inez Janger at the counsel's table with Raymond Kuntz. Inez Janger was one of the two well-coifed women Kligerman had noticed, and she was passing notes to the school district's attorney, helping him in the case against Amy. Clifford had not recognized Janger right away, and Nancy had communicated with him as they sat down in the courtroom. "That woman," she said, signing and speaking and indicating Janger with her hand, "is the mother of a deaf child. I know her." Nancy could not believe it, a parent against a parent. She knew that Inez Janger had the oralist viewpoint, but she still could not imagine her testifying against Amy.

At the opposing counsel's table, with Raymond Kuntz, was Paul E. "Pete" Sherman, attorney for the Commissioner of Education of the State of New York. He was the man who had written the decision for the commissioner upholding the impartial hearing officer. He was there because Judge Broderick had joined the commissioner's office to the case, in effect making it a party to the Hendrick Hudson defense. Deaf individuals had crowded in to take available seats, and Sherman felt anger directed at him boiling up around him. It was unmistakable. His glance in the direction of these people was met with a withering stare. He felt that this hostility was misdirected. Why didn't they pick on New York City, he wondered, where there was so much to quarrel with in the schools? Why pick on this school district, which seemed to him to be doing a wonderful job with Amy? He was sure that the Rowleys were being used as a test case cooked up somewhere else. Why else would all these deaf people be here in the courtroom? Of course, it was possible that the district wanted a test case, too. From where he worked, in Albany, it was impossible to know.

Inez Janger was a parent–advocate working at Lexington School for the Deaf in New York City, developing and managing a referral service and attempting to secure an "oral option" for parents of deaf children. Although change was in the air, Lexington had long been regarded as a bastion of oralism, which meant that sign language had been strictly forbidden. Janger did not regard herself as a formal, unyielding oralist in the mode of some teachers at Lexington. Once, when teachers from Clarke, another oralist school, visited Lexington, she had the job of introducing them around. One of them remarked, not in the friendliest of tones, that for a parent of a deaf child she used her hands a lot while speaking. She realized with a shock that she was being chided for interfering with the lipreading skills of her child by the use of her hands. She set herself apart from people who thought that way.

On the other hand, she was raising her own child orally, without sign language, and felt strongly about her right to do that. The passage of the Education for All Handicapped Children Act of 1975 raised what was for oralists the specter of deaf children being mainstreamed with hearing children in a total communications mode with sign language. She did not regard herself as "anti" sign language but neither did she think that oral education and total communications could be taught in the same class. The alternative, many thought, might be "segregated" private schools for the oral option.

Janger was one of the victims of the rubella epidemic, and Michael, the youngest of her three sons, had been born deaf. After he had been diagnosed, she was told that they would give him a hearing aid at the age of four or five. She saw him disappearing into a school for the deaf and emerging with no oral skills. In effect, she saw him disappearing from her world. She became, to use her own word, "hysterical" over that.

She set out to educate herself about oralism and when the time came, she and her husband pulled every string they had to get Michael into Lexington. Her expectations for him in terms of speech were set back severely when she met a widely known, profoundly deaf oralist psychologist. When she heard this woman's voice she burst into tears. The psychologist's voice was good but flat, very "deaf." Janger began the process she would later describe as growing up, meeting other parents of deaf children, making common cause with them no matter how little like her she felt they were. And while Michael was getting an oral education, Janger and her husband let their son know that it was always his decision if he wanted to learn sign. She refused to denigrate it as so many of the oralist persuasion did.

When the school district asked her if she would visit Amy in school and consider testifying in the case on the side of the school, she felt ambivalent. She had met Nancy and respected her. She thought the Rowley family was remarkable. But she also felt an obligation to go to Furnace Woods and observe Amy. What she saw there convinced her that Amy was doing very well. She wished that her Michael, who was then eleven, had been as articulate and verbal as Amy was when he was her age.

Taking the stand to testify for the second day, Barbara Kligerman could not help but glance again at the two women who were with school district attorney Raymond Kuntz. She could guess that they were from Lexington without having to be told. She very nearly took a job at Lexington once herself.

Back in the 1960s, deaf education *was* pretty much oral education. She and her husband had gone out to California so that he could get his doctorate at Berkeley. Shortly after the rubella epidemic, she found herself diagnosing deaf babies at the Children's Hospital Medical Center of Northern California in Oakland. She helped form a support group for hearing parents of deaf children and found herself fascinated by these children. She noticed how dull and oppressed they seemed when they were prohibited from signing with one another and how eagerly they burst into bloom when they were allowed to sign. She observed, also, how poorly many of them spoke, even after much training. She came to believe something that was also observed in numerous studies in the late 1960s and

1970s—how much better prepared were the deaf children of deaf parents who had sign language from infancy as a first language upon which to build English as a second language.

By 1967, when she and her husband returned east, Kligerman had strong doubts about the exclusion of sign language, which had been the basis of oralism. With these doubts, and with two small children at home, she turned down an opportunity to interview for a job at Lexington. When the job at the Westchester Medical Center came open in 1972, she applied and got it. Two years later she was introduced to the little girl who was responsible for her sitting in a cold, uncomfortable wooden chair and looking out nervously at Kuntz, waiting for him to speak.

Kuntz began a line of questioning that apparently sought to distinguish between speech discrimination and speech comprehension. In the ensuing exchange, Kligerman found herself instructed several times "just to answer the question, please," when she felt the question could not be answered by a "yes" or a "no." At one point, Kuntz appealed to Judge Broderick to instruct the witness to confine her answers to the questions. The judge gently complied with the counsel's request. After drawing from Kligerman the statement that "schoolbook vocabulary tests" could be described in terms of "comprehension," Kuntz took off on another tack.

"You described Amy as scoring lower when she used the FM wireless system than when she used hearing aids apparently used by her outside the classroom, is that correct?"

"Her own hearing aids."

"When you conducted the test, did you make a calibration test or any other kind of test on the FM device to see if it was functioning properly?"

"In fact, it was not functioning properly. It was intermittent and we had to make sure that it was functioning—she had to sit still and to make sure that it was functioning at that time."

"Could its functioning have been intermittent during the time that it was utilized when the test was going forward."

"It could have been."

And then Kuntz was, suddenly, finished. Sherman had few questions and Barbara Kligerman found herself excused from the witness stand. It had not been the ordeal she had feared. Neither attorney had asked her a single question about her main testimony: the tests she had performed to establish the level at which the child could comprehend verbal speech. She felt unexpectedly set free and in a way wished she could remain for the rest of the day, as it appeared that an outside "expert" on deafness—who was himself deaf—was getting ready to take the stand.

The deaf expert witness was Martin Sternberg from the Deafness Research and Training Institute at New York University. Brought up in the South Bronx during the Depression, he was one of four children of a sheet metal worker who had spent three years out of work. Martin had lost his hearing from spinal meningitis at the age of seven, when he was in the third grade. His parents were horrified. Like so many hearing parents, their reaction was one of denial. They put Martin back in school for an abortive attempt to "carry on" despite the disability, but the school didn't seem to know what to do with the boy. Martin was finally relegated to P.S. 47, the city's public school for the deaf.

In one way, Martin was fortunate. He had developed language fully before he became deaf, and he could survive in the oral milieu in which he found himself. But he was an unhappy boy, his dreams of a career in music dashed, his parents still struggling to "shield" him and, in the process, distance themselves from the reality of his deafness. His father caught him trying to learn finger-spelling from a deaf teenager in the neighborhood and slapped him in the face for his trouble. With his parents spurring him on, he went to a hearing high school in the city. At this level, Martin had a difficult time, struggling to copy notes from students on either side while trying at the same time to get something out of lipreading.

Still, he graduated, attended City College of New York, and worked for the Red Cross part-time during the war. His breakthrough occurred when he was offered a part-time teaching job at Gallaudet while working for his masters degree at nearby American University. He discovered the first day at Gallaudet that he could not do without sign language there. He was fortunate to come under the aegis of a kindly, elderly professor named Elizabeth Peet, who belonged to the illustrious line of teachers of the deaf for whom Peet Hall at the New York School for the Deaf had been named. For five years, she met with him almost daily in her quarters on campus teaching him American Sign Language. He found the experience utterly transforming. From being an oralist, he was converted to total communication.

Sternberg returned to New York University later to work in the program that eventually became the Deafness Research and Training Institute, getting his doctorate in deafness rehabilitation there. His parents lived long enough to see their son a respected professor at N.Y.U., but not long enough to share the achievement represented by the publication of his *American Sign Language: A Comprehensive Dictionary*, the best-known publication of its kind and currently in its tenth printing.* His father and mother never said so, but Sternberg believes they came to understand that they had been wrong in those early years. But, of course, what they reflected was the common experience of hearing parents who had no one to turn to for information or advice.

Sternberg knew the Rowleys through contacts at Gallaudet, and when Michael Chatoff asked him to testify for Amy in court, he said that first he would have to meet Amy. Mindful of the stress she had been under, the Rowleys wanted to make the meeting as little like an interview as possible.

The result was an occasion all agreed was serendipitous. Nancy, Clifford, Amy, and Sternberg met at an ice cream parlor, made small talk, and got comfortable. Gradually, Sternberg steered this warm, signed, and spoken conversation to Amy's schoolwork and her views on how it was going. Amy didn't hesitate to tell him what she told anyone who asked, that she was doing all right but would be doing better with an interpreter in class. Pressed for detail, she cited her increasing awareness of conversations among students and between the teacher and students. Sternberg, who had not had a sign language interpreter until his work at the doctoral level, had no problem in understanding this. After all, he had spoken and heard the English language before he lost his hearing; Amy had not.

On the witness stand, Sternberg used a classroom trick that always got the students' attention. When Chatoff asked him to comment on lipreading, he noted that only 26 percent of sounds are visible on the lips and many words appear virtually identical to the lip-reader. He asked everyone to pay attention to his lips and told them that he would say the words "amuse" and "abuse." Twice his lips moved.

"How many of you think I said 'abuse' first? How many think I said 'amuse' first?" he asked, pausing and looking about the room for a raised hand. "I have no takers," he continued, "but that's all right. The point is that I said the same word twice. Nobody knows the difference." Sternberg was pleased to see that the little demonstration held the courtroom participants, including the judge, in rapt attention. In the rear, the deaf spectators, receiving the trick in sign language, were smiling delightedly, pleased to see such a point made of an everyday problem in lipreading.

---

* New York: Harper Perennial, 1994, originally published in 1981.

Later, Chatoff asked Sternberg whether he relied on lipreading in court or the interpreter. With a smile and bow to the interpreter working with him, Sternberg said that interpretation was essential to him. Then Chatoff asked Sternberg to comment on a statement attributed to a member of the school's District Committee on the Handicapped to the effect that the "first grade is not important enough to require an interpreter."

Sternberg paused for a moment and responded: "I disagree emphatically with that statement in the light of my experience. I believe that the deaf child should be exposed as early as possible to meaningful additional input. . . . The first five years of life, as most of us know, are the most important years for linguistic development. When we are deprived by reason of inadequate input during these formative years, we are going to suffer irreparable harm educationally as we continue to grow up."

After establishing that Sternberg had recently spent time with Amy and her parents discussing the school situation, Chatoff asked the professor, "In your opinion, does Amy need an interpreter in her classroom."

"Most definitely, yes."

"What do you think about the present arrangements?"

"I think it is a sad commentary on a school system that it would permit a situation whereby a so-called mainstreamed child is receiving the equivalent of one hour a day of special assistance from a resource teacher, three hours of therapy [weekly], and the remaining six hours a day with no supportive services whatsoever."

In his cross-examination, Kuntz attempted to draw a parallel between the oralist and total communication approaches. He and Sternberg had this exchange:

"Dr. Sternberg, you told us that total communication is a philosophy of approach. Is that correct?"

"Yes."

"I take it that when you characterize it as a philosophy it is not then a method."

"Correct."

"As a philosophy, has it received unanimity of acceptance among educators of the deaf?"

"Since its introduction approximately fifteen years ago, 50 percent of the schools for the deaf have adopted it and the number continues to increase steadily."

"If there is a parallel philosophy or another philosophy, what is that other philosophy called or how is it named?"

"I would say how it is named. It is not a philosophy. The others are called methods . . . all methods of actual presentation. They are not philosophies, however."

"Are you telling me that there is no oral philosophy?"

"Not in the same sense as there is a total communication philosophy. We are talking now in terms of semantics."

"Yes, we are. And I wonder if you aren't reluctant to dignify the other approach with the nomenclature of philosophy and by that device downgrade its importance."

"No. Such is not the case, because the total communication philosophy obviously was intended to involve methodologies, namely the oral, the manual, and the combin[ation,] together with written communication and auditory amplification. All of these are per se methods."

Under re-direct examination, Chatoff returned to the subject.

"Is there a difference between the acceptance of total communication by deaf educators of the deaf and hearing educators of the deaf?" he asked Sternberg.

"Yes, there is."

"Who prefers the use of total communication, deaf or hearing educators?"

"The deaf educator will tend to prefer total communication."

"Why is that?"

"Their experience."

Later, Taras Denis, Clifford Rowley's former teacher, took the stand. A classmate of Sternberg's at P.S. 47 (although they had not known one another at the time), he had experienced, at the New York School for the Deaf, a sign language epiphany similar to Nancy Rowley's and had gone on to earn graduate degrees from Gallaudet, Columbia University, and Hunter College.

He testified that Amy needed a sign language interpreter and warned that she could suffer real damage if the service were delayed. "I've always believed that the most important years of a deaf child are when that child is very young. . . . Maybe while she is young, Amy will not have many problems at first. But as time proceeds, the gap of communication gets farther and farther apart and problems that could be social, cultural, psychological, not just academic, set in."

Under cross-examination by Kuntz, Denis told of his own experiences with a note-taker in college. He drew the distinction between what the lecturer said, which he could get in one form or another through the note-taker, and the class discussions. "With an interpreter, Amy can possibly go further, even participate normally, and that's a very important thing in a child's growth and development. Amy is brighter than most and she needs this."

"Aside from the issue of the provision of the sign language interpreter," Kuntz finally asked, "are you aware of any deficiencies in Amy's current academic program or performance?"

"No," Denis responded. And then he thought, as Kuntz excused him, that the question was an odd one. After all, the whole issue before the court was the sign language interpreter. That was all the Rowleys had ever asked for.

I put down the transcript of the district court hearing I have been reading. For the second time, something that Denis said triggers a memory. I see a boy standing in the middle of a big, empty room. He is sweeping a rug. I am in this image too, advancing on the boy, notebook in hand. I have come to see Jimmy, the deaf youngster off the streets of Charlotte, one of the seven youths in the study I am doing. On a spring morning in 1980, I have dropped in, without announcement, on the Comprehensive Employment and Training Act program in which he is participating. I am to meet Gary Beene of the Charlotte Council for the Hearing Impaired, who is working with Jimmy, at this former motel, which is being converted into a home for the elderly. I have arrived early and caught Jimmy in the midst of his duties and, as he looks up at me, I realize that I have not given a thought to how to communicate with him.

Here is no verbal, articulate deaf person. Here is a deaf boy with little language and no speech. On his face, as I approach, is the look of someone who thinks he should know the person bearing down on him but has not the slightest idea who that person is. I mouth my name as I put out my hand to him. He has to shift the broom from one hand to the other to shake my hand and tries to bring a smile to this maneuver.

In my mind, I pull back from the remembered scene to observe it in all its comical splendor. I feel the huge, cathedral quiet of this immense anteroom and now see two figures at stage center, one with a broom tucked back under his armpit, the other gesticulating and apparently speaking with lips bared and teeth and tongue thrust forward. From above, they are tiny figures, a few inconsequential lines of sketching, in naked relief. They are nodding furiously at each other, but a closer observer could see that not the least jot of communication is taking place between the two.

One of the figures in my tableaux has begun scribbling on his pad while the other figure continues nervously shifting the broom back and forth from one hand to the other. My note reads, "Where are your fellow workers?" Jimmy looks blankly at the question. He attempts a smile again, accompanied by a shrug. I am changing the wording, "Where are the others, working with you?" The response is a Mack Sennett, hands-up shrug, face screwed up into a question mark. More scribbling, "Where is your supervisor?" and then the last word scratched out and "boss" written over it. Another blank look from Jimmy. For the first time in many years of being a reporter, I feel a sense of panic. I look about desperately, and my stars are in a winning configuration. Here comes Gary Beene now, accompanied by a sign language interpreter.

Intuiting my distress, Beene and the interpreter begin signing with Jimmy, who is by now nervously shuffling his feet. It is clear that the interpreter is going too fast for Jimmy's modest signing skills. She slows up. Beene calms Jimmy down, hand on his shoulder. Jimmy begins signing back. "He's saying that the other boys don't want him with them," Beene tells me. "We'll look into it, could be a simple mess-up." After a considerable time, with Beene off to find the project's supervisor, I try again with simple pencil and paper notes. Jimmy tells me that he's OK. Yes, really. How has he communicated with his boss? By giving him notes, he writes. How has that worked? Jimmy shrugs, turning away, his attention span apparently spent by all the questions he has been answering.

Thinking about all this now, as I sit with the district court transcript still in my lap, I remember Gary's words to me about Jimmy. "Only rudimentary signing, no voice, poor lipreading skills, but much worse, no vocabulary and very little ability to read." Thumbing back over Taras Denis' testimony, I come to the words that had sparked that recollection.

"I've always believed that the most important years of a deaf child are when that child is very young. . . . But as time proceeds, the gap of communication gets farther and farther apart and problems that could be social, cultural, psychological, not just academic, set in."

I think I can really grasp what Denis is saying now as I had not before, certainly not while talking with Jimmy at the time. Where would the words come from to express Jimmy's frustration at having been separated from the rest of the young workers in this work-training project? Where would the language come from with which to mediate against the blows of life, to celebrate triumphs, to share fully in the human experience? Denis is asking us to understand that without a word for it or a sign for it, without the ability to communicate, an elemental human emotion like anger eventually could become unbearable.

———

When court convened again on Friday, September 28, 1979, the board of education's attorney, Raymond Kuntz, rose to address the court. Face flushed, voice tense, Kuntz said that in sixteen years as a trial lawyer he had never had the kind of experience he had had in the past twelve hours. He began to describe to the court a situation in which the two women who had been assisting him, Inez Janger and Carol Blumberg, a teacher at the Lexington School for the Deaf, and who were to testify on the district's behalf, had been instructed to withdraw from the case by Leo Connor, the head of Lexington. This had come about, Kuntz said, as a result of protests from members of the deaf community over the women's testifying against Amy Rowley. In particular, he added, a group comprising a deaf community action board, which had been supporting a mental health clinic for the deaf, had threatened to withdraw support if the women testified.

"It seems to me that the plaintiffs in this case, and I'm not sure of how it has been done or why it has been done, have decided that the people who were here as witnesses posed some sort of threat to them and have apparently counterthreatened in some fashion, so that I am no longer able to conduct this trial in the way that I intended to when I first began it."

After some discussion between Kuntz and Judge Broderick as to how to proceed, Chatoff arose to ask permission of the court to speak.

"I believe that this entire statement should be stricken as self-serving hearsay," he said, "by someone who was not even sworn. I think basically it is an indictment of an entire community, and under these circumstances, if it was stated to a single individual, it would be slander. I can't understand a statement like this being made in court."

Judge Broderick noted that Kuntz had said he would try to find a substitute expert witness for the case, and that time would be provided for that purpose by allowing Pete Sherman to go ahead first with his case once Chatoff had concluded. At the end of the day, referring to the incident again, the judge said that whatever had happened, he intended to see that nothing like it happened again.

Sherman, attorney for the Commissioner of Education of the State of New York, began by establishing a major tenet of the state's case. He moved for dismissal of the Rowleys' suit on grounds that no evidence had been introduced that the district was providing an "inappropriate" education to Amy Rowley. "We have heard testimony," he said, "that perhaps the district is not providing the best education for this child through an interpreter. Of course, that can be debated, and obviously we are debating that. But the standard is not the best education, it is an appropriate education, in line with federal guidelines. . . . We are willing to concede that this child, and perhaps every child in the state, is not getting the best possible education they could get, but they are getting an appropriate one." Kuntz joined in the motion for dismissal, arguing that there had been no showing of immediate and irreparable harm. Judge Broderick reserved judgment on both motions.

Sherman's next witness was Norman Doctor ("Dr. Doctor, is it?" Sherman asked, and the witness responded, "I try not to use it."), a regional associate for the State Department of Education with responsibilities for monitoring the education of handicapped youth. In addition to his doctorate in education of the deaf, Doctor was certified as a teacher of the deaf. He testified that he and an associate visited Amy in class on Monday past, observed her for twenty minutes, and chatted with her for ten more.

Asked by Sherman for an opinion, Doctor stated, "I did not do an extensive observation of her to any degree, all right? I'm basing my opinion on the information that was available in the child's school record and a very small observation. She was learning, she was interacting with the children in her class. My opinion would be from that observation and so on that she is in fact receiving an appropriate education." Later he added a further caution, "I would have to say that it is very difficult to draw conclusions in terms of issues that are taking place here. Whether in fact Amy could follow an instructional lesson with a new vocabulary being introduced as compared to the simple conversation we were having, I could not testify." He added that Amy was a very good lip-reader with residual hearing in the lower frequencies, "so in terms of her using her residual hearing and using her lipreading ability, based on the audiogram and based on my impressions of Amy, I feel she would be able to function in an auditory oral approach."

Doctor went on to elaborate on the residual hearing issue. "Amy has a good island of residual hearing in the lower frequencies. All sounds are divided into frequencies. The vowel sounds, which are the sounds most difficult to lip read because they are not on the surface of the lips, are the sounds she is most likely to hear. The high-frequency sounds, which is where her most severe part of her hearing impairment is, are the sounds that would be easiest to see."

In cross-examination, Chatoff established that Doctor could not sign, had no "great" knowledge of total communication, and had never recommended a child for mainstreaming with total communication ("because no resources were available for that at the time"). Doctor conceded that in the twenty minutes he observed Amy, no group discussion went on. "If there is a general discussion going on in the class," he testified, "it is more difficult for a deaf child to lip-read because there are more people talking either at the same time or usually one after the other. But it is not impossible."

Doctor's companion for the brief visit to Amy's class was Ed Cortez, another regional associate for the State Department of Education. Cortez signed a little, had done illustrations for books on signing, and had taught Hispanic deaf children. He based his testimony that Amy was receiving an appropriate education on records of the case, on his observations, and particularly on the affidavit from Jack Janik, Amy's kindergarten sign language interpreter for two weeks. Chatoff drew from him the acknowledgment that he was not familiar enough with affidavits from Michael Deninger and Mary Sheie, who had concluded that Amy was missing a great deal in class, to answer questions about them and that he had thought the sign language interpreter experiment took place during Amy's first-grade year in school.

When court reconvened almost a week later, Michael Chatoff was using a state-of-the-art TTY at his desk with a typist to keep up with the proceedings. Raymond Kuntz had replaced his two missing witnesses with one of the best-known oral educators of the deaf in the country. This witness was Dr. Ann Mullholland of the Lexington School for the Deaf, but she was perhaps better known for her many years of work at Columbia University with an oralist program. Most of the deaf spectators assembled again in the back of the courtroom knew this hearing witness as perhaps the most effective opponent of sign language in the current generation of educators.

First, Furnace Woods Principal Joseph Zavarella testified that the education being furnished Amy Rowley was "more than just an adequate education" because of the teachers' interest in Amy as a person. Under cross-examination, Zavarella recalled that, of the two tests given to students at the end of the first year of school, the Metropolitan had been given in the classroom, but the Stanford had been given to Amy by Sue Williams, who had used sign language in giving instructions. Chatoff also drew from Zavarella the fact that although Amy and Janik had had a "discussion" prior to the interpreter experiment, no orientation was conducted for the class.

Under re-direct examination, Kuntz had Zavarella read into the record Amy's Metropolitan and Stanford Achievement Test scores. On both tests, Amy scored well. She stood at the second grade level, with scores running from 2.1 to 2.5 (with the decimals standing for months beyond the grade level) in the Metropolitan, but her scores in the Stanford ranged up from 3.5 for a reading test to 4 for mathematics, 4.5 for mathematics computation, and 5.7 for "listening comprehension."

Judge Broderick interrupted. "I think you are going to have to explain that to me," he told the witness. "Obviously, Amy does not listen. Will you tell us what 'listening comprehension' has tested?"

"I see the contradiction in that your honor," Zavarella responded, "but listening comprehension with Amy would be through visual means. Rather than saying the word, the word was signed. See, she received a clue from the teacher and the youngster has to respond by selecting the appropriate symbol on the paper. By receiving the signed clues, she then responded on the paper. That was listening comprehension."

Then Ann Mullholland was on the stand, testifying as to her two-hour visit to Amy's classroom the previous Friday. She said that Amy seemed to understand everything that was going on, that Amy's socialization in class was good, and that her records indicated solid progress. She credited a good bit of Amy's success to her residual hearing in the lower frequencies. She said that once Amy, wearing her FM receiver, had turned around in response to her name being called by the teacher from three rows behind her. "In my opinion," she said "I have not yet seen any school system provide what has been provided in this situation. I was very pleased about that."

Kuntz took her through Amy's test scores and Mullholland said that they were very good. Then he asked her if, in her judgment, a sign language interpreter was needed in Amy's second-grade classroom.

"In my considered judgment, there is no need at this time for a manual interpreter. I do not preclude that being a valuable asset in the future, but at this time I do not see that she needs an interpreter."

Offered an opportunity to amplify, she said, "One of the reasons is that I am looking at Amy as an individual child in a particular educational setting.

And in that setting, which I have described as formal and teacher-directed, I'm not sure what an interpreter would do. Amy is free to turn around and talk, and she is communicating, and there is no intermediary through whom she must go. She relates directly to the children, she relates directly to the classroom teacher and to all of those with whom I saw her in contact. It may be that as the work becomes more complex, it would be valuable to her to have a manual interpreter."

Kuntz asked whether a sign language interpreter at this point might actually prove harmful, and Ann Mullholland answered that it might. She gave as an example an incident in which Amy sat on the lap of her teacher, which—Mullholland speculated—she might not have done if an interpreter was around.

Under cross-examination, Chatoff asked about Mullholland's testimony that Amy had considerable residual hearing in the lower frequencies. "Isn't it true," Chatoff asked, "that people talk in the higher frequencies, higher than the frequencies at which Amy scores well?"

Mullholand asked for the question to be repeated by the court reporter. Her answer was, in full: "Speech sounds do include high-frequency components. For example, the sound of *S* is a high frequency sound; *Sh* would be another one. If one were to look at the phonemes plotted against an audiogram, one would see in some instances there are two places on an audiogram perhaps where sound will occur. For example, I will say *D* off the top of my head. You will find that does have a harmonic, and therefore, that appears in two peaks of acoustic energy. You will find also that the sibilants, the high frequency sibilants, may be interpreted by deaf people differently from the way we hear them. And this is what I was referring to earlier on when I talked about acoustic cues."

With the case for the school district and the state presented, Chatoff had an opportunity to insert a kind of "substitute" witness of his own. Donald Moores had not been Chatoff's first choice as an expert witness, but the Rowleys' attorney was having trouble getting a videotape produced by his first choice introduced into the record. Moores had been suggested to him as someone who was not only an expert who had researched and written widely on deafness, but also an articulate hearing person who understood and used total communication. Chatoff asked and Moores was pleased to testify.

Moores had grown up in Connecticut and as a teenager had worked part-time in summers at schools for the deaf back when these schools were farms. He continued this kind of work at Amherst College as an undergraduate. He was majoring in psychology and playing college football, so the superintendent of the school for the deaf nearby asked him to work with that school's football team during the summer. It was a fascinating experience for Moores. He developed "survival skills" in communicating with deaf football players, picked up enough signing to get along, and further developed his interest in deafness and communications. After taking a graduate degree at Gallaudet, he had taught in New York, Connecticut, and California, got his doctorate at the University of Illinois, worked as a research director in a teacher-training program for eleven years at the University of Minnesota, and then moved on to direct special education at Pennsylvania State University.

After the preliminaries, Chatoff asked Moores to discuss the results of the two tests that had been presented so painstakingly by the school district's witnesses. Moores quoted several of the scores, noting that on virtually every scale, Amy had done better on the Stanford.

"Assuming that these tests were given in a valid way, these are really significant differences," he noted. "I would suggest that the individuals who gave them consider whether the higher scores on the Stanford test were not due to the fact that the test was administered by a teacher of the deaf who used not only oral communication but manual communication. . . . Given Amy's I.Q., reported at 122, it would be my guess that she is probably a precocious child, and that the Stanford test is probably closer to an estimate of her ability than the Metropolitan score."

Chatoff wanted the judge particularly to see how sign language looked and how well a hearing person could use it to communicate with the deaf. He asked Moores to discuss the development of total communication, using signs along with his voice. The interpreters realized that many of the deaf persons seated in the back of the courtroom were now looking past them for the first time; the interpreters turned around and saw the witness speaking and signing fluently.

Moores traced renewed interest in sign language to the rubella epidemic of the 1960s when studies showed that preschool programs for deaf children, virtually all strictly oral at the time, were largely unsuccessful. No matter how the children were educated in the classroom, they used signs in interactions outside the classroom. Moores also discussed successful mainstreaming efforts in which deaf children were being placed in the classroom with hearing children profitably, with a sign language interpreter. Who were the deaf children who could use this service best, Chatoff asked. Moores said they were those with better speech, good signing, and good residual hearing.

Finally, Chatoff wanted Moores to testify to the effect of all this learning on current teaching of the deaf. Moores referred to a study for the year 1977–78 in which 6 classes changed to oral only while 481 changed from oral only; 537 classes were changing to total communication and 8 from total communication. "So the net finding was that 481 classes stopped using oral only and 537 started using total communication."

In his cross-examination, Kuntz attempted to call into question the credibility of studies that had found total communication more effective than oral-only teaching for the deaf. He cited a particular article from 1975 that argued that these studies were not designed to test the difference in effectiveness between the two approaches and that they were flawed in other ways.

Kuntz asked Moores: "Do you consider this criticism of the research as valid?"

"Not really," Moores responded. "I think it was self-serving."

"Are you familiar with the article?"

"Yes, I am. Do you want me to continue to respond?"

"No, thank you."

Kuntz moved to another line of questioning. "Is there any situation that you could hypothesize where a deaf child would not require, in your opinion, a sign language interpreter in a second-grade classroom in order to be a successful student and receive an adequate and appropriate education?"

"Certainly."

"Would you describe that for us."

"If the teacher could sign."

"Any other circumstances?"

"It would have to be an ideal situation. No deaf child that I have seen, no."

After Kuntz had finished, Judge Broderick had a question for Moores. "Dr. Moores, is there not some correlation between the scores which Amy achieved on this test, this Stanford Achievement Test, and the appropriateness of the education which she received in the last two years at Furnace Woods school?"

"To some degree. . . . I think it is also quite possible that in the regular classroom give-and-take she misses quite a bit from the teacher. If she is missing quite a bit and if it is true that some of the difference or all of the difference between these two tests might be due to the fact that she didn't understand the directions, what we are finding here would be a difference between what she is capable of doing under ideal conditions and what she does when she is not completely sure."

The judge leaned back and said he was pleased to have the answer, but that he wanted a response to his question of whether Amy's achievement on the Stanford test might not reflect an appropriate education in the Furnace Woods School.

"I would say it would be, yes. I think the question is would it be better, even more, with the additional service."

Judge Broderick had one more question. He noted that Moores had been present during Mullholland's presentation of Amy as an unusually well-adjusted child socially. The judge wanted to know if Moores would comment on whether that should be valued perhaps against more complete communication.

"I don't have any evidence to suggest that the provision of interpreter services would detract from her communication skills or her socialization skills," Moores responded. "When I say 'her,' I should put it in a more general way, from a deaf child's socialization skills. I think most deaf as they grow, far better than hearing people, understand that they live and deal with hearing people and deaf people in a variety of settings and most develop effective ways of doing so."

The judge continued. "But for a child of six or seven or eight, isn't it very important that if it can be achieved, that she function in an atmosphere which, as far as the children she is functioning with, is as normal as possible?"

"Certainly."

"And doesn't the introduction of a sign language interpreter make that more difficult?"

"I don't think it would be any more difficult than the introduction of the auditory training unit which the children pass around. The question is what is needed to make it effective. Each time you introduce something, there is an element of danger, whether it be an auditory training unit or whatever. . . . The question is can it be done without disrupting the give-and-flow, the give-and-take, the everyday flow of communication. I think a sensitive interpreter can do so."

The judge thanked Moores and the witness stepped down. He was Chatoff's last witness and, although there was further discussion between the lawyers, including an agreement to submit briefs in lieu of final arguments, the federal district court hearing in the Rowleys' suit against the school district and the state was over.

A tall, slender, broad-browed man, Judge Vincent L. Broderick was a product of Harvard Law School who had served as a captain in the United States Corps of Engineers during World War II, as chief assistant United States Attorney for the Southern district from 1961 to 1965, and as police commissioner for the City of New York from 1965 to 1966. He was considered to be a top-flight judge who was invariably courteous and fair. He could be impatient, but lawyers understood how judges use their available impatience to keep from being "motioned" to death. He had the reputation of not being afraid to try cases and of writing well, although not necessarily of delivering his opinions swiftly. He was an inveterate pipe smoker and over the next weeks as he thought and read his way through testimony and, with his clerk's help, went over the legislative history of the Education for All Handicapped Children's Act and related acts, pored over court precedents, and examined the final briefs, his pipe did extra duty.

Broderick had every intention of making a prompt decision in this case. He was convinced that Amy was at some risk as time went on of losing significant portions of her educational opportunity without a sign language interpreter. He felt he had learned a good bit about deafness from the testimony and found himself musing about his only early contact with the subject, a distant memory, rising smokily from the streets of New York City like steam from the pipes below. He saw the deaf boys in their uniforms at 165th Street and Riverside Drive, walking toward the New York School for the Deaf in the years before it moved out to "Fanwood." He and his chums had watched the boys' silent marching, as though it proceeded from another world. He recognized something mysterious, even alien, about the scene as he filtered it back through his youth's consciousness. What did he and his friends make of this uniformed column? The answer was lost in the mists of childhood.

The judge did not want to delay his verdict any longer than necessary. For one thing, the school was trying to find Amy a teacher of the deaf under its old IEP, when a sign language interpreter was what the judge intended to require, and that might well be a different person. On December 28, he issued a two-paragraph order:

This court heard evidence in the above captioned matter on September 26, 27, 28, and October 4, 1979. Upon the bases to be set forth in the opinion to be filed herein, I find that the plaintiff has established her right to the relief requested. According, the decision of the Commissioner of Education dated April 10.1979, is reversed, and it is hereby

ORDERED, that the defendants provide the plaintiff with the services of a certified interpreter for the deaf during any school period in which academic subjects are taught." *

Someone in the judge's clerk's office called Chatoff on a borrowed TTY with the news. Excited, Chatoff got on his TTY. He first tried to reach Nancy Rowley and, when he got no answer, he tried Taras Denis, who also was away. Then he tried Martin Sternberg, with no better luck. Desperate to find someone with whom to share this good news, he punched out the Rowley number again. There was a long pause and, just as Chatoff was about to hang up, he got a response and quickly typed in his name: "Michael calling. GA."

Another pause. Then: "Michael, this is Nancy here. Johnny answered the phone. How are you? GA."

"Fine, thanks. Are you sitting down? GA."

"Yes, just in from outdoors. GA."

"I just heard from the judge's law clerk. We won. Let me repeat. We won. GA."

"Oh, boy. Hooray, and I'm really relieved. Relieved is the word. GA."

Chatoff explained that the order with the judge's reasoning would follow within weeks. They chatted excitedly for a few minutes, and then Chatoff said he was going down to dinner. Nancy said she couldn't wait to tell Clifford and that meanwhile the children were running all over the room cheering as loudly as they could.

Both children were excited, sharing youthful high spirits at the idea that their family had triumphed over that big, impersonal system known as school. But their reactions came from very different personal wellsprings. Amy felt that the decision would help her and allow her to lead a more normal life, at play and at home as well as at school. Johnny felt triumphant, personally vindicated.

---

* United States District Court, Southern District of New York, Amy Rowley by her parents v. Hendrick Hudson Central School District, December 28, 1979, p. B-1.

It was not that Johnny didn't care about his little sister. Indeed, he felt that she had been treated poorly by the school, that she should have had the interpreter from the start. Johnny's problem was that he was getting the flack from the other school kids. Two years ahead of his sister, he was the target of the resentment that these older boys and girls picked up in school, at home, and elsewhere over all the "special" treatment Amy required. Friends he thought he could count on were cool when they weren't outright hostile. He found that he had to defend his parents' right to seek a better chance for their daughter.

Clifford and Nancy understood, to their very real pain. They sat Johnny down to talk with him about it, but Johnny didn't really want to talk about it. It wasn't that he didn't agree with his parents, but that the subject had begun to dominate his life at school. It didn't seem fair that he had to listen to all the ugly talk at school and then come home and deal with more needs.

Johnny had come to terms with being the only hearing member of this family. It could be a pain to have to answer the telephone every time it rang. Whenever it was not a TTY call to his parents, he had to take careful notes of what was said and pass this information along to his parents or his sister or all three. He had learned enough sign language to do this well because he would feel that it was his fault if anything went wrong, if there was a misunderstanding, even if his parents would never blame him.

And there was another side to being the only hearing person in the family. The responsibility that felt burdensome from time to time sometimes also felt good. He never doubted—as other children might—that he was needed. Being counted on had its drawbacks, but Johnny didn't mind. He saw at first hand how remarkably able his parents were and that the way other people thought about deafness was a greater problem than his parents' deafness. They were overcoming their disability just fine.

That's another reason it cut him so deeply to hear false charges against them—that they were making demands on the school that parents shouldn't make; that they didn't care about Amy, but only about their own theories of how things ought to be. Johnny understood how much anguish his parents had been through and how deeply they believed that Amy's best interests hung in the balance. He had been in more than one fight over it. Now, maybe, with the court decision in the Rowleys' favor, it would all go away. We won, he exulted. They will have to back down now: They were wrong and we were right.

With the school district gaining a stay of the judge's order, pending appeal to the United States Court of Appeals for the Second Circuit, Judge Broderick made haste to file his full opinion on January 18, 1980. All parties had agreed that Amy Rowley was getting a free public education in the least restricted environment. The judge had said that education was not, however, an "appropriate" one. The judge's task was to define an "appropriate" education in this context under the Education for All Handicapped Children Act.

In his brief, the Rowleys' attorney, had tried to shed light on the word "appropriate." Chatoff noted that Amy's education had been "adequate" according to Ann Mullholland and "more than adequate" according to Joe Zavarella. Neither term, Chatoff contended, was close to being synonymous with "appropriate," a word to which he applied the dictionary meaning of "suitable to a specific purpose" or "especially suitable." That, he argued, was something more than the education Amy was getting.

Although Congress had not further defined "appropriate," it had defined "special education," which constituted the services under the umbrella of the act, as "specifically designed instruction . . . to meet the unique needs of a handicapped child." Judge Broderick sought a reasonable standard that would meet a handicapped child's "unique" needs with an "appropriate" education under the act.

He began by rejecting two extremes that had been suggested in legal arguments and in the legislative halls and that were, respectively, below and above the standard he sought.

An appropriate education could mean, he wrote, deliberately using words the school district had used about Amy's education, "an adequate education—that is, an education substantial enough to facilitate a child's progress from one grade to another and to enable him or her to earn a high school diploma." That definition he found too limited.

On the other hand, an "appropriate" education could also mean one that enabled the handicapped child to achieve his or her "full potential." That definition he found too ambitious.

He then elaborated a standard that seemed proper to him. "Between those two extremes," he wrote, "is a standard which I conclude is more in keeping with the regulations, with Equal Protection decisions which motivated the passage of the Act, and with common sense." His standard would require that

*each handicapped child be given an opportunity to achieve his full poten-
tial commensurate with the opportunity provided other children.* (Author's
emphasis)

The judge amplified this: "Since some handicapped children will un-
doubtedly do better than merely progress from grade to grade, this standard requires something more than the 'adequate' education described
above. On the other hand, since even the best public schools lack the resources to enable every child to achieve his full potential, the standard
would not require them to go so far."

The judge then took account of a difficulty with the standard. "It requires
that the potential of the handicapped child be measured and compared to
his or her performance, and that the resulting differential or 'shortfall' be
compared to the shortfall experienced by non-handicapped children." He
observed that the school had used a variety of tests and observations in concluding that Amy's performance had lived up to the standard of the act as
they understood it. Based on these tests and observations, Amy's hearing
teachers, teacher of the deaf, and the principal had concluded that this deaf
child understood virtually everything that was being said in class. But the
audiologist who had tested Amy since infancy, Barbara Kligerman, had
said that it would not be possible for Amy to understand more than 59 percent of what was said in any classroom. In most noisy classroom settings,
she had added, Amy would apprehend considerably less. Judge Broderick
concluded that Amy was missing a great deal.

This raised the issue of where a student like Amy, with an I.Q. of 122,
"ought" to stand in her class. One of the plaintiff's witnesses, Donald
Moores, had noted sharp discrepancies in the test scores she had posted in
the Metropolitan Achievement Test and the Stanford Achievement Test.
The school itself had testified that sign language was used one-on-one in
giving Amy instructions for the latter. Judge Broderick took account of
Moores' testimony that Amy might be a "precocious" child and that the
Stanford test was a better index of her potential than was the Metropolitan.

"Moreover," the judge continued, "Amy's I.Q. does not represent the full
measure of her potential. The defendant's own witnesses have established
by their testimony Amy's energy, her intellectual assertiveness, her rapport
with her teachers and her interest in learning. These are significant ele-
ments of her potential which are not reflected in her I.Q. but which are un-
doubtedly reflected in the results of her achievement and other academic

tests. It seems likely that much of Amy's energy and eagerness goes into compensating for her handicap; if the need for some of that compensation were eliminated, her energy could be channeled into greater excellence in classroom performance. It is unfair and contrary to law to penalize her for her own efforts and those of her parents, by which she has remained slightly above the median of her class." With a sign language interpreter, witnesses for the Rowleys had noted without contradiction, Amy could understand potentially 100 percent of what was said in the classroom.

To Judge Broderick, this all added up to a legally mandated need that was not being met. "Taken as a whole," he wrote, "this information establishes that Amy is a very bright child who is doing fairly well in school. It also establishes that she understands considerably less of what goes on in class than she could if she were not deaf. Thus she is not learning as much, or performing as well academically, as she would without her handicap. While I accept the defendant's evidence that an interpreter is less necessary for the transmission of mechanical skills in the early grades than for the increasingly academic instruction of higher grades, I also find that anything missed in the classroom early in the learning process will have far-reaching consequences."

The judge disposed of the argument that "no child understands 100 percent of what is said in a classroom." He wrote: "While it is true, as defendants contend, that no child understands 100 percent of what is taught in class, the failures of other children can be attributed either to lack of intellectual potential, in which case there is no shortfall relevant to the standard prescribed, or to a lack of interest and energy, factors which can be controlled and which it is the purpose of a school to develop." The fact that Amy clearly could understand less than 100 percent of what was being said in the classroom at the present was the "shortfall" that the judge found the act was intended to remedy. Undisputed testimony demonstrated that a sign language interpreter could eliminate this shortfall and give Amy an opportunity equal to that given her classmates.

The last issue to be dealt with concerning Amy specifically, in the judge's view, was the question of whether a sign language interpreter would be accepted by Amy in the classroom and, if so, whether the interpreter would be a distraction to the other children. He referred to the trial use of the interpreter Jack Janik in kindergarten and to testimony that Amy refused to follow Janik and instead continued to look at the teacher. "There is no indication, however," the judge wrote, "that Amy was adequately coached to respond to this change in her classroom setting, or that she was given enough time to adjust to it. It is hard for me to believe that a child who has been raised with the use of total communication cannot be taught to follow an interpreter.

"One of the plaintiff's witnesses, Dr. Donald Moores, who has had experience with interpreters in the classroom, testified that a sensitive interpreter can minimize this disruptive impact on the classroom. In addition, he pointed out that the FM wireless currently being used by Amy in class, which operates through a transmitter, which students pass from hand to hand when they are reading aloud, is also potentially disruptive and also draws that attention of other students to Amy's handicap. All of the testimony offered by both sides, however, establishes that Amy's classmates have adapted without difficulty to the presence of the wireless and have accepted Amy as their peer. There is nothing on the record to suggest that they will respond to the presence of an interpreter any differently."*

The judge also decided to admit into evidence the affidavits submitted by Michael Deninger and Mary Sheie, the experts who had evaluated Amy in the classroom and found that she was missing a good deal of what was being said. Both Kuntz and Sherman had objected vigorously to this evidence being admitted, as these affidavits were submitted to the commissioner of education after the impartial hearing, which meant that neither expert was available to the defense for cross-examination. The judge's decision on this matter was, in effect, a ruling that the affidavits should have been considered by the commissioner.

Sitting in my home office seven years after the fact, with benefit of a pile of testimony from Judge Broderick's court on a table beside me, I was struck by what seemed to be an unusual, and possibly significant comparison. The courtroom case for Amy Rowley, a deaf child brought up on sign language, involved testimony by deaf as well as hearing people, including numerous hearing people who signed fluently. By contrast, the case for the school district and the state employed no deaf witnesses nor anyone who was even close to fluent in sign language. The school's chief expert witness, Ann Mullholland, on the contrary, was someone whose major experience had been with oral programs that banned sign language.

* The quotes on pp. 88–90 are from United States District Court, Southern District of New York, Amy Rowley by her parents v. Hendrick Hudson Central School District, December 28, 1979, pp. 1–18.

It would have been difficult, I found myself thinking, for the deaf individuals who packed the courtroom to think of the proceedings in any way other than "them" against "us." Indeed, the anger that spilled over and was felt by Sherman, the attorney for the commissioner of education—and surely others on the school's side—was evidence of that feeling. I could identify that anger and even credit it, but I was aware of not fully understanding it. There was a history here I needed to know about, a past obviously involving conflict and bitter disappointment for deaf people.

The other thing that struck me in reading the testimony of the people who taught Amy Rowley was their conviction that she understood what they said, that she was "getting" what they were teaching. But, of all Amy's regular teachers, only Sue Williams had any experience teaching deaf children, and Williams was not that often in the classroom with Amy and frequently used sign language with her outside the classroom.

It fascinated me that members of the school staff saw Amy's efforts to recruit academic help in her classroom as "socialization" and expressed pleasure with how other children helped her. To them, this was a sign that mainstreaming was working. Would they have been thrilled to learn that their own children felt compelled to go to classmates for help in understanding the lessons? To Nancy Rowley, as to other deaf people attending the hearing, this was a sign that mainstreaming was failing once again for lack of supportive services.

The deeper implications of the case lay in Judge Broderick's opinion. If the Congress of the United States meant to confer equal opportunity to learn on the children with disabilities admitted to public schools, it did not matter where Amy stood in her class. The question was, as Broderick had put it, how much better might she do given the same chance as the children sitting on either side of her?

But that was the wrong question—if the majority of the Supreme Court had fairly construed Congress' intent in passing the Education for All Handicapped Children Act. I would have to understand that intent as fully as possible and I would need the help of both lawyers and members of Congress in that effort. Even then, I thought, I would still have to understand the anger of the deaf audience in that courtroom and why, in spite of it, the school district had so clearly excluded all deaf people from taking any part in its case. It seemed to me that the key to unlocking the mystery I was trying to solve would be found by understanding the attitudes that underlay this behavior.

5

A Case about Amy

In the aftermath of Judge Broderick's order and opinion, Charles Eible, a quick-smiling, affable man who had succeeded to the post of superintendent of schools, became chief spokesperson for the Hendrick Hudson Central School District as the local press began to follow the *Rowley* case. Eible told the *Peekskill Evening Star* that both the district and the state boards of education would appeal Judge Broderick's decision.

He was quoted as saying that the decision could have "enormous implications." He elaborated thus, "Amy is a bright girl, very articulate, performing well in the upper group of her classmates. If Amy Rowley requires sign language interpretation, then the position is all deaf children require it." Although, he said, the matter of cost could not be an issue in the court case and was not the district's "overriding factor" in its decisions on Amy's supports, he estimated that an interpreter could cost $20,000 a year at an hourly rate of $13 to $15 for a 7-hour day, 180 days a year, plus benefits. He noted also that the district had graduated a deaf student the previous year who was doing "very well" in college. "Those parents would have objected to sign language interpretation," Eible told the reporter. "They argued that it was not the real world their son had to adjust to."*

In ensuing weeks, Eible's estimate of the cost of a sign language inter-

---

* *Peekskill Evening Star* (N.Y.), January 19, 1980, p. 3.

preter dropped first to $18,000 and later to $12,000 a year. The local press was not entirely sure what to make of the matter, but the consideration of costs for an interpreter did not go unnoticed. In an editorial, the *Croton-Cortlandt News* placed the *Rowley* issue against a backdrop of what it called "impending federal mandates." The editorial continued, "Will ramps and elevators have to be built at the Croton Municipal Building or local school buildings to assist the wheelchair-bound handicapped? Will sign language interpreters have to be provided at all town and village board meetings? Will public speakers have to be provided to interpret what a citizen with a speech impediment has to say at these meetings, but can't?"*

Albeit the intent of federal laws was commendable, the editorialist wrote, "There is a fear that all of a sudden handicapped people are going to start making inordinate demands for ramps and elevators and interpreters—and all at public expense. We don't think that's what will happen, but some very fine lines are going to have to be drawn as both the public and the handicapped come to know each other a little better." Finally, the editorial praised Amy for her intelligence and rapport with her teachers, concluding: "While there may be difficulties ahead, we can't think of any better reason for 'normal' people to go the extra distance in making life a little easier for them."

The editorial drew a letter from a reader who chastised the writer for being "sadly uninformed." The letter-writer described the growth throughout the country of the "disabled community," which had become a civil rights movement. The purpose of the federal laws cited by the editorialist, the letter continued, "was not to 'make life a little easier for them'—they resent and do not want charity, but insist on their human dignity, and on their right to have architectural and other barriers removed which would prevent them from earning their living and from participating in and contributing to American society."

As for looking at the costs of all this, the letter writer continued, better to look at that issue broadly. "It is obviously much cheaper in the long run to enable disabled people to be self-supporting taxpayers rather than to maintain them through life-long public or private assistance."†

* *Croton-Courtland News* (Croton, N.Y.), January 31, 1980, editorial page.
† *Croton-Courtland News* (Croton, N.Y.), February 2, 1980, letters to the editor.

The deaf youth Charles Eible mentioned to the press who had graduated from Hendrick Hudson High School the previous June was Robert Collender. He was at that time twenty-one years old. His mother, Ann Collender, had feared that he might be deaf when he was born, for she had been diagnosed in pregnancy with German measles (rubella). But the attending doctor told her, drawing a curtain around them in the nursery recovery room, that her son had a heart murmur, possibly a serious one.

Despite her fears about his hearing, the doctors attributed his early unresponsiveness to speech to laziness, not deafness. His mother proved right and her early attention to the problem resulted in Robert's being fitted with a hearing aid at eighteen months. Then, Ann Collender set to work as soon as possible to help her son learn to speak.

When Robert was four and one-half, the Collenders sent him to the New York School for the Deaf. They chose "Fanwood" because they wanted him to be home on a daily basis, and a sympathetic school superintendent had waived a rule limiting transportation of children to older children so that Robert could be taken to and from school every day. He did well in Fanwood, which was still in the early 1960s essentially an oral-only operation. The Collenders were told to forbid Robert to learn signing, which they were told would surely prevent him from learning to speak. Robert's early training in speaking worked in his favor as did the fact that he was not profoundly deaf.

His heart condition did not improve significantly and when he was eight, it was decided that open-heart surgery was necessary. The Collenders tried to prepare Robert for it, but neither knew the procedure and nobody who did was available for help. They drew pictures, wrote descriptions, but Robert did not really know what was in store for him when his parents took him to Presbyterian Hospital in Manhattan in 1967. As they were leaving the hospital the evening before the operation, an African American woman they did not know caught up with them, took their arms, and explained that her son had been through the open-heart procedure recently and was now doing fine. Ann Collender thought it was the kindest act anyone had performed for her in her memory.

The next day, through a hospital mix-up, the Collenders sat in the waiting room for more than an hour after Robert had come out of the anesthesia. He was upset, startled to find tubes implanted in his body, and worried and angry because his parents had left him there alone for so long.

Then, the orderlies wheeled Robert into the patients' elevator to go downstairs for another procedure. As the Collenders took the visitors' elevator down, they could hear Robert's hysterical screams; his mother was sure that he had misunderstood and thought he was going to be operated on again.

Robert recovered and progressed reasonably well at Fanwood; he repeated some grades—not uncommon with deaf children—and reached the sixth grade when he was fourteen. At that time, the school considered him a candidate for mainstreaming, and his parents were glad to have him closer to home. He was enrolled at Blue Mountain Middle School. The principal, Frank Thomas, got on the public address system the first day of school and notified the students that they had handicapped students in school now and that they had better treat them right. The students did that for the most part, and Robert did well enough at Blue Mountain.

High school was another matter: in a mainstreamed situation with limited communications skills, Robert was barely getting by. Socialization was difficult, too. It was during this most difficult time in Robert's life that Sue Williams came on the scene. She was working as a teacher of the deaf at that time with Amy Rowley, Robert, and one other deaf student out of the district. She saw in Robert an artistic boy, with his father's bright, outgoing personality and a need for contact with an adult outside his family. He really did have a talent for design, which she was sure he could develop. She saw his father, particularly, as having a typically male difficulty in accepting his child's deafness. For his part, Robert saw Williams as someone with knowledge of deafness and of the ways of the outside world, his link with both realities.

Ann Collender worried that the high school was merely pushing her son out through the slot marked "graduation." He had a C average but his language skills were utterly lacking. She and her husband looked at Robert's writing, with its tortured syntax and poor spelling, and wondered how he would progress. Yet he got an A once in high school for English, an event his mother could only chalk up to a young teacher's fascination with raw effort. And it was clear that he was going to pass English no matter how poorly he did. Robert's real talent showed up in mechanical drawing class, where he did so well that he was apprenticed to an engineer one summer and helped redesign the community center. At twenty, he marched in the graduation ceremonies and was even given an award for his summer work, coaching in the Little League, and other community activities.

To realize his ambition to become an architect, Robert would have to go to college, but he had no chance of getting into a mainstreamed school or even Gallaudet, which required better skills in English than Robert possessed. Sue Williams suggested the National Technical Institute for the Deaf in Rochester, essentially a vocational college for the deaf, and drove upstate with Robert and his grateful parents. This was the college Eible had referred to in his example, but at that time, Robert was *not* doing well: he was struggling, and his mother was wondering whether it would not have been better, after all, if he had stayed in the New York School for the Deaf.

Michael Chatoff was concerned about the delay in getting the sign language interpreter for Amy Rowley, who was already in the second grade. He was also concerned about his ability to continue to argue the case without better assistance in comprehending what was going on in court. The experiment with the TTY that last day in Judge Broderick's court had been sobering. The typist simply had not been able to keep up. Chatoff felt that the time had come when he needed more particular help in the courtroom.

Born in 1946, Michael Chatoff had grown up in Queens, New York, the son of a successful clothier, a bright, athletic boy with the boundless future of the white, middle-class male youth of post–World War II America. Small but wiry and well-coordinated, he succeeded as well on the tennis court as in the classroom, and through an accelerated program he graduated from Jamaica High School at sixteen.

One of his oldest friends, Arlene Ratzabi, maintains that his hearing problems began as early as thirteen or fourteen, when his friends noticed they had to repeat things. In those days, the Chatoffs' solid, two-story brick house in Jamaica Estates was headquarters for his friends, many of whom lived in less affluent Queens Village. They played pool in the basement and enjoyed backyard barbecues. Chatoff was outgoing but had, at the same time, a kind of reserve that verged on formality.

His years at Queens College, where he enrolled in 1963, were full of cheerful success. He and a friend founded a house plan (a kind of fraternity without national affiliation) and put it in sound condition financially. Gary Ackerman, in later years a congressman from New York, was editor of the house newspaper when Chatoff showed up looking for work as business manager. It was hard to find anyone interested in the business end, and Ackerman regarded the popular, Joe-College Chatoff as sheer good luck. Ackerman's new business manager was a tough taskmaster, but after the paper had been put to bed on deadline evenings, Chatoff relented and they all went out to eat Italian. One night, however, as the group walked back from a rock concert, Michael lost his balance and fell to the ground. "We knew he was having hearing problems," Ratzabi says. "We used to joke about it and he would laugh."

By his senior year, when Chatoff was working part-time in an accounting firm in Manhattan, the hearing problem had noticeably worsened. At a school awards ceremony at which several people were seated around a table, Chatoff kept asking what had been said. His grandmother told his mother, "Michael can't hear." His mother rebuked her, "Don't you ever say anything like that. Of course Michael can hear." During the summer of 1967, Chatoff took his cousins who lived in Riverdale out to dinner. In the restaurant, a deaf couple was signing. Chatoff was shocked and embarrassed for them. How could people make themselves so obvious—and in public?

Later that summer, their parents sent Michael and his brother, Peter, who had graduated from Hofstra, off to Europe as a graduation present. In England, the two young men stood together beneath Big Ben on the hour, and Michael wondered aloud to his brother why so famous a clock didn't strike. Dumbfounded, Peter stared at him. The clock was striking as they spoke. For the first time, fear edged into Michael Chatoff's consciousness. In September, he enrolled in Brooklyn Law School. Almost from the beginning, he felt his hearing slipping and his balance deserting him. He went to several ear specialists who told him that he had nerve damage and would have to start wearing a hearing aid and learn to read lips.

But Chatoff had a notion that something else was wrong. In the summer of 1968, he told his friends, "There's a problem with fine tuning." He went to one more specialist at the Long Island Jewish Medical Center. This doctor concluded that the problem was not in the inner ear but between the inner ear and the brain, the province of neurology. The neurologist he referred Chatoff to suggested that he enter the hospital for a series of tests. The tests revealed large tumors wrapped around each of Chatoff's auditory nerves, a condition known as bilateral acoustic neuroma. The doctors said that they could only remove the tumors one at a time, the larger one first. They said nothing either to Chatoff or his mother of what the results might be.

Arlene Ratzabi, got this news from Chatoff's brother Peter over the phone. Obviously distraught, Peter told her that they were expecting eight to ten hours of surgery, and the outcome was not sure. Ratzabi wept. When Chatoff awoke from the operation, it was to a nightmare moment in his life. He could not hear. He had a tube in his throat that made it impossible for him to talk. The eye where the surgeon had cut the facial nerve was stitched shut. He was in pain. He was lying on his side, unable to use a pillow. He could not raise his head. Hear no evil, speak no evil, see no evil, he thought silently to himself.

He understood that he would be able to see once the stitches were removed from his eyelids and that he would speak, although how well was a question that did not occur to him at first. But it was just as clear that he had lost virtually all hearing in both ears, not just the one operated on, and nobody was promising him that his hearing would return. His mother was shocked by her son's appearance. His face seemed to have drooped from the cutting of the facial nerve around which the tumor had wrapped.

Chatoff was in the hospital three weeks. When he finally did manage to get out of bed, it took two people to hold him up. Someone had to help him upstairs and downstairs in his parents' home. He slept fifteen hours a day. He had weighed 125 pounds when he went into the hospital but only 75 pounds when he came out. Ratzabi thought he looked like a skeleton. On election day, 1968, when he was old enough to vote for the first time, he was still so weak he had to be virtually carried to the polling place across and up the street from his parents' house. But he was determined to vote for Hubert Humphrey, a man he much admired. And he was determined to be ready for reenrollment in Brooklyn Law School. He took his law books to Puerto Rico, where his parents sent him for rest and recuperation.

He had entered the world of the deaf fully unprepared. Brooklyn Law School, like most, didn't feel any need for a deaf student, although it did have a blind student. The blind student got to classes, took notes and, reading in Braille, took exams like anyone else. But deaf was different. Chatoff's parents discovered this when they visited the dean of the law school to defend their son's right to return to school. The dean suggested that he should look into some other line of professional pursuit. The Chatoffs were adamant. They simply would not go away. They were ready to make a fuss if necessary. In the end, Michael was readmitted.

It was a jolt for Chatoff to discover his new status and to realize what it meant. In the eyes of others, he was "handicapped," and this meant that people had begun to view him in terms of his disability, rather than his abilities. He found that, for most people, to know that someone was "deaf" was to know all it was necessary to know about that person. He could feel people shrink discreetly away from him. He asked himself if he had held that attitude himself before becoming deaf and he remembered his discomfiture at the deaf people signing in the restaurant. He could think of no deaf people in his experience of growing up. Nobody at Queens was deaf. Nobody in the neighborhood was deaf. For the first time in his life, he asked himself: Where were all the deaf people?

Suddenly, he had become one of a group that had been missing in his life's experience. He felt no kinship with the deaf, yet he could not avoid the conclusion that he had lost something that had placed him happily in that amorphous group who considered themselves "normal" people. One old friend from college days came by during his recovery period, had difficulty communicating with him, and never returned.

He told himself that he did not have time for friends with the task set before him now of graduating from law school. He had to study in a new way and harder, he had to take therapy for his speech, which had not returned in its old strength and clarity, and he had to learn sign language. There were not enough hours in the day. Besides, he had one friend he knew he could count on: Harvey Barrison.

———

Harvey Barrison went back with Chatoff to Queens College, to 1965, a classmate who had chosen the same law school. The connection was more professional than social at Queens, where they were both in student government. At Brooklyn Law School, in Chatoff's first year, they were merely classmates. But when Chatoff returned to school after his operation, he asked Barrison to help him by taking notes in class. Barrison said sure.

Barrison had grown up in Brooklyn and in the Woodhaven section of Queens in a family with no disabilities. His willingness to help had nothing to do with any grand sense of duty to his fellow man, nor was it a conscious decision to become involved in problems of disability. He was Chatoff's friend, and Chatoff was asking for a simple kind of help. Barrison was taking fairly complete notes for himself. Why not make them available to his friend?

Chatoff's deafness seemed to Barrison to be a misfortune not different from those many other people had suffered through, although perhaps a greater one than most. He knew Chatoff well enough to feel certain that he would overcome the problems posed by his deafness and continue with his career. Chatoff was tough and, Barrison felt, resilient. The idea that deafness might prevent a man like him from becoming a lawyer seemed absurd to Barrison. So did the idea that deafness could interrupt or end a friendship. It took a little more time to communicate, true. They wrote notes when that was necessary, and Chatoff began to read lips better as time went on. He had lost lip movement on the right side, but he was still easy enough to understand. It just took a little more time. If a person was worth it, Barrison figured, you simply overlooked a problem like that. There were plenty of other things about people that one had to overlook in the name of friendship. Barrison sat in the back in Judge Broderick's court and took notes, conferred with Chatoff between sessions, and repeated this assistance later for the appellate court hearing.

To Chatoff, Barrison's early help was particularly welcome. He badly needed someone who was willing to be there for him as he struggled with the unfamiliar barriers created by the loss of a sense. And he was far from back to full strength physically. As he resumed his law school work, he was able to attend classes for four or five hours, go to therapy, nap for a while, and then hit the law books for several hours—a ten-to-twelve-hour day. He graduated from Brooklyn Law School in January 1971. At the graduation ceremony, Mayor John Lindsay made a speech about a blind man in Chatoff's graduating class. Nobody apparently had bothered to tell the mayor about Chatoff. It hurt his mother's feelings.

In June 1971, Chatoff had the second operation. It was no easier to bear and no worse than the first, but when it was over, he had lost the ability to use his lips for speech altogether. Henceforth, he would have to create words in his throat and expel them with no help from his lips to form them. Moreover, while he was definably deaf before this second operation, he was afterward, in popular parlance, stone deaf, unable to hear even the loudest sound.

And again he faced a long recuperation. It was January before he felt able to go to work. His aunt helped him get a job with a Chicago title insurance company. At the same time, he decided to go to night school at New York University to get his master of law degree. Getting into New York University proved no simple matter either. He had made an appointment to be admitted and had an interview with the instructor. Before he had even gotten home from this interview, his parents had a telephone call from the instructor. Did they know their son was deaf, she wanted to know? Yes, Chatoff's mother replied, they were aware of that. Well, the instructor said, how can you expect him to get through the program at N.Y.U.? The

Chatoffs pointed out that their son's deafness had not prevented him from graduating from Brooklyn high in his class. In the end, reluctantly, the school agreed to admit him.

The entire experience seemed to settle on Chatoff's shoulders. As he retreated from the rebuffs he felt around him, he found it difficult to keep up his usual good spirits. One evening, sitting around the dinner table, feeling the even deeper isolation that comes from being cut off from easy communication with his own family, Chatoff got up and went to his room. His uncle came up after him, sat down at his desk, and began typing a note. It read something like this: "There are billions of people in the world. If someone won't speak to you, forget him. There will always be others who will not be intimidated by your deafness." Chatoff decided to take the advice to heart and to deal with the world one person at a time.

It is my first meeting with him, in the fall of 1984. I have come to his apartment in Floral Park, on Long Island, high up in one of three stone-and-glass towers off Grand Central Parkway. Downstairs, the woman at the desk has explained to me that they would alert him that he had a visitor by ringing his apartment, which would activate a blinking light. When Mr. Chatoff saw the light, she continued in the voice of a tour guide who has been through the routine once too often, he would come downstairs to meet me.

The system worked smoothly enough, and Chatoff appeared shortly to greet me. He was smaller than I expected, and I remembered that the image fixed in my mind was a photograph of him standing on the Supreme Court steps. The New York Times photographer had shot up across his body to capture the building in the background, which elongated his figure. He walked a little as though taking precautions for each step, measuring it and placing his feet precisely, as though on a high wire.

I wanted to use a tape recorder, but it was clear that I would have to do extensive back-up note-taking. Listening carefully, I could understand most of what he said, but he had trouble understanding me. For all of this, Chatoff turned out to be the best kind of interviewee, an anecdotalist with a strong memory for detail, and I found working through the background questions easier than I had imagined.

Afterward, we repaired to a restaurant nearby for a mid-afternoon snack. We found a table and a waitress came up to take our order. She said something without looking up from her order pad, and of course Chatoff could not pick it up. What is the protocol, I wondered? Should I tell her that Chatoff was deaf or would he resent that? I said nothing and ordered instead. She looked at Chatoff, who was still studying the menu. "Anyou?" she asked, a little huffily. When he did not look up, she repeated the question, clearly impatient, and of course, still looking at the menu, he did not respond. I had to speak. "He's deaf," I said, "but he will understand if you get his attention and speak clearly to him." At this moment Chatoff looked up and ordered what sounded to me like a glass of milk and a Coca-Cola, although with the background noise of the restaurant, it was hard to be sure. The waitress looked at me warily: "What did he say?" she snapped. I asked Michael to repeat the order, which he did while the waitress continued to stare intently at me. "He wants a glass of milk and a Coca-Cola," I said. Strange order but then we all have our eccentricities.

When she brought the order, she once again spoke only to me. "Here's your order. Anything else?" I could see that Michael was puzzled. When he finally got her attention, she still would not look at him. As he spoke she looked at me, exactly the way, I thought, a stranger would look at the owner of a pet dog to learn what the animal's barking might portend. This time I understood. He had ordered a glass of milk and a chocolate cruller. I so informed the waitress, who was livid. "You," she screeched, "told me he wanted a Coca-Cola." I confessed it was true, I was sorry. She flounced off, spilling Coca-Cola in her wake.

The waitress had effectively made Michael Chatoff disappear in this exchange. She had willed him out of existence rather than deal with his deafness. I was with him and I could hear, so she would deal with me. It struck me that most of us do that most of the time. I had done that with the blind man who came to my friend's Christmas parties, pretending that I did not notice him. It seemed to me this could be the purpose of our reaction to a person with a disability: to make that person disappear. But what if the person refused? What if, like Amy Rowley, that person continued to show up day after day in a situation in which she could not be ignored, as, for instance, in attending public school? Was the school district's adamant, negative reaction to the persistence of Amy and her family what could happen when an individual with a disability continued to demand an even footing with other people? And if so, what attitudes lay behind the school district's reaction?

Judge Walter R. Mansfield, a compact, silver-haired man with a reputation as one of the best federal appellate judges in the northeast, sometimes dominated the process of questioning attorneys in oral argument. That was the case on May 1, 1980, when the *Rowley* case came up on appeal before the Second Circuit in the U.S. Customs Courthouse in New York City. Mansfield's fellow justices were William H. Timbers from the circuit, a graduate of Yale Law School and a dog breeder, and a district court judge, Dudley B. Bonsal, an international lawyer who later succeeded to the circuit. It was Mansfield who bored into the presentation of Sherman, the attorney for the commissioner of education, to get at what he considered the core of the question before the court.

Mansfield wanted to deal with the issue of what an "appropriate" education for a handicapped child might mean under the Education for All Handicapped Children Act. "Does it mean a program that will allow a child to reach his or her maximum potential, or does it mean a program that will enable a child to become as independent as possible from dependency on others, or does it mean, as the district judge thought, that the child must be given an education that will develop the child's potential to the extent comparable to the development of the potential of other children in the district?" Sherman never got a chance to answer this question. To Judge Bonsal, Judge Mansfield's characterization of Judge Broderick's opinion was lacking in a most important detail.

"If I understand," he interposed, "an *equal opportunity* to obtain that education. Isn't that the standard?" He intentionally leaned heavily on the words "equal opportunity" because his reading had convinced him that this was the crucial point in the Broderick opinion.

Sherman now had to respond to a somewhat different question and he did. "We certainly feel that handicapped children should be given an equal opportunity to attain an education," he said. "We have a lot of trouble with the lower court standard. He [Broderick] said how you apply this standard and to determine whether the child is getting an equal opportunity is that you compare the child's—this is the handicapped child's—potential with that child's actual performance." It was this test that the commissioner felt was incorrect and unworkable, Sherman told the court.

Much was made of Judge Broderick's language about tests later on by Raymond Kuntz, the school district's attorney. In fact, Kuntz said in the appellate court hearing that day, "We have no great disagreement with that [equal opportunity] standard but it is inevitably coupled with the discovery process of how the local district may determine it is meeting that standard . . . in utilizing the judge's standards we come up against an impossible task."

Mansfield wondered aloud whether it was not essential to compare Amy Rowley in some way with other students in making the determination that she was receiving an appropriate education. Sherman said he didn't think so and followed up by observing that numerous cases had demonstrated that school districts and state education agencies "don't have to maximize the potential of children." That got Judge Bonsal stirring again.

"I don't know whether potential comes into it but the handicapped child should have an *equal opportunity* with unhandicapped children to receive whatever it is the school can offer," Judge Bonsal said.

"I think that is true," Sherman responded. "There is no requirement that nonhandicapped children be provided with an education that will maximize their potential."

"No," agreed Bonsal. "I think that is it. If they get the equal opportunity, then from there on it is up to them."

"Well," said Sherman. "I think that if you take a look at this child's performances . . . "

"I say I don't know why that matters," broke in Judge Bonsal again. "Suppose the child's performance is very good. Isn't the test really whether this child had an equal opportunity with others to learn the things that were taught in the classroom?"

"Your Honor, there was absolutely—the record is devoid of any evidence indicating what opportunity has been given to the nonhandicapped children in this district. It would seem that the burden would rest with the plaintiff to demonstrate that she, in fact, was being denied that opportunity."

"The record indicates that she's a handicapped child," Judge Bonsal said.

"Yes, it does."

"Sure."

When his turn came, Chatoff moved back to the equal opportunity ground he had occupied from the impartial hearing on up through Judge Broderick's court. "It is their [the Rowleys'] position that if she's going to have an equal chance to succeed as a student and to succeed in life that she has to receive the same information as everyone else. Basically, their position is that she's entitled to an even chance . . . Amy is a good lip-reader but lipreading is a very imprecise science. Only 26 percent of spoken words are visible on the lips. I am considered a good lip-reader. I can't understand anything that is going on in these proceedings using the lipreading alone. That is why I have a note-taker and an interpreter here with me."

Judge Mansfield was paying close attention. There was a question he particularly wanted to ask. "What is your answer," he asked, "to the argument that provision of a sign language interpreter might adversely affect the education of a child by diverting it from the other methods of understanding what is said, such as lipreading and this discrete FM apparatus and make the child more dependent upon the interpreter than upon the type of situation that the child will be confronted with throughout his or her life?"

"I think it was made very clear in the record," Chatoff responded, "that the use of total communication by a deaf child improves all communication skills. Amy speaks more clearly than 99 percent of deaf children her age because of the use of total communication. Total communication provides a child with an opportunity to receive information, places information in the child's brain, and stimulates a desire to learn. I don't believe it has any detrimental effect whatsoever on interaction with hearing people in school or in later life."

Chatoff seized the opportunity to say something else he thought important for the judges to hear. He spoke as slowly and as carefully as he could. "I think deaf people, better than hearing people, understand that they live in a hearing world. Deaf people will make a considerable effort to make themselves understood to a hearing person. They will go well over half-way but they cannot go all the way. . . . They cannot learn to hear. It is important that the other person make some adjustments for deafness as well."

Judge Mansfield then wanted to know whether it was Chatoff's position that every deaf child must have an interpreter in his or her class.

"Definitely not," Chatoff responded. "It is my position and the position of the plaintiffs that the parents of a deaf child have the right and duty to determine how to raise their child and if the parents determine that their child shall be raised strictly by oral methods, shunning total communication entirely, that is their right."

Judge Mansfield had paid close attention to the note-taker Chatoff was employing and to what Chatoff said about lipreading. The judge, himself, had been losing a significant degree of his hearing over the years, perhaps going back as far as service in World War II. Some time back, he had purchased a hearing aid. Even now, in the courtroom, he felt the strain of keeping up with the testimony, and that worried him.

As I thought about Judge Mansfield's hearing loss, I could visualize my father's hearing aids, in the ear, attached to the eyeglasses, in their cases, and I remembered conversation in my parents' home about hearing aids. I remembered, also, my wheelchair friend Elisabeth Hudson's reaction to learning that my mother was hearing impaired as well as blind and that my father had suffered loss of hearing in his later years. "Maybe that's why you picked Jimmy to write about and then, later, Amy. You ought to think about that."

I found myself thinking instead about my father, that preeminent gadgeteer, whose collection of hearing aids and hearing-aid parts had been strewn around the house and on the desk in his study in the years between 1964 and 1972, when he died. He had been losing his hearing gradually for some years prior to 1964, but for a long time he seemed unwilling to face that fact. The sure way to arouse his ire in those days was to mention in the company of others that he was losing his hearing.

I don't know what eventually caused my father to deal directly with his problem, but I suspect someone in his corporate workplace spoke to him about getting a hearing aid. Whatever the reason, he plunged into the world of hearing aids with typical gusto. A man with no visible mechanical gifts, he was nonetheless a sucker for any small object whose purpose one could engage by pushing a button or sliding a lever. He dutifully studied the literature, whether about electric can openers (my parents' kitchen was studded with the latest electric or mechanical labor-savers) or hearing aids.

But my father never was pleased about having to wear a hearing aid. He had a sense of humor about it, as he did about everything, but I can remember his confiding in me once that people treated him differently now that he had to wear one. "Everybody is always shouting at me," I remember him saying. "And you know, I think they simplify their language because they are afraid I won't understand them. Sometimes, I feel as though I [am] being treated like a not-too-bright child." I didn't think about this at the time but I have since, and also about the curious differences in the popular perception of hearing impairment as compared to sight impairment.

Eyeglasses correct for deficiencies of sight, just as hearing aids correct for deficiencies of hearing, but insofar as public perception of the wearer is concerned, there the similarities end. Eyeglasses have been the object of teasing and still are, particularly among the young, but on the whole among adults they are so common that we treat them as much as an adornment as a necessity. The opticians' trade markets style, even elegance, with the product of improved vision. Respect due a person of learning may accompany eyeglasses, a particularly desirable outcome for professional women. Once the eyeglass selection is made, the wearer tends to be treated as he or she would be without glasses. Why, then, is the wearer of the hearing aid suddenly a problem to her- or himself, the family, associates, and casual acquaintances, when the wearer is merely correcting for weakness of a different sense?

It may have something to do with our perception of the kind of sensorial loss involved here. Problems with vision are accepted as the norm. The word "disability" does not occur to anyone in this connection. Eventually, most adults who live long enough come to wearing glasses, again without experiencing any sense of threat. Most important, wearing eyeglasses does not imply that one is "losing" one's sight.

Substitute the hearing aid for the eyeglasses and see how different this script plays. The child wearing a hearing aid is perceived as having a "disability," which is to say that the perception—although, again, not necessarily the truth—is that the hearing aid does *not* restore the child's hearing to normal. This sense of irrecoverable loss carries over to adulthood and affects both the wearer of the hearing aid and those who perceive him or her. Far from being an article of apparel conferring respect, the hearing aid may be considered by the wearer as a label of misfortune to be hidden away insofar as possible inside the ear—the less conspicuous the better.

We have to take eye tests so that we can learn in school and do no harm on the roadway. We do not have to take hearing tests and so we do not take them, preferring to conceal our hearing loss for as long as possible. If we were as rational about hearing loss as we are about vision loss, many more of us would wear hearing aids, perhaps stylish, gemlike accessories to dress the ear. But there is something else to be considered as well. We are not much affected by another person's limitation of sight. That loss is invisible to us. But a limitation of hearing on another person's part is immediately our own personal communication problem, as I believe my father's colleagues eventually had to tell him.

My father worried about his hearing but he was deeply apprehensive for mother in her worsening condition. She was losing her hearing and could not compensate by using a hearing aid, all varieties of which she maintained were unbearable to her because of their magnification of the incidental static of conversation and household noise. In this perilous position, he confided to me once, she was also losing her sight to cataracts, first, and then to glaucoma. He would not lose his sight but he had an operation for glaucoma, too, and suffered a third and fatal heart attack during the recovery period. He came sprawling to his bedroom floor out of an afternoon nap while reaching, we surmised later, for his eyeglasses and hearing aids, which he had placed on the bed table.

The period between the oral hearing and the Second Circuit Court's opinion was stressful for Nancy Rowley. The school year was winding down in early June, and there was pressure to have tests (SAT) administered to Amy. The problem was that Sue Williams, who had Nancy's confidence as a signer—despite her earlier testimony against the Rowleys in the impartial hearing—had left her job with the district. Her replacement had come from an oral-exclusive teaching program and was only now learning signing.

To Joseph Zavarella, the principal, this seemed a minor problem. The new teacher of the deaf was to administer the tests and she had no problems doing it, although she agreed with Nancy that it would be better if a more skilled signer were available. Zavarella got a letter from a staff member at BOCES saying that the new teacher of the deaf was qualified and sent it to the Rowleys. It arrived on the day Amy came home to report that she had been tested. Nancy was furious. She got on the TTY to Michael Chatoff, who advised her to get a letter from September Polk, staff assistant–interpreter for the Westchester County Office for the Disabled, who was teaching sign language to the new teacher, saying that her pupil was not up to instructing Amy on taking tests.

It all seemed totally unfair to Nancy. The Rowleys had won their case in court and yet Amy seemed farther away than ever from getting the services they had fought for. Another whole school year had passed without a classroom sign language interpreter, and now Amy had nobody who could even use total communications with her in the school. It seemed to Nancy that the school was going out of its way to be difficult. She got her letter from Polk saying that the new teacher of the deaf was not yet ready to serve as an instructor using sign language, but that merely underscored the problem.

September Polk was a sophisticated witness to all that was happening in these days. A native of Oklahoma City, she was in pre-med at Maryville College in Maryville, Tennessee, when she had the opportunity to take a three-week crash course in signing. After five days, she signed so well everyone in her class thought she was deaf. A fan of actress Shirley MacLaine, she speculated—pleased with the effect that it had on others— that in an earlier life she really was deaf. She got her degree in deaf education, taught the deaf at St. Joseph's in the Bronx, worked briefly for BOCES in Westchester County, and moved over to the Office for the Disabled soon afterward.

Polk liked the Rowleys and sympathized with them. She felt that Amy deserved and definitely needed a sign language interpreter in her classes. But she also felt that Nancy was sometimes her own worst enemy. An outspoken person herself, Polk would tell Nancy she had to learn when to shut up. But even if Nancy sometimes came across as unyielding, Polk thought, the truth was that she had to fight for Amy's needs and was still fighting, with nothing but signed legal opinions to show for it. The issue of the interpreter had begun to poison the atmosphere outside the classroom. The problem came to a head in June when Zavarella received instructions from the District Committee on the Handicapped to hold a meeting to review Amy's IEP and establish goals for the following year.

Nancy insisted on having an interpreter for meetings over Amy's schoolwork, and the school had always paid for this service. But September Polk became ill and could not serve as interpreter. Given such short notice, Zavarella could not find a substitute. It seemed to him that Nancy was being stubborn by insisting on the interpreter in that situation and so he asked her to find one. It seemed to her that he was simply passing the problem along to her for solution. She gave him telephone numbers to call and when he didn't succeed in finding an interpreter and announced that the meeting would still be held, she called Chatoff for advice. He told her to refuse to participate without interpretive services.

Nancy fretted about the upcoming June 18 meeting for days beforehand. Despite what others might think, she had no real taste for confrontation. She wished that Clifford could be with her, but he was unable to attend meetings in the afternoon. She showed up filled with dread and found herself and Zavarella center stage, with other school staff sitting about without participating. Nevertheless, she asked that everyone write down what they said so that she could follow the discussion. When Zavarella said that he would take notes, Nancy produced a piece of carbon paper and said she wanted a carbon of his notes. He refused and said it was clear she didn't trust him. She said that was right, not after all that had happened.

She described all this in a TTY conversation with Chatoff—her nervousness, the fact that Zavarella did not ask her to sign anything, her expression of disapproval of the whole affair. Chatoff said he thought the principal was just following orders from above.

At one point in their conversation, Nancy reported, "He even said that I don't care about Amy and that they are very concerned. I told him I'm concerned even though I'm here without an interpreter. He said I could leave the meeting if I'm not interested, but I refused. I told him he is hurting Amy more and more."

Zavarella wrote up the minutes of the meeting. "Mrs. Rowley does protest the lack of an interpreter but we asked her to get one if she could. We thought Mrs. Rowley would be interested in the progress made by her daughter over the past school year but she felt she could not proceed because she needs an interpreter."

Norman Gross, then a lawyer in the office of the Department of Education for the State of New York, had an associate who liked to say that one of the basic rules in writing a legal document in defense of a school district's action is never to use the first name of a child. It tended to create sympathy for the child, whether or not that sympathy was justified. Gross had cause to remember this when the Second Circuit Court of Appeals handed down its two-to-one decision on July 17, 1980, affirming Judge Broderick's decision in the *Rowley* case. Gross often said later on that you had only to read the first sentence of that decision to know who had won. "This case is about Amy," the opinion began.

The majority opinion continued: "She is eight years old. She is deaf and has been since birth. She needs a sign language interpreter in her classroom to enable her to have the same educational opportunity as her classmates. The district court, Vincent L. Broderick, district judge, held that she is entitled by law to have such an interpreter. We agree and accordingly we affirm the judgment of the district court." *

Gross had written the amicus curiae brief of the New York State School Boards Association supporting Hendrick Hudson's position in the case. He was not particularly surprised at the verdict, but he was mildly surprised

---

* United States Court of Appeals, Second Circuit, Amy Rowley by her parents v. Board of Education of Hendrick Hudson Central School District, July 17, 1980, p. 4513.

that the entire opinion signed by Judges Bonsal and Timbers was barely three pages long. It went on to say that evidence before the district court indicated that, without a sign language interpreter, Amy did not have the opportunity her classmates had to understand. That was about it. No discussion of the meaning of "appropriate" education, no probing of the legislative history of the act. And then, after this bare-bones, summary opinion, a final paragraph:

"Finally, we wish to emphasize the narrow scope of our holding. This is not a class action in which the needs of all deaf children are being determined. The evidence upon which our decision rests is concerned with a particular child, her atypical family, her upbringing and training since birth, and her classroom experience. In short, our decision is limited to the unique facts of this case and is not intended as authority beyond this case" (p. 4517). Here, a footnote referred the reader to a rule of the court intended to preclude citation of a specific decision as an authority in any other case.

Gross was aware of Rule 23, which had the effect described above. It was a controversial rule in the legal community wherever it was applied at the circuit court level. Some argued that it was impossible for a court to put limits on how other courts might use its decisions. But Gross had another reason for thinking that such a ruling would not be limited to the case at hand. He assumed that the Rowleys intended their daughter's case to be a "test case" for the new standard of assistance to handicapped children in school. He assumed advocacy groups supporting the Rowleys wanted that test. For his part, he thought Hendrick Hudson had a solid case of its own. It was not one of those "horror stories" all attorneys in education had heard, where the school people allow handicapped children to be mainstreamed with no services at all. Hendrick Hudson, in his view, had done quite a lot. If limits were not set on a school district's responsibilities to handicapped children, he thought, the cost of such education would be staggering.

He and others of like mind were more than pleased with Judge Mansfield's dissent. It ran to nineteen pages and was a powerful document in its passionate defense of the school district. After describing the district's efforts on Amy's behalf as "Herculean," and her success in school as "remarkable," Mansfield wrote that Judge Broderick had mistakenly alluded to the regulations of the Rehabilitation Act of 1973 rather than those of the Education for All Handicapped Children Act. With this observation, he noted that the earlier act referred to the services of sign language interpreters while the 1975 act did not—"showing that when Congress wished to provide such services, it knew how to do so." He observed that the standard that Judge Broderick had adopted—"that each handicapped child be given an opportunity to achieve his full potential commensurate with the opportunity provided other children"—had been borrowed from an article in a law review.

He concentrated—as Raymond Kuntz had concentrated in his argument and brief—on what he called the "impossibility" of tests he said Judge Broderick wanted to impose on both handicapped and nonhandicapped children to measure the shortfall between their potential and their performance. Judge Mansfield conjured up the image of a "battery" of such tests, which he said would be too expensive to impose and would prove inconclusive in any event.

Later on, he disposed of as speculative the position taken by Judge Broderick that Amy's I.Q. of 122 did not represent the full measure of her potential and went on: "On the opposite side of the ledger is the view that provision of a sign language interpreter would not prepare her for later life in a world in which she will not have such an interpreter available at her elbow but will be forced to achieve self-sufficiency in society through lipreading and maximization of the effectiveness of her residual hearing."

As to Amy's inability to hear 100 percent of what was said in the classroom, Judge Mansfield observed that some of her classmates "probably hear less than 100 percent too, due to inattention, daydreaming, and other causes."

But the heart of Judge Mansfield's dissenting opinion was his own standard for the Education for All Handicapped Children Act of 1975. Judge Broderick had found equal opportunity to be the standard that correctly comprehended the intent of Congress. For Judge Mansfield, nothing that ambitious was intended by Congress.

"Congress visualized a much more practical objective," he wrote, "i.e., an education for each handicapped child that would enable the child to be as free as reasonably possible from dependency on others, would enable the child to be a productive member of society, and would hopefully promote academic achievement that would roughly approximate that of his or her nonhandicapped classmates."* He concluded that a handicapped child's

---

* Judge Mansfield's quotes on pp. 111–13 are from United States Court of Appeals, Second Circuit, Amy Rowley by her parents v. Board of Education of Hendrick Hudson Central School District, July 17, 1980, pp. 4518–34.

112

"unique" needs were served whenever that happened, and that it was clearly happening in Amy Rowley's case.

In these paragraphs, Judge Mansfield took dead aim at the heart of Judge Broderick's decision. Mansfield did not read the act as providing the equal opportunity that his two colleagues on the Second Circuit and Judge Broderick before them believed it did. If the case were appealed, it would presumably turn on this issue. What did Congress intend to do for the education of children with disabilities when it passed the Education for All Handicapped Children Act of 1975?

A "Voice" in the Classroom

The Rowleys thought that the Second Circuit Court of Appeals decision was well timed, given that Amy had already been through another school year without a sign language interpreter. Coming in mid-July, the decision meant, to them, that Amy would have her interpreter by the start of school, when she would be in the third grade. Their attorney, Michael Chatoff, was concerned about the intransigence of the school district, which was going about the business of readying an appeal to the Supreme Court. Nothing was done about an interpreter until after school began and the appellate court vacated its stay of Judge Broderick's order. Then Chatoff was able to get a more-than-willing Judge Broderick to set a deadline, and the school district hired a sign language interpreter. It would do this but under no circumstances would it recommend a sign language interpreter for Amy Rowley. The school's legal position for future as well as past reference would continue to be that Amy didn't need that service.

Some bright spots were showing up outside the official school family, however. Nancy was pleased and surprised at the school open house to be warmly greeted by a number of parents she and Clifford knew only slightly. It seemed to her that the court's legitimization of their efforts on their daughter's behalf had made it possible for other parents, some with grievances of their own and some without, to express support for the family's efforts. The Rowleys met Charles and Helen Brooks, who had been fighting for services for their son Charlie, a district high school student with a learning disability. Nancy also renewed acquaintance with a hearing woman who had impressed her in earlier meetings on Amy's behalf, an advocate for children and a parent of a deaf child who was preparing herself for law school. Best of all, Louise McQuade had said she would be willing to accompany the Rowleys to the meeting that would be held with the pupil placement committee to determine Amy's IEP.

Louise McQuade had a deaf son and a daughter with a speech impediment caused by a cleft palate. Working to try to improve her son's chances for an education, she had become president of the New York State Council of Organizations for the Handicapped, an umbrella group of about forty-five organizations. It was a group, as she put it, run by mothers out of their kitchens. She worked for no pay, and her chief frustration was that, without a law degree, she could not bring matters she was involved in to closure. She was an oralist, herself, but she believed that the Rowleys had an equally valid communications style. From her own experience, McQuade felt sure that if you ignored a deaf child's natural mode of communications, you blocked that child's input.

Her son Douglas had been in public school in another Westchester County district some years back. He had an I.Q. in the 140 range, but she calculated after some study of the matter that using lipreading he was getting no more than 60 percent of what was being taught. With no legislation on the books, there was little she could do about that. The school, she felt, expected her to be grateful that they had even allowed him to attend. In fact, the school suggested the next year that the McQuades try the New York School for the Deaf.

Fanwood was a disaster in Louise McQuade's judgment. Total communications had arrived but only in the lower grades, and she saw hearing teachers who didn't sign and deaf teachers who didn't speak, along with others who spoke so poorly that Douglas couldn't lip-read them. He began to pick up a little sign language, but in her view it was too much to ask him to learn a new language at the same time he was learning new subject matter. She believed that the average reading ability in her son's class was barely above the kindergarten level. This was in 1977, when New York State had passed its companion legislation to the Education for All Handicapped Children Act, and it seemed to McQuade that Douglas could be returned to public school with more support than he had had before. But in public school, she found that problems remained. Teachers wouldn't talk directly to him so that he could lip-read to the best of his ability, and he was not always placed advantageously in the classroom. At the end of the day, he needed catch-up help from the resource center teacher.

McQuade agreed to help the Rowleys because she realized how doubly difficult it would be for a deaf couple, entangled legally with a school district, to win an argument about educating a deaf child. She considered the Hendrick Hudson District, in her experience, to be one of the most difficult to deal with. Usually, she was able to reconcile differences and get a District Committee on the Handicapped to agree to do something it had said it would do. It hadn't worked that way before with Hendrick Hudson.

For their part, the Rowley were convinced that they would get nowhere at this point without a specific listing of what they expected as a result of Judge Broderick's order. Michael Chatoff insisted that Amy's IEP contain a reference to a "qualified" sign language interpreter for all academic subjects and that the definition of academic be broad enough to cover such subjects as music. He also wanted the school to discontinue sending Amy out of her classes for work with a teacher of the deaf. So the Rowleys put together a laundry list of fifteen items they wanted the school to provide. These varied from use of the sign language interpreter in assemblies and field trips to a training program in mainstreaming a deaf child for officials, staff, and hearing parents.

The pupil placement committee meeting on October 6 went on for three hours and ended without some of the Rowleys' points even being discussed. McQuade spent a good bit of time explaining to the Rowleys various points made by others despite the presence of a sign language interpreter for them. She thought that Amy's teachers were open-minded but that Zavarella became increasingly agitated and angry. She thought he had been particularly rude to the Rowleys as well as to her at this meeting. He had asked her why she had bothered to get involved with something of this kind and why she thought the Rowleys needed her help.

From Zavarella's point of view, the meeting was at an impasse before it got under way. Actually, he felt powerless to act as soon as he read the Rowleys' fifteen points. He told Clifford later over the TTY that he had specific instructions to provide the interpreter only for academic subjects, which had been defined to him as what went on in Joan Conklin's third-grade class and any library work associated with it. He wrote a memorandum the day after the meeting to Marilyn Goodman, the new DCOH chairperson, concluding: "As you can see, we are at an impasse at the building level simply because many of the requests are out of our domain. I respectfully ask that the case be placed on the DCOH agenda as soon as possible."

116

The Rowleys, Chatoff, and McQuade arrived at the school district office at 12:15 P.M. on November 24 for the DCOH meeting. As they sat in the waiting room, they could see members of the committee in the meeting room in deep discussion with Teresa Kuntz, Raymond Kuntz' wife and a member of his law firm. It was after 1 P.M. before the Rowley party was admitted to the meeting room and introductions could be made around the table. Louise McQuade noted that in addition to the note-taker, an even-dozen members of the committee were present in the room—three times the number of the Rowley party. Louise had attended DCOH meetings with more than half of the approximately 375 families she had worked with in the preceding four years in Westchester and surrounding counties. She had observed this phenomenon, which she described as "stacking" the committee room, many times before. Sometimes as many as twenty professionals attended these meetings, and the intent was clearly, to her, to intimidate the parents. She had put an end to the practice in her own district by bringing more parental support on the side of her clients so that they outnumbered the school professionals. At that point, she observed, the school district stopped playing the numbers game.

A tape recorder was set up, and an interpreter was available for the Rowleys and Chatoff. Louise McQuade kept private notes which later formed the basis of a sworn deposition. She observed that the chairman of the DCOH, Marilyn "Mitty" Goodman, ran the meeting by reading statements from several typed pages she had before her. When Goodman asked questions or made motions, McQuade noted, she read them from the pages. Motions were always seconded and the votes went swiftly to the affirmative. When points were unclear, Goodman conferred with Kuntz and then continued. Additionally, McQuade thought that the way the meeting was being run was designed to keep comment and questions from the other side of the table to a minimum. Several times, she observed in her deposition, questions from the Rowleys were cut off or ignored. The verb that she used in her deposition was "bulldog"—as in the chairman's trying to "bulldog" the meeting.

What struck McQuade as most unfair was the committee's ignoring the obvious need of the Rowleys and Chatoff for more time to keep up with the proceedings. With so little time allowed for digestion and review, it was clearly impossible for these deaf individuals to keep up with what was going on in a crowded meeting, in which they also had to take notes in order to respond. In these circumstances, the interpreter's and the note-taker's jobs were also nightmarish. Twice in the twenty-seven-page transcript the note-taker asked for time to catch up and once was reminded by Goodman that there was a back-up tape. That tape indicates that the note-taker frequently did not understand or could not transcribe accurately or completely the infrequent remarks the Rowleys made or the questions they asked.

A good bit of time in the meeting was taken up in a discussion of what Judge Broderick meant in his order to supply Amy with a sign language interpreter for "all academic subjects." Chatoff and Kuntz argued over the legal ramifications of the term. Were assemblies to be included, Chatoff asked. Goodman promptly responded that it had been decided that the principal would determine whether the subject materials in the assembly were "academic" and see that an interpreter was provided when they were. Clifford Rowley wondered why Amy should be in assemblies without an interpreter when she got so little out of it. "True," Goodman responded, "but that was not the court order."

The meeting's heaviest contention was reserved for the issue of whether Amy should be taken out of classes to work with the teacher of the deaf. This matter had galled the Rowley all along and now, with a sign language interpreter at last working in the classroom with Amy, it made absolutely no sense to them for her to continue to leave class. Here was an issue on which many educators could easily sympathize with the parents' view—even Zavarella had praise for the Rowleys' plan to phase out use of the teacher of the deaf—but once again the legal view would prevail: that the present use of the teacher of the deaf was legally correct, had worked successfully, and should not be changed.

As the meeting began to wind down, with the chairman pushing toward adjournment, tempers began to fray. Clifford Rowley asked someone to tell him what had been accomplished in the meeting. Goodman said that the Rowleys' list of "suggestions" had been reviewed, although not with a vote taken on each of them; that the committee was prepared to give guidance to the pupil placement committee on Amy's IEP; and that the committee had voted not to change the original recommendations, which did not include a sign language interpreter. Clifford then asked why the meetings never were pleasant.

"I think," said Zavarella, "that it might be appropriate for Cliff and . . . [me] to have an off-the-record discussion. It might be pleasant. Whenever we get into a formal discussion, there are always people such as Mr. Chatoff and Mrs. Kuntz and Mrs. McQuade around that makes it somewhat unpleasant. The point is," he added, looking at Clifford, "if you want to have a more pleasant conversation, see me as a father who is interested in dealing with the needs of your daughter, not as the father of a deaf person who is advancing the rights of all deaf people. Then you and I could have a very pleasant conversation. On that note, I think I better shut my mouth."

But the Furnace Woods principal did not quite succeed in this resolve. Dr. Leonard S. DiBart, the school physician, brought up the subject of the New York School for the Deaf. "Maybe they can offer Amy better than we are [offering] here. And that ought to be investigated . . . and maybe the decision should be made as to what place she should go for her education."

Zavarella could not resist. "We seem to be running into all kinds of difficulties," he said. "Maybe they are set up better than we are to handle these difficulties. It's just the parents who are not really satisfied with what we are doing here."

Nancy Rowley spoke briefly on the old and oft-discussed subject of why "Fanwood" was not for Amy. Zavarella listened and responded once more, "You tell me that Amy is better off here. But you keep giving requests for more and more services. . . . There is another facility available and, if you are not happy here, maybe we should go to this other facility and work there."

It was time for adjournment, McQuade realized sadly. She was sure that there would be no budging this district short of a mandate to action from their attorneys. She felt sorry for Nancy and Clifford. She felt sure they were right about Amy's needs based on her own experience. The third grade, she remembered, had been difficult for her Doug. For deaf students, it was where the water suddenly got deep.

Goodman, however, left the meeting with a different impression, one that, if anything, became more of a conviction with the passage of time. She left the school district a few years after the Supreme Court decision in the case and moved to Florida. Remarried, and now Marilyn Penner, she was as convinced as ever that the school district had been right in the Amy Rowley matter. A former elementary schoolteacher with a master's degree in special education herself, she thought the school was doing very well by Amy and believed that, if the child had begun to "struggle," the district would willingly have provided her with an interpreter.

She did, indeed, remember this meeting of the DCOH. It might have begun late, she said, as many of their meetings did. Yes, she was reading regulations in answer to questions. "After all," she noted, "we were deep, deep in a legal battle by then." But she saw nothing wrong with the way the meeting was conducted and described McQuade as "hostile." Finally, she offered the opinion that Amy Rowley made "a bad test case of the law." When I asked why she thought it was a test case, she responded that she did not believe that the Rowleys were acting on their own but that they were involved in an activist effort on the part of the deaf community at large.

—

Amy couldn't believe it. Here, at last, was a woman, a funny-looking, funny-talking woman, standing in her classroom, signing perfectly to her, so that she could understand everything. And this woman was positioning herself so that Amy could keep her and the teacher, Joan Conklin, in her line of vision at the same time. Best of all, this woman, Fran Miller, was fun to be around, made her laugh, and made the rest of the class laugh. Miller was outrageous. She was zany. But Amy knew she was using humor to hold their attention.

Fran Miller had grown up with deafness as the constant, the one thing reliably to be dealt with as a daily fact of her life: mother, father, brother, two cousins, aunt, uncle—all hereditarily deaf. She was that rarest of hearing persons, one for whom signing was a first language and English a second. She often found herself talking from a "deaf perspective" and once told Nancy Rowley that she did not entirely trust hearing people. Nancy was a little shocked by this but she liked Miller and was impressed that the interpreter used signed English with Amy and worked hard to get every word understood.

More than all but a tiny minority of hearing people, Miller had experienced the isolation that afflicts the deaf. In an odd reversal of roles, the isolation came from the sensation that she was systematically losing her family because of deafness. Her older hearing sister seems to have departed from home quite early. She saw her deaf father, a computer specialist, begin a slide into mental illness that culminated in institutionalization. Separated from her husband, Miller's deaf mother eventually moved her and her brother from Poughkeepsie to Connecticut. Then her deaf brother, only eighteen months older, was packed off to St. Mary's School for the Deaf in Buffalo. Miller simply did not understand. She realized that he was deaf—sometimes in her child's life this took the form of a sudden awareness that she *could* hear—but why did this mean that they had to be separated? When her high school prom beckoned, Miller refused to go if her brother couldn't go as well. Startled by the request, the school nevertheless acquiesced. Miller's brother promptly found an attractive girl at the dance and she was deserted again, but that at least was something she could understand.

Her sense of humor helped her through, but she became keenly aware of the mortal enemy of the deaf and families of the deaf: ignorance, the ignorance of hearing people of the deaf and of deafness. It was this ignorance that made her fearful and a little mistrustful of most hearing persons. Most did not care to learn about deafness at all. Their instinct was to shun or ignore the deaf and hope they would go away.

As someone who had interpreted mainly for deaf adults, she found working with a third-grade deaf child exciting and challenging. She also understood quickly that this little girl was a perfectionist, which was a blessing for Amy because third grade was so hard, so many new words, so many words that sounded the same. Amy had to deal with "which" and "witch," with "to," "too," and "two." It was necessary first for Amy to know she was dealing with a new word. For "which," Miller signed "witch" and then signed "not this word—a word that sounds like this." Then she would finger-spell the new word. This technique eliminated a kind of catch-22 for a deaf child trying to understand. Without the signing and the explanation, she might figure out a new word through its context, but often the context depended on the meaning of that word.

Miller felt that Amy had other needs that she could fill. Amy needed to develop her signing skills, and Miller's sessions with her provided that opportunity. Then, Amy sometimes displayed a lack of attention that troubled Miller. It was no worse than that exhibited by the hearing students, but Amy couldn't afford it. Finally, Miller worried that Amy sometimes used her status as a "deaf" student in a hearing class as an excuse for not doing all she could. The interpreter kept a diary while she worked in Furnace Woods, and one entry reads: "This is a hard day for her [Amy] but if I am going to work in this room, she is not going to use deafness as her way out of things, nor be treated any differently [from] any other child in class. This is a very important stage in life. There are a lot of building tools given and she has to learn them now before getting into other classes where she wouldn't keep up due to her own frustrations."

To Miller's delight, she found herself working with someone she regarded as an excellent teacher and one who seemed to understand Amy's needs. Joan Conklin had been chosen from the third-grade teachers for Amy's class in no small part because of her talent and commitment. There

121

were times when Miller couldn't work with Amy. She was not allowed to interpret for the child in music, as the school's official position was that music was not an "academic" subject. Amy still had to leave her class to work with her teacher of the deaf on a daily basis, something that Miller saw as a distinct disadvantage for Amy. Miller found ways to occupy herself usefully, grading papers or creating educational "crossword puzzles" that students could work on after they finished their assigned work. The students loved them and competed for time with Miller. She also located a few educationally needy students in the class and found a variety of ways to help them. Without setting out to do it, and certainly without an official directive to do so, Fran Miller was fulfilling the role of interpreter-tutor that Nancy Rowley had laid out for Hendrick Hudson school officials long before Amy had entered kindergarten.

For their part, the children in the class responded with admiration for this new figure in their school lives. Marjorie Augenblick, for example, had established herself in first and second grade as a friend who would help Amy whenever she had difficulty understanding. Marjorie realized that while she and Amy both were bright, Amy did not always understand what was going on in class. When Amy flashed her a puzzled look, Marjorie would explain what had been said. Sometimes teachers had asked Marjorie to help Amy. Because she habitually sat next to Amy, Marjorie readily noticed the improvement in Amy's ability to comprehend after Fran Miller began signing for her. Like others in the class, Marjorie was fascinated with the process of signing and even more with this entertaining and often most helpful woman. For Marjorie, Fran Miller added a dimension that the classroom had not possessed before. She drew word pictures on the blackboard. She helped everyone—not just Amy—understand. She made it possible to visualize what otherwise was a purely oral exercise. Words, Marjorie thought, came flutteringly to life in Fran Miller's hands.

Like most of Amy's classmates, Marjorie did not make much of Amy's deafness. It was a simple fact to be absorbed, more important, perhaps, than Amy's wearing her straight, blonde hair in ribbons that matched her outfits, but nothing to treat her differently about. The girls became close friends, and Marjorie spent a good bit of time at Amy's house. Once, when John was not home, Marjorie was asked to telephone an automobile repair shop to find out if the family car was ready. It was a thrilling experience for a preteenager, and she teased her mother about it, asking why she didn't get to do that at home.

Andrea Marino was another of the students in Conklin's class who appreciated Fran Miller. She found herself concentrating more in class with Fran there. She saw other students competing for attention from Miller when Conklin was not actually in front of the class teaching. She saw Amy's confidence grow as the experience of the sign language interpreter became the accepted norm in the classroom. This pleased her because she liked Amy and admired Amy's parents.

What impressed Miller was the number of parents who came to her during parent–teacher meetings and told her with enthusiasm that their children had become interested in sign language as a result of seeing it used. Miller decided that what negative feelings existed were coming from other parents, not based on experience but, quite the opposite, on inexperience. That old devil, ignorance, rearing up again. Miller thought that, if she could have her way, she would always work exclusively with children. They were so much more adaptable; they had so little mental baggage to unload before they could learn.

In this period, the Rowleys, Miller, and Conklin were interviewed by a *New York Times* reporter about Amy's progress. Amy told the reporter that she was doing better with the sign language interpreter, and Nancy and Clifford concurred. Joan Conklin told the reporter that Amy was getting used to Miller and was using her more and more in the classroom. "She's reading fine and writing fine," Conklin was quoted as saying. "The only weak area is math, but she has company there," the teacher added. Then, in a final note, she observed that since Fran had come along the other children did not rush to Amy's aid as they had done before.*

But the *Times* story was not inspired by Amy's progress so much as by the appeal the school district was readying for the Supreme Court. "School districts have civil rights, too," Zavarella was quoted as saying in the same story. "We had always said to the parents that if we found that she was failing we might make a recommendation that a sign language interpreter was necessary. She's been doing exceptionally well."

In response to the Rowleys' contention that Amy was doing significantly better with Fran Miller's help, the *Times* reporter quoted Paul E. "Pete" Sherman, the state commissioner of education attorney: "My son would do better [too] if he had four teachers. He's got a great I.Q. but he's getting Cs and B-minuses."

---

* *New York Times*, October 22, 1980, p. B-2.

The school district's adamance over her not being needed raised personal problems for Fran Miller. These problems had begun at her first meeting with Zavarella, on September 24, after which she was sure that her duties were outlined as including interpreting for Amy in auditorium assemblies, for speakers, movies, and on field trips within school hours. In her opinion, she could not do justice to Amy with less exposure than that. Amy needed her in the classroom, but also in the out-of-classroom learning experiences. If the classroom materials were more important, it was also true that the out-of-class situations were even harder for Amy to comprehend without help. Miller was certain she had also understood clearly, at a meeting with school fiscal and administrative officials, that they had agreed to pay her $300 a week. But the two people involved on the school side seemed just as certain that the offer was for $250 a week, and one told her that if she persisted in asking for more she might as well give her notice.

Miller had been troubled by an ulcer before and she soon found that old enemy in full revolt. An assembly on the history of jazz took place on October 16, and Miller expected to interpret for Amy there. Before the assembly, Zavarella took her aside and explained that she could not interpret because the assembly was for entertainment, not educational purposes. To Miller, this decision was in conflict with the job description they had agreed upon. Worse, it put Amy in a situation where she would have a very hard time understanding what was going on in the assembly.

Equally baffling was the decision made about an assembly session on November 12, "Bill Robinson's Animals from Africa." She was called out of the faculty room on that occasion and rushed into the auditorium. There, Zavarella asked that she sit next to Amy and interpret. She explained to the principal that the side-by-side position was not conducive to interpreting, and they compromised by putting Miller in the aisle facing Amy. It seemed to Miller that the principal had wanted to avoid at all costs putting her in a position where the other children could easily see her.

Miller felt keenly the day-to-day uncertainty about her role. One day she was a few minutes late and missed the bus for a field trip. She didn't even have an address for the planetarium where the children were headed, but she finally found it. When she got there, she had to borrow a flashlight to find Amy and then sit on the floor with her in the dark, using the flashlight to interpret what the show host was saying. Amy had not brought along her FM transistor hearing aid, which had been malfunctioning, and, without Miller, she would have sat in the dark literally and figuratively, for two hours, recovering later only what her schoolmates and Conklin could tell her in the limited time available for that exchange.

Miller's diary catalogues the end of her stay at Furnace Woods. She had been in touch with Nancy during most of this time, dropping by to keep her posted, or talking with her over the TTY. Michael Chatoff thought that what Miller had experienced ought to be part of the court record and asked her to do a notarized statement, which she did on December 15. She also sent a letter to the administration on the subject of her salary. She noted in her diary: "I told her [an administrative assistant] that since I've worked here they've been able to upset my ulcer with their 'you will' and 'you won't' special events interpreting, never knowing what is going to happen. I spoke to Joe Zavarella to let him know that I have sent in this letter. He wants me to stay, but I'm not a ball that can be bounced around. The money thing is just a principle thing anyway because $50 is not that much money." Miller felt that $12,000 a year, which is what the school was paying for her services, was too little even for an interpreter in an ideal situation, let alone for one in the cave of confusion into which she had fallen. Both parties agreed that it was time to part company. The school district's view was that Fran Miller was too political, by which they clearly meant that she was al-lied with the Rowleys' cause and the cause of the deaf generally. Miller's view was that she could afford to lose the dispute over her salary but she could not afford the continued visits to the doctor.

The students of Conklin third-grade class created cards for Fran Miller, wishing her well. Virtually every one of those cards thanked her for help given. One boy wrote, "Thanks so much for teaching me some sign language. I really like it a lot. If you come back to the school, come to fourth or fifth grade. By." In the packet, Joan Conklin added a note of her own, thanking Fran Miller for her "extra special help . . . understanding, and sensitivity." Af-ter leaving, Miller cried and could never afterward be sure to what degree the tears were of sorrow and to what degree relief. But she kept the cards and the notes and a letter, which Nancy received later from a parent of one of Amy's classmates, who said that Fran's work had added extra enrichment to her son's appreciation of a December assembly in which carols from around the world were sung in various languages. This parent's letter concluded, "He and many of his classmates have learned a good deal of sign language this year. I think, too, that he has grown in character as he has become aware of those around him who have to adapt themselves to various handicaps."

1

"Full Potential" in the Court

With the decision of the three-judge circuit court favoring the Rowleys and the strong dissent of Judge Mansfield, the case had begun to attract the attention of the major media. Two days after the decision was announced, the *New York Times* carried a lead editorial with the arresting title, "Going Wrong with Handicapped Rights." It was a curious editorial, which did not mention the Rowleys by name and gave few particulars of the case. It began in the familiar "sounds good . . . but" editorial vein.

"It sounds humane for a Federal Appeals Court to rule that the schools of Peekskill, New York, are legally obliged to provide a personal sign-language interpreter for a bright, partly-deaf 8-year-old pupil. But even the judges who so read the Education for All Handicapped Children Act of 1975 recoiled from the precedent; they were not saying *all* deaf children, they insisted. Maybe not. The trend, however, is alarmingly clear. A humane Federal benefit is turning into a state and local obligation with no sign that the Federal Government means to pay for what it decrees."*

This "viewing with alarm" tone was sustained throughout the editorial. The *Times* noted that New York State's outlays had "doubled" (from when was not clear) to $300 million a year. The federal government, the editorial writer noted, was paying only 12 percent of the additional costs of special education nationally, rather than the 40 percent it had promised to pay. After noting, almost as though in passing, that handicapped children had

* *New York Times*, July 19, 1980, p. 16.

126

been neglected by our educational system in the past and that they are "entitled to the best possible instruction," it got down to its conclusions.

"It is perverse for Congress and the courts to define an 'appropriate education' only for the handicapped and write rules that result in the deprivation of other children. The allocation of scarce local resources is necessarily a political matter, best left to local government. If Washington wants to help, the right way would be through special education grants that can be used at local discretion. It is no favor to the handicapped to make them the beneficiaries of unique rhetorical rights and the object of local resentment."

The editorial was given immediate circulation among members of the Hendrick Hudson Board of Education by Superintendent Charles Eible, who noted that the *Times* had editorially "expressed its concern" over the Rowley decision and that "Judge Mansfield agreed with the position taken by the district and in fact praised the district for its major effort on Amy's behalf." He added, that after studying the decision with school district attorney Raymond Kuntz, he would call a meeting of the board "to review various options and decide on a future course of action." *

From Floral Park, on July 21, Michael Chatoff sent a letter to the *New York Times,* in which he chided the editorial board for its description of Amy. "She is not 'partly' deaf, whatever that means. She is severely deaf—she cannot process linguistic communications through hearing alone." Chatoff then attempted to set the record straight on what the Rowleys sought. "You talk about providing handicapped children with the 'best possible education' but the plaintiffs never argued for such a standard and the district court and court of appeals specifically rejected such a standard. They adopted the standard enunciated in federal law, that each child is entitled to an equal educational opportunity, that child's disability notwithstanding. In the case of a child who is deaf, that means the provision of services that will provide the child with the same opportunity as other children to understand what is said in the classroom. A more reasonable standard cannot be imagined." The *Times* did not publish the letter.

In the light of what subsequently happened, the *Times* editorial is worth a closer, critical perusal. First of all it minimized the disability involved, Amy's deafness, by describing her as "partly" deaf. Then it singled out individuals with disabilities as having been placed in a category of need above and beyond all other students. What could one make of this sentence—"It

* Memo to Board of Education, Hendrick Hudson Central School District, from Charles Eible, July 21, 1980.

is perverse for Congress and the courts to define an 'appropriate' education *only* [author's emphasis] for the handicapped and write rules that result in the deprivation of other children"—other than that children with disabilities had been given an unfair and confiscatory advantage over other children? Finally, in order to sustain this theme, the editorialist necessarily ignored the clear "equal opportunity" thrust of the court decisions.

As for the issue of cost—that gray area for legal consideration—it shone brightly through the fabric of the editorial. Interestingly enough, in this same period, a brief for the commissioner of education for the State of New York had said that losing the case would cost New York $100 million a year in public education money, a figure that Pete Sherman said he had arrived at by multiplying the number of deaf children of school age by a single interpreter cost of $20,000 annually.

Because media commentary focuses on specific events, there was little to note about *Rowley* in the major media until the Supreme Court announced, on November 2, 1981, that it would accept the case for review. *New York Times* reporter Linda Greenhouse wrote a story in which she stated that the district court originally had found that the Education for All Handicapped Children Act meant that "each handicapped child be given an opportunity to achieve his full potential."*

Ever-vigilant, Michael Chatoff wrote to Greenhouse the next day, objecting. "Judge [Vincent] Broderick did not hold that each handicapped child be given an opportunity to achieve his full potential," Chatoff wrote. "Indeed, he specifically rejected that standard."

Greenhouse responded promptly on *Times* letterhead that she should have added the last eight words of Judge Broderick's decision, immediately following the word "potential"—"commensurate with the opportunity provided to other children." However, she added in her letter to Chatoff, "that would have required further discussion that I did not have space to pursue and that I doubt would have enlightened the readers significantly."

It was not the first time these words had been taken out of context by the press in connection with *Rowley*. Back in February 1981, the *School Lawyer*, had used "full potential" the same way.† But the *Times* reference was the first in so influential and widely read a publication. And this language was picked up on the news wire and ran in a number of newspapers, including the *Albany Times-Union*. The fact that a decision that had stressed equal

* November 3, 1981, p. 13.

† Published by Educational Information Services, Alexandria, Va., February 1981, p. 5.

opportunity for children with disabilities now was being read as giving children with disabilities a unique opportunity to achieve their full potential was not lost on disability advocates. To them, news that the Supreme Court would review *Rowley* was not good. A decided majority of the cases that this Supreme Court was reviewing had resulted in reversals.

The truth was that many advocates for individuals with disabilities were becoming vocal about their dislike of the *Rowley* case at the same time that they set to work on amicus briefs supporting Amy and her family. To lawyers like Norman Rosenburg, of the Mental Health Law Project, it was the wrong case at the wrong time. It was not sufficiently compelling factually or emotionally, he felt. Amy was not a poor kid or one failing sadly in school or one whose needs were woefully ignored—"although you could argue from the other point of view that here was a deaf kid with potential, deaf lawyer defending her, etc." But the timing of the case was particularly upsetting to him and other advocates. Working with their own interpretation of what was meant by an "appropriate" education, the lower courts had generally been looking favorably upon the cause of children with disabilities, particularly in public schools. The last thing that was needed now, advocates like Rosenburg felt, was a case that could result in the gutting of the Education for All Handicapped Children Act.

At least one advocacy agency's attorneys elected to argue along more conservative lines in the hope that they might trace a path this Court could consider following. This brief argued that Congress, in enacting the legislation in question, had found the states seriously deficient in providing satisfactory education for individuals with disabilities and had carefully drafted legislation to correct this problem. The Supreme Court should not now reshape what it took the Congress hundreds of witnesses and years of deliberation to achieve, this brief argued. Jane Yohalem, one of the lawyers who wrote that brief, recalled that, with the equal opportunity issue covered elsewhere, they felt that they had the luxury of trying an approach this Court might be more likely to buy.* Obviously *Rowley* scared the advocacy community out of its collective wits. What might *this* Court do?—that was how they put the question when the case was discussed among them.

By *this* Court, they meant a Supreme Court far removed from the "liberal" Warren Court that had reflected twenty years of Democratic presidency during the Roosevelt era, capstoned by Republican President Dwight

* Brief of the Association of Retarded Citizens of the United States et al. in the case of Hendrick Hudson Central School District v. Amy Rowley by her parents, January 30, 1982.

D. Eisenhower's appointment—one he later publicly regretted—of Chief Justice Earl Warren. When the advocacy attorneys tabulated the possible scorecard on a case like *Rowley* in October 1981, shivers of apprehension ran through the group. The list of dependable conservatives in this Court included Chief Justice Warren E. Burger, Justice Lewis E. Powell, and William H. Rehnquist, all appointed by President Richard Nixon. It might be assumed that the group had been swelled to four by the seating of President Ronald Reagan's first appointee, Justice Sandra Day O'Connor, the Court's first woman justice. All the school people needed, it seemed, was one more vote to have a majority. The only dependable liberals were Justices Thurgood Marshall, a Lyndon Johnson appointee and the Court's first African American; and William J. Brennan, Jr., another "Eisenhower liberal." That left a generally centrist group composed of Justice Byron R. White, a Kennedy appointee; Harry A. Blackmun, another Nixon appointee; and John Paul Stevens, appointed by President Gerald Ford. The advocacy attorneys concluded that they needed all three of these "chancy" votes to win.

In January 1982, as briefs were being sent up to the Supreme Court on both sides of the *Rowley* case, *Harper's* magazine published an article by Roger Starr of the editorial board of the *New York Times*, entitled "Wheels of Misfortune." The article took the position that individuals with disabilities did not have any "rights" as a result of their condition and suggested that they would have to compete for heavy costs of rehabilitation with other social concerns that might be more pressing. Starr concluded, "In establishing federal standards for the treatment of handicapped children, just as in the case of establishing federal standards for transporting handicapped people of all ages, the national government has put its name on an obligation it simply cannot meet."

The article attracted damning letters from a variety of readers, but it got support as well. "Public schools, buildings, and transportation," wrote one reader, "are being held hostage by the handicapped special interest group, which probably is out of touch with the wishes of its members and probably is more in touch with the grantsmanship-funds generation. My local supermarket has six parking spaces reserved for the handicapped and I have never seen a wheelchair in the grocery."

What was happening nationally seemed fine tuned to the timbre of Starr's article. With that issue of *Harper's* still on the newsstands, on January 27, 1982, the Department of Justice circulated unpublished guidelines for Section 504 of the Rehabilitation Act that seemed to members of the disability community to undercut severely the campaign they had fought barely five years before. In addition to requiring a complainant to prove intent to discriminate—often very difficult to establish—it was feared that the changes would call for deletion of the word "appropriate" from the guarantee of free, public education for children with disabilities.

Cheston T. Mottershead, a Vietnam veteran in a wheelchair who ran a model school for children with disabilities in Rocky Mount, North Carolina, thought he saw a way to bring some of these issue into focus and rally the troops. Noting that Starr had already begun making speeches based on his article, Mottershead invited the writer to debate the subject with Frank Bowe, a distinguished author and lecturer who was deaf, as part of the International Year of the Disabled meeting in Greensboro, North Carolina. Because I had been looking at Mottershead's programs as part of my work for *Seven Special Kids*, he suggested that I sit in.

I was interested in hearing both men. I was not aware of the *Rowley* case at this point, but I had read Bowe's *Rehabilitating America* (1980) and was beginning to understand something about the costs of our maintenance system for disability. The hotel where the debate was to be held was jammed with individuals in wheelchairs, deaf people with sign language interpreters, blind men and women, people with cerebral palsy, and others with various disabilities. They were all busy with petitions, phone lists, and banners. Their enthusiasm and the zeal of a sizable coterie of advocates, most of them young people going at top speed, were impressive. Starr elaborated on the position he had taken in his article. "Rights is a tricky word," he told the overflow audience, which had turned silent as he appeared on the podium. "The Constitution says that all moneys spent by the government come as the result of bills originating in the House of Representatives, and you need a popular majority to get this or that piece of money. . . . The right doesn't exist except as a decent society provides it within its economic ability." He concluded by warning advocates not to argue that an effort could pay for itself.

Speaking next in a slightly stiff but otherwise ordinary voice, Bowe, a slender man with dark, piercing eyes, went to the "rights" issue immediately, arguing that legislation and court rulings of recent years had provided evidence of "a decent society proceeding according to priorities which we have decided are rights." On the subject of the cost of helping individuals with disabilities move into the mainstream of society, he challenged his opponent directly and forcefully.

"You ask me how we can justify these things," Bowe said, turning to look at Starr, who was sitting on the platform to his left. "You justify them because it is more economical than not to do it. I am an example. If I had not worked last year, I would have collected $10,000 in federal taxes. I *did* work and I paid instead $10,000 in federal taxes. I am one person. There are millions of people in my situation. . . . To my mind the question is how can we justify spending what we are spending—$50 billion a year on handicapped people, and of that almost $47 billion is on federal assistance cash subsidies (Medicare, ssi, etc.) and only $2.5 billion is going to education for them or jobs for them. That's $25 in handouts for every dollar spent making them productive. The question is not whether we can afford to help the handicapped get jobs but whether we can afford not to. . . . I say we can't."

It was Bowe, naturally enough in the circumstances, who drew the applause at the end of his presentation. I remember being struck with the heated fervor expressed by this group, largely composed of individuals with disabilities. There was an element of vehemence to it, a sharp, angry edge. It was as though what was being expressed was as much aimed, with the force of a collective verbal blow, at Roger Starr as it was applauding the words of Frank Bowe.

Years later, poised in my research at this moment in the past—the days before the Supreme Court's hearing of the oral arguments in *Rowley*—I found myself making connections I couldn't have made then. I had from Barbara Kligerman her recollection of the applause she had received in Judge Broderick's court. I wondered if there was not as much frustration and anger in that outburst as there had been in what I had heard after Frank Bowe finished speaking. What Pete Sherman, the commissioner of education's attorney, had felt in Broderick's courtroom almost as a raised fist at his back suggested to me that this was so. I found myself thinking of Elisabeth Hudson's earlier reference to the Wild Boy of Aveyron and I wondered if a history of deaf education might help me understand better. With this in mind, I began reading Harlan Lane's *When the Mind Hears*, from which I have drawn much of what follows here.* Nothing is known of the

* *When the Mind Hears: A History of the Deaf* (New York: Random House, 1984).

origins of the Wild Boy of Aveyron, but after some years of living in the woods in the French province of Aveyron, he wandered into civilization one morning in the winter of 1800. He became celebrated as someone grown to near-adulthood in isolation from any human contact, who might teach us what we owe of our formation to society and what to biological inheritance. Here was a boy who seemed as much creature as human being, one who neither spoke nor responded to speech, rejected clothing on the coldest of days, and appeared to be utterly without emotional baggage. He was packed off to Paris to be studied and taught.

His teacher was Jean-Marc Itard, an ambitious young doctor. Ignoring the presence of a significant, well-developed signing community in the area, Itard determined to teach Victor, as he called the Wild Boy, through the application of purely oral methods, to understand and speak. When he failed in his initial efforts to get Victor to imitate the sound of words, he set about to teach him the written names of objects. Here he had some success. Victor learned to distinguish among the metal letters Itard had placed before him, and to spell out simple needs. But while this triumph made Itard famous and brought him worldly success, years of work with Victor did not produce much more in the way of communications. Several times Victor tried to escape and return to his former life. Finally discouraged, Itard turned the Wild Boy over to a woman who agreed to board him for a stipend. There, Victor died in his forties, in 1828, still half-wild and unable to speak.

It seemed clear to me why Elisabeth Hudson had thought of Jimmy in connection with Victor. Jimmy had been found living wild under porches in a poor section of Charlotte, uncared for, his teeth yellow and his hair matted. Now, he was struggling in school, mainstreamed more in name than in fact, attending only physical education and homeroom classes with hearing students. He was far behind and showing no signs of catching up. The school thought that he had a learning disability in addition to his deafness. He was put in a class of multihandicapped children and, in the opinion of his adoptive parents, not pushed to learn. Attempts to get him to learn speech through training were not successful. He had begun to exhibit antisocial patterns of behavior at home, raising problems for the Walcotts and their two sons. More than once he had wandered away as though seeking the life he had led before, returning to the Walcotts' house only when he was desperate for food and shelter.

Jimmy was deaf and the Wild Boy of Aveyron was not, but the similarities between them were far more interesting than this difference. Both grew up living wild, on their own. Victor's isolation served to rob him of language, as Jimmy's deafness and lack of training did for him. Both had lost out during the critical, formative years of early childhood when most children process hundreds of new words, impacted with meaning, every day in simple conversation. Both were linguistically and culturally bereft.

For a long time after his work with Victor, Itard managed to compound his errors. As a hearing person, he had labored for years to transform deaf people into hearing ones. He blamed the sign language these deaf students used for what he regarded as their unwillingness to learn speech. If he had isolated them, he believed, as he had isolated Victor, that would have prevented them from signing to each other and forced them to learn speech.

Itard's deliverance from this view of signing came from a deaf pupil brought up in a hearing home without sign language. This bright young man, Eugene Allibert, was the object of five years of intensive training by Itard. Despite Allibert's considerable residual hearing and persistent efforts, which resulted in his hair turning gray at age eighteen, all labors failed. He could be understood only by his relatives and he could not himself understand oral address. But when Itard allowed him to go to school each day for an explanation in sign language of the texts he was studying, his progress was dramatic, and not many years later he became a university professor.

Pupil had turned instructor. Itard was at last convinced and proved grateful. From being a strict oralist, Itard progressed to a view of deaf education based solidly on sign language. Moreover, he observed that the use of sign language was the rock upon which any written language for the deaf rested. Yet despite Itard's discovery of truths ordinarily known among deaf educators, and despite the spread of sign language in this country and abroad in succeeding years, half a century later schools for the deaf using sign language were at the point of extinction. If it could ever be said that one man was responsible for a major turning in the tide of opinion, it might be said of Alexander Graham Bell. The inventor of the telephone was a eugenicist who believed in selective breeding in humans as well as livestock. Having grown up with a hard-of-hearing mother and married a deaf woman who shrank from her disability, Bell also believed in teaching deaf children to forget they are deaf.

He considered deaf people who used sign language failures and urged that sign language itself be abolished. He believed all deaf individuals could be taught intelligible speech. He thought that intermarriage among deaf people posed a threat of creating what he called "a deaf variety of the human race" and set about to find a way to prevent such marriages. He had little success with this goal or in eliminating "socially unfit" classes like the deaf and blind from "the human stock," but succeeded to a considerable degree in his effort to wipe out schools for the deaf that taught sign language. These efforts culminated in the Congress of Milan, in 1880, when proponents of speech communication for the deaf—virtually all hearing people—overwhelmed their opposition with evidence of oral-training success that seemed to some neutral observers to be all too well rehearsed.

When Bell came to this country from Scotland, half the teachers of the deaf were deaf themselves. Twenty years later the proportion had shrunk to one-fourth. It continued to shrink, as pure oralism won the day, to one-fifth by World War I, to a mere one-eighth in the 1960s. And even as this was happening, Bell's ideas fell, one by one, into discredit. Deaf children continued to use sign language, deaf people continued to intermarry, and the great majority of the deaf were born to hearing parents. None of this, however, affected the sweeping growth of pure oral schools for the deaf. More and more, deaf education became the private province of hearing people.

The anger this inspired among the deaf was smothered, self-suppressed, during these years. It was this deeply held, clutched-to-the-chest anger that was breaking out in the fourth quarter of the twentieth century. It was coalescing around the idea that the hearing world had stolen their language and was holding them prisoners in schools where that language was being prohibited with an eye toward its eradication. As in most revolutions, the full potency of that suppressed anger was emerging just as those in power were being forced to offer concessions that seemed clearly, to those they were intended to pacify, to be far too little and much too late.

It was Helen and Charlie Brooks' first visit to the Supreme Court, and they were, in their separate ways, very much in awe. To Charlie, a senior in high school, the building at No. 1, First Street, Northeast, seemed sprung to life from an educational television show. His mother Helen was impressed with her first look at the sixteen columns of white Vermont marble supporting the Corinthian portico and the architrave above bearing the legend: "Equal Justice Under Law." But she was impressed, too, with the fact that, at least technically, it was as a member of the press that she was about to attend her first Supreme Court oral hearing.

The *Croton-Cortlandt News,* unable to send a correspondent, wanted someone who planned to be there to take notes for a story. So, unpaid but credentialed, Helen planned to file some kind of report later in the day. To her surprise, as she parted with her son to find her way through the crowd to the press box, she was given a place of honor as a member of the "local" press. On this morning of March 22, 1982, the press box was jammed, its red-cushioned, red-backed, wooden frame seats filled with reporters anxious to share history being made. Out in the corridor was a computer, and in the courtroom a terminal sat on the desk of the Rowleys' attorney, Michael Chatoff; it would flash before the deaf man's eyes the words being spoken by members of the Court and opposing counsel. Nothing remotely like it had happened before—it was the first time a deaf lawyer would plead in the Supreme Court and the first use of recording equipment permitted on these premises. Helen Brooks was particularly pleased that her son had wanted to come with her to the hearing. Charlie was bright but he also had a learning disability and had suffered through difficult times at school in the Hendrick Hudson School District. Helen and her husband, Charles, a railroad executive in New York City, had spent many hours trying to get better services for Charlie, and this made them sympathetic to the Rowleys, with whom they had become friends. Inspired by Charlie's interest, Helen had assembled briefs for the case and articles about Chatoff, all of which her son had dutifully read.

Both mother and son were optimistic about Amy's chances of winning her case. As a handicapped child, she was a member of a minority and she was also an unusual child who was extremely well motivated. Brooks thought that Amy might eventually take law training herself. She chuckled to herself as she thought of Amy's response to a newspaper interviewer who had asked her what she wanted to be when she grew up. "I did want to be a lawyer," this ten-year-old had said, "but I think right now I'd like to be a judge."

Michael Chatoff was less optimistic than the Brookses. He and his lawyer friends had also done the arithmetic on the probable votes of the justices. But while his mind was focused sharply on what he had to say in the courtroom on this day, he could not help but worry about communications. In that sense, it was a moment he had been dreading even as he welcomed it. In an ordinary court setting, with someone at his side taking notes, he could at least function. But in the Supreme Court, where any one of nine justices could ask a question without notice, reliance on such tactics would be folly. Chatoff had called his friend Robert Davila at Gallaudet University about the state of the art of what was being called "real time translation." The call led to a series of contacts with systems and program people who decided that, with the help of Gallaudet, they could equip Chatoff for the Court contest.

While not really ground-breaking, what was proposed amounted to a neat trick. Whatever was spoken in the courtroom the stenotypist would enter in the stenographic code, which permits of speeds not possible in English. Normally that coded product would await translation by the stenotypist into English and the resultant typing out into the verbatim record. But in this system, the code would go instantaneously from the machine into the computer stationed in the corridor outside the courtroom. Using a sophisticated program, the computer would immediately convert the code into its English equivalent and transmit it to the display terminal on Chatoff's desk, where it would appear on the screen as printed English. This whole process would take only a few seconds. Then, alerted by Harvey Barrison, who this time would sit beside him, Chatoff could read what had been said and respond to it.

A neat trick, but would it work in actuality as it had in a rehearsal? And would Chatoff's voice—that ventriloquist's projection the operations had left him—be understood? Moreover, Chatoff was unused to courtroom appearances, having argued only one other case in his life, albeit successfully. He was not surprised that his knees were shaky as he walked out to where Clifford and Nancy Rowley sat to shake hands. They felt his nervousness but they also noted that he radiated a kind of internal concentration that boded well for his presentation.

To Chatoff's left at the respondents' (the Rowleys') table was Elliott Schulder, a young lawyer representing the United States Department of Justice, who himself had reason to be nervous. He had entered the case late as a substitute for the attorney who had prepared the brief for the Solicitor-General's Office. He had plunged into the case vigorously and had satisfied himself that a fair reading of the legislative history indicated that Congress had intended the Education for All Handicapped Children Act to provide equal opportunity for children with disabilities. He planned to stress that point. But it was not as though it had been his case from the beginning. He did not own every detail of background as part of his memory reaction bank. He had not lived with his argument that long.

With the Reagan winds blowing harshly over the cause of individuals with disabilities, many people wondered that the Justice Department, in March 1982, was siding with the Rowleys at all. The answer lies in its immediate past history. The Justice Department had been involved in the cases of individuals with disabilities for some time and had built up a supportive record. A key figure in this phase was a dark-haired, solidly built, plain-spoken young lawyer named Peter Buscemi. While he did not consider himself a "liberal," he was someone the office often turned to when civil rights cases arose.

Buscemi observed that these cases were essentially different from the ones that had involved African Americans. In his view, the prejudice against African Americans had expressed itself in rejection plain and simple: we will not hire them, educate them, or let them live here. And the courts had eventually responded in corresponding spirit: yes, you will. In cases of individuals with disabilities, Buscemi observed, there was a generally professed willingness to provide services and employment. But to do so, special accommodation usually was necessary—changes in procedures and modifications often with costs—and the resistance, at least for the record, focused on unwillingness to make those changes. Buscemi termed this point of view as one in which everything is given except the one thing of value asked for.

His position on this point was sharpened by a case involving deafness already considered by the Supreme Court. Walter Camenisch had been appointed acting dean of students at the Texas School for the Deaf in 1977. To obtain a permanent appointment, he needed a master's degree. He enrolled successfully in graduate school at the University of Texas, asking the university to provide a sign language interpreter for his classes. He pointed out that the university accepted more than $31 million in federal aid annually and, as a condition, had agreed to comply with Section 504 of the Rehabilitation Act, which forbade recipients to discriminate on the basis of disability. Still, the university refused to pay for the interpreter.

In the brief on Camenisch's behalf, written by Buscemi and filed by the Solicitor-General's Office, the government argued, as it had before, that Section 504 required affirmative action. Only a niggardly reading of Section 504 could conclude that it was intended to get an individual with a disability into an educational institution and then leave the student without a means of education, ran this line of argument. But because Camenisch had finished his program before the case reached the high court—incidentally paying much of his interpreter costs himself—the Supreme Court disposed of the case as moot.

While *Camenisch* focused on Section 504 of the Rehabilitation Act, the Supreme Court in the spring of 1981 had two cases it could choose between for its first review under the Education for All Handicapped Children Act. One of these was *Rowley*. The other was a case involving severely mentally handicapped children in Pennsylvania whose parents had argued that they needed more than the state could provide in its 180-day schedule of annual public school instruction. The lower courts had ruled for the parents, but the district court's logic was not upheld in the appellate court. The Supreme Court declined review in this case, *Scanlon v. Battle*.

This left *Rowley* and, despite the timing of the Supreme Court's decision to hear the case, there were reasons the Justice Department would continue to argue for a school client who had a disability. The election of Ronald Reagan had signaled not just a new administration, but a new party in power, always a major sea change in Washington. Such a political transformation leaves a degree of chaos in its wake. Appointments take first priority, and other agendas may lag behind. During the many months of settling in, what to do about *Rowley* was a source of considerable debate between the Department of Health, Education and Welfare and the Department of Justice. In the end, the Solicitor-General's Office did what many governmental agencies do in a period of turmoil: it kept on keeping on, in this instance, electing to look to the laws passed by Congress as containing considerable protection for individual citizens. Buscemi, once again, became involved, this time reworking a draft brief of the department's position written by another Justice Department lawyer.

He had no problem with the assignment and expected to continue to be involved with *Rowley*, but events conspired to remove him from the case. He got a job offer that he couldn't refuse. He had put in his time at Justice and had been looking for a position with a prominent private firm. He turned the case over to Elliott Schulder with his blessings.

Nobody had to sign to the deaf students, grouped in the first two rows on the left in the audience section, to tell them to stand up when the marshal rose to intone, "Oyez, oyez, oyez. God save this honorable court." Jackie Epstein had trained her seventh-, eighth-, and ninth-grade students painstakingly on Court protocol. They were watching the marshal and rose as he rose. Epstein had taught them the federal court system, the history of *Rowley,* and the peculiarities of life for a spectator in the Supreme Court. "You must not touch *anything.* Keep your hands in your laps at all times." She had even reviewed the *Camenisch* case with these deaf students, mainstreamed in the schools of Montgomery County, Virginia. There, all of them had sign language interpreters and they assumed Amy would keep hers. How would they have done without a sign language interpreter, Epstein had asked these thirteen- to fifteen-year-old students in class one day. They had set to writing: "lots of frustration." "can't understand," "can't lip-read all day, too tiring," "can't see when teachers turn away their heads," "teachers talk while we write notes," "miss a lot of what hearing kids get," "miss all of the announcements." "miss fire drills," "have a lot of problems catching up with hearing kids." Jackie Epstein was shocked to learn from her husband Aaron, a Supreme Court reporter for United Press International who was also present in court that day, that no sign language interpreter would be furnished her children by the Court. She brought her own and saw that Gallaudet University had done the same. It bothered her that, if Amy lost her case, she would have to find a way to explain it to the children.

The school district's attorney, Raymond Kuntz, began oral argument by characterizing the dispute before the court as a not-unusual disagreement between parents and a school board. Sitting at the petitioner's table, Gwenn Gregory, assistant general counsel for the National School Board Association, was pleased with this beginning, which she had favored. She thought the Court would understand that sometimes parents were unreasonable in such matters. At least this notion would be easily grasped by Justice Powell, a former school board member and former president of the Virginia State Board of Education.

Kuntz then began to recite the school district's position in the case in detail. He emphasized the services supplied to Amy—the sign language course taken by school personnel, the TTY installed in Principal Joseph Zavarella's office, the choice of a first-rate kindergarten teacher, and positioning Amy where she could see what was going on. He continued by describing visits by the District Committee on the Handicapped to other settings for teaching deaf children and its decision to provide Amy with an FM wireless, the services of a teacher of the deaf an hour a day, and of a speech therapist three times a week. The result, he told the court, was "outstanding academic and social success for Amy . . . she had equivalent class rank. In other words, Amy placed in her class exactly as you would expect her to place, given her I.Q. . . . The school district built bridges of meaning to Amy and the court dismantled those bridges and substituted a different program based on what we contend is an inaccurate view of the Act and its requirements."

As Kuntz continued with virtually no interruption from the justices, entirely different reactions were being experienced by the attorneys committed to opposing sides in the case. Norman Gross, one of the attorneys for the State School Board Association, remembered the "bridges of meaning" phrase years later, still impressed with it. He felt that Kuntz had struck just the right note, setting the Hendrick Hudson School District aside from those school districts that did not even provide basic services to handicapped children.

Not far from where Gross was sitting was Marc Charmatz, a tough-minded young lawyer for the National Association of the Deaf Legal Defense Fund, one who asserts that advocates ought to lose a case if they cannot prove that the child would benefit from services sought. He felt Kuntz's presentation was crucial, too, but reacted very differently. He could not believe that the justices would take seriously a recitation of facts that had been insufficient to carry the day in the trial court. "I was sitting there thinking . . . they are saying it's not so bad, not so bad. And I knew the facts, brought out in court, that Amy could understand only half of the material lipreading and that with other communication she could understand 100 percent. They portrayed a school district doing a lot. And they got away with it because if you didn't know all that and were listening to it for the first time, it sounded good and there were no questions asked."

But Kuntz knew there were questions out there, waiting to be asked. He was particularly concerned about one question he thought Justice Stevens might ask, and after some preliminary questioning, the diminutive Stevens shifted slightly in his chair and squared his shoulders preparatory to speaking.

"Mr. Kuntz, may I ask, is it your view that a federal judge may merely require compliance with the *procedures* specified in the Act and that there is no *substantive* standard that the federal judge may apply to define what is a free, appropriate education? . . . Supposing you had in this case a teacher with a loud voice and nothing more, or something like that, that most people would clearly say was not sufficient. Could the federal judge correct anything at all substantively?"

The question struck at the heart of the argument Kuntz had proposed to make to the court as late as the day before. He had proposed to say, in effect: The State of New York had submitted a compliance plan to the United States Department of Education that did not specifically provide for sign language interpretation. The secretary had approved that plan. The federal district court and the appellate court—by approving a sign language interpreter—had effectively amended this plan, thereby interposing the judiciary into matters legislative and executive.

It was a clean argument and one Kuntz thought had appeal. But it had a weakness that had grown in his mind. What if a justice—and Stevens came to mind—asked what role the courts might have if a school district clearly was not meeting the needs of a handicapped child? Could he, Kuntz, tell the Supreme Court that because the New York State plan did not specifically provide for an interpreter, a court could not intervene on behalf of a child in a situation where one was needed? He had sat up past midnight the night before wrestling with that question and had re-configured his argument.

"I would think," he responded, "that in that particular situation that the first thing that would occur is a finding that the procedure had not been followed . . . the Act requires that the local school districts plan for the unique needs of that child. I think that's a procedural requirement. . . . I tend to think that in your situation, your example, that you would find so many procedural errors in arriving at that determination that there would be no need to get into a substantive determination."

Kuntz did not expect that would be enough for the bulldoggish Stevens and it was not. "Well," Stevens continued, "supposing the board had a meeting and said, we really can't afford to buy the FM wireless and we can't afford to have our teachers take the time off to take sign language training, as you did. . . . We're just going to do the best we can . . . for reasons that very well might make good sense for a board that has a tight budget?"

The school board attorney had decided beforehand that this bullet had to be bitten. "I would hate to think that there would be no situation where the courts couldn't step in and cure a totally arbitrary and capricious act."

Justice Stevens nodded. "The problem I have with the case is as soon as you acknowledge that there's some substantive review, then what's the stopping point?"

In deep water, Kuntz had decided to take the "imperfect world" approach. "I totally agree with you . . . but I truly believe that Congress did not in this particular statute move in and determine for each local school district that ultimately what is to be the governing philosophy is what a court, federal or state, tells the agency. And I'm afraid that is what happens when you carry the logic to the extreme on the other side."

At this juncture, Kuntz got a soft, medium-speed pitch right over the center of the plate. Chief Justice Burger interrupted, "Is it your view that this school has done more than they were required to do?"

Kuntz went after the justice's pitch. "Yes they did. They not only complied with the state plan as it specifies services for deaf children whose audiological loss is within the range that Amy's is, but they provided extra services far over and beyond what they were required to do. I think . . . that the program they [the school district] developed worked and that the program the court substituted does not particularly appear to the school district to be much better. As a matter of fact, the school district believes that ultimately, in the long run, it does Amy a disservice because it does not take advantage . . . and promote use of her residual hearing, of her excellent ability to lip-read. And these skills will atrophy."

Nancy Rowley was not sure she fully grasped the argument over the procedural and substantive aspects of the act but she felt deep in her bones anger welling up at this hearing person who she believed had demonstrated that he knew nothing of deafness preaching to the court what was to her a long-since discredited sermon. It was amply apparent to Nancy that Amy had done significantly better since she got her interpreter. The idea that Amy's lipreading skills would atrophy as a result was a hurtful as it was, in her mind, absurd.

In his years on the Supreme Court, Justice Marshall had affected a sleepy look on the bench, never more so than when he was about to ask a question. His lidded eyes widened as he put his hands down on the bench and addressed Kuntz, "But this Court of Appeals limited its decision to the facts in this case."

Kuntz took it as a question and attempted to answer, . . . "Yes, I think because they . . . "

But Justice Marshall was not finished. "So it wasn't any broad, general sweep like you're talking about, was it? It said that you were *wrong*"—the justice leaned hard on this word—"in this case for the facts that were before it at that time. What's wrong with that? Isn't that the normal way to decide a case?"

For the first time, Kuntz hesitated slightly. "Then it becomes a case about Amy, as the court said in its opening sentence: 'This is a case about

Amy.' It's also a case about the law, and every case that's decided by the Court of Appeals is precedent. I simply don't know how any court is going to distinguish Amy's case from the case of any other deaf child. Amy's situation is not an unusual situation."

Marshall continued: "Well, aren't all constitutional rights individual?"

"Yes, I believe that they have to adhere in the individual in order to be effective. But I also would say that all decisions of the Court of Appeals become precedent for all other factual situations which are similar in content and nature to the one addressed by the court."

Again, Chief Justice Burger leapt in with a helpful question. "Do you think they were afraid of it as precedent?"

"I think . . . they were somewhat leery of the precedent that they were creating and were attempting to limit it. I don't think they were deciding on the law. I think they were deciding on the facts of this particular case and out of sympathy for Amy."

What followed after this exchange was a series of questions put to Kuntz by the justices dealing with—as Justices White and Stevens phrased it —"the full potential standard." Both justices used these exact words several times. Justice Stevens concluded the exchange with another question for Kuntz, "Don't you necessarily have to attack the standard because you do have the district court and the court of appeals both agreeing that the sign language interpreter was required to satisfy the full potential standard?"

"The full potential standard is an impossible standard," Kuntz responded. "The tests devised by Judge Broderick to determine whether the full potential had been met are simply unworkable tests."

Reading his monitor intently as this was going on, Chatoff realized that he would have to work hard to overcome the impression that this case was somehow about a "full potential standard." This was the same misleading linguistic shortcut the press had taken up, now coming off the lips of justices who of course knew better. He had never argued that the school was responsible for Amy's realizing her "full potential." Judge Broderick had specifically rejected that, or the attainment of any specific educational level, as a responsibility of the school. Chatoff felt that the record would survive these various misstatements, but he knew he had to drive home the important two words that both the district and appellate courts had based their decision on, and which had not yet been uttered in this courtroom: *equal opportunity.*

On his feet, Chatoff felt less nervous. He was particularly conscious, however, of having to split his half-hour allotment with the Justice Department. It meant that he had to make every word count. He began with a recitation of Amy's and her parents' deafness, with Amy's early training in total communication, and with the finding by the lower court that Amy could understand less than two-thirds of what was spoken in class without an interpreter, and 100 percent with one. He then turned to the responsibilities of the school.

"Recipients of funds under the Education for All Handicapped Children Act commit themselves to provide each handicapped child within its borders with a free, appropriate education. A free, appropriate public education is specially designed instruction to meet the handicapped child's unique needs in order to provide that child with an *equal educational opportunity.*"

Others had leaned on words for emphasis and Chatoff took this opportunity to do so himself. Helen Brooks, sitting in the press section, thought that by this time the attorney had everyone in the courtroom riveted to the sound of his voice, which seemed to her to be clear enough for good understanding.

The other word Chatoff particularly wanted to stress was "unique," as in a child's "unique" needs, from the definition of special education in the act. "Amy's unique needs are obvious," he said. "The shortfall in her comprehension is precisely the deficiency Congress had in mind when it directed recipients to provide for the unique needs of each handicapped child. Amy needs a visual depiction of oral communication. She can't learn if she can't understand, and she can't understand if material is presented to her in a way that is closed to her. An interpreter merely provides Amy with access to the same education as available to every other student, no more and no less."

"Mr. Chatoff," Justice O'Connor sat erect, leaning forward only slightly, as Harvey Barrison tugged Chatoff's coat and pointed in her direction. "Did the evidence show at the trial court level that the school district had found that having an interpreter present was a distraction to the child, and that she did not need it?"

Sarah Geer, a young attorney for the Center for Law and the Deaf at Gallaudet, had the sensation that the whole courtroom was holding its breath at this first real test of the electronic equipment in the court. Dr. Roz Rosen, herself deaf and coordinator of the Education for All Handicapped Children Act at Gallaudet, was aware that Chatoff had been asked a question and was looking anxiously at the Gallaudet interpreter, hoping to see his answer signed for the deaf spectators. Four seconds, no more, elapsed, according to Sarah Geer's count, but she "felt" the pause as a kind of jolt to her central nervous system. Then Chatoff looked up and faced Justice O'Connor.

"The trial court found that the school district said that providing an interpreter would be a distraction to Amy. However, relying on expert testimony and written statements in the record, the trial court determined that an interpreter would not be a distraction for Amy," he said.

Geer thought the answer was a particularly good one. Not only had Chatoff said that an interpreter would not be a distraction, but that the district court had found that to be the case. After all, the Supreme Court had to defer to findings of fact of the lower court unless clearly erroneous. Chatoff went on:

"Amy is not special because she is deaf. Amy has special needs resulting from her deafness. It is those special needs Congress directed recipients to accommodate in order to fulfill obligations under the Act. If Amy is special—and even the witnesses for the petitioners concede that she is—she is special because of her creativity and her enthusiasm and her rapport with others.

"I don't believe anyone would question the fact that there have been past deficiencies in the education of deaf children. But that's all water under the bridge. We can't correct past deficiencies by providing Amy with anything on a silver platter. This is a tough world. It's going to be as tough for Amy as it will be for every other child. She'll have no preparation for that world if things are handed to her on a silver lining [*sic*]." The reporters in the press section were scribbling furiously, for this was good, quotable stuff. When Chatoff said the world was tough, he spoke from knowledge, not just of Amy's case, but of his own profoundly difficult experience and that of millions of individuals with disabilities in the country.

"But if she is going to compete in the world, she must receive an education equivalent to that of other children. This Court said that education is the principal instrument for preparing the child for later professional training and helping that child to adjust normally to its environment. Once Amy gets an education, an equivalent education, what she does with that education is up to her. The school district has no obligation to guarantee her any particular level of achievement, only the same opportunity to achieve as everyone else."

Barrison was tugging at Chatoff's sleeve again, but the Rowleys' attorney could see Justice Stevens wriggling in his chair, preparing to speak. "May I interrupt, Mr. Chatoff, will your interpretation of the statute require every school board to provide a sign language interpreter for every deaf child in the country?"

Here was the question Chatoff had expected, and from Justice Stevens at that.

"Definitely not. The statute requires an individual determination of the needs of each handicapped child. The deaf community is not a monolithic entity. Although deaf children have in common their hearing loss, their other characteristics are all different. Every child is different. Every child is brought up differently. Some use strictly oral methods of communication. Some use speech . . . some use what is called American Sign Language."

Chatoff saw his opportunity to dispose of the idea, fostered by the school district and just repeated in the courtroom by Kuntz, that Amy was a "typical" deaf child. He believed this was said, in part, to support the school's position that she did as well as could be expected in her studies without an interpreter and, in part, to seed the fear that anything gained in her case would be demanded for all deaf children. "Not every deaf child can be educated in the public schools," he said. "In fact, very few can. Amy happens to be one of those very few. Children who are educated in special schools or resource rooms have no need for interpreters. Children raised using the oral method have no need for interpreters. It will be only very specific instances. This case does *not* establish that any or every other deaf child is entitled to an interpreter. . . . This case involves Amy and only Amy and does not go beyond Amy's particular and individual needs."

Helen Brooks had pointed out the Rowleys to members of the press corps, and now a number of them were looking over in the direction of the family, trying to spot Amy. Helen was certainly not going to break the court's rigid protocol with a stage whisper, and the reporters' attention turned back immediately to the bar, where Chief Justice Burger was recognizing Elliott Schulder on behalf of the United States Department of Justice. A tall, slim, dark-haired man with a mustache, Schulder was dressed in the formal garb that the solicitor's office had affected immemorially in addressing the Court: cutaway, striped pants, winged collar. Schulder's preparation had centered his argument on congressional intent in writing the act, which the attorney felt was the centerpiece and main strength of the Rowleys' case. Unfortunately for him, he was not allowed to develop his argument as Chatoff and Kuntz, to a lesser degree, had been. Questions flew swiftly at him from the bench, beginning with one from Justice Rehnquist.

"How does one get . . . to the standard that apparently the district court used and that the court of appeals was willing to see used in this case, that each handicapped child be given an opportunity to achieve his full potential commensurate with the opportunity provided to other children?"

At least Rehnquist had not used the "full potential" shorthand, Schulder thought, and had instead placed the words in the context of equal opportunity that Judge Broderick had established. But Schulder's instincts were that Rehnquist was really only hearing "full potential" and that these two words seemed to stand implacably in the way of an understanding of the Rowleys' and the government's position. He had decided, on this account, to skirt the "full potential" barricades and concentrate on "equal opportunity." Accordingly, he responded: "Your honor, we do not agree with that particular part of the district court's opinion."

"It came out of a law review article, didn't it?" Rehnquist asked.

"I believe it did," Schulder responded. "The court of appeals, however, did not rely on that part of the district court's opinion. On page 6-A of the appendix to the petition, the court of appeals quoted that part of the district court's opinion that stated that under the Act, the educational authorities are required to bring Amy's educational *opportunity* up to a level of educational *opportunity* being offered to her non-handicapped peers. In other words, the emphasis is not on potential or shortfall from potential, but on making available to handicapped children the same opportunities that are available to non-handicapped children to benefit from the regular educational program that the state or local authorities provide." Later on, in answer to another question, he added "and the legislative history of the Act clearly supports this reading of the statute."

Justice Powell, a slim, neat man who held himself militarily erect on the bench and often used a pencil on the bench in front or in the air to emphasize his points, spoke with a soft, Virginia accent. Near the end of Schulder's time, he asked a question, "Is there any recognition in your submission that the degree of disability varies widely? Sadly, there are some children with I.Q.s of 40, deaf and dumb. What is a state required to do with respect to such a child?"

UPI reporter Aaron Epstein had chosen his seat in the press box to be as close as he could to his wife's class of deaf children. Hence he could actually feel the shock that Justice's Powell's words, "deaf and dumb," had sent through this group and the larger Gallaudet contingent behind them. There was that old bugaboo word "dumb," with its archaic connotations, here on the lips of someone as eminent as a justice of the Supreme Court. The justice not only appeared insensitive as to what those words might mean to a group of deaf people, but actually seemed to be using "dumb" to mean lack of intelligence rather than muteness. Helen Brooks could not believe that any educated person could use such a term. Nancy Rowley, reflecting the heavier disapproval of the term held by deaf people, concluded that it showed that Justice Powell "had not done his homework" and probably should not have been sitting on the case. One veteran Court observer was saddened, reflecting that Justice Powell was one of the nicest men on the Court.

———

In the course of interviewing numerous persons who were present during the Supreme Court hearing, I got various descriptions of Amy Rowley's appearance in court. She was dressed in blue with a white ribbon in her hair. She was her usual bright, alert self, eyes flickering here and there, taking in the scene. She was quiet, almost solemn. She was an appealing figure, sitting between her mother and her father.

The truth was that Amy was not there. The decision about Amy and John—typically, Nancy and Clifford made the same decision about them both—was relatively easy. The crush of the press was something the Rowleys wanted to spare both their children. Amy, at ten, would have been the center of a glare of attention from television cameras. The Rowleys had left Amy and John with friends at Gallaudet.

The notion that Amy was at the hearing probably was given currency by photographs of her in the *New York Times* prior to and just after the hearing, including one over the headline of the next day's front-page story; and possibly it was furthered inadvertently by an interview conducted by National Public Radio Supreme Court reporter Nina Totenburg, who came upon Jackie Epstein and her deaf students outside the Supreme Court. The students were in some distress. For the first time they were asking Epstein seriously: Could they lose their interpreters? Epstein was reassuring them when Totenburg came on the scene, looking for someone to interview. Epstein had thought this might happen and had already settled on fifteen-year-old Roxanne Diamandis, who spoke well. The students surrounded Totenburg and Diamandis, and the interview began. Totenburg took note of the fact that while she was speaking slowly and carefully to Roxanne, the child still looked to her interpreter to get the question in sign language.

How important was a classroom interpreter to Roxanne?

"I must have an interpreter in my class because if I don't have an interpreter, I can't get the complete sense of what you're saying, only about half."

How did Roxanne think Michael Chatoff had done in court?

"I think he did a great job," Roxanne answered. "I am really proud of him."

Totenburg interviewed Chatoff and Kuntz and used clips of each of them in a story about Amy—Kuntz repeated his contention that Amy's communication skills would atrophy with the use of a sign language interpreter, a service he likened to use of a "crutch." Later Totenburg received numerous calls of congratulations from public radio stations around the country for the interview with Roxanne Diamandis.

Probably some spectators leaving the hearing were misled into thinking that the child being interviewed in the circle of deaf children was Amy Rowley. That was the case with Gwenn Gregory, the attorney for the National School Boards Association. She passed the group on the way out and felt a pang of guilt as she looked at Roxanne, thinking she was Amy. Gregory had worked at the Department of Health, Education and Welfare in the past, and while she felt that the school district's position was correct, she never wanted to be a judge in a case where the child with the disability was in front of her.

At L'Enfant Plaza, a celebration was going on. Kuntz had been interviewed and photographed, once with his father standing behind him to memorialize the first time he had heard his son argue a case. Now the attorney and his group of board members, office staff, and other interested parties were gathered for a luncheon. Kuntz was expansive. It was a moment to be remembered, he told the gathering, whatever the final decision of the Court would be. The case could have an enormous impact on the future of litigation involving schools and handicapped children. He thanked those present for their contributions. In an upbeat mood, school board member Eileen Curinga felt confident that the district's position would be upheld. So did Daniel Horan, chairman of the board of education.

Afterward, Horan wrote out a statement recounting the experiences of the day, the awe inspired by the courtroom and the justices, and the work Kuntz and his wife Theresa, who had assisted him and sat beside him in the courtroom, had done. At the end of the statement, Horan wrote: "In arriving at Amy's program, the district experimented with many options, including sign language interpretation, before determining her appropriate placement. Mr. Chatoff's argument for the Rowleys was based on the premise that the program must be designed to meet each handicapped child's unique needs so as to completely overcome all deficits caused by her handicap. He indicated parents, court should be arbiters of what constitutes a free, appropriate education for each child."

Meanwhile, Michael Chatoff was basking in unaccustomed publicity. He was interviewed outside the Supreme Court Building. Later, in a press conference at the Hyatt Regency Hotel, he was besieged by television and news reporters. With the issues surrounding the case of Amy Rowley suspended for future settlement, the press had as its main fare a commanding story about a deaf adult who had the courage of his personal convictions. A secondary angle was how a piece of the communications future had come to the staid Supreme Court. The press conference had been set up by Translation Systems, Inc., the Rockville, Maryland, company that had put together the computer system Chatoff had used. But Chatoff, not the bulky machinery that symbolized the effort to provide "real time translation" for the deaf, was the center of attention. As his parents stood quietly proud in the background, Chatoff attempted to use the events of the day to further the cause of the deaf and of individuals with disabilities in general.

"Handicapped people can do what other people can do," he told one of the television people. "Some will do it well and some will not." Fred Thomas, of Newscenter 4 TV in Washington, began his coverage of the day's events: "Rights of the handicapped child were almost overshadowed by the manner in which the argument was presented," he said. Asked how he felt when he learned that he would be deaf, Chatoff responded. "That my career would be limited by the fact that I was deaf. . . . I proved to myself today that I was a good lawyer, that I can do what any other lawyer can do. . . . I feel good because I've proved that I'm capable. That's really what life is all about." Thomas wrapped up the interview: "Whether or not Amy Rowley wins her case, Chatoff already has won a great victory not just for himself but for many handicapped people in this country."

Television coverage was not uniformly sensible to the position the Rowleys had taken in the case, however. Several nationally viewed news programs contained questionable versions of what Chatoff had argued. One of the more arresting of these came from CBS's Fred Graham, one of the most respected media commentators on legal matters. Graham had Chatoff arguing that "school systems should be required to provide whatever was necessary to put handicapped children on the same level as normal children." Chatoff fretted over what he saw as further evidence that the press simply did not understand what this case was all about.

The theme of Chatoff's triumph in court, however, was reinforced the next day when the *New York Times'* front-page story featured a picture of him and employed as a lead the dramatic presentation made by the first deaf lawyer ever to argue before the Supreme Court. Chatoff was pleased with this, as were the Rowleys. Efforts had been made to discourage Chatoff from making the argument on behalf of his clients, and behind these efforts lay, all three were convinced, the suspicion that the lawyer's deafness would prevent him from doing the job well. Now everyone could see numerous abilities where before they had seen only one disability. "I'm not a 'deaf attorney,'" Chatoff was quoted more than once as saying, "only an attorney who happens to be deaf."

But he was not optimistic about how the Court would rule. The press continued to present the case in terms unfavorable to the Rowley cause. On April 3, the *Times* wondered rhetorically on the editorial page: "Should an appropriate education merely attempt to impart skills? Or must it enable a child to attain his or her fullest potential—as argued recently in the Supreme Court by a deaf Westchester County girl who seeks a sign-language interpreter? Would that not entitle every learning disabled youngster to an individual tutor? 'Normal' children who underachieve enjoy no comparable right."

The *Times* with this editorial had arrived at referring to the issue in terms of "fullest potential," language never used in any context in the courts dealing with *Rowley*. And here the specific message was that the lower courts were requiring schools to attain this goal only for children with disabilities. Add to this the strong, underlying implication of staggering costs involved—"every learning disabled youngster . . . an individual tutor"—and the *Times*, with three questions and one declarative sentence, had created out of Amy's case a nightmarish thicket of danger that must have been compelling to any reader unaware of the facts of the case.

Chatoff responded to this editorial April 5 with his most blistering letter, reciting once again the fact that Broderick had specifically rejected "achievement" of any sort—much less achievement of "fullest" potential—in favor of "opportunity." In a second paragraph, he wrote: "If you knew your editorial was inaccurate before you went to press, then you performed a distinct disservice for your readers. Certainly, your actions reflect poorly on the newspaper industry as a whole and in particular on the *New York*

Times, which used to, and in theory at least still does, take pride in its accuracy and objectivity."

This letter didn't make the *Times'* letters to the editor column, but a letter by James C. Francis IV appeared on April 20. Francis chided the newspaper for "erroneously assuming that a single policy could adequately serve all handicapped children" and went on to note that in the *Rowley* case, "her lawyer did not argue that she was entitled by law to attain her maximum potential. Rather, he contended that she should be permitted to have the same *opportunity* [his emphasis] to achieve as her peers who are not deaf. . . . Under the law, the [school] district cannot ask her to start the race 40 yards behind her classmates."

Chatoff knew what the potential readership of the letters column was compared to that of the editorial columns and he had a good idea which would have more credence. He thought the wisest policy was to hope for the best and prepare for the worst.

When the Court's decision was announced on June 29, 1982, Raymond Kuntz was among the first to hear the good news. His friend, Gwenn Gregory from the National School Board Association, had a law clerk who had been calling the Supreme Court every day. When she got the news that morning, she called Gregory, who called Kuntz. Gregory said just one word over the phone: "Congratulations." Then Ray Kuntz was screaming over the phone and swearing he was getting on a plane right away for Washington. She offered to express him the opinion, but he said, no, he'd come and get it himself. That's the way lawyers behave when they win one in the Supreme Court, Gregory told herself.

Nancy Rowley heard the bad news a good bit later. Two calls did come to her home that morning but they were voice calls and John was away at camp. She could only speak into the soundless (for her) phone and ask the caller to go to the TTY, knowing that person probably would have no idea what she meant. As usual, she fretted over who might have been calling, how she or Clifford could find out with John away, and whether the calls might be important enough to require immediate response. She finally heard the news from Clifford, who got it from an enterprising reporter who called him at his office. Nancy was bitter and upset. "I can't believe it," she told a *New York Times* reporter who had made her way to the Rowley house. "This is a setback—way back—for deaf people and perhaps all the handicapped. Are they going to take away the Braille books for the blind and the ramps for people in wheelchairs?"* Nancy showed this reporter Amy's report card for the fourth grade, the second year in which Amy had an interpreter (Fran Miller had been replaced by a capable interpreter named Beth Freed). It showed that Amy had worked at fifth-grade level in vocabulary and science, at sixth-grade level in reading comprehension and language, and at eighth-grade level in spelling and mathematical concepts. "As long as she had the interpreter, she did fantastically," Nancy told this reporter. "Without it, everything is hard. She will get only half as much from her classes and it will get harder as time goes on."

Amy absorbed the news increment by increment, trying to understand what it meant for her. It was only as she stood with her mother as she talked with the *Times* reporter that Amy got it all clearly. She would no longer have a sign language interpreter. Never. No more. She felt a cold knot at her stomach and began the process of mental detachment, similar to the backward steps a child takes from a frightening situation, trying somehow to reverse time, before turning to run in panic. She found herself staring at the reporter, an ordinary-looking woman whose full energies were concentrated on comprehending Nancy. Who was this person? Amy asked herself. By what right is she here—this stranger—explaining to my mother what will happen to me? The reporter took on the persona of a distant, dark stranger, an unknown who had imposed this defeat on her family. Amy could feel the vibrations of her mother's unhappiness. It had all been for nothing. She knew that there would be sad talk between her mother and father that night and that John would go to his room to get away from it all. Staring hostilely at the reporter, it seemed to Amy that people like this had stolen her childhood.

Michael Chatoff's parents heard about it when most other interested people did. They picked it up over a radio newscast in a shopping center in Maine, where they were visiting their daughter. Shocked, they went to their car to listen to the full story and then began calling their son. He was very down. To make matters worse, they couldn't talk with him directly as they had not taken their TTY along on the trip. They had to talk to someone who relayed the message to Michael and his message back to them. It was all so unsatisfactory to Leona Chatoff at a time when she felt so keenly the need to communicate her disappointment and concern and support, but it was the best that could be done.

* *New York Times,* July 4, 1982, p. 8.

Charlie Eible, the superintendent of schools, heard about it early, from Kuntz' office, and got out a press release. For most of that day and the next, he responded to inquiries from the press. He said that the district was pleased that "the highest court in the land supports the position that we had taken for some time that the district was providing the necessary and appropriate services for Amy to not only function well but to receive an excellent educational program." As for the district's legal fees, he said that it just happened to fall to this district to define "free appropriate education" for the whole country.

Daniel Horan, chairman of the board of education, heard about it that morning as well and got some calls from the press. In answer to a question, he told one reporter that the litigation cost the district about $100,000.

Although a hearing person, John Rowley got the news last of all. He was away at camp and didn't learn about it for several days. When he did find out, he thought, Wouldn't it be great not to have to go back to school in September?

The court's decision turned on congressional intent. The majority opinion, joined by five justices, concluded that Congress' aims were satisfied when the state provided personalized instruction with sufficient support services to permit the handicapped child to benefit educationally. Four justices (Justices Brennan, White, Marshall, and Blackmun) concluded that Congress meant to provide equal educational opportunity for handicapped children. Justice Blackmun, however, determined that standard had been met in Amy's case and thus concurred separately in the majority's opinion. Justice White, in a dissent joined by Justices Brennan and Marshall, believed that Amy had not received an opportunity to learn commensurate with that afforded her hearing classmates.

Allowing for Justice Blackmun's differing conclusions on the meaning of the facts in the case, the opposing views of the majority five and minority four justices on Congress' intent moved off in different directions, exclusive of each other more than gripping one another in opposition. The majority saw the act as one primarily permitting access to public school for handicapped children. It rejected Judge Mansfield's view that "self-sufficiency" was the standard sought, but adopted the remainder of the appellate court dissenting opinion, down to concluding that services calculated to achieve passing marks, progress from grade to grade, and some unspecified degree of educational benefit were generally sufficient to satisfy the act, so long as procedural requirements were met.

At times the majority opinion spoke as though the issue had been to "maximize a handicapped child's potential," and, at other times, it provided a somewhat fuller context—"maximize each child's potential commensurate with the opportunity provided other children." But neither of these descriptions made it clear that this "opportunity" had no attainment strings attached to it. All children, Judge Broderick had written, deserved the "opportunity" to achieve up to their full potential. Nothing less, nothing more. In this way, the majority opinion skirted the "equal opportunity" issue completely, observed that the lower courts "should not have concluded that the Act requires the provision of a sign language interpreter," reversed the appellate court decision, and remanded the case "for further proceedings consistent with this opinion."

The dissent charged that the majority opinion ignored congressional intent. To this point, the three dissenters noted that the Senate report said that the act "does 'guarantee that handicapped children be provided *equal* educational opportunity,'" and quoted a dozen members of congress to that effect. It pointed to the definition of "special education" in the act, which included calling for "specifically designed instruction . . . to *meet the unique needs*" (emphasis in the dissent) of the handicapped child. It was clear, Justice White wrote, that Congress meant for the handicapped child to be given "an equal opportunity to learn if that is reasonably possible." With these points, Justice Blackmun, in his concurrence, agreed. Additionally, White relied on language used by Justice Stevens—who joined the majority—during oral argument. By the majority's standard, White wrote, the act would have been satisfied in Amy's case by "provision of a teacher with a loud voice."

The press picked up on this last quote, but only, in most stories, in the bottom half, after the lead and recitation of the majority view. But virtually all of these next-day stories used the "full potential" shortcut now and sometimes even the word "opportunity" was left out. Interesting in view of her earlier exchange with Michael Chatoff was Linda Greenhouse's front-page lead story in the *New York Times,* on June 29, which numbered among the latter. She wrote that the Court had concluded that schools were not obliged "to provide services that such [handicapped children] need to reach their full academic potential." *Time* magazine used similar language.*

* July 12, 1982, p. 53.

On July 30, the *Times* carried on its editorial page an article by Harry Schwartz, a former member of the newspaper's editorial board who was, at the time of the article, writer-in-residence at the College of Physicians and Surgeons at Columbia University. Schwartz interpreted the Supreme Court decision as meaning, "There is a limit on how much public money should be spent on one child, and that limit was less than was required for Amy to do as well as possible." He carried the construct of the parents of children with disabilities cheating other children by asking for too much a step further: "The true callousness is to demand that a particular child or an adult get everything he or she desires while ignoring the fact that to do that denies others what they need and want." Finally, he likened disability to sickness: "Our society is simply not rich enough to give every handicapped or sick person every bit of help that is economically possible."

Sick children, selfish parents asking for too much: what these parents and advocates really wanted—in the opinion of these writers—may have been summed up best in an editorial in the *Washington Post* on July 1. After quoting Justice Rehnquist to the effect that the case was about providing services sufficient to maximize each handicapped child's potential, the editorial concluded: "Of course it can be heart-wrenching in a case like Amy Rowley's to say no. But there are limits to what society can afford, limits which suggest that the goal of some handicapped rights groups— that people with handicaps be able to function as if they did not have them—is simply not attainable."

In other words, parents of children with disabilities want to be just like "us," they want their children to be placed in a special category higher than that of "normal" children, and they want "us" to pay the bill for it.

Given the ugly edge of this tone in the media's discussion, the disability press may be forgiven for drawing a collective sigh of relief that the decision in *Rowley* was no worse than it turned out to be. A few carefully reasoned articles stressed the point that the Supreme Court had left room for the lower courts to decide that this or that service was needed for a child with a disability to progress satisfactorily. One article by Reed Martin, a respected legal mind in the disability field, published by the Association for Children with Learning Disabilities, actually described *Rowley* as a "victory" for handicapped students. This article reflected better than most the fears that beset lawyers in advocacy circles at the time the case was heard. For Martin listed the things the Supreme Court "could have done" and included among them (1) holding the act an unconstitutional intrusion into

157

state affairs; (2) holding that "appropriate" was a term so loose as to be meaningless; (3) holding that the funds appropriated by Congress were insufficient to commit the states to the expense of appropriate education; or (4), holding that if schools deemed a requested service too costly, that service would be considered inappropriate.*

This last possibility Martin considered "most potentially devastating" to the cause of individuals with disabilities. It raised the issue of cost, carefully screened away by the language of the Court's decision, but just as obviously on the justices' minds and on the minds of a large majority of the reading public.

A handful of articles from advocacy groups took the position that the decision was a severe blow to the hopes of individuals with disabilities. Typical of these, one advocacy group for the deaf opined that the decision gave deaf people the message that they are not equal to hearing people under the law and wondered whether the schools paying for sign language interpreters would use the Supreme Court's decision to back out of their responsibilities.

More detailed reviews of the decision trickled out in the months afterward, one of the most scathing of which was written by Bonnie Poitras Tucker, an attorney prominent in the education of the deaf. She argued that the Supreme Court majority had "deliberately ignored" the intent of Congress to provide equal educational opportunities. She thought cost was the court majority's main motivation. "This case," she wrote, "clearly indicates that in the area of handicapped rights the Court reigns supreme, and, at least in the present political climate, the Court does *not* [her emphasis] intend to give recognition to the Civil Rights movement for handicapped persons. It does not bode well for the future of handicapped persons in general or deaf persons in particular."†

But only relative handfuls of Americans read articles in the disability press. By August 1982, the general media had concluded that the *Rowley* case was about parents' efforts to "maximize the potential" of their deaf child in a mainstream school. The words "equal opportunity" had been made to disappear. But while I could track the disappearance of words and the substitution of other words as I reviewed this performance by the media, I could not answer the question that dogged me as a former newspa-

---

* *Newsbriefs* (September–October 1982): 20–23.

† "Utter Chaos," *Journal of Law and Education* 12 (1983).

perman with a considerable residue of faith in the major media's efforts to be fair: Why? Why were so many newspapers and television stations making plain misstatements of facts in a single case at law? Why was it so important to say "no" to Amy Rowley?

———

The future did not look good. The *Rowley* case could be seen as a kind of backdrop against which the Reagan administration was attempting to roll back the advances made by individuals with disabilities. The real threat, in the minds of many advocates, was executive and legislative rather than judicial. "It is expected that the administration will introduce legislation to repeal Public Law 94–142 [the Education for All Handicapped Children Act] in its entirety or to repeal some of the key provisions of the law," the *Disability Rights Review* had reported in its March 1982 issue.

By August 1982, the Reagan administration was ready for a frontal assault on disability law. On August 3, Secretary of Education Terrel H. Bell placed in the *Federal Register* the proposed new regulations for Public Law 94-142. In a news conference he stressed that the changes would be beneficial because they would give the states more discretion. Besides, he said, they were only tentative and could be changed after the ninety-day comment period. Ten hearings were scheduled around the country.

Essentially, the changes proposed were: (1) elimination of the requirement that schools must have parents' written consent to educational plans for their children; (2) leaving to the school systems decisions on placements in the "least restrictive environment" as close as possible to the mainstream of school life; (3) making optional, rather than required, related medical services from the schools, including eyeglasses, insulin injections, or other medications; (4) elimination of thirty-day deadlines for states to evaluate a child and set up an Individual Education Program; (5) dropping the requirement that evaluation personnel be required to attend all meetings with parents on education plans for children; and (6) deleting the definition of "qualified personnel" for dealing with handicapped children in school.

These proposed changes immediately met with strong and bipartisan opposition in Congress. The *New York Times* reported that, in a hearing before the Subcommittee on the Handicapped of the Senate Labor and Human Resources Committee, members of both parties took potshots at the proposed changes. Senator Robert T. Stafford (R-Vt.) told Secretary Bell and others that the proposed changes "would seriously erode the rights and protections afforded handicapped children and their parents." Then-Senator Dan Quayle (R-Ind.) said he was concerned that some schools would interpret "disruptive" behavior too loosely, perhaps deciding that a child in a wheelchair was a case in point. He argued as well that parental involvement would be weakened.

The harshest critic was Subcommittee Chairman Lowell P. Weicker, Jr. (R-Conn.). He candidly expressed his suspicions about the philosophy that lay behind the proposed changes. The administration had to date, he said, "sought to gut special education," urging reductions of up to 30 percent. "Now," added the chairman, "we are being told that the same people who asked us to decimate the law and to slash funding are selling a regulatory rewrite as an improvement for the disabled. We shall see today whether that is the case or whether the Administration is attempting to do by regulation what it has been unable to do in Congress: To eliminate our nation's system of special education."*

These words captured the fervent spirit of the debate. As they suggest, the issue had become one of good faith, and the reaction against the proposed changes reflected the lack of good faith on the part of the Reagan administration felt among parents and advocates. The public hearings bore this out. The one in Washington was typical. "People were crying and screaming," recalled Paul Hippolitus of the President's Committee on Employment of Individuals with Disabilities in an interview. "It was hard to get through any individual's comment without tears. It was an emotional affair."

It didn't take long for the administration to react to the political beestings it was suffering. On September 29, Secretary Bell appeared before the Subcommittee on Select Education of the House Committee on Education and Labor to withdraw the major recommendations of the proposed regulations. "According to testimony received at the hearings on our proposed regulations," he said, "the impression is widespread that we are diminishing the basic rights of handicapped children through these proposals. It is essential that we establish at the outset of this testimony, and for the record, the extensive protections of these rights that have been maintained in our proposed rules."

Still, Bell didn't manage to satisfy everyone at the hearing. He insisted that some "technical or editorial" changes might yet be made in the regulations. Representative George Miller (D-Cal.) responded: "It's your sense

* *New York Times*, August 11, 1982, p. A-19.

of 'technical changes' that got us into this problem. . . . Before this law, these wonderful local people on the school boards were locking these children up in basements and closets. . . . Rights were vested in the states before this law, and they didn't do a damn thing for these students."*

Miller's statement with its bristling civil rights imagery might just as well have been the last word on the subject. On November 3, 1982, the Department of Education published in the *Federal Register* a "Modification of Notice of Proposed Rulemaking," in which the six areas of proposed change in the regulations were withdrawn. In the meantime, other changes considered as onerous to many advocates for children with disabilities, such as the rewrite of Section 504, simply vaporized and were heard from no more. A knowledgeable observer of the scene described the routing of the effort to modify the legislation by new regulations as a historic moment for handicapped people.

Of all the things that had happened, as far back as she could remember, losing her interpreter after having had interpreter service in her classroom for two years, seemed to Amy Rowley the most unthinkable. But next to that, close to it in terms of worry, was the idea being broached during her fifth-grade year in the fall of 1982, of moving away from Peekskill, from all her classmates, all her friends, to a strange, new place in another state. Her mother and father had sat Amy and John down and talked it over with them more than once. She would be better off in Mountain Lakes, New Jersey, because she would probably have an interpreter in some if not all of her classes. John would be better off because the schools there were familiar with deafness; one school in the public system specialized in teaching deaf children. No one would taunt John about coming from a deaf family. It was a real option, and Nancy and Cliff wanted both children to understand it was being seriously considered.

Amy could see that John was miserable and she had to admit that she was unhappy now that she had no help in the classroom. Her parents had exerted so much effort on her behalf that they deserved some relief from the constant hassle. But that was overbalanced in her mind by the prospect of losing the familiarity, the comfort of known friends and home and classmates—Marjorie Augenblick, Andrea Marino, Heather Fromme, and others. Another grievous thing was that she couldn't tell her classmates

---

* *Washington Post*, September 30, 1982.

what was going on. They would ask why she didn't have a sign language interpreter this year and she would say that the school wouldn't give her one, and they would ask why was that and she would say she didn't know. In her heart, it was true—she really didn't know. She couldn't tell them that her family was moving. Her mother and father had asked her not to. The court process was still going on in some way she didn't quite understand, and because of that she couldn't prepare her friends—really, prepare herself through them—for her leaving. It had come down to a matter of evasion and lying. Then one day her good friend Marjorie had asked her if she was going to bring a lunch box to school next year, an option on entering middle school and the sixth grade. She couldn't lie to Marjorie, she had to tell someone. Tearfully, she said she might not be back; her family was considering moving away, but Marjorie should tell no one.

She was torn between fear and guilt. She feared the unknown in the move to New Jersey. She felt guilt about the loss of her interpreter. The only way she could explain to herself not having the interpreter this year was that she must not have used the services properly. She thought of times she had not been as cooperative with Fran Miller and, later, with Beth Freed, as she should have been. She worried now that, as much as she appreciated them and had tried to tell them so, perhaps she had not succeeded. She felt herself slipping academically, particularly in mathematics. She was beginning to feel in the classroom the way she did on field trips. Without the help of an interpreter there, it was impossible for her to keep up. When the camping trip to Ashokan came along in the spring of 1983, she was ready to stop trying to communicate and adopt the role of the lone explorer, close to a new world of nature.

While Nancy and Clifford Rowley were reasoning with their two children, they were also battling the costs of the court case. Chatoff had taken no money; he worked on his own time, vacation time, and whatever time he could get from his employer. But now, having had to go to the Supreme Court and having lost, the Rowleys were faced with additional costs. Clifford had written the Gallaudet Alumni Association for help with the $949.79 cost of printing the briefs. Neither this group nor the National Association for the Deaf, for various reasons, was able to help.

Other efforts at fund-raising had been equally unavailing. Occasional small checks appeared from sympathetic individuals including one for $15 from a penitentiary inmate who had read about Amy's case and thought she had gotten a "stinking deal." Nancy wrote the man a thoughtful, grateful letter telling him that the money would be put in an account for Amy's education, along with any other money that came in.

While Amy fretted in her fifth-grade classes, her court case had clung precariously to life as though on support systems. Michael Chatoff had to ask Barry Felder, an amiable and capable lawyer in private practice—who had written an amicus curiae brief on behalf of the Rowleys for the Supreme Court that Chatoff had admired—to take over for him when he became ill again. While vacationing in Europe after the oral hearing, he had experienced dizziness, and back home, he learned that the tumors had recurred. Felder took over while Chatoff recovered from the nightmarish procedure of repeating the two operations. Once recovered, Chatoff gamely threw himself back into the fray.

Back in the fall of 1982, as Amy entered fifth grade, her lawyers had sought another school-based impartial hearing on the grounds that the Supreme Court order dealt with four-year-old evidence and test scores and that Amy's need for an interpreter had become far greater. Reporters Jon Craig and Dorothea Smith, covering the story for the *Citizen-Register,* a Gannett chain newspaper in Westchester County, found school board attorney Raymond Kuntz noticeably angry about the new development. "What the Rowleys are doing," they quoted Kuntz as saying, in a story published November 12, "is appealing the Supreme Court's decision, something that was fundamentally decided last spring. It makes very little sense to appeal it at this point." It was all a "ridiculous" effort and "a great waste of taxpayers' money." Kuntz put the cost of the legal battle to the school board at $100,000, not including the new round of hearings.

The issue of cost came up in a different way through the reporting of Craig and Smith. Nancy Rowley told them that she and Clifford had offered to pay for Amy's interpreter for the school year and been turned down. When the reporters talked with various members of the school's administrative, teaching, and legal team, nobody could remember such an offer, Craig and Smith reported on November 12. They had asked Teresa Kiernan Kuntz, the school district attorney's wife and a member of his firm; Joan Thompson, director of special education and chairperson of the District Committee for the Handicapped; and Steven Hall, a reading teacher at the school and member of the DCOH. "We have no documentation of such an offer," Thompson told the reporters.

For the November 19 issue of the *Citizen-Register* Craig wrote that the Rowleys had supplied the newspaper with a tape of a DCOH meeting on

August 31, 1982, in which the offer was clearly made by Mrs. Rowley, through an interpreter, and repeated. "Suppose we provided the interpreter, would you accept?" they reported Nancy Rowley as asking. And then, asked to repeat, "If we provide the interpreter and the cost of the interpreter, would you accept?"

Craig's story records Hall as answering, "Money is not the issue to me so that's irrelevant. . . . I would feel that if it is in Amy's best interest to provide an interpreter in those [group] situations, I would want to recommend it and take responsibility for it. If it isn't, then in my judgment it isn't. And regardless who provides it, I would still feel that it isn't." The summarized minutes of the DCOH session did not mention this exchange at all, the reporter noted.

At the impartial hearing, Smith remembers the hearing officer, an acting village justice in Hastings named Earle Warren Zaidins, as chatting amiably with Raymond Kuntz and members of the school board in court before proceedings began. The hearing focused on sharply differing versions of how well Amy was doing in her classwork. William Brett, Amy's fifth-grade teacher, said that when Amy didn't understand anything, she always let him know. Harold Smelter, her math teacher, testified that she was ten pages ahead of her class, doing above average work, and that "when Amy doesn't understand something, you can see it on her face." Joel Ziev, executive director of the New York Society of the Deaf, assisted Chatoff and told Craig and Smith later, "I really feel the district is doing what they perceive as correct, but they don't understand the needs of a deaf person in a group situation" (November 19 issue of the *Citizen Register*). He said that Amy's FM wireless hearing aid amplified "flat sounds," but did not produce the stereo effect of normal hearing that would allow Amy to remain oriented, identify other speakers, and follow a conversation in the classroom. Nancy Rowley maintained that Amy was not understanding so much as she had been with the sign language interpreter in her class. "Everything's changed since last year," Nancy testified. "She's not getting everything she could be getting."

Zaidins ruled in favor of the school, saying that he was most impressed with the teachers' testimony. "My heart goes out to Amy," Smith quoted Zaidins as saying on December 9 in the *Citizen-Register*, "but I could see the case objectively. I think the school has done fantastically for her." Zaidins had other comments quoted by Smith. "She's a nice lady but I think she's carrying this a bit far," Smith quoted him as saying about

Nancy Rowley. "I think they are doing an injustice to Amy by not letting her be as normal as possible." Told that Nancy Rowley questioned his objectivity in the case and wanted to know who had hired him, Zaidins responded, "I'd have to check my records, but I get paid one way or another, no matter what decision I come to. I have no loyalty to one side or the other."

Chatoff made one last effort as Amy was theoretically getting ready to begin sixth grade in the Blue Mountain Middle School in the Hendrick Hudson Central School District in 1983. His argument was that procedural errors, not ruled on by Judge Broderick, had been committed by the school by not involving the parents in the decision on services for Amy. But the Rowleys disclosed on the first day of the hearing that they were moving to Mountain Lakes. The school presented witnesses including Special Education Director Joan Thompson to testify that Amy was making good progress in school. Zaidins' decision in favor of the school district seemed, however, a foregone conclusion. After it had come down, and it was clear that matters between the family and the school district had moved to conclusion, Smith quoted Superintendent Eible, in the *Citizen-Register* for September 2, 1983, as saying: "From six months before Amy started school until now, the Rowleys have lodged a steady, continuous stream of charges against this school district." Smith quoted Nancy Rowley: "All handicapped children have educational and human rights. They should have equal access to education. . . . We feel Amy will have free access to learning when we move to our new school district."

As the Rowleys waited for moving vans to take their possessions to their new home, they learned that a lien had been placed on their Peekskill house for $4,600 in Supreme Court costs, to be taken from the proceeds of its sale.

Michael Chatoff's legal colleague, Barry Felder, told himself that he wasn't sorry to have been extricated from a case that he felt was probably over before he got on the scene. At the same time, because he believed strongly in his client's cause, he had hoped for a chance to be more helpful. His law firm and he himself had a reputation for supplying pro bono services. But there was another, more personal reason for Felder's involvement. The education of a deaf child was of vital importance to him, because his only child, his daughter, was profoundly deaf, too; and in October 1981, when

Felder agreed to write the amicus curiae brief in the *Rowley* case, she was in preschool therapy.

Felder had grown up in Atlantic Beach, Long Island, the son of a lawyer, and had married his high school sweetheart, Robyn Wallen. Melissa was born on May 18, 1980, and the discovery of her deafness parallels other stories of the slowly confirmed suspicions of hearing parents. And like other hearing parents, the shock of the news betrayed unsettling fears. "We thought what had happened would isolate her from the rest of the world," Robyn Felder recalled in an interview. "To us, the child we had was gone and this was another child. She was not going to be anything we had dreamed she would be. She was going to learn sign language, and she would be isolated since only such a small percentage of people outside the deaf community know sign language."

While the parents wrestled with their emotions, Robyn Felder's father got on the phone and put them in touch with the Manhattan Eye, Ear, Nose, and Throat Hospital, where someone told them about the New York League for the Hard of Hearing. Robyn was told that, all things being equal, Melissa would be able to go to a regular school with other children by the time she was three years old and would not have to learn sign language. The Felders visited the Lexington School and were not impressed with the speech capabilities of these orally trained deaf children. They noticed the children signing to each other out of class. The league encouraged them to point Melissa in the direction of an oral education and mainstreaming in public schools, with the most powerful amplification of sound she could get.

When Melissa was enrolled in Lakeside Elementary School in Merrick, Long Island, the school supplied an aide—not a sign language person—in class with her. The Felders, determined not to allow extra help that Melissa might come to depend on, said they did not feel that this person was necessary. But the school insisted and later Melissa told her parents that the aide was a big help not only to her but also to other students in the class.

Barry Felder was on the board of the New York Society for the Deaf and so was in touch with deaf culture. He also had a sister who had become a sign language interpreter. She felt strongly that Melissa ought to learn sign language, and the subject produced heated conversations whenever she visited the Felders. The Felders' own viewpoint was far from antisign. They felt that when and if Melissa asked to learn sign language would be time enough for it. Robyn Felder even considered learning sign language to prepare for that day.

Barry Felder saw Amy's case as entirely different. "She grew up in a home with a total communications atmosphere," he said. "That was her learning mode. She needed an interpreter and her parents wanted her to have an interpreter. I've never doubted that that was necessary for her to get an equal opportunity to make the best of her education or that this was what Congress intended in passing the act."

But in the milieu of suburban Long Island, where the Felders lived, they knew of no deaf child who was not being educated orally. By the same token, they knew of no deaf child who did not have hearing parents. It was their perception that Melissa was doing well in her classes and so they felt the course they were following was reasonable. "You're out there," Robyn Felder said, "with a problem and you're just stumbling around, not knowing where to turn. . . . It seems that there should be some objective resource center where a person can find out the alternatives and make some kind of educated decision rather than just going through the phone book and calling everyone under that category."

8

Maybe It Wouldn't Happen Today

When I began my search, years afterward, for the people I needed to help unravel what was still, to me, the mystery of the *Rowley* case, I found that I had quite a list of "missing persons," people who had moved and might be difficult to locate. But fortunately, many of the major actors in the drama were still clustered in the network of old villages on the Hudson—Buchanan, Peekskill, Montrose—in Westchester County. Much of this prosperous area could be described as a series of lightly interconnected suburbs surrounding crusty, little towns where commerce is still warmly confined to shops. Typical of these suburbs is the quiet street where the Rowleys lived in a two-story, white house not far from where Clifford Rowley grew up in Croton-on-Hudson. Most of the homeowners here were, like Clifford, professional people who worked elsewhere, in New York City or, via the Tappan Zee Bridge, in New Jersey.

But for all the change swept in by American mobility of the 1970s and 1980s, there remains something settled, smugly secure about these towns: they strike the visitor as tiny, carefully preserved organisms from an earlier day, now feeding off the burgeoning suburbs around them. The word "village" leaps to mind as one walks in downtown Croton. When you ask for history, you are directed to the village historian, a woman who works in a bookstore full of books about the town. Anyone you ask can tell you about her, and if you tell her who sent you, she will probably know that person as well. She is ready for anything in the way of questions but suspects that one about Washington Irving lurks, waiting to be asked and answered, and is always prepared with books, a map, and a suggested drive.

If the towns seem outsized by the suburbs, the geographical focus for modern Westchester is not in the county, but in the megalopolis, New York City, downriver. A sleepy, Dutch town like Clifford Rowley's Croton made the typical transformation from farming, shipping, and flour- and brick-making in the nineteenth century to the twentieth century, with the help of the construction of a huge dam on the Croton River to supply millions of gallons of water to Manhattan daily. Along with Irish and Italian settlers in those years came a diametrically different strain that was to cast a shadow of disproportionate length. John Reed, the American convert to communism, and Louise Bryant moved in, bringing their baggage of free love and women's rights with them. The most notable of the backlashes against these "radicals" were the famous Peekskill riots set off in 1949 by the concert appearance of Paul Robeson, the great African American singer, who had also embraced communism. More than one hundred and fifty people were injured in the melee that broke out when those in attendance were ambushed by a mob composed in part of townspeople.

Croton, today, is diverse but essentially blue-collar, with descendants of the railroad- and dam-builders mingled with some of the art colony's spiritual, if not actual, descendants, along with upper-middle-class professional people who found it too costly to educate their children in New York City's private schools. Westchester is rated the second-wealthiest county in New York State, a bastion of conservatism where the ethic of individual freedom relates intrinsically to the ownership of property. An oldtimer in the area told me that practically everybody he knew in town had been called a "Communist" at one time or another.

As I made my way around the area, interviewing key people in the Rowley story, I found myself wondering whether any of this history was significant in forming the opinions I encountered. It was relatively easy to find people who said they respected the Rowleys, but difficult to find anyone who believed that their efforts to get the school to provide a sign language interpreter for their daughter were justified. I found that the farther away I got from the few people who were principals in the making of the *Rowley* case, the more tenuous was the grasp of the facts of the matter. One older couple, close to Clifford Rowley's family as he grew up in Croton and in every way disposed favorably to support the family's cause, told me that Amy Rowley was provided sign language interpreters by the school in several of her classes and that the case went to court only because her parents insisted on having them in all of her classes and for assemblies. If people friendly to the Rowleys believed this, I wondered, how many others not so friendly would gladly believe it.

The law offices of Raymond Kuntz were located on the second floor of a building in a small shopping center in Bedford Village, New York, not far from Peekskill. As I sat in the anteroom, waiting for him to appear for our interview, I observed that the Hendrick Hudson School District's attorney had a wall posted with mementos of the *Rowley* case. There was a caricature of Kuntz arguing before the Court with the justices' faces looking in at him. Then there was a photograph of Kuntz being interviewed by the press outside on the steps of the Court. To the left was the petition for certiorari for the October, 1980 term of the Supreme Court.

Kuntz was a slim man, elegant looking from his closely cropped dark blond hair to his well-polished shoes. A native of Westchester, he had undergraduate and law degrees from Fordham University. Graduated in 1962 and married that same year, in 1965 he had the opportunity to take over representation of the Hendrick Hudson School District from an older lawyer. By 1969, he had his own firm and was representing several school districts in the mid-Hudson area.

Voluble and articulate, Kuntz was willing to recite his version of the history of the *Rowley* case in detail. He told me that the Rowleys had signed a document agreeing to test various means of teaching Amy and then had turned around after that and filed their civil action with the Department of Health, Education and Welfare. He also told me that the Rowleys had not insisted upon a sign language interpreter for Amy at first. He recited the services the district had provided, the TTY, the teacher of the deaf, the speech therapist, the special attention given by the kindergarten teacher. Amy was doing, he said, as well as anyone would expect a child with normal hearing to do given her I.Q. A sign language interpreter had been tried and failed. As he spoke, he warmed to his subject, gesticulating here to stress a point, raising his voice a few decibels there to underscore another. I felt as though I were sitting in a jury box, listening to a summation delivered expertly by a passionate advocate.

He considered that the Rowleys and the advocates for their cause were relying on a premise based on their philosophy of deaf education—"that every deaf child does better with a sign language interpreter"—and that the school, without interest in causes or disputes over the education of the deaf, simply had tried what made sense to them, and it had worked.

He said he remembered the *New York Times* editorial of 1980 without my having to show it to him. He didn't think, however, that it had been particularly influential in helping the district make up its mind to appeal to the Supreme Court. "I think the board was concerned, first, to do the right thing. The district's decision was not unanimous. The one or two board members that were not in favor of going to the Supreme Court wondered why the school had not taken the approach suggested by Judge Broderick. They had severe doubts about the case. Ultimately, all those doubts were resolved." I asked whether he personally had taken it upon himself to look into issues of deafness in connection with the case and he said he had a shelf of books on deafness that he had explored. Later on, however, in describing sign language interpretation, he said, "Of course, if you're familiar with this, sign language is not by any means an interpretation of exactly what is going on in the classroom, but rather a shorthand of what transpires. It probably only conveys a fraction of what is said. It's simply like one of those foreign films where you hear two minutes of dialogue and what you see underneath is the words, 'Hello, there.'"

Kuntz also believed that Amy could hear more than was generally thought. "That's because she does have near-normal hearing in the lower frequencies," he told me. "When her name is called, she turns around. This is a kid who is adept at what she is about, which is getting information from other people."

At one point, I asked Kuntz if anyone had bothered to ask Amy if she thought a sign language interpreter would help her.

"No," Kuntz responded. "Of course not . . . not when the case had become a cause célèbre." I asked him when that had happened, and he responded that it was so from the very beginning, that the Rowleys had organized support for their case in the community through their church. "They courted the news media," he said, "and they publicized their case."

What about the Rowleys' offer after the Supreme Court decision to pay for the sign language interpreter if the school would permit one? "The superintendent and the board decided that they wouldn't do that because cost was not the prime consideration. They felt that having a sign language interpreter was not best for Amy. That's not to say that there were not other considerations involved in making that decision."

I asked what other considerations he had in mind.

"In one respect, having taken the case all the way to the Supreme Court, and then saying, OK, we'll put in a sign language interpreter, wouldn't have made much sense."

I wondered if I was right to think that he and Eible were the real leaders in the school district's effort. "I think it would be a misperception to say that it was Mr. Eible and I who led the board to appeal, because I don't think that's true. There were people on the board who thought that an appeal was something that should be attempted ultimately to verify that the school had done the right thing. They weren't looking for vindication. It didn't have that emotional flavor. They thought they were right. They were also influenced by the fact that the State of New York, represented by the commissioner of education, had tentatively determined that they would go ahead with an appeal."

The school district's attorney also expressed a feeling that I was to encounter, in different words, more than once in my interviewing. "It's been my experience that [in] any group which considers itself oppressed or looked down upon, whether it be police officers or teachers on strike, or any one of a number of groups that feels that society is not giving them their full due, there is a note of righteousness that creeps into their attitudes . . . Doubts about whether or not a particular course of action is entirely correct . . . are resolved in going ahead and doing it anyway because we've been taking this for all these years, so we've got a right to do this."

Kuntz suggested that I talk with Linda Carmody-Roberts, who he thought was president of the school board at the time the decision was made to appeal to the Supreme Court. I caught up with her on a later trip to the area, after my wife and I had gone through the school's files on Amy. We showed her the "confidential draft" memorandum from October 26, 1977, in which the board had heard from Kuntz that the Rowley matter would go to an independent hearing officer for settlement, and where trial of a sign language interpreter was described by the note-taker as having "an element of risk but . . . could strengthen our hand." I asked if the language of the memo did not suggest to her a group whose mind was already made up to go to court.

A neat, personable attorney who had lived in Montrose all her life, she looked at the memo for a minute, then noted that she was present at the meeting but did not remember it clearly. "It sounds like we're already in court," she said. "However, I believe the determination was made that we should explore all possibilities before we eliminated any of them. If we eliminated the idea of having a sign language interpreter before even trying it, we couldn't say that we had tried all the possibilities. I don't think this board had quite as closed a mind as you may think. There were some who said, 'Fine, let's do it.' Others said, 'Let's investigate it further. Let's see what is not only appropriate for Amy but also for other deaf kids.' "

To her mind, the Rowleys were the intransigent ones. "They came across as saying that every deaf child should have a sign language interpreter in the public school. That's what their association believed." What association was that, I asked. "I assume the Association for the Deaf . . . . We felt we had to consider the other fifteen to twenty children." Asked what she meant by that, she responded: "The disruption, particularly in kindergarten. The ability of socialization of a five-year-old who always has an adult with her." She told me that, based on her experience as an attorney, the *Rowley* case was a good one for an association of the deaf to choose to test the Education for All Handicapped Children Act. I asked her why. "Because you had two deaf parents of a deaf child," she responded.

But Carmody-Roberts was not actually president of the board at the time of the decision to appeal to the Supreme Court. That distinction belonged to Warren Button, another veteran whose membership went back before Amy's kindergarten year. I met Button in a restaurant outside downtown Croton one morning. He turned out to be a pleasant man, with degrees from Cornell, Pennsylvania State, and the Harvard School of Business, who had moved to Cortlandt in 1958 and eventually established a business manufacturing insulated, thermocoupled wire. With five children of his own, he was a model of parental interest, teaching Sunday school and working with the Boy Scouts. He joined the school board in 1966 and served fifteen years.

To Button, the *Rowley* case was as simple as it was significant. It was a test of whether a school board or an interest group would prevail in an important educational dispute. He remembered early on, during Amy's first or second year in school, asking someone—he believed it was the school district's attorney, Raymond Kuntz—who would decide what an "appropriate" education was, and getting the response that the National Association of the Deaf says, "We decide." That, Button said, simply wouldn't work because interest groups have no taste for arbitration. "It seemed clear that there was no guidance in the law; we were plowing new ground, and Kuntz said we could take a stand on this, and he was very open—'You have the unfortunate burden; probably this is a serious constitutional issue that can go all the way.' "

Button conceded that he had proceeded on hearsay, but it was clear that, years after the fact, his conviction remained as strong as it had been in the beginning. "It's my understanding the case was politicized. It was being funded by the NAD on the Rowley side. It's my understanding they were looking for a case where there was a youngster who was bright, who was really capable of doing well in school in a district where the district wasn't strapped for funds, and it fell to us." I asked him if he was saying that the Rowleys were selected in some way for their role. "Yes," he responded, "selected, or if not, at least through their involvement, volunteered." He was convinced, also, that had the Rowleys lost at the district level, NAD would have appealed.

Button guessed the litigation cost the district $75,000 to $80,000, but against this cost, he put the cost of a sign language interpreter at $12,000 a year for twelve years or $144,000. "We're talking several deaf children and given the importance of the precedent I think the lawyer hit it right, early on, when he said you have the misfortune of carrying this burden." I asked how Button had concluded that "several" deaf students would be involved. "Well, it's like the judge's [Judge Broderick's] decision. If you supplied enough resources, they all could. The sky's the limit. Why not? . . . We had five other deaf children, four in one family, which didn't have the support of the NAD, didn't have the outspoken parents, that were going to the school for the deaf."

Button also struck a note that Kuntz and Judge Mansfield had made much of, that Amy would become dependent upon an interpreter and that would be a disservice to her after her school life, when she no longer had one.

Daniel Horan, the high school social studies teacher who had been elected to the school board in May 1980, was one of the board members who had serious questions at first about appealing Judge Broderick's decision. I asked him what had persuaded him, and he showed me the editorial in the *New York Times*, which he had clipped and saved. He also spoke of Judge Mansfield's dissent as having had an influence on him. "It seemed to me to be a strong opinion," he said. But even before that, he was beginning to feel that the district's position was strong and that perhaps Judge Broderick had "overstepped his authority." Then, he added, some members of the board "felt some sort of discomfort at the whole idea of the sign language interpreter." I asked why that was.

"Well," he said, "first of all the object, as I understand it, of the handicapped act in terms of a free and appropriate education is to make the education for handicapped youngsters as similar to that of the nonhandicapped population as possible. I think many of us were concerned that the presence of a sign language interpreter tended to isolate Amy from the rest of the class and also could provide distractions for the other youngsters in the class." The theme that denying Amy Rowley a sign language interpreter in the name of "mainstreaming" provided positive benefits to her that would otherwise have been lost recurred in a number of my interviews with members of the school board. Eileen Curinga, a board member with three children in school, including one who at one point had been classified as having a learning disability, said that the board was aware of evidence presented in court that Amy could not possibly understand more than 60 percent of what was said in the classroom. "I had a little trouble with that," she told me, "because most children don't hear 100 percent of what is going on."

I asked her if she thought that Amy could understand as well as the children on either side of her, and she said she did not think so. But she added, "From what we were told, the children and the class itself were making an effort to include Amy and help her. And I think that's one of the things about mainstream education. She could be going to a school for the deaf and be getting 100 percent of what is going on, but there are trade-offs. Mainstreaming is allowing them to adapt and interact with normal children that they're going to go through life with in spite of their handicap."

Later Curinga observed, "I don't think we [public schools] have the resources to have every child work up to his or her potential." The issue of bringing children with disabilities up to their "full potential" came up in other conversations I had with members of the community. One person talked to me about his "bright" son who had an I.Q. of 160 and was not being brought up to his full potential. A woman who had lobbied hard but unsuccessfully for her son to receive extra tutoring because of his artistic talent compared his case to that of Amy Rowley. If her son could not receive "special treatment," she asked, why should Amy?

More than once during these talks, I was told that Amy was an "excellent" lip-reader who had "near-normal hearing in the lower ranges." Several times I was told that if you spoke her name behind her back, she would turn around. On a number of occasions, I heard that while Clifford Rowley was someone who had adjusted well to deafness, Nancy Rowley, having lost her hearing gradually, was bitter about her deafness and, in consequence, unreasonable. Nancy took the position, as one person put it, that "somebody's got to pay." Once I was told that Nancy did not care one whit for Amy, but was using her child to wreak revenge on the hearing world. More than once I was told that Nancy and Clifford had neglected John, casting him off as a hearing child and, so, not their kind. What I remember most from these comments was the raw anger in the voices of the individuals commenting.

———

Charles Eible, the Hendrick Hudson superintendent of schools, had had a career that seemed hand-crafted to fit him for the position he occupied. A lifelong resident of the area, he had his bachelor's degree from Manhattan College and his master's from New York University. He had taught physical education and sixth grade, served as assistant superintendent and then superintendent in a nearby school district, and had come to Hendrick Hudson to fill a newly created position as assistant superintendent with responsibilities for curriculum. Finally, he had succeeded to the superintendency when his predecessor moved on.

Eible reacted much as Kuntz had to my question about whether it would be fair to characterize him as a key player in the school district's opposition to providing a sign language interpreter for Amy Rowley. As superintendent, he argued, he was not even in the decision-making loop. The responsibility for decisions of that sort rested first with the District Committee on the Handicapped to determine the services to be provided and, then, with the board of education to approve the IEPs and determine what action to take in response to a decision of parents to go to court to seek further services.

"Now for me to say that the board didn't ask me at certain given points in time, 'What do you think, Charlie?' that isn't true. Of course they did." And Eible was quick to accept that his role was that of spokesman, the person the press would call up and quote in the newspapers.

His recollection of how the *Rowley* case began was that Dr. Thomas Jenkins, his predecessor, had set up a meeting, at which Eible was present and in which the Rowleys, concerned that Amy would be sent to the school for the deaf, pleaded that she be placed in a mainstreamed setting. In fact, Eible said, their fears were without substance. "We had every intention of having Amy come to school, because we recognized Amy as socially alert and as a bright young lady. For reasons known only to them," he continued, "they filed a complaint against the school district pre–her enrollment in our schools, with the federal government. An investigation was done, and their allegations were not upheld."

I reminded him that the Rowleys had gone to Furnace Woods Principal Joseph Zavarella as far back as eighteen months before Amy's enrollment in kindergarten with only one request—that Amy be mainstreamed with a classroom interpreter–tutor. He agreed then that that was "part of their initial complaint."

Eible then volunteered that he had a nephew who was deaf and had been educated at the New York School for the Deaf, had graduated, and was employed at this time in the printing business. Eible described this young man as speaking and signing and said that his (Eible's) sister-in-law signed, too, but that he did not see her signing to her son "because he is such an excellent lip-reader." Had Eible made a study of deafness or read about it as a result of his nephew's deafness, I asked. He had not, he said.

I asked Eible about deaf children subsequently enrolled in the Hendrick Hudson School District. Had any of them asked for or received sign language interpretation in their classrooms? Of the half-dozen or so deaf children in the district, two were at that time in the public schools, without interpreters. The others were in the New York School for the Deaf, receiving sign language services there. With the exception of Amy Rowley, no deaf child in the district had ever been given a sign language interpreter in a regular class. I asked Eible if he could describe a situation in which an interpreter would be appropriate in such classes.

"A deaf child who has all the potential of being able to progress at a normal rate through a mainstream program with the kinds of services we provide, who is not progressing at that rate because of communications problems in the classroom."

"But you haven't had that kind of kid?"

"Or if we have, the child has been placed in the New York School for the Deaf."

I noted that the district had been at pains to employ sign language interpreters for school conferences attended by Nancy and Clifford Rowley, both of them good lip-readers. Was that so the parents could understand as much as was possible of what transpired? He agreed that that was the reason. Why, then, did the district not provide an interpreter for Amy in the classroom for the same reason?

"We didn't think that was the intent of the law," he responded, "that a school district had the absolute responsibility of providing the absolute maximum, optimum, or whatever parents might decide was the optimum, for handicapped or nonhandicapped children."

The distance from Charles Eible's office to Joe Zavarella's lair in the basement of the F. G. Lindsey School in Montrose is barely beyond the limits of the proverbial stone's throw, but it would be hard to imagine a more vivid contrast of place and personality. Zavarella had moved from the principalship of Furnace Woods Elementary School to a position as district curriculum coordinator by the time I interviewed him. This heavy-set, mildly disheveled man emerged like a hibernating bear from under a stack of papers to greet me in his comfortable, stripped-down space, which looked as though it might once have been used for storage, and made of the interview a conversation punctuated with asides, useful digressions, and fascinating contradictions.

From his very first words, it was clear that the *Rowley* case lay heavily upon him. "The interesting thing about it," he began, "is that this district was considered as very-far-into-the-future in terms of doing what was best for kids. We had a focus on individuals at Furnace Woods. Our whole effort was focused on doing what was best for each individual kid. . . . Everybody was thrilled about Amy's coming. We were very psyched up about this. Everybody fell in love with Amy. She was such a loving kid. We really dove into the whole project."

Zavarella's memory of early meetings with Nancy Rowley was no more accurate than that of the others, as he, too, at first remembered only Nancy's request that Amy be mainstreamed rather than her insistence that Amy have an interpreter–tutor in the classroom. Despite the fact that this single issue of the classroom interpreter, on which neither side ever gave an inch, was the sole serious point of contention, Zavarella spoke as though Nancy had steadily increased her demands for service. "It became obvious that whatever the school agreed to do, there was always another thing that Nancy thought was necessary."

But for all the anger still burning over these battles with the Rowleys, it was clear that Zavarella had regrets. He had liked Nancy upon first meeting, and he and the teachers rushed to try to do the best possible job with Amy. Zavarella retold the story of the sign language classes taken by teachers and by him—which he conceded were not sufficient to supply any real help to Amy in the classroom—the TTY "direct line" to the Rowleys from his office, the efforts to place Amy in an advantageous position in the classroom and get her the best possible teacher for her kindergarten experience.

All this eventually washed out, he said, shaking his big head sadly. The hostility created by the Rowleys' civil suit against the school provided a backdrop against which he felt helpless. "I was a person who had to adhere to what my boss—the superintendent, the board—was telling me. There was an entrapment. . . . We ended up on the wrong side of this issue—all of us, the teachers, and anyone who feels very strongly about what we should be doing about kids. . . . From another perspective, as an administrator and bureaucrat, we had to look at it as a situation that had very strong implications for the world. . . . If we did this, what else would we have to do? How much would these things cost us?"

Zavarella did read carefully Nancy Rowley's information about total communications; a term he had never heard before meeting her. He looked into some books on the subject. He nosed about and looked at some programs. He became a convert. "I got involved more and more in the total communications approach and saw it as the only way to go for the general population of deaf people." He came to understand the principle of community education about deafness. "In those days," he said, "people looked on deafness as retardation because the people talked funny." It was his private idea that if Nancy had just been more patient, she would have gotten what she wanted.

"That would have been a sign language interpreter for Amy?" I asked.

"I think eventually the school board would have entertained the proposal from the principal of Furnace Woods school, and if the staff had been allowed to pursue this thing normally and make the recommendation, I have the feeling she would have had an interpreter by the second grade without the need for hostile engagement. I believe that. . . ." His voice dropped lower and he shook his head again. "What was taken away from the whole case was the school's view, its educationally sound view of what could be done for Amy in a mainstreamed setting. These views were taken away because of the politics in that situation. Whenever we presented a view, we had to think about what it would do to us legally."

At times, the former school principal reverted to defending the school district's position. He said that he had supported the determination to appeal Judge Broderick's decision. He was especially bitter about the Rowleys' filing of the civil suit with HEW. "If you want to determine who fired the first shot, ... this was the first shot." From Zavarella's perspective, with this action the case became a crusade sponsored by powerful national forces aligned behind the needs of all deaf children.

He was especially struck by Sue Williams' testimony that Amy did not seem to need an interpreter, at least at the time. He cited the "failure" of the test of the sign language interpreter in kindergarten. But, I asked, how much preparation did Amy and her classmates have for an interpreter to appear suddenly in their midst? Zavarella nodded and shrugged. Had the principal ever asked Amy if she wanted an interpreter?

"Oh, yes. She always said she did."

If that was the case, I continued, why wasn't another effort made to test the use of a sign language interpreter after kindergarten, in the more structured classroom settings?

"By that time, backs were up . . . the Rowleys, the board of education, the superintendent's office. I guess you might have to say there was some resistance on the part of the school because we were so conscious of a youngster growing up. It became so embroiled, all this stuff, but we never lost sight of the fact that Amy was a youngster. . . . But [in] the case that was won in the Supreme Court [it] seemed that it was the institution against the child, and that's alien to those of us who work every day with children. We were forced into that position."

And if the case had not come up when it did, but did come up now, I asked, would it come out differently?

"I really believe that it would. . . . You've got to appreciate the fact that we're talking 1975 here, when [Public Law] 94–142 was enacted. Having been enacted, it now had to sift down through the state education departments and eventually down through their bureaucracies to the grass roots at every school. That took five years. In the midst of all that we were dealing with the *Rowley* case . . . ."

"Sure, a sign language interpreter would have been helpful," he continued. "But is it cost effective? Is it money that makes people reach that kind of decision? Yes and no. Every issue has a dollar sign attached to it. . . . It was always my contention that we were delivering Amy Rowley an appropriate education. Was it the best education possible? Probably not, but you could say that about any kid in the district."

Zavarella paused: "I have to say that I always thought I was the Rowleys' friend. There was an adversarial relationship, but we never had any angry words. Cliff and I parted as friends, I think. I've tried to search through my behavior during those six years, and I can say with confidence that my intent was to do what was good for the kid. The parents . . . I don't think they actually hated me, but they did see me as a genuine obstacle to their goal."

"And as someone who would not necessarily be consistent at all times?"

"OK. That was politics working—I can say that in retrospect. Consistency was hard because I was being torn between the needs of these parents and that kid and the needs of the school board and the super saying you will do it this way. Nobody issued orders. No one ever said, 'Joe, you will do it this way.'"

"Was there no occasion when that was said?"

"That was said, for example in, 'We will do what Judge Broderick's decision says and nothing more. If it's interpretive, we will err in favor of the conservative side.'"

"That is, not doing it?"

"Right. The reason was we couldn't commit to anything that would present itself later. It was known at that time that we would appeal the case."

"And this was right after the decision came down? There was never any question about an appeal?"

"Yes. In fact, I believe the decision was made before Judge Broderick's decision came down. If the decision went against the district, they were discussing an appeal to the Supreme Court even then."

"By 'they,' you mean Eible, Kuntz, and the board of education?"

"Right. Again, the legal view was very much at work here."

9

What Amy Hears

At age twenty, already a sturdy young man, Jimmy Walcott finished high school in Charlotte, North Carolina. The school gave him a certificate saying that he had completed twelve years of public education. His reading skills were at second-, possibly third-grade level. His math skills were closer to first- or second-grade levels. His comprehension, when he paid attention, extended just beyond that of a first- or second-grader.

His foster parents, Wayne and Donna Walcott, had a hard time accepting all this. They had his I.Q. tested twice and it was right at 100. Yet for all the efforts educators had made and for all of his foster parents' considerable efforts at home, here was a young man who began adding rather than subtracting his checks when his account reached zero—and became angry when his mistake was explained to him. He had an American Sign Language style that might employ a series of nouns first followed by a string of verbs, followed by any stray conjunctions left about, so that one could never be sure whether he was describing something that had happened, was happening, could happen, or merely something he had seen on television.

This was not what the Walcotts had hoped for when they took Jimmy out of the North Carolina School for the Deaf in Morganton, where he had been diagnosed as having a learning disability, put in a class of multihandicapped kids, some of whom had mental deficiencies, and was not pushed to learn at all, in their opinion. Jimmy had two dedicated teachers in Charlotte, and it turned out that he did not have a learning disability, but the

182

teachers still warned the Walcotts not to expect much. Jimmy made no progress in learning to speak and seemed to see no point in making the effort. He had no sense of planning even from hour to hour; to him, life sprang anew moment by moment, and he did what he wanted to do and expected others to support him in whatever that entailed.

But Jimmy wanted that certificate from high school. His foster parents explained that it would say only that he had been through twelve years of public education, but he had been told that he would wear a cap and gown just like the other kids, and Jimmy wanted to do that. After his public schooling, the Walcotts found him a place in a group home for young, deaf people who were taught life skills—meal planning, shopping, cooking, banking, bill-paying—and worked at Goodwill Industries to learn trades. Jimmy couldn't abide the rules there any more than he could at home, where he had clashed with the Walcotts' younger biological sons, Eric and Corey, who eventually tired of his throwing his dirty clothes to them to put in the washing machine. Jimmy was expelled from the group home and ended up back at the Walcotts', where he got a job bagging groceries in a food store, opened a checking account, wore out one car, and, when the Walcotts got him another, paid Wayne $40 faithfully every month. The Walcotts thought at last the concept of responsibility had taken hold.

But Jimmy's bossy, domineering ways around the house continued to be an irritant and he fell in with some young men who drank. When he started coming home drunk, the Walcotts told him that, much as they regretted it, he would have to move out. By this time, he had become openly belligerent with them, and his anger seemed a breathing thing, lying just below the surface of his normal sociability and ready to spring forth. They found him a trailer located within walking distance of the grocery store, but he soon lost his job because he wouldn't work when he didn't feel like it. If his parents gave him money, it usually went for liquor. So they brought him groceries even though they thought it demeaning to him. Jimmy started drawing Social Security Income (ssi) benefits but sometimes didn't show up to collect them. One day the trailer was boarded up and Jimmy was gone.

Since then, in the summer he has lived mostly outdoors. When the weather turns cold, he goes back to his foster parents' home, and they take him in and listen to his stories. He had been employed at a skyscraper going up, and he was the worker who walked far out on the edge of the building with nothing on either side of him but a deadly drop. Or a construction boss had been teaching him to operate a crane. He had been in jail with two other youths who had stolen a car—he would never steal a car but he went along with them. They had driven to Washington, California, Hawaii, and back through Georgia—all in four days. And so on.

Jimmy has run through a series of jobs the Walcotts found for him, the most promising of which was as a carpenter's apprentice. He had natural aptitude for the job and delighted in it at first. The Walcotts tried to get through to him that he had the skills to be a full-fledged, professional carpenter, if he would just apply himself and, please, stick to it. But soon he was unemployed again.

Now when the Walcott family is together on holidays with their college-age sons, they all talk about the different foster children they have had in their home. The conversation always turns to Jimmy because he stayed much longer than the others. Wayne does not think anything will change for Jimmy. Donna refuses to give up, but her hopes are not high. "Everything with him," she says, "is someone else's fault."

"I wish it had been different," Wayne says. "I wish Jimmy would have succeeded. I wish I could look back and say that we took this little kid off the streets and gave him a break in life, sure I wish that. We can't do that but at the same time we can't dismiss the fact that he lived in this house all the time as our son, he still is that. We still all hug each other when he comes home. He still cries in our arms and he still wants our sympathy and wants us to relive his exploits, however wild they may be."

Sometimes the Walcotts talk about Morganton. What if they had left him there? What if they had let that be the central experience of Jimmy's learning life? Would it have made a difference? They had thought he was only being warehoused there, but, Wayne now says, "Anything that Jimmy could have got that could have given him some society and cultural values, a set of mores that he doesn't have now, would have put him in a better position. Anything that would have left him less angry with the world. Morganton might have come closer to giving him that than our house, where he could come and go." And Wayne no longer is sure that the kind of deafness Jimmy experienced isn't responsible for his situation today. "It's true," Wayne says, "responsibility, the work ethic, those are concepts, too, and they have to be developed out of language Jimmy doesn't have. So maybe it does come back to his being deaf and being cut off from school and parental support so early."

Frank Bowe, the teacher and author, who is deaf, had the parental support Jimmy lacked and a good home and relatively happy childhood as well.

But in his book, *Changing the Rules,* he tells how soon the deaf child's hearing parents, siblings, even friends begin to talk with him or her only when necessary.* And because the deaf child in a hearing family is communicated with so little, she or he learns words at a rate alarmingly short of that of hearing children. Where lipreading is most overrated, Bowe writes, is in school, when so many words—so many concepts—are new for all the children. New words are mysterious on the teacher's lips, no matter how careful the teacher may be. As I read that, I thought of the sign language interpreter Fran Miller explaining to Amy the difference between "witch" and "which."

For Bowe, the third grade was a shattering experience. He could not believe the third-grade reader he was given by a trusted teacher. He didn't know the words in the stories. He had to confess this to his teacher, who told him with sorrow that the average hearing child in the third grade has a vocabulary of thirty thousand words and is picking up about thirty-five new words every day of the week, most of them outside the classroom. Bowe's only hope was to bury himself in the library and read voraciously, far longer than any of this hearing friends would consider doing. Even with this effort, Bowe's progress through elementary school was a fierce struggle for academic survival. He missed most of what was said in the classroom, despite strong lipreading efforts. He stopped asking questions for fear of exposing his ignorance of what had been going on. Instead, he captured the teacher at every break and asked for help.

In the library one day, he discovered the signs that the deaf use to converse in a Boy Scout manual. Thrilled, he ran home to his mother with the news. She was petrified. He would have to speak with his father. When he did, this otherwise generous-spirited, supportive man informed him that every doctor they had visited had told them, above all else, not to let their son learn sign language. If he did, these doctors assured the Bowes, the boy would never learn to speak. He would only be able to converse with others who used "that hand language." Reluctantly, young Frank returned the Scout manual to the library.

By the seventh grade, he was dealing with a half-dozen teachers every day, some of them extremely difficult to keep up with, as they read far too swiftly from notes, or looked away from the class, or had—as one did—a mustache, a tiny mouth, and bad teeth and could not be lip-read successfully even under the best of conditions. Somehow, working twice as hard

* Silver Spring, Md.: T.J. Publishers, 1986, chapter 7.

as the others, Frank Bowe made it through school, on to Western Maryland University, and then to Gallaudet University in a master's program. There he learned sign language and experienced what Nancy Rowley had experienced at that same school—a mind-expanding, thrilling new vista of possibilities. For the first time in his life, he knew what conversation was and could take part in it.

—

These three people, as different as they can be, still represent a kind of spectrum of education for deaf children: Jimmy Walcott, a neglected child of hearing parents, whose crucial early years were lost; Frank Bowe, a highly intelligent child of supportive hearing parents who were discouraged by experts from making sign language available to their son; and Amy Rowley, a child of supportive, deaf signing and speaking parents, capable of learning in a situation fully integrated with hearing classmates. What was the explanation? How was it that deaf children of deaf parents with sign language performed so well? Or, to put it differently, what great advantage did they have over other deaf children?

Fortunately, there are studies and books that are helpful in answering this question to the extent it can be answered. One such source is *They Grow in Silence: Understanding Deaf Children and Adults* by McKay Vernon and Eugene D. Mindel.* The authors conducted extensive tests of deaf children from hearing and from deaf households and reached conclusions:

"Among all the students tested from both hearing and deaf households, we found a strong relationship between ability to understand signing in the context of either signed English or ASL and ability to read. Thus, the greater the student's comprehension ability in either signed English or ASL, the greater his or her reading comprehension. We previously found that students who received no sign input at home were unlikely to develop above average sign comprehension skills in comparison to their age-matched peers. It follows that these same student were also unlikely to develop excellent reading skills." The authors had some special observations for children brought up with signing. "If the parent of a deaf child is also deaf, the language of choice usually is ASL. Upon entering school, this child will have to learn either another pedagogical sign system or oral language, as pure ASL is not usually used for instruction." This was why Clifford and Nancy

* Silver Spring, Md.: National Association of the Deaf, pp. 94–95.

had made sure that Amy had signed English, which literally translates English words into signs, rather than ASL, which has its own structure and syntax. They knew she would learn ASL from them and from other deaf friends as well.

Understanding this helped me to account for Amy's performance in school, but I still didn't know how many deaf children were in schools for the deaf, how many were mainstreamed in public schools, and how many of the latter had sign language interpreters. For these data, I went to the Center for Assessment and Demographic Studies at Gallaudet University. Arthur Schildroth, an amiable and patient man, a researcher there, and author of books on deaf education, was my guide through the maze of numbers available. While the center's annual survey of hearing impaired students' participation in education is voluntary, Schildroth is convinced that the 60 percent response is representative of the state of deaf education today.

For the 1989–90 school year, the survey turned up 47,973 hearing-impaired children, of whom *26,788* were deaf (hearing loss of 70 decibels or more in either ear).

Of these 26,788 deaf children, 12,144 were in residential and day schools for the deaf, and *14,514* (54 percent) were in "local" schools, heavily public systems, but including some private schools with hearing pupils.

Of these 14,514 "mainstreamed" students, *8,587* (65 percent) were actually attending one academic class or more with hearing students.

And of these 8,587 students attending one or more academic classes with hearing students, *5,535* (64 percent) were receiving the services of a sign language interpreter or had a teacher who used signs. The rest included small numbers using cued speech or oral interpreters, and *2,639* (31 percent) using no interpreter and learning in a strictly oral setting.

Amy was at the very top of the top-level group of 8,587 deaf students attending one or more academic classes with hearing students, those who were mainstreamed in *all* academic classes with hearing children. This was a category not used in the survey, but one that surely represents a small percentage of all deaf children being educated today—let alone years past when Amy went through public school.

While the numbers of children utilizing sign language in all schools have increased, the numbers of deaf children integrated into public schools has increased more dramatically. Between 1960 and 1990, for instance, the ratio of deaf children educated in public schools rather than schools for the deaf has reversed from roughly 30:70 percent to 70:30 percent. For all of this movement away from the exclusionism of strict oralism, it is important to remember that the number of deaf children utilizing sign language interpreters in public schools *for one or more academic classes,* by these figures, is still only 21 percent of the total of deaf children receiving special education today—one child in five. Fifteen years after Amy's entrance into public school in Westchester County, New York, a deaf child capable of being integrated into *all* academic classes and able to use a sign language interpreter—in effect, an intellectually apt and fully bilingual deaf child—remains in a small minority.

The large majority of deaf children fall between the levels represented by Amy and Jimmy, with the average far closer to the latter than the former in terms of prospects for learning. In their book *Can't Your Child Hear?* Roger D. Freeman, Clifton F. Carbin, and Robert J. Boese note that educationally, the majority of deaf high school graduates, despite average intelligence, have a reading level comparable to a nine- or ten-year-old child.* The idea implanted by the school district, and stressed by attorney Raymond Kuntz in his Supreme Court argument, that Amy's was not an unusual case and that she was a typical deaf child, was incorrect. Taras Denis' court statement that Amy was one of the "rare ones" who could profit from a sign language interpreter in her classroom is much more accurate.

———

Mountain Lakes, an old, up-scale suburb ambling around a series of lakes in northern New Jersey, northwest of Montclair, was to the Rowleys a garden of limitless prospect. Their new home on a wooded lane with the fairy-tale name of Rainbow Trail dropped down from the hilly road with enough depth for the pond framing their backyard below. Clifford, good with his hands, could imagine a deck overlooking this yard and a garage for the cars and his woodworking tools. Clifford had hated leaving Croton far more than he ever let himself express; he had grown up there and his sense of home there was lifelong. But in Mountain Lakes he was actually closer to his job as a chemical engineer for Lonza, Inc., 45 miles away in New Jersey. And the children and Nancy—everyone would be better off.

Nancy felt the pressure on her ebbing away until, one day, she realized how much of it she had dealt with over the years. She was bitter at first about the money the family had to pay the school district from the sale of

———

* Austin, Tex.: Pro-Ed Publishers, 1981, p. 16.

their Peekskill house for Supreme Court costs, a matter of injustice being compounded by further injustice in the family's reckoning. But she could not deny that over the years the battle had depleted her store of energy and optimism. It was good to have it behind her and, yes, at a geographical distance as well. Then, there was the matter of the children, where the change was dramatic enough to be perceived daily.

John had secretly welcomed the flight from Peekskill, where misery had led to more misery at every turn. But he had not fully apprehended the depth of the change beforehand. He had been prepared to fight, waiting for the first slur with fists screwed tight to his side. These new classmates not only didn't know about the court case, but wouldn't care about it if they did. And—miracle of miracles—they were scarcely interested in the fact that he had a deaf family. John picked up quickly on the fact that Lake Drive School, a part of the Mountain Lakes public school system, was for deaf children, with full resources for teaching them. Deaf children came from all over New Jersey to attend Lake Drive; deafness in Mountain Lakes was no big deal.

Amy sorrowed over the loss of her old friends, but lingering in the past was not part of her nature. She was assigned to Briarcliff Middle School, where she was one of a handful of the approximately sixty deaf children from Lake Drive to be accepted for full integration into academic classes. She showed up cheerfully for psychological testing, which determined that she was cooperative, self-confident, expressive, and had an I.Q. near the middle of the superior range of intelligence—124 on the Performance Scale being regarded as more indicative than 112 on the Verbal Scale, given her handicap.

To his recitation of Amy's I.Q. scores, the Mountain Lakes school psychologist added, in a school memorandum, a couple of notes. Despite her avid reading and gifted writing skills, Amy's vocabulary was only average, well below the level that would be expected of a hearing child with her intellectual capacity, particularly as her memory and attention were excellent. She had simply not processed the same number of words the hearing pupils had. The second note had to do with mathematics, which pulled down her score because of the extra time she needed to do problems and because of difficulties she had with fractions.

Under "Conclusions," the school psychologist wrote: "Amy is an eleven and one-half year-old girl of superior intelligence, who has an endogenous hearing impairment. Even though she is equipped with hearing aids, her registration of sound and speech does not approximate that of a physically normal youngster. Hence, even under optimal conditions it is necessary to repeat words, phrases, and sentences partly because she does not adequately distinguish what she hears and partly because she is not sure what she hears is correct. This condition of uncertainty exists in a face-to-face situation and is amplified in a group setting." The psychologist recommended further tests to see if she would benefit from a sign language interpreter and such tests were forthcoming. Results mirrored those from Grasslands in Westchester County. After three months, she received sign language interpretation in all classes, a note-taker (a student who customarily took the most complete notes, so that Amy could concentrate on what was being said without having to look down to write), and speech therapy and auditory training as well. She also had a tutor to help with math.

One of her classmates in the sixth grade was Emily Shannon, an alert, inquisitive girl who already had one deaf friend, Veronica "Roni" Lepore. Roni did not speak as well as Amy, but Emily had begun to pick up sign language from her. When Emily met Amy, she started to expand her knowledge of sign language, and she and another hearing friend who was also in the fifth grade, Margaret Higgs, began to talk with one another in sign language as well. Soon, their fascinated classmates began to pick up words here and there. Then Amy would come along and teach them some more. Margaret Higgs got a TTY from supportive parents to be able to communicate with her deaf friends and had captions on her television set for them, too.

Emily was delighted to learn that American Sign Language was far more than a collection of word symbols. She found it a real language, just like the French she was learning, with a full-fledged syntax and all the various tenses and moods languages have. She thought signing was pure beauty and marveled, as other friends had before, at Amy's energy level.

Emily also observed that some of the other students showed prejudice toward Amy. They would mouth meaningless words to confuse her. That angered Emily, who thought Amy was just like any of them except with a different language. Emily couldn't imagine how Amy had gotten on without an interpreter. Emily didn't find that any students were distracted by the interpreter in their classes. She noted, though, that Amy was not above using the interpreter as an excuse once in a while when she failed to do a homework assignment on time. "I didn't get that from my interpreter," Amy would tell her teacher, wide-eyed, and Emily and Amy would think it was funny, but Amy did get the assigned work done, usually by the next day, anyway.

All was not harmonious for Amy as a student, however. Her math problems were sticky enough so that her math teacher worked with her one-on-one. Then, Richard "Rich" Morgan, who was on Amy's child study committee when she arrived in Mountain Lakes and later taught her science in the eighth grade, observed that as bright and cooperative as Amy was, she was hurting herself with absences from his class. As much as she tried to make up for these absences—which were chalked up to "stomach problems," which he translated as stress—she was disappointed not to be able to take honors biology largely on that account.

But Morgan was not surprised when Amy began to do better. His first impression, walking around Briarcliff with her and her parents, had been that she was overcompensating with wit for her nervousness. Usually, new, young students, particularly girls, were quiet, even a little timid. Here was this very bright little girl strung tight as a violin string. He figured she would take time to ease into the routine of the new school and that her competitiveness would give her stressful moments. He worried, too, about John, but discovered soon that if you sat down with this lad and quietly explained things, got his assent to something on the basis that it was reasonable, he would do whatever he had agreed to do without further complaint.

Rich Morgan had grown up in Pennsylvania, the son of a steelworker; neither parent had gone beyond high school. He was asked to tutor a friend who was in an iron lung and couldn't attend classes, and this early experience in teaching through a disability lingered in his mind. He got his bachelor's in science and his master's in guidance, counseling, and administration. He and his young wife came to Mountain Lakes, where he found himself well suited to teaching and particularly to his work on the child study committee, which was responsible for the testing and placement of special education students.

He watched with pleasure as Amy blossomed after her early attendance problems. To his mind, her exceling on the field hockey team was a turning point—from then on she felt that she belonged. One could tell in walking through the halls which students were fitting in and feeling good about themselves. There was Amy, giggling with friends all about her. He was delighted with Amy's obvious respect for her parents and found between Amy and John a bond that was stronger than most he had seen between brother and sister. His experience with children with disabilities was limited. He had taught a deaf child briefly, as a substitute teacher, and discovered that he had to repeat a great deal in science, where words new to students tumbled out of the textbook like nasty surprises, page after page. He wondered how deaf children could learn at all without interpreters.

What most interested him was the process he came to think of as enrichment: not so much Amy's enrichment, which he never doubted, but his own as well as that of the entire class. Having to teach "different" children—two other hearing-impaired children were in his science class—meant that one had to stretch one's skills, and that was a learning experience for the teacher. He noted that while the interpreters had no special duty or assignment with hearing children, they served as accompanists for the teacher, another pair of eyes and hands ready to help out in dozens of small ways. Most important, he watched somewhat bemused as signing bloomed as a kind of language planted row by row in his classroom. Margaret Higgs was flat-out good; even the interpreters' noses were out of joint over her. Others began to sign. Sometimes at the end of class conversations were going on that eluded him, and he walked out of the classroom grinning sheepishly.

One day an interpreter took sick and was absent. Morgan felt a moment's panic when he discovered this, but his educational instincts took over. He enlisted the best signers on his behalf, simplified the day's lesson a little, and used the hearing students who could sign to help teach the hearing-impaired members of the class. In the midst of all this happy, noisy brew and in the buzzing fascination of the students with what was going on, Morgan had an apocalyptic moment as a teacher. He shook his head years later trying to describe the memorable dazzle of it. "There are these moments," he said, "in teaching, and they don't happen very often, when you know you are *doing* it."

For Amy, the experience of learning with deaf as well as hearing children was critically important. She hit it off immediately with Veronica Lepore, and they went ice skating and to sleep-overs and movies together. Roni's path to an integrated classroom with hearing students was very different from Amy's. She had started out in an oral school in Cincinnati, was still being taught orally when the family moved to Illinois, and entered Lake Drive School when the family moved to Rockaway, New Jersey. She was integrated into a number of mainstreamed classes with hearing children in the sixth grade and there met Amy. But Roni was in a class of four, all deaf, for English, the result—her mother was convinced—of a slow start in oral education without sign language.

When the family had moved to Illinois, her mother began to learn sign language. "We have four children," she said. "I saw that the kids weren't communicating with each other. Illinois is a total communications state. That's when I started learning sign language. And all the kids learned it." Asked whether her conversion to total communications was a difficult one, Roni's mother shrugged, "It's all part of accepting it." She paused. "I think it comes from that process of burying that child you thought you were going to have and accepting the child you now have and realizing that you have to take that child and bring him to the highest goals and use the child's way. It's letting go of who you are and letting the child lead you. That's the part that's really hard. It's scary."

For her part, Roni's friend, Margaret Higgs, was becoming more deeply involved in the world of the deaf every day. Signing was so natural to her that her mother thought she was more comfortable with it than with her native English. Margaret began sitting with Roni at lunch and, as her skills increased, she began translating for her friend. As the girls spent more time with each other, as they went on trips and even vacations together, the tie between them bound more tightly. The trouble was, Margaret thought, that Roni was greedy for knowing; she wanted Margaret to translate everything, to make sense of the entire bumble of voices around her. That wasn't in Margaret's power, and she began to resent the burden secretly. Why couldn't Roni see that she was asking too much?

What saved the friendship for Margaret was her involvement with Roni, during high school years, in the Northwest Jersey Association for the Deaf. Here was the other side of the wall whose existence Margaret had recognized before only intellectually, never emotionally. Here she, not Roni, was the stranger. Here she was dependent upon her friend as Roni had been upon her. The reversal of roles was healthy, even curative, both girls felt. And the world of deafness burst upon Margaret with the splendor of the discovery of a new civilization. These people were so expressive, so completely open. She felt a thrill when someone asked her if she were deaf or hearing. The question was signed with an accompanying "it-doesn't-matter-but-I-was-curious," and it meant acceptance at a level Margaret was just beginning to dream might be possible. What was happening affected Margaret's family. When they took vacations, they visited deaf schools—in Montana and China, for example—the way other people visited museums.

Somewhere around this time, it occurred to Margaret Higgs that she had chosen a career without knowing it, without even considering it in quite that way. After high school, she got her quality assurance certification as a sign language interpreter from the State of Florida and broke the news to her parents. She wanted to go into deaf education and after that teach either in a school for the deaf or in a mainstreamed public school situation. Her father was not thrilled. Her mother said, in effect, "If it's for you, go for it."

When I caught up with Margaret, she was at Flagler College in St. Augustine, Florida, a freshman, with a sixteen-hour-a-week academic load and an additional eleven hours of sign language interpreting in the classroom. It was a heavy load. When I asked her if it was easy living on both sides of the wall, she responded, "In school, I was accepted fully as hearing, and at the Northwest Jersey Association for the Deaf, I was accepted fully by the deaf and it didn't matter whether I was hearing or not; but when you mix the two worlds it becomes complicated." Searching for a way of describing it, she came up with this, "For instance, the jokes of hearing people are plays on words, sometimes double meanings, while the jokes of deaf people are plays on visual experience. We laugh at hearing jokes and they laugh at deaf jokes."

I wondered what Nancy Rowley had meant, for she had said it more than once, "I would like for you to hear what Amy hears." To hear what a deaf person hears. Ah, I thought, playing with the words that deaf people use to distinguish, here what I was hearing fell sadly short of understanding. What could Nancy be thinking about? I asked her one day over the TTY.

She had a classmate at Gallaudet who went on to become a well-known audiologist. Somewhere she had heard that if you had an audiogram of a deaf person, you might construct a recording of what that person actually could hear with and without amplification. She had the telephone number of Dr. Jerry L. Northern, whom she had not seen in years, at the University of Colorado School of Medicine. He knew, she thought, little or nothing about Amy or about the court case.

Jerry Northern turned out to be, first of all, a hearing educator with a great deal of experience with the deaf. He had been raised in Denver by deaf grandparents, both Gallaudet graduates, and consequently signed fluently from an early age. Both his father and an aunt had spent their lives educating the deaf and Northern's own major at Gallaudet was deaf education. He decided that to pursue it professionally would be too much like the life he had experienced in the past. Instead, he became an audiologist. In 1974, he and Marion P. Downs published the first textbook in pediatric audiology, in its fourth edition at the time I talked with him.* He reported to me with obvious pride that his hearing daughter was also studying education of the deaf.

He had lost touch with the Rowleys and was unaware of Amy's situation or even details of the Supreme Court decision. But he did know of a laboratory that might be able to reconstruct auditorially the level at which Amy could hear. He asked for an audiogram, and I sent him copies of all the audiograms in my possession, including the last one, which had been done at the request of Furnace Woods school, by an audiologist in Spring Valley, New York, in October 1982. After examining them all, he thought that one would be the best to use, particularly as it was done with and without a hearing aid. Looking at the audiograms, he told me, "Here's a kid with a really considerable hearing loss."

I decided to check out a perception, based on what he had just said. That being the case, I asked him, what is one to make of the evidence presented by various school people at Furnace Woods that, wearing hearing aids, Amy had been known to turn around in response to her name being called from behind. He chuckled over the phone. "Ah," he said, "that nice, fat vowel sound. She would hear a hard AAAAAA."

What about another assertion, then, that the school's witnesses had put forth, that Amy was lucky because she had her best residual hearing at the lower frequencies, where the vowel sounds were. She could—so they said— hear the vowels and lip-read the consonants. "Theoretically, that's right," he said. "You make the consonant sounds with your teeth, lips, visibly, whereas the vowel sounds are made from the throat, deep back, where they cannot be seen. But the truth is that Amy's audiograms do not sustain that she could get that much out of any 'residual' hearing she had. Given the audiograms, you would have to say that, even if she had a 160 I.Q., she would have been struggling to understand."

Was this a rebuttal of the ability the school thought she had to use her residual hearing at the lower frequencies, I wondered. "Again, I'm looking at these audiograms," Northern said. "Frequency levels for human speech range from about 500 to 3,000 cycles. When they talk about Amy's residual hearing in the lower frequencies, they are talking about 125 to 150 cycles, well below the 500-cycle lower limit of most human conversation. Even if Amy's hearing went up to 750–1,000 cycles, she would still be missing a great deal of conversation that starts at around 1,500 cycles."

* *Hearing in Children* (Baltimore: Williams & Wilkins, 1974).

I thought of Michael Chatoff's challenge–question to Dr. Ann Mull-holland on the stand in district court about whether Amy's residual hearing was not at a level below where human conversation took place, and Mullholland's convoluted and unresponsive answer. Chatoff later became fond of attacking this presumption publicly by observing that if the school had hired a dog to bark rather than a teacher to speak, Amy might have used her residual hearing at the lower levels effectively.

What, then, of reports from teachers in the school that she "understood" what was going on? From his classroom experience in days after Gallaudet, what did he make of that? "Some can get, with assistance, the nuts and bolts of what the teacher has said. They miss—without a sign language interpreter—the machinery as a whole. They miss the vitality of the class, what's going on around them, and the exchanges between teacher and other students, students and other students. It's like putting a one-legged runner in a race with other runners and expecting him to keep up. No way can he keep up. If he gets farther and farther behind, which is what can happen from grade to grade, he can finally lose heart."

He had promised to send me a copy of the letter he got from the Starkey Laboratory in Minneapolis, where the cassette of Amy's hearing was being made. The letter arrived, written by Dr. Jeremy Agnew, director of the firm's product development. Dr. Agnew also spoke of Amy's "large audiometric loss" and noted with regret that it would not be possible for the laboratory to approximate the additional "unpredictable cochlear distortions present in sensoneural hearing loss." I asked Northern about that. He described the distortions as a kind of heavy static that the deaf have to deal with along with any sounds they hear, aided or unaided. The cassette product would thus be better than anything Amy actually could hear, he noted.

The tape was made with three recordings, each with a preceding announcement of what it would be. First a man's voice read a message of about a paragraph in length at a volume that would have sufficed to reach a classroom of hearing individuals. Then that same message, read at the same volume, was reproduced as Amy would hear it without her hearing aids. Finally, it was reproduced as she would hear it with her hearing aids.

I telephoned Northern after each of us had had a chance to listen to our copies of the recording. We agreed that in the recording approximating what Amy would get with hearing aids, it was possible to make out some of the words, although not all the sense of what was being said, at a distance of six feet or so—my wife and I had measured out the distance in our living room. But at eight feet, very little was distinguishable. Then Northern talked for a few minutes about the radical difference between what Amy got with the hearing aids and without them.

Again, we agreed, but I could not tell him the feeling that I had, nor could I begin to describe the look that had passed between my wife and me when we had listened to what Amy heard without her hearing aids. After the message had been read first by the male voice at normal volume, we heard the announcer saying that next we would hear what Amy heard without her hearing aids. We waited, six feet away from the machine, through what seemed like long moments, although it could not have been more than a matter of seconds. It was only when the announcer's voice came on again to say that the next reading would be what Amy heard *with* her hearing aids that we realized that, unwittingly, we had gotten the message. Without her hearing aids at that distance, Amy heard nothing. The silence was pure, unbroken by the least sound. Only by pressing our ears to the machine on the replay could we distinguish a sound, and it was a voice without words, as of a hummingbird buzzing softly outside an open window on a summer evening.

10

A Matter of Growth

I had Judge Walter Mansfield on my list of prospective interviewees but before I could call him he died, in 1987. Three years later, I decided to track down what I could about the judge through his law clerk. That call led to others. Everybody was friendly and helpful and I found myself learning a little about a man highly admired by many, including Judge Vincent Broderick, the district court judge in *Rowley*, whose opinion Judge Mansfield had dissented with so vigorously and, I thought, with something curiously approaching passion.

The son of a former mayor of Boston, Mansfield had an interesting career, having been plucked from regular Marine service during World War II by Major General William J. "Wild Bill" Donovan, for whose law firm he had worked in civilian life. The general headed the Office of Strategic Services (OSS) and had some nervy reconnaissance in mind for young Mansfield, who was parachuted behind German lines to work with guerrilla forces in Yugoslavia. Later, Mansfield jumped behind Japanese lines to assist General Chiang Kai-shek in China. After Mansfield's death, a diary he kept of his experiences in these ventures was found and transcribed by his longtime secretary, who said that the writing was infinitesimally small, as though the major had feared he would surely run out of paper.

Although a Republican, Mansfield was appointed by President Lyndon Johnson to the district court bench in 1966. One of his most famous decisions held that McSorley's Old Ale House, on East 7th Street in New York

City, a 116-year-old, much-celebrated tavern, could not continue to exclude women. In 1971, he was elevated to the court of appeals for the Second District of New York. When he died, by-then Chief Justice William Rehnquist sent his widow a copy of the resolution of the Judicial Conference of the United States commemorating his faithful and outstanding service. Appended to that note is a handwritten postscript in which the chief justice recalled an enjoyable boat trip on Lake Washington in Seattle with the judge and his wife in August 1984, on the occasion of Mansfield's address to the Ninth Circuit Judicial Conference.

When Judge Mansfield's widow, Tina, first met him, she thought it odd that the judge regularly wore half-glasses, the type usually associated with reading. Then she discovered that they were attached to a hearing aid. But nothing about the judge suggested to her that he was denying this disability. To the contrary, his associates agree, he didn't hide it, didn't stress it, and was capable of making sport of it. His widow remembers him snatching off his glasses in the middle of a tennis game and saying, "Can't see and can't hear."

One of his law clerks at the time of the *Rowley* case, Los Angeles attorney Rob Knauss, remembers Judge Mansfield as being a laid-back man, easy to work for, a courteous gentleman of the old school, but also capable of sternness, as "someone who was raised in the Depression and felt everyone had to make his way." Knauss recalls having to make some noise on entering the judge's office when he was working so that the judge could put his hearing aid back in his ear. He tells a story about having to confront the judge about an employee in the office who was giving everyone grief. The judge listened politely and lectured him gently about the hard life this person had led. Besides, the judge added, "When she gets to be too much, I turn off my hearing aid."

Rob Knauss didn't remember the *Rowley* case when I first reached him by phone in Los Angeles. When I sent him a transcript of the oral hearing and the judge's opinion, he decided that this was one the judge had probably written himself. "He wrote strong opinions," Knauss recalled, noting that several of them had gone up to the Supreme Court. All he remembered from the day of the oral argument—after rereading the transcript—was that he thought Chatoff was taking the position that the parents were the primary authority on educating the child with a disability, and that was wrong. The year following the appellate court's decision, Knauss was clerking for then-Justice Rehnquist of the Supreme Court.

The Mansfields' next-door neighbor in New Canaan, Connecticut, happened to be an audiologist, a longtime friend of Mrs. Mansfield's, Dr. Patricia Bollard, then associate director of the Rockland County Center for the Physically Handicapped. The judge looked to Bollard for advice on his hearing loss. She talked with him and then sent him to the Monzon brothers in New York City, Mario and Robert. Mario was the businessman and technician, and Robert was an audiologist. From 1977 on, they gave the judge advice, tested his hearing, sent him hearing aids, and later, in 1985, developed a system for his courtroom that made it possible for him to understand more of what was said there.

Mario Monzon became the judge's friend as well as someone to whom he looked for advice. The judge dropped in on Mario on 42nd Street before going to his chambers downtown. The two would discuss problems of hearing loss and deafness. At first the judge deeply feared losing his hearing completely. With the benefit of brother Robert's audiograms, Mario Monzon was able to assure him teasingly that he would still be hearing at a hundred and ten. Monzon remembers that the judge reflected a strong conviction that people with a hearing loss should maintain their independence and not be given a crutch of any kind—that would be bad for them. Could the judge have extrapolated from that feeling about himself that giving a deaf child like Amy Rowley a sign language interpreter would be harmful for her, I asked. Monzon said he thought that was possible, although the judge never discussed the *Rowley* case with him.

At some point, Mario Monzon remembered, Judge Mansfield began to spend time at the New York League for the Hard of Hearing, down on 23rd Street in Manhattan. When I called, the league's office had no record of the judge's having been a client and the league's position in the 1970's, I was told, was no longer exclusively oral. But a number of deaf people I have talked with maintain that the league came very slowly to its acceptance of sign language. All agreed that a man like Judge Mansfield would not have been likely to have received any information about sign language or total communications from the league at that time. All agreed, too, that his contact with deaf people through those offices would have been minimal or nil.

Judge Mansfield did not discuss the *Rowley* case either with Bollard, who describes herself as "primarily an auditory-oralist," but also as someone who has contributed a chapter on total communications to a textbook—"which I wouldn't have done if I didn't believe in it." She began to change and broaden her view of communications for the deaf in 1970 when she learned firsthand how many deaf children taught with strictly oral methods spoke poorly. "They went into the world and were not understood as they had been told they would be by oralist teachers." No wonder they had developed their own language, she thought. She also began to run into deaf children who were, in her opinion, not good candidates for oralism, children from deaf families who signed well and were otherwise well-developed for communication. She remembered the *Rowley* case only vaguely and had not read the judge's opinion at the time, possibly because she did not want to have to comment on it to him. She was, however, willing to read court transcripts and the judicial opinions, which I sent her.

After reading these materials, she indicated in a letter that she did not think that his hearing loss had affected Judge Mansfield's decision, although she conceded that no one but the judge, and possibly not even he, could know that for sure. She saw him influenced favorably by the school's efforts and by the apparent failure of the kindergarten experiment with a sign language interpreter. But she made no bones about what she considered to have been Amy's needs, as indicated by the audiograms and the facts of the case brought out in Judge Broderick's court. Amy, she observed, was a bilingual child. "While a typical bilingual student," she wrote, "can ultimately obtain the language proficiency and then be able to understand 100 percent of what is being taught, the hearing-impaired bilingual or monolingual (oral) student can never understand everything that is said in the classroom. Hearing-impaired deaf students should therefore be provided a means of receiving all the information being provided by that teacher. . . . The Rowleys wanted an equal chance or equal opportunity for their child to obtain all the information presented in class and that could only have been done through total communication, an interpreter, or a voice-activated TTY, which would supply Amy with an ongoing written transcript of everything being said in class. . . . All children are entitled to an equal educational opportunity."

When I finally found Sue Williams who had moved to California, she (now calling herself Susan) was working for the Scripps Clinic and Research Foundation in a health program that, among other things, was designed to help obese people lose weight. Amy's first teacher of the deaf was willing to make the sometimes painful probe back into the past, into the world of the Rowleys and Furnace Woods school, and the impartial hearing, at which she had testified that she did not think Amy needed a classroom interpreter. She told me that she had sealed all that away in a deep, secluded part of her mind where memory might eventually have died, but that my letter—full of references to what had happened and with news about Amy and her family—had broken through and allowed it all to spill out again. Over the next weeks, in letters and phone conversations, and after study of the documents of the *Rowley* case, she told me about the Sue Williams of 1978 and what she thought had happened to that person then.

"I grew up in East Tennessee, father in the Air Force, and we traveled a lot. I did my undergraduate work at East Tennessee State, major in English. One of my older sisters had done some work with deaf students; that was right after the rubella epidemic, and I got interested in what she said about it and did my master's in special education for the hearing impaired. . . . I guess one other reason for that might be that my mother had been a hula dancer, and all the hula dancer's stories are told with the hands.

"Finished graduate work in 1968 and got married, my husband in the Army, and we went to El Paso, and in the next five–six years I had three babies and no jobs outside the house. By that time, we were living in Westchester County, and I was working with hearing-impaired kids part-time. I did some tennis instructing and met Nancy Rowley that way. I was hired to be Amy's teacher of the deaf, Amy's and two other deaf kids'. The first meeting was with Joe Zavarella and some others. They outlined what was going on, that the mother was getting pushy, although of course within her rights to look after her child, and was insisting on an interpreter, and they didn't think she [Amy] needed one. I did feel like I was getting a message from them. I was supposed to find out what was going on and come back and report. But I was very immature. I had been an abused child and I had my own troubles with my marriage at that time and was locked up in those things and couldn't see what was going on very well. Because of my childhood, I felt the need to bond with Amy, and so we would meet as often as possible and spend time [together] out of class. When I would ask her what was going on, she would always say everything was fine but of course I knew that what she didn't like was being taken out of class. . . . She was afraid of losing ground, of missing even more in class as a result of coming out with me. For me to be able to help her I had to know what she had missed, and that just happened or it didn't. I guess, thinking back on it, I was playing into their [the school district's] hands. . . . Dr. Z [Zavarella] would ask me what about this and I guess I did say that from the standpoint of the child, an interpreter didn't seem to me to be what was wanted.

"More and more my own wounded child came out. I understood her anxiety, or perhaps I translated it into my own. I had been abused and I thought I could understand her feelings of being powerless in the grip of circumstances in the world. I didn't understand about deafness. I didn't understand that the first five years leave such an imprint on our lives—especially with deaf kids—and that this was happening to Amy and she didn't really know what the effect of it was going to be. I guess, in the testimony I gave in the impartial hearing, I was being used, although at the time I thought what I said was all right.

"The long and short of it was that I was trying to make an emotional attachment with a little girl who was in some ways like the abused little girl who once was Susan Williams. I don't think I was very effective for her. Maybe better as a counselor than anything else.

"The other kid I worked with in the district was Robert Collender, and I feel as though I let him down, too, in a way. His parents were typical hearing parents and did not think well of the idea of his signing. He needed reassurance. He knew that I thought he was really talented and he needed to hear that. He called me up one time. He had had emergency surgery and he wanted to come over. I was going through the worst of my divorce. The whole thing wasn't right for me. I am afraid that he was hurt because I wouldn't meet with him then. He has a great personality, though, like his dad, and I'm not really worried about him. He'll be OK."

Several months later, Susan Williams called me from Yuma, Arizona. She had moved there to work with deaf junior high school kids. "It's all your fault," she laughed over the phone. "If you hadn't reminded me what I was supposed to be doing, I might never have gotten back to it." She was working mainly with poor, Hispanic children mainly whose parents were even more in denial of their children's deafness, she said, than most hearing parents. But it was a good group, with two to three hundred people in the deaf community. She had started up a sign language course. All in all, Susan Williams sounded happy.

Robert Collender, Williams' other deaf student in the Hendrick Hudson School District, was twenty years old when he graduated from high school and, at thirty-one, was an engineering draftsman in the Veterans Administration Center and a part-time student at Westchester Community College. He transferred to Duchess Community College and got a degree in architectural technology the next year. He still wanted to be an architect but saw the road ahead as a difficult one. He was freelancing as an architectural designer when last I talked with him.

He had good feelings about his education, but also some reservations. His years at the New York School for the Deaf had put him in touch with sign language and the deaf community, while he still maintained hearing friends in his neighborhood. But for years he struggled with English grammar, which mystified him. It was, he was sure, because of his deafness.

He still believed that his parents had done the right thing to enroll him in public school as a mainstreamed student. He had made many hearing friends and got a good education, except for English. He had one regret, he said: "I should have had a sign language interpreter in high school. I learned a lesson because I had an interpreter later in Westchester Community College, and it was easier for me."

In the nursing home where my mother lives is a young woman I will call "Alice" because I do not know her name. In her early thirties now, she was in an automobile accident when she was a teenager, and she reclines in a wheelchair, her neck in a brace, her eyes closed or slitted open. Until I was told differently, I would have guessed that she could not see. The nurses tell me she can smile and, what seems to me more remarkable, that she sometimes does.

What would I do if Alice smiled at me? The pride I once held in my communications skills has withered with hard experience. I have taken up sign language three times, once with a private tutor who left to go to another city, once later in a class of women who outdistanced me shamefully in the first two weeks, and once still later with a video tape. Somehow, the commitment to continue is not there. Michael Chatoff, who will never win an award for diplomacy as he often has occasion to say, has written, after reading an early draft of this book, that I avoid talking with deaf people. He writes of my "dislike" of deaf people, a manner of expression that depresses and angers me.

When I mention my difficulties to Elisabeth Hudson, my friend in the wheelchair, she looks at me oddly and commences a line of questioning sufficiently maddening to have pleased old Socrates himself. Why do I want to learn sign language? Why, to converse with deaf people in their language, of course. Which deaf people in particular? Well, I don't know, those I come upon in the course of writing this book. Am I not communicating easily enough with the Rowleys in person, she wonders, and do I not have a TTY and letters to communicate with others? Yes. Well, then—Elisabeth Hudson shrugs—you need to find out what you are trying to prove.

A hearing woman in Washington, D.C., fluent in sign, tells me that the way to learn is to involve oneself with a number of deaf people in one's community. Go to their meetings. Study their signing. Learn from them. I know in my heart that I will not do that. I am the kind of person who must be dragged by the heels to civic or even public interest meetings filled with strangers. Still, I know that I am conscious now of the need to make a greater effort and that this consciousness is relatively new to me. I know that I care about the Rowleys as friends and that I can smile back if Alice smiles at me, but I don't know much more than that.

I find myself in this mood, awake one night, thinking about an old colleague named W. H. "Dub" Hipps, who was in the newsroom when I arrived at the *Norfolk Virginian-Pilot* as a young reporter back in 1953. Hipps had cerebral palsy and was four-foot-something tall with a hunched back, a precarious, swaying walk, and a nasal, choked voice. He edited copy at one of the desks and rolled out to the composing room on that drunken sailor's walk. He lurched into the newsroom cussing one night, fresh from the bus station where he had bought a milkshake only to have a woman passing by drop a quarter into the cup. "Ruint a damn good milkshake," Hipps sputtered. He had, however, retrieved the quarter. On another occasion, on his way back from the bus station, someone from a crowded, passing car had hollered "Quasimodo" at him. Recounting the story in the newsroom later, Hipps commented, "Literate son of a bitch." I remember one party during those space-obsessed days of the 1950s, during which several of us had repaired in various stages of alcoholic disarray to an apartment roof with a dummy rocket, which we had told Hipps he would man on a trip to certain infinity. Hipps went along with it until close to the moment of truth when, with a gesture as commanding as he could make it, he declared, pointing to the newsroom beauty, "If I go, she goes with me."

So why was I suddenly thinking about Dub Hipps, dead these long years? Surely he was one of us, certificate to our lack of prejudice against individuals with disabilities. And yet no matter how hard I tried, I could not think of another newsroom party he had attended. He had never been to my house, nor I to his apartment. Nor had I seen him anywhere else in the young-married and bachelor digs in which we morning newspaper people—proudly alienated from the mainstream of the world by our nightlife work—kept one another awake in the hours before dawn. As far as social life was concerned in this most inwardly sociable of working-class societies, Hipps was invisible.

Prejudice against individuals with disabilities is different from the prejudices we typically bring to mind. Nobody says derogatory things about individuals with disabilities as a group. Nobody would dream of saying he "hates" them. We say we are saddened by what we see as their misfortune. We may even "pity" them, while, at the same time holding them at a safe distance, unwilling to make any effort to understand how they perceive their situation. Prejudice against individuals with disabilities takes the form of exclusion and isolation. The exclusion breeds further ignorance and, unless something happens to alter perceptions, the cycle of discriminatory behavior renews. Our "pity" saddens, mystifies, and eventually angers those for whom we hold it.

So deep below the surface of our emotional conscious are these feelings of pity and unrecognized revulsion that it is only in recent years that discrimination against individuals with disabilities has been recognized at all. Gordon Allport's classic, *The Nature of Prejudice,* first published in 1954, lists fourteen groups against whom prejudice was being practiced, and individuals with disabilities ("handicapped people" in the language of that day) are not mentioned.* It was 1980 before John Gliedman and William Roth, in their groundbreaking book, *The Unexpected Minority,* could write of "a new idea . . . that handicapped children and adults are an oppressed minority group" and of "outright prejudice against handicapped people of all ages, job discrimination against disabled adults, and well-meaning but destructive misconceptions that exaggerate the true limitations of many handicaps."†

It was the revisiting of Allport's book that helped me understand what I had done in my infamous column about the deaf protests over the film, *Voices,* in 1979. Allport wrote of the "overlapping normal curve," by which, he noted, it is possible to see that intellectual achievement of African American children, while still lower overall than that of Caucasian children, overlapped to the point where demonstrably many African American children achieved at a higher level than did many Caucasian children. The

---

* Reading, Mass.: Addison-Wesley, 1954, pp. 99–102.

† New York: Harcourt Brace Jovanovich, 1980, pp. 3, 23.

principle of the overlapping normal curve is the deadly enemy of prejudice because it demonstrates that it is not possible to think of "all" of one group as inferior to "all" of another group. Once that comfortable stanchion of prejudice is knocked loose, general discrimination against a group based on "inferiority" survives only with heavily footnoted exceptions. Eventually, it loses its appeal and power.

Reading my *Voices* column again ten years after it was written, I could see that the writer simply couldn't conceive of *any* deaf actress being as good as *any* hearing actress for the part, because he could not conceive of a real actress who also happened to be deaf. This writer saw, read, and conceived of deafness, the disability, as a defining term, sweeping away all possibility of talent. He thought that only an act of charity could result in the choice of someone deaf to play the role of a deaf person. When the deaf complained that one of their number had not been chosen for the part, he saw their anger as the irrational reaction of a mother whose tone-deaf child had not been chosen as a soloist in the school choir. It had taken the experience of writing *Seven Special Kids*, meeting the Rowleys and the other deaf people I had come to know, seeing the National Theater of the Deaf, and, perhaps, viewing the work of deaf actress Marlee Matlin as well to disabuse me of this idea.

My mother could be considered, in a sense, lucky. Regarded at the nursing home at first as a multiply disabled person to be worked around (for which read "avoided"), she is now understood to be merely one of the elders in need of communication as well as nursing care. Her attendant, Maggie Ray, an African American woman who has recently had a hip transplant, has won over the staff to her charge, and my mother has enjoyed in her life a second, late-blossoming into a figure of queenly influence, someone in her nineties revered for her simple humor and acceptance of her lot—and occasionally feared for her fiery temperament. A group of her admirers are gathered in her room one winter afternoon, we later learn, attracted by Maggie Ray's hearty laughter, to watch a scene and bewilder and delight my mother later with applause. Ray described it to us, "I mean you should have seen the looks on their faces, crowding in here. The record player going and in the middle of the floor, this old, blind white lady teaching this gimpy colored lady how to dance."

The recovered scene has to me qualities embracing the ironic as well as the divine, for in her active life, my mother had exhibited prejudice toward

African Americans that, while not unusual for the era in which she had grown up, was nevertheless a powerful force. Her attitude toward Ray sometimes embarrassed my wife and me. This woman who had been fortunate enough to have a housemaid–cook (always an African American) over the last twenty years of her life before the nursing home, was convinced that Ray was stealing clothing, including small, marginally useful articles—once even a single shoe. Ray understood that these were all the possessions left to mother in the world and empathized with her powerlessness, I think, better than we did. She withstood my mother's accusations with a pride that was stronger for the wounds inflicted on it. "I can handle it because I love her," Maggie Ray told us, "and in her way, I know she loves me."

And in her way—I never doubted that my mother did. She clung to her prejudices as though to life itself; they were, after all, a part of the past where she had place and power appropriate to her place. But in the nursing home, there was no power, for the sisters and their nurses, nurses' aides, and orderlies ruled as gently as the zephyrs of spring. In this atmosphere, mother gradually loosed her grip on the ways of the world in which she had grown to adulthood. She fretted over Ray's children, one of whom suffered terribly from sickle cell anemia, as though they were her own, and worried about how Ray could tend to them, keep working so hard at the nursing home, and still maintain her health.

Eventually, we had to let Maggie Ray move on to another patient when the money put aside for the nursing home began to run low. My mother accepted it as she accepted everything now; it happened, it could not be helped. But Ray continued to visit my mother at odd times, checking up on her, looking in for a few valuable minutes of conversation and, always, a hug. When Ray's son Mike died of sickle cell anemia a year later, Ray decided at first not to tell Mother. She told my wife and me that it might "confuse" her, but I thought that perhaps she was just having a hard time talking about it. Some months later, on one of our biweekly visits, my mother mentioned that Maggie Ray had told her about Mike's death. Mother shook her head sadly, her blind eyes filling with tears. "You know I love Maggie," she said, "and I miss her now. I miss her a lot."

It came to me that prejudice could not so easily survive the raw, human need of the nursing home. In the close, day-by-day passage of life to death, prejudice becomes old hat, an abstraction no longer relevant. Surrounded by her cadre of invisible helpers—"Now who are you, dear?" she would ask as they administered her pills or brought her water or food—mother was outliving it.

———

Looking back, Inez Janger said, in the living room of the Jangers' airy, Hastings-on-Hudson house, it was hard to tell what she actually believed in 1982 about Amy Rowley's present and future need for a sign language interpreter in her classes. One thing came through clearly to me as I listened to her talk: she knew she was not now the same person who had come to federal district court prepared to testify for the school district against the Rowleys.

"Growth," is the way she explained it, with a nod toward the kitchen, where her deaf son, Michael, was foraging for food. "I've done a lot of growing up." She still believed in the sanctity of the oral option for those who wanted it and she did not regret having brought up Michael in a strictly oral program—"although *always* with the idea that if he wanted sign language later he could have it"—but she had to think herself back to the person who sat at Raymond Kuntz' side during the first days of the hearing in Judge Broderick's courtroom.

She had observed Amy as a bright, articulate child, obviously doing well by any standards an untrained visitor might apply. She had been told and believed that the school was constantly reviewing Amy's status and would supply a sign language interpreter when one was needed, certainly by the time new information was flowing heavily from the teacher to the students. At the same time, she said, she wished she had been more aware of what the Rowleys wanted, rather than getting only the school district's version of it. "I would have loved to have seen more informational things before it got to be a court case. I don't know why it got into court. I think that we [she and Carole Blumberg, the other intended witness from Lexington] might have looked on it . . . as in some way validating oral education."

She was aware now of wishing that her son was as socially adept, verbal, and articulate as the Amy she saw, and that this might have affected her opinion of Amy's needs. She devoutly hoped that she had not come across as someone who opposed Amy's ever having an interpreter in school. She saw how well bright, deaf kids who had sign language "as a mother tongue" did. At the same time, she found it hard to believe that it is a realistic expectation for a hearing family to bring up a deaf child bilingually. "Michael has two hearing brothers. It was far more doable for all of us to try and create an environment for Michael where he could as much as possible understand what was going on around him."

As is so often the case with hearing parents, the crucial lesson for Inez Janger came from her deaf child. At seventeen, Michael attended the National Association of the Deaf convention in Chicago. Both oral and sign language interpreters were there, but Michael found the oral interpreters less than adequate. He came home talking for the first time about learning sign language. Janger scrambled about but couldn't find a course in the evenings that summer while Michael was working during the day. Then he took a year off from his coursework at Brown University to work in Washington, serving, among other things, as an intern for Senator Edward Kennedy's Select Committee on Education.

Michael was headed for Brown the next month on the August day I dropped in to visit the Jangers, and he expressed confidence that he would be able to get a sign language course once he got to Providence. I asked him exactly why he felt that he needed such a course, and he said that he could not converse with his deaf friends any other way. He could lip-read his hearing friends pretty well, but that was out of the question with his deaf friends. He felt cut off from them and that was bad.

Janger understood. She was serving on the board of the Alexander Graham Bell Association for the Deaf and was involved in that organization's efforts to preserve deaf children's rights to the oral option. At meetings, there were oral deaf people she had severe difficulty understanding. She had often thought it would go much better if she signed. "I feel bad about that. Do I feel bad enough to learn how to sign? I guess not."

On the other hand, if it came down to a need that was closer to home, she might feel differently. At the time we spoke in the Janger home, Michael was planning to visit a deaf young woman in Atlanta whom he had met at Alexander Graham Bell. She is oral, but it's possible, Inez Janger said, that Michael might some day bring home a deaf young woman who was not oral. "If that happens," she said, "guess who's going to be learning sign very quickly."

One thing Inez Janger did remember clearly from the trial of the *Rowley* case before Judge Broderick was the thick anger she felt settling at her back, emanating from the section of deaf people sitting behind her. This anger was gathering into a form of group outrage. The thought that people with deaf children, who themselves worked in a school for the deaf, could be in court to testify against a deaf family's efforts to provide help for their deaf child was almost too much for these deaf people to bear. Worse, to the deaf spectators present, the fight that was going on in Judge Broderick's court was something very much less than a battle of philosophies, as the school district was suggesting. It was about nothing more and nothing less than money. It was another chapter's worth of the refusal of political powers to pay attention to a deaf child. It was as simple as that to them—and as crass. Young Phillip Bravin, also deaf, was shuttling back and forth between the courtroom and Wall Street, where he was beginning a successful business career, and he was as furious as everyone around him. His anger focused on Kuntz as the spokesman for the schools. It seemed to Bravin that the point of view represented by Kuntz had nothing to do with Amy and everything to do with the almighty dollar.

When I reached Bravin, then an executive at IBM, it had been ten years since the events surrounding the *Rowley* hearing in Judge Broderick's court. He recalled that telephone calls had been made to Leo Connor, head of Lexington School for the Deaf, where Janger and Carole Blumberg were employed. He was not sure how many, or even if he himself had made one. "Essentially, we got the deaf community mindful of the fact that there were two witnesses from Lexington appearing in court against the Rowleys and that this would not put the school in a good light. Several of them expressed displeasure to the school and that was the end of it as far as I was concerned. . . . It was a long time ago. I was very young." One thing Bravin did remember was that they went out of their way to keep the Rowleys out of the protest. "Any suggestion that they took a leadership role in it is incorrect," he said.

Carole Blumberg remembered the morning after her second day in court vividly. While Inez Janger was a volunteer at Lexington back then, Blumberg was a full-time professional, an educator of educators, someone whose job, working out of Lexington, was to help regular public school teachers without expertise teach mainstreamed deaf students. So when Lexington Superintendent Leo Connor had asked her and Janger to go up to Westchester County to observe Amy Rowley for a day, she was doing nothing more than she usually did in her work. She had heard of the Rowleys and was even more impressed with them when she met Amy. She couldn't help but make comparisons. Ten-year-old Amy's language was so much richer than that of her own deaf fourteen-year-old daughter, Lori. Furthermore, based on her own experience, Blumberg felt that Amy was doing fine and receiving satisfactory ancillary services.

211

She was prepared to continue to assist Kuntz and, at the proper time, to be a witness for the school district. On the morning of the third day of the trial, however, she was stopped by an official at Lexington and told that she was not to report to court that day, that she and Janger were off the case. She asked why and was told that it was the result of pressure from members of the deaf community. She was distressed at the news but felt that there was no alternative to complying with the order.

Remembering that, when I first called her years later, she reflected on it. "We were political pariahs, caught between the school and the deaf community," she said. "But I truly didn't understand the problem back then. I didn't understand the oral language deficit the deaf community starts out with and how they have to deal with that. I do now. My deaf daughter educated me." Back then, she was a hearing person all of whose training had come from hearing people, working in a strictly oral setting at Lexington. She recalls with a chuckle that Superintendent Connor was called "Dr. No Hands."

Blumberg had a deaf child by one of those astounding life coincidences that are too fictional to make fiction. At sixteen, she had met a young woman from Lexington who was a speech therapist and she had run all the way home to announce to her parents that this was what she wanted to be. Later, when she and her husband adopted a child, she had every reason to believe the child would have normal hearing.

She remembers speaking to the pediatrician over the phone after he had examined the infant, and his expressing relief that the child bore no obvious signs of rubella syndrome. While he seemed relieved, she was staggered. Rubella? What rubella? Didn't the obstetrician tell you, the doctor said, his relief replaced with alarm, that the mother was exposed to rubella? He had not. Blumberg took Lori home when the infant was three days old, having paid the hospital bill and bearing heavily in her heart the fear that her child would be blind. Her pediatrician examined Lori when she was four months old and found no problems. By the time Lori was seventeen months old, Blumberg was convinced her child was deaf. Tests revealed that she was right, and she asked a specialist the question that works like a nettle into the skin of hearing parents of deaf children: Will my child learn to talk? The specialist said that the best the child could do would probably sound like the speech of a child with a severely cleft palate. Tears streaming down her face, Blumberg told him that he would see, five years from now, *he would see.*

She said her prayers and vowed never to say never. Lori learned to talk slowly, with difficulty, but with success, too. They could have conversations. "She has done everything I ever expected her to do," Blumberg says now. After Lori decided to attend the National Technical Institute for the Deaf in Rochester, she found cause to learn sign language. Her deaf friends all used it. Blumberg herself took a course. Later on, Lori fell in love with a man who was hard of hearing.

When I talked with Blumberg, she was planning a wedding. Because all Lori's friends were deaf, there would be several interpreters involved, so that everyone would know what was going on. Meeting Lori's friends has been an important experience for Blumberg. She noted that the deaf marrieds in the group all had hearing children. They were experiencing a role reversal from that of Blumberg and other hearing parents of deaf children. These small children who could hear were absorbing sign language so that they could converse with their deaf parents. "These hearing kids will all be bilingual before they're five years old," Blumberg reflected.

She now considers that having a deaf child turned her from a "typical 1950s kid, a marshmallow" into a focused individual capable of pursuing a desired goal to a desired end. "I had to grow up fast." Her first husband, unable to cope with the idea of a deaf child, had left her. "It was a turning point in my life. All of a sudden, it all depended on me." Since then, she has served on a citywide task force in New York and as liaison to a District of Columbia task force whose function was to interpret P.L. 94-142 to various government bodies in the northeast.

The *Rowley* case and 1979 seemed long ago, but she says that if she had known then what she knew now, she probably would have declined to get involved in court. "In a way, it's a blessing that my name is not in that court transcript as a witness," she says. "I understand now what the Rowleys were trying to accomplish and I honor it." As for the story of the teenager who fell in love with deaf education and then adopted—accidentally—a deaf child, she used a Yiddish word by way of explanation. "All that was *bashert*," she says. "It means *destiny*."

Michael Schwartz wanted one thing beyond all others. He wanted to clerk for Judge Vincent L. Broderick. Sitting in Judge Broderick's courtroom during the trial, he was impressed with the judge's control of the courtroom, particularly his determination to hold proceedings at a pace at which everyone including the deaf participants could keep up. He was amazed and delighted with the judge's sensitivity to the problems of the deaf. Broderick's opinion afterwards seemed to Schwartz to be a remarkably egalitarian document. Faithfully, Schwartz attended the later hearings in appellate court and in the Supreme Court.

Schwartz had never met Judge Broderick and he did not attempt to at that time, but one of Schwartz' law professors at New York University called the judge about his student. This professor was in the habit of grading final examinations before looking at the names. There were two failures in Schwartz' class and the professor had assumed that Schwartz, deaf and at a disadvantage, was one of them. To the contrary—he discovered that Schwartz had one of the top grades. The law professor told the judge that Schwartz had made it clear that he would clerk for no one but Broderick.

The judge was touched and interested. The *Rowley* case had been an education for him in deafness, one that made him think of ability rather than disability. He interviewed Schwartz, finding a young man who did not speak particularly well but who had a keen mind and that rare quality without which he would never have risen so far: an unquenchable determination to succeed. He told Schwartz that he would be glad to have him for a clerk.

Michael Schwartz was another in the floodtide of rubella babies, diagnosed as deaf at the age of one. A year later, his father resigned as professor of social work at Ohio State University and moved with his social worker wife, Michael, and his older, hearing brother to Chicago, where Michael could attend the Northwestern University Speech and Hearing Clinic.

For the next ten years Michael Schwartz' mother took him to speech therapy and encouraged him to work at home while attending regular classes in public schools. After graduation from public school in New Rochelle, New York, Schwartz went to Brandeis University, where he graduated cum laude with a bachelor's degree in English. In 1975 he was back at Northwestern for graduate work. The building in which he had studied earlier had been replaced, and in the new edifice they were using total communications. Schwartz set about to learn sign language. "I learned speech there at age two and sign language there at age twenty-two," he liked to say later on.

I visited Schwartz in the Criminal Courts Building in Manhattan, where at that time he was serving as an assistant district attorney. A solid, big-boned man with a gracious smile, he greeted me there and we conversed. He turned out to be a remarkable lip-reader who did not speak well in spite of all the years of tutoring and hard work on his part. When I did not understand him, or when he was afraid I would not, he wrote things out on a legal-sized pad on his desk. Five years before, he had stood before the judges of the First Appellate Court, a young attorney not that long out of law school, and introduced himself in sign language, assisted by a voice interpreter, an occasion described by the presiding judge as a "historic event of which we are proud to be a part." Since then, he had represented New York State on appeals from criminal convictions.

He talked glowingly about Judge Broderick with whom he frequently lunched. For Schwartz, the pipe-smoking judge always remembered to put his pipe aside so that his lips could be read. Learning sign language, Schwartz told me, was his way of at last coming to terms with his deafness. As he talked, he emphasized his words with occasional blows of his fist on his desk, an action that brought to mind at once the lawyer and a man who was not aware of how loud the sounds he was making actually were. I asked him what he would do if he had a deaf child now.

"If I had a deaf child today, I would teach that child to sign and speak. My emphasis would be on that child's developing language. Whatever it took for the child to learn, that's what I'd do." He started to say something else, paused, and began writing on a pad. "So you'll understand me better," he said apologetically. This is what he wrote.

"I have paid a heavy price for my success as a deaf person in a hearing world. Because my parents were so determined for me to speak, I felt it as a rejection of my deafness. Every child knows when he is being rejected. As a child, I could not distinguish between the rejection of deafness and the rejection of me as a person. I came to feel that somehow I was defective, that something was wrong with me. The pressure seemed to be to overcome deafness, not adapting to it. If I had it to do over again, I would say to my mother and father, do exactly what you did but don't reject my deafness. I internalized it and I rejected my deafness. I had years of therapy to overcome that. I was very angry as I grew up. My father was a wonderful man but impossible to live with. He was tough on himself and tough on me, and I was tough on myself."

As she chugged along in her bronze 1983 Toyota toward Gallaudet University on the morning of Monday, March 7, 1988, Mary Malzkuhn was surprised to find the West Virginia Avenue gate closed. She drove around the corner to the Florida Avenue gate, where she saw a line of students and a line of cars blocking the gate. The students were shouting something and waving at cars passing by. When she pulled up and stopped, she saw these students signing, "If you want a deaf president, honk." Deaf herself and blessed with a keen sense of humor, Mary Malzkuhn pressed down heavily on her car horn and laughed aloud at the idea of deaf students asking for noise as proof of support. She had been working furiously at home on her dissertation and, obviously, had missed something that had happened on Sunday. A student she had never seen before came over to her car and signed to her, "Just go home and finish your writing." It sounded like a good idea to Malzkuhn. It was clear she would teach no classes this day.

She was shocked to see that the students actually had shut down the university, but she was also thrilled. She came back later that afternoon with a colleague and talked with a number of the student leaders, who were still on a "high" over their actions. She had agreed with them that things had to change and she had attended their rallies, but she had never imagined that they would convert their convictions into action this radical. She wanted to make sure that they did things properly now. The more radical the action, the more important that it be done with restraint as well as pride.

On that Sunday, a crowd arriving at the Gallaudet field house for an 8:30 P.M. announcement of the name of the new president of the nation's only university for the deaf had learned that a news release had been sent two hours earlier from the Mayflower Hotel, where the board of directors was staying. The release proclaimed that the school would have its first woman president, Dr. Elizabeth Zinser, vice chancellor of the University of North Carolina at Greensboro. The announcement did not have to say it—everyone knew that Dr. Zinser was hearing. It had happened again. Of the three candidates, two perfectly suitable deaf people had been passed over and the hearing person chosen. And one, moreover, who, like hearing board members, could not sign, could not even speak the language of the deaf. The anger was building, and soon, to the vast confusion of the district police, a sizable, simmering crowd—students, staff, faculty, alumni—was marching up to the Mayflower. The marchers had no permit, but the police decided it was better not to challenge a steamed-up body of people who couldn't hear them, anyway. So they blocked off Florida Avenue and provided the marchers with an escort.

At the Mayflower Hotel, the crowd petitioned for the opportunity for student leaders to talk with the board chairman, Jane Bassett Spillman. After some time, this was arranged, and in the ensuing conversation, Spillman either did or did not tell the students, through an interpreter: "Deaf people are not ready to function in the hearing world." The outraged students gave this quote to the capital press, which used it extensively in the Monday morning news and subsequently. While the outcome of the protest that lasted all week probably would have been the same, the quote served as a rallying point for what quickly became the Deaf-President-Now movement.

Later on, I tried to get to the bottom of the mystery of that quote, so apparently raw and intolerable. Getting a comment from an interpreter is a bit like getting a transcript of a confession from a priest. But for the vital communication link they serve, sign language interpreters consider that they actually are not even present and so are incapable of comment. Joyce Fitzpatrick, one of the directors of the public relations firm working for the Gallaudet board in the crisis, maintains that the consensus of most people in the room was that Spillman had actually said: "I'm not saying that deaf people are not ready to function in a hearing world," and that, stunned at the almost physical revulsion the remark drew from the students, she had turned to the interpreter and said: "What's wrong? What did I say?" Later Spillman told a newspaper reporter she had used a double negative.

One of the students present was Tim Rarus, a junior from Arizona, majoring in American government. Rarus and the other two students to whom Spillman was speaking got only one negative from her sentence. They maintain they asked her to repeat what she said and again got the offensive statement that they repeated to the press after the meeting. "I'll remember it for the next seventy years or maybe in my coffin," Rarus told me.

Rarus was one of four undergraduate students at Gallaudet who sparked the week-long protest that culminated with the withdrawal of Zinser as president, the resignation of Spillman as chairman of the board, and the appointment by the new board through its new chairman, Phil Bravin, of the school's first deaf president, Dr. I. King Jordan, who had been one of the two deaf candidates nominated. Rarus was exhorting fellow students to stand firm at about the same time Monday that Mary Malzkuhn and her friend were pulling up to the Florida Avenue gate. He was also keeping a fascinated eye on another scene. The district police were moving toward the demonstrators in an oddly uncertain way, their very postures betraying ambivalence. They stopped, finally, short of the barriers and the gate, and Rarus noticed them passing each other significant looks. Then they turned around and walked back in the other direction, across the street. It struck him then that these African American police officers were thinking: Martin Luther King, Jr. They may have been confused about what the deaf protesters were so fired up about, but they were not willing to play the part of a white, southern police force putting down a student-led demonstration that, for all they knew, might involve those students' civil rights.

Rarus was well acquainted with the events of the civil rights movement in the South. He and two others of the four student leaders had taken Mary Malzkuhn's course on civil rights, Government 351, a case-law course that she had taught every spring for the previous eight years. Two things she had hammered home: don't be afraid to speak up; abide by the law. Her students would use her name again and again to reporters over the next several days as someone who had inspired them, given them self-confidence, focused their attention on problems of the deaf. She shrugged this off in a conversation with me: she was born at the right time, in school at the right time, she could pass along the information—that was all. She was at pains to point out something else. The four students who had been the leaders were all deaf children of deaf parents.

"Having deaf parents definitely had something to do with their being leaders," she said. "Look at Rarus. His mother's a leader in her own right [principal of a deaf school in Tucson]. Tim grew up watching his mother, so he learned a lot from her. Bridgetta Bourne's parents are Gallaudet alumni, and her father works for the government, so she grew up watching him as a model. They were very much exposed to political process and analysis. James Covell—I taught his mother. She came to school late, like me. James saw her problems and has seen the problems of deaf people. Greg Hlibock [president of the student body] was never my student, but I know his parents. They talk about the problems all the time. The kids are very much exposed. I'm not surprised that all of them are leaders today."

As I listened, another thought flashed across my mind. Along with politics and activism, these young people had gotten that rich language that hearing parents heard from Amy Rowley and envied. They had had sign language as well as spoken English from their earliest memory. These deaf young people were indeed bilingual, with all the advantage that term implies. Not only did they have role models, involved parents, and motivational teaching, but also the means of communicating to others their frustrations, desires, and faith as well.

In her class, Malzkuhn gives her students more than a sense of their powers and responsibilities. She uses a figure called Hope to give them strength. Her Hope comes from the legend of Pandora's box in Greek mythology. The first woman on earth, Pandora, ("all-gifted") was sent by Zeus to exact vengeance upon man. Endowed with all the feminine charms, but also with curiosity, drive, and deceit, she was to marry Prometheus' simple-minded brother. She brought a box with her, which she was forbidden to open. When she did open it, all the evils that have attended mankind in its history escaped, with only Hope remaining inside. As Malzkuhn signs the story broadly and dramatically to her students, the hearing people of the world leave the box with the evils while the deaf, hearing no commotion, remain. Hope, she tells her students, thus remains with the deaf students. There is always Hope, no matter how desperate the situation. Inevitably asked why Hope remained behind, she shrugs, "Either Hope is very compassionate, or she, too, is deaf."

Malzkuhn's doctoral dissertation was on the *Rowley* case. I thought, reading it, how, in their different ways, Amy's case and the Gallaudet uprising both illustrated how hard the deaf work to bridge the communications gap with the hearing world, and how little effort is returned to them by hearing people. In the end, it did not matter what Spillman said or did not say to the deaf students that Sunday night at the Mayflower Hotel. She was not understood because she had not learned how to communicate with the students in the school whose fate she had presided over. She did not speak the language. To Rarus, it was simple. She had said they could not function in a hearing world, but, "obviously," he said, "she could not function in a deaf world."

The Gallaudet story ends on a grace note. Elizabeth Zinser, who had begun working on sign language before being chosen president, realized after two days on the scene—unable even to gain access to the campus—that she could not serve. Moreover, she came to understand the students' fervently held aspirations not as a personal insult to her but as a significant moment in a long struggle of the deaf to gain a voice for their legitimate aspirations. Zinser concluded the announcement of her withdrawal as president by flashing to the students the "I-love-you" sign. Young Hlibock, the student body president, later wrote her a letter wishing her great success and noting, "You were, of course, an innocent victim and unfortunate target for our collective anger."

In Greensboro, she was welcomed back to her old post with a considerable show of affection by the university. Members of the school for the deaf in that city created a "name sign" for her, with an "E" for Elizabeth over a heart, indicating that her heart was in the right place.

Amy in Oz

Robert Coultas was having second thoughts, and they were all doubts. His first thought had been one of those midnight lightning ideas that now seemed to be evanescing under the weight of day. How could he have thought that a deaf teenager could be the answer to his local Rotary International's quest for "special" young people to bring into their international educational–cultural exchange program? Special was one thing, deaf was something else. Now he was on his way to an interview with a deaf family, at which an interpreter would be present. The international exchange program required teenagers of a special sort, those kids who had the acumen to adjust to an entirely new country, able to hurdle cultural and language barriers. How could a deaf person, however able, be expected to manage that?

These gloomy thoughts assailed Coultas one chilly afternoon in November 1988, as he and his friend, Mike Rabasca, made their way west from Florham, New Jersey, toward Mountain Lakes on Interstate 80 in Coultas' white 1986 Audi. His big mistake, Coultas told himself unhappily, was listening to Elmer Rowley, a fine man and a splendid Rotarian but, also, this candidate's grandfather. Coultas told himself he never should have agreed to the interview. The truth was that generally wherever Amy went as an exchange student, there would be no interpreter. This deaf girl would be strictly on her own. Coultas' heart went out to her. He and his wife had had sixty young students from foreign lands living with them in the Rotary exchange program over the past twenty years, and although they

220

knew the joy this had brought them, they were also aware of the difficulties students faced in a strange land.

An hour and a half after arriving at the Rowleys' house in Mountain Lakes, Coultas and Rabasca said their goodbyes to the family and walked back up the winding, wooden stairway to where they had parked their car. They opened the car doors, sat down, and looked at each other in frank, open disbelief. Then, realizing that they were both wearing the same expression, they broke into delighted laughs. "My God," Coultas expostulated to his friend, "what a kid!"

The two parents had been most cordial and asked good, probing questions about where their daughter would be, with whom she would be staying, and how they would know how she was doing. But Amy was far beyond what they could have imagined beforehand. In a one-on-one conversation, face-to-face, she understood them and they understood her. She conducted a conversation with them, charmed them with her brightness, and sold herself utterly, with a sense of humor that made it all feel right.

Before the meeting, Coultas had it in mind that if this deaf teen-age girl had any chance at all, it would be in one of the English-speaking countries in which the Rotary program was lodged: South Africa, New Zealand, or Australia. His interest had quickened when it turned out that Amy had been living a distant love affair with Australia for some time. She definitely wanted to go there. She was sure she would love it and thrive on the opportunity. The two men listened, and Coultas began to think, It won't do to write letters over there or to anyone here about this kid. I will have to get on the phone to these people myself and let them hear how excited I am, how sure I am that this girl and the program were made for each other.

For Amy, "Oz," as many Australians call their country, was a case of love at first sight. She had made up her mind not to expect anything of it, on the theory that this was a good way of fighting culture shock. But coming out on the jetway, feeling the hot wind blasting at her, that was something she couldn't have conjured up from the snows of Mountain Lakes in January. Amy took a sniff of the spicy air and started smiling. Across the Melbourne Airport tarmac, she could see palm and pine trees growing side by side. Crazy, she thought happily, I'm in another world.

As she walked over to the car park, she experienced a moment of panic. She had seen photographs of the people who were supposed to meet her, but no one there looked right. The hot wind was making her clothes stick to her body. She could handle it if she had to—she could find someone to put her in touch with the local Rotary club, but after thirty-three hours on airplanes she was ready for something that looked like home. Then she saw the man and the woman in the photographs, and then they were smiling and moving toward her. By the next afternoon, she was swimming in their backyard pool. The next day, with Bob and Marg Sansom—her host family—she took in a charity tennis match on the eve of the Australian Open and saw Pat Cash, Ivan Lendl, and John McEnroe play.

Amy fell on Australia as though the whole continent was her picnic fare. She fit in snugly at Berwick High School, found the students and everyone else in Australia as friendly and accessible as the ice-blue, beckoning sky, and took on each new day as a personal challenge. Her host family folded around her like a comfortably worn robe; she was one of them, sister to Lisa and Karen and foster daughter to Bob and Marg. She and Karen, who was in her grade at Berwick, got up together each morning to catch the school bus. They wore each other's clothes so frequently that "Mum" Marg commented in a letter to the Rowleys that it was "first up, best dressed." The Sansoms forgot about Amy's deafness to all intents and purposes, with sister Karen even complaining once that she had called home and Amy had let the phone ring without answering it.

For their part, the Sansoms recognized that while Amy had a knack for fitting in, she also had a fierce independence. She's got a mind of her own, Bob Sansom told people, with a mixture of mild bafflement, amusement, and admiration. Owner, with his wife, of a company manufacturing low-voltage garden lights, Sansom was also a deeply committed Rotarian who had looked forward to meeting Amy Rowley ever since his American friend, Bob Coultas, had told him that this was an exchange student he shouldn't miss. Coultas had been right, Sansom knew soon after meeting Amy. One couldn't hold on to stereotypes of deaf people or disability very long with someone like Amy around.

Experiences heaped about Amy. She went with the Sansoms to the Grampian Mountains, observed a sheepshearing, visited a farm in the bush. She was introduced to cricket, which she liked and played at Berwick, and to Australian-rules football, which puzzled her. She ran like fury and scrambled to catch up on her studies. In the required monthly reports to the Denville Rotary club back in New Jersey, she frequently ended her summaries with "Do I have to go home?" a line meant partly as a plaintively humorous compliment to the people responsible for her visit and partly as a marker for the time that was passing all too swiftly for her. She sprinkled these reports with Australian slang. "Oz" was "totally fairdinkum" (genuine). She was "mucking about" (having a good time) here and there. Now and then she encountered a "boofhead" (someone not too bright) who asked her silly questions, like whether America had any Catholics or whether Christmas was ever celebrated there. That last one, she reported, put her on her "bum" with laughter. (She had not thought it funny at all, however, when someone in her first days in the country had asked her how she learned to talk—*nobody* had ever asked her that before.)

A grand, memory-making experience was her "debut" at Berwick high in May. The Australian debut is a cross between a prom and a "coming out" party for debutantes in America. Amy wore a borrowed dress. In the pictures she sent home, she glowed in this long, white dress, her hair tied up in a white bow. She learned exotic dances such as the "evening freestep," and the "progressive barn dance," and that grandperson of Australian debut dance steps, the "Pride of Erin." Marg wrote the Rowleys to tell them what a delight Amy was, how warm and loving.

Another highlight of the visit was the two-week camping safari into Central Australia. Amy found it thrilling and firmed up friendships with students from other countries that served her in good stead when she made a European trip with her brother. Later, she went far north with the Sansoms to Port Douglas, in Queensland, where Marg's sister lived. She snorkeled off the Agincourt Reef and was delighted by the multicolored fish and coral. During this time, she also began to make speeches to Rotary clubs. In September at the local Dandenong Club in Victoria, she had her first smash hit. The club had invited deaf students as a kickoff to a month devoted to youth activities. Amy began her talk by saying, "I am happy to be here in crocodile-infested Australia." The president of the club, Bruce Fletcher, described the impact of this speech in a letter to the Rowleys:

"Amy addressed the club in what I guess you would accept as her usual enthusiastic, humorous, and fantastic way. Amy's story is an incredible one and left her audience of approximately seventy-five people absolutely spellbound. Amy received a standing ovation at the end of her address, which is a first for the club. Many of our senior members indicated that Amy was the best guest speaker they had ever heard." The speech was so well received that Amy was invited to speak at a local college into which twenty-four deaf students had been integrated. The Dandenong Club made a video of her speech for use with students with disabilities who, as one club member put it, "will be able to see just what is possible with determination."

Back in Victoria, Amy went into a work experience that distinctly broadened her outlook on her professional future. She worked in South Melbourne at the State Coroner's Office and the Victorian Institute of Forensic Pathology—the place, as she said, where they find out whether a death was a murder. Her enthusiasm for science and biology, always strong, matured further here, in large part as a result of an interest expressed by a man named David Stevens. She told friends at home later that he had made a positive impact on her life by giving her the freedom to be herself and to learn. She found that, under these conditions, what she was doing did not seem like work. When she left, Stevens gave her a coroner's knife with her name engraved on it to take home to the States.

Amy dreaded leaving. It was not that she didn't miss her family back home, but she had put so much of herself into Australia and her new friends that she knew it would be painful to leave. In effect she was leaving the three families with whom she had stayed at various times during the year. But leave she did, and I called her on the TTY on January 12, 1990, two days after she had returned. I had been told that friends in Mountain Lakes had gotten up a party for her eighteenth birthday, which she had celebrated in Australia the week before. She didn't want to talk about the Mountain Lakes party, but about her departure from Oz. More or less verbatim, this is what she told me:

"It was a very nice party. I invited seventy people but a lot more than that came and we partied, and after the party a few good mates stayed with me, and after a bit we proceeded to get emotional. I mean eeee-motional. I was packing and crying and unpacking and crying some more and then everyone else was packing for me and we all were crying. We had to take my South African mate to the train station to get to where she was staying. . . . Then we went for a last spin in my brother Steven's [Archibald] go-cart. Then we went out to the airport and even more friends showed up there. I didn't expect that. And one of them signed to me, "Friends forever." Then my host dad, John Archibald, and Steven had to leave, so it wasn't easy to say 'see ya,' but mission accomplished, two down and a million to go. Tried to thank Margaret and Bob Sansom and tried to thank everyone else. It was a scene and we were going through customs and I kept crying until I got on the plane. Then it was worse. I saw all of my mates on the observation deck in the airport. I saw them but I didn't know if they saw me but one girl, Kelly, she is my best friend in Australia, she looked really sad, she wasn't talking to anyone else, just standing out there, she was in a way separated from everyone else and I was making the plane flood up. . . . I really miss all of them, and on the flight to New Zealand the stewardess says to me are you all right, do you want a drink of something strong? Hmm, now I am eighteen and legally old enough to drink so I had something strong and then a couple. Yuck. . . . But the flight to Auckland was so bad. Then I got to Auckland and then on to Los Angeles, twelve hours during the night. You couldn't really sleep and it wasn't very nice. Then I got to Los Angeles and had to go through customs. No worries, I had everything legal but actually you don't have to declare anything under $1,400. At the airport I met my mom's bridesmaid, Carol, and stayed with her seven hours. That was great fun, and I caught another airplane to New York and another night without sleeping. I arrived at JFK finally and walked out into the airport but there wasn't anyone there and I was scared and worried and everything else at the same time but I found out they weren't allowed past a certain door, so I finally found them and everybody was crying. We came home after leaving a note on my best friend's car at school. . . . I still haven't seen her. . . . And gave my brother a big hug and a kiss and I've been putting the house through turmoil, and tomorrow I am going to have another party. Then I'll piss off and go back to Australia and never come back."

Being back home again turned out not to be the easiest of adjustments. She missed Australia, her friends, her foster parents, everything. She felt torn out of her element. She took out her frustration on her parents, and they asked Bob Coultas to come and talk with her. Coultas gave her a straight talking to, and Amy listened and promised to do better, to be more considerate. Gradually, the pain of separation from Australia—the place, the continent, that world—eased. She knew she had to buckle down to her studies. Getting a transcript with grades that would satisfy the requirements of Mountain Lakes High School had become a problem.

The truth was that she had not performed academically up to her standards in Australia—her mind was "blown" by the thrill of her independence and exciting, new surroundings. Her education there had come from what classroom teachers would call "distractions," the everyday activities that occupied her new life. As if all this was not classroom handicap enough, Amy had had no sign language interpreter in school. It was not a provision the

Australian school she attended was prepared for. Amy learned what she could, got help from whomever she could in class, and didn't complain. But she did recognize that old slipping-behind feeling again and promised herself she would work twice as hard when she got home again. Worst of all was the sensation that mathematics had eluded her grasp completely.

Back home, it seemed that all these problems in class had magnified and were made even more difficult by a modest portion of fame that had come to her. She was in demand on the Rotary club circuit as a speaker, and as one guaranteed to delight the faithful. Her triumphs at lunch were counterbalanced by problems at dinner. She found that she had picked up an Australian accent that was as baffling to her hearing brother as it was to her lipreading parents—it did occur to her, not without an inward chuckle, that she had undergone an amazing transformation and was now playing Mr. Brett, her old fifth-grade teacher, to her befuddled parents, who found themselves in her old position.

But with these problems came a new kind of serenity, once she had come down off her Australian high. She was finally able to tell herself that Australia was a private coming-out in life for her that nobody else need understand. She found she had more patience with everyone in school. She was not so dependent on a small clique of friends. Her new interpreter, Doreen DeLuca, monitoring the teachers' lounge for the inside word on Amy, began to pick up good vibes. Teachers were talking about how much calmer Amy was since getting back from Australia. Another of the young women drawn to sign by its beauty, DeLuca, who had grown up in Florham Park, had feared working with a kind of celebrity, but found Amy a joy. So powerfully focused was Amy's attention that for the first time in her experience, DeLuca had the disquieting sense of being somehow responsible for the news she bore. Interpreting a film about Vietnam, DeLuca found herself speaking the words almost as though she had assumed the personae on the screen, the dying soldier and his war-numbed companions. As Amy's plastic, expressive face registered the pain the information gave her, DeLuca felt a pang of guilt. It's not my fault, she found herself close to blurting out.

It was by far the hardest academic year Amy had put in since leaving Furnace Woods, but she got her Australian grades honored and managed, with DeLuca's help, to make up a degree of what she had missed in the classroom Down Under. I flew up to Newark Thursday, the day before her graduation, and rented a car to get to Mountain Lakes. Elmer and Bunny Rowley, Amy's grandparents, were coming in on Friday, and the only other family expected was John, who was visiting a girlfriend in Virginia Beach. Amy and I talked about John on Thursday. She told me, reflecting on her Peekskill days, in a different way from ever before, "It was harder on John than anyone else. Much harder, because my brother lost all his friends in the school. He kept changing himself around to suit other people. He lost himself there for a while. He suffered much more than I did in all this."

John was supposed to drive to Mountain Lakes Thursday, but his car had developed transmission problems, and Thursday night he got word to his father that he would not set out for Mountain Lakes until the next morning. Elmer and Bunny arrived early Friday afternoon, just in time to learn, with the rest of us, that John had finally set out for Mountain Lakes around 2 P.M. Amy was in the room when this news arrived, and I saw her duck her head for an instant before shrugging and leaving the room. Later, Bunny told me that Amy had said to her that it didn't matter if John didn't make her high school graduation: he'll be there for my college graduation. John's always been told he has to do things because of me, she told her grandmother.

The Amy I saw in June 1990, was indefinably different from the teenager I had seen the year before her trip to Australia. The old giddy, skipping ebullience was toned down, and in its place was a young woman who looked at people earnestly and long as though "listening" for the clue to who they were. She shocked me by bringing up John and discussing him as she had done, but she was equally candid about herself. "I learned it was a tough world long ago," she said. "You have to work for everything because it is not going to be given to you. I think maybe the experience [her school years in Peekskill] may have helped in the long run. That may have had something to do with my desire to go to Australia, that the idea didn't scare me. After what had happened to me, I felt I was prepared for anything." Her feelings for her parents had, if anything, deepened. She said she loved them more than ever before, but now wanted to take them with her back to Australia, where she also had friends and a newer family.

As the seniors filed into the auditorium that night, I noted that seating on the stage had been arranged with Amy at the end of a mid-row to the right so that DeLuca had room to function in front of her without blocking the spectators. I was focused in on them when I saw Amy give a start, begin to rise, think better of it, and finally settle for a hasty wriggling of her fingers at something happening behind us. Turning, I saw John come in, dressed in a black sweater–shirt and slacks. As he walked, he held his fingers in the

"I-love-you" sign high over his head so that Amy could see it. Later, DeLuca told me that she was getting shivery watching Amy's eyes well up as her brother walked down the aisle in the auditorium.

Amy had been worried that she would not know when her name was called to come up for her diploma, and DeLuca had promised to take care of it. She did not sign the names of the other students (Amy knew them anyway), and when Amy's name was called, she signed it and lifted her hand slightly to indicate "stand up." Amy got up, and moved across the stage to get her diploma. "I wanted to go hug her." DeLuca said later.

On the back of the program, where the names of the students who had won awards were listed, Amy's name stood beside the I. King Jordan Scholarship, named for the new president of Gallaudet, who had taken his post after the Deaf-President-Now movement had succeeded two years earlier. Amy was going to Gallaudet as her parents had before her.

12

Equal Opportunity Writ Large

In his law offices, former Senator Charles McC. Mathias of Maryland talked about his boyhood in the Monocacy River town of Frederick, the home of patriot Barbara Frietchie and once a settlers' stop on the road to the Ohio Valley. Around the dinner table in the Mathias home, the conversation was often about civic and school affairs and the dominant educational institution in town, the Maryland School for the Deaf.

These conversations were lively ones, for young Charles' father was for many years a member of the board of visitors of the school for the deaf. The issues of whether sign language should be used or not, and if so, when and how, were frequently raised around the Mathias table. Frederick was not a big city, and the deaf students were a common sight on the streets and in the stores. So was signing and the obvious fact that not all the signers were deaf. Charles grew up with a sense of these deaf students as willing and able and as a part of the community, not only educable but taking full advantage of their opportunity for education. Now in his seventies, a ruddy-looking man with big, heavy-knuckled hands, Mathias mused about the impact of these early years. "My wife became the first woman member of the board of visitors of the Maryland School for the Deaf," he noted, "and so the conversations went on in my own home."

Enclaves of enlightened discussion of problems of disability were extraordinarily few in those days, and even after World War II, when Mathias returned to Frederick after service in the Pacific Theater. As late as 1958,

229

for example, the year in which he was elected to the General Assembly of Maryland, the Illinois Supreme Court had held that establishing programs for the handicapped did not require that free public education be provided to a mentally impaired child. In many states at that time, legislation permitted the exclusion of any child whose presence in a classroom was determined by school authorities to be, for any reason, disruptive. Until as late as 1969, a North Carolina statute made it a crime for a parent to persist in efforts to enroll a handicapped child in school after the superintendent had determined to exclude that child.

In 1965, congressional hearings revealed that fully two-thirds of the nation's children with disabilities were either totally excluded from school or sitting, unserved, in regular classrooms. Congress passed the Education of the Handicapped Act the next year, establishing a program of grants to the states to encourage improvement of services for persons with handicaps. In 1970, the program was expanded and funding increased. In 1973, more eye-opening hearings were conducted. In none of the states in which hearings were held were services available to meet the needs of children with disabilities adequately, even including those states that had enacted laws providing public education for these children.

While these hearings had a powerful effect on Congress, so did the mounting number of court cases in the early 1970s, chipping away at the worst areas of neglect—often involving mentally retarded children, who were barely out of the attic even at this late date. Mathias recalls reading, in 1974, *Maryland Association of Retarded Children v. State of Maryland,* in which a circuit court judge held that Maryland law required the state to provide a free education to all children with handicaps, particularly including mentally retarded children. In his decision, the judge pointed to the language of a Maryland statute requiring local school boards to maintain a public school system "designed to provide quality education, and equal educational opportunity for all youth." By this time, Mathias was a member of the United States Senate and in a position to look for opportunities to do something more far-reaching about an issue that had always interested him. "That opinion inspired me," he recalled. "It fired me up."

Another person who read the decision with great interest was Richard Schifter, then vice president of the Maryland Board of Education. His interest had been captured two years earlier by *Mills v. Board of Education,* a federal case in the District of Columbia in which the holding was that all children were entitled to a public education regardless of mental, physical, or emotional disability. As a former member of the board of visitors of the

Maryland School for the Deaf, Schifter knew Senator Mathias. When the judge's decision in the *Maryland Association of Retarded Children v. State of Maryland* came down, Schifter was attending meetings with Blair Lee, then lieutenant governor, with legislative responsibilities for education. Schifter used those meetings to advocate, in the strongest terms he could summon, that the decision not be appealed. His plea carried the day.

I corresponded with Schifter and telephoned him in an effort to discover circumstances that might have led to his taking such a strong, egalitarian position at that time. He was not, he wrote, an advocate for children with disabilities or any other group and had no history of disability in his family. "I had read the decision and thought that it was wrong to go along with the . . . appeal. I would have taken the same position if another group had, in my opinion, not been dealt with properly." He noted that his law practice had focused for many years on the representation of Native American tribes. And then, as though in an afterthought, he said, "I am a refugee from Nazi Germany. My mother and father were killed in a death camp."

When the *Maryland Association* decision came down in 1974, the United States Senate was considering Senate Bill 6, sponsored by Senator Harrison Williams of New Jersey, chairman of the Committee on Labor and Public Welfare, and shepherded by Senator Jennings Randolph of West Virginia as head of the Subcommittee on the Handicapped. The bill did what Senator Mathias wanted done, but the $6-billion price tag made the senator and other supporters doubt that it could pass the Ninety-third Congress. If it did, there was a strong possibility it would be vetoed by President Gerald Ford.

Senator Mathias got Schifter and Colbert King, a member of the senator's staff, to work up an amendment with a formula that would keep initial costs under control and then persuaded Senators Williams and Randolph to let him sponsor this much less expensive, more politically marketable amendment to the Education of the Handicapped Act as a stopgap measure. In his speech to assembled senators, he left no doubt as to what was intended. "No other concept," he said, "is as widely accepted by the citizens of our country as the concept of equal educational opportunity. . . . If, however, we believe in the basic premise that equal educational opportunity must be provided to all handicapped children, then our nation is a long way from achieving that most desirable goal."*

* The remarks of United States senators appearing in this chapter come from the *Congressional Record*, Senate Proceedings, Ninety-fifth Congress, 1975.

Then Mathias introduced another important element of the language being used in the consideration of legislation in Congress. Referring to the education amendment bill, he noted that it stated that "every citizen is entitled to an education to meet his or her *full potential* [author's emphasis] without financial barriers and limited only by the desire to learn and absorb such an education." Years later, in his office, I showed Mathias a number of quotes from members of Congress approving this use of the term "full potential." He nodded. "We were talking, of course, as your quotes show, about developing *all* students to their full potential as far as possible."

While he gratefully supported the Mathias amendment, which passed successfully, Senator Williams was determined to press for a new education of the handicapped act during the next term of Congress. A child of the Depression, Harrison Williams had grown up in Plainfield, New Jersey, son of a small manufacturer of concrete burial vaults. With the necessity of burial a constant, the family was insulated from the worst aspects of the national economic blight, but young Harrison vividly remembered idle men sitting on benches and others who came to the kitchen door to beg for food. "Here I was, a kid," he recalled, "wondering what their kids were doing for food."

After service in World War II as a pilot and trainer of pilots in the Navy, he decided on Columbia Law School, but first went to work in a midwestern steel mill for the experience. After law school and a brief fling as a country lawyer in New England, he came back to Plainfield in 1949 to practice law. He got into Congress by running for the unexpired term of a Democrat in a Republican stronghold. By his third term in the Senate, in 1971, Williams had succeeded to the post of chairman of the Committee on Labor and Public Welfare. He had two groups he wanted to help: the addictive alcoholic and the handicapped. A recovered alcoholic himself, he had firsthand experience of the limited access alcoholics had to help. Then he, too, had been impressed with one of the court cases of the day, *Pennsylvania Association of Retarded Children v. Pennsylvania,* another declaration that equal protection of the laws would not allow exclusion of handicapped youth from public education.

When he arose to address the Senate of the Ninety-fifth Congress on behalf of his new act in 1975, he had a copy of a Supreme Court opinion in his hand. He waved it for emphasis as he spoke: "Twenty-one years ago, in 1954," he said, "the Supreme Court of the United States fully opened the door for all children to be guaranteed equal educational opportunity." He then quoted from the decision of the Warren Supreme Court in *Brown v. Board of Education:*

"In these days it is doubtful that any child may reasonably be expected to succeed in life if he is denied the opportunity of an education. Such an opportunity . . . is a right which must be made available to all on equal terms."

Speakers following Williams were eloquent in varying degrees and addressed different aspects of the problem and the bill's potential for solving it. One by one, they also stressed equality of opportunity.

Senator Robert T. Stafford of Vermont, the ranking minority (Republican) member, observed: "We can all agree that education [for a handicapped child] should be equivalent at least to the one those children who are not handicapped receive." Later, in an article in the *Vermont Law Review,* he began this way: "Every American child has a right to an equal educational opportunity."

Republican Senator Jacob K. Javits of New York, who was worried about the difficulties faced by handicapped children, was willing to go further. "Handicapped children, while entitled to the same opportunity to an education as all other children, are nonetheless a unique group . . . the benefits of early identification and education are so great as to justify emphasis on pre-school education for handicapped children."

Senator Alan Cranston, Democrat of California, echoed others in worrying about whether, in view of then-current constraints on federal fiscal policy, it would be possible to fund the act fully. Nevertheless, he supported it. "Its enactment would signify a new beginning and the broadening of equal opportunity for our children."

Senator Lowell Schweiker of Pennsylvania, another Republican, picked up on the language of the *Pennsylvania Association* case, which had established the right of mentally retarded individuals to a "free, appropriate education," To this language, which ultimately emerged as key in the Education for all Handicapped Children Act of 1975, he appended this definitional observation: "Congress must take a more active role under its responsibilities for equal protection of the law to guarantee that handicapped children are provided equal educational opportunity."

Senator Hubert Humphrey of Minnesota put it as simply as it could be put: "Handicapped children have a right to equal and free education."

And to be sure that these numerous individual statements emphasizing equality of opportunity were not ignored, the Senate Committee on

Labor and Public Welfare wrote the words simply and plainly in recommending passage of the act. "It is this committee's belief that the Congress must take a more active role under its responsibility for equal protection of the laws to guarantee that handicapped children are provided equal educational opportunity."

What might this "equal educational opportunity" mean in the case of a deaf child like Amy Rowley, mainstreamed in a school with hearing children? This was suggested clearly later on, in hearings prior to passage of the Rehabilitation Act amendments of 1978, and noted by Michael Chatoff, the Rowleys' attorney, in his memorandum of law to Judge Broderick before the district court hearing on *Rowley*. Senator Stafford, with the concurrence of Senator Randolph, had stated that the amendments would "guarantee that properly trained interpreters would be available to our school-age deaf population." Senator Williams put it more bluntly: "The Education for All Handicapped Children Act requires that each state make available teachers, interpreters, and financial assistance necessary to assure every deaf child . . . an appropriate education."

Rereading the transcript from the Senate debate on the Education for All Handicapped Children Act seventeen years later—and noting that the House debate was not significantly different—Senator Williams shook his head. "If the Supreme Court had been looking for congressional intent, it's all here, spread through the entire hearing," he told me. "You can't miss it. It spells out equal opportunity in those very words again and again. The court was doing just what they said they were against. They were creating new legislation in the review process. They were not looking at what we did. They were creating a whole new concept. The grade-by-grade thing [a portion of the majority opinion defining "sufficient benefits" of the act as grade-by-grade progress of handicapped youth]—where did they get that? It's not in the legislation."

Senator Williams sent me to Lisa Walker, then director of the Education Writers of America, but in 1975 a member of his staff who was generally regarded as the chief architect of the act. She agreed to reread the materials relating to the case and the Supreme Court decision to jog her memory of what had happened. "I have no question that what we were about was equal opportunity—a parallel to equal protection of the laws under the Fourteenth Amendment," she said after her review. "In re-reading the majority opinion of the Supreme Court, it seems to me that behind this language is a sort of implied notion, something like what can we be expected to do for these handicapped youngsters. Reading it feels like reading the language of discrimination."

Looking through my interviews with and the testimony of educators who had worked with Amy Rowley or observed her in Furnace Woods school, I became fascinated by how many of them thought that, at some point in the near future, Amy probably would need a sign language interpreter in her classroom. It was not a matter of whether-or-not to these individuals, but when. Amy's teachers and tutors and her trial sign language interpreter in kindergarten—most of them people who had testified against the Rowleys in the legal proceedings—fell into this category. Even Ann Mullholland, the school district's chief witness, had suggested that a day might come soon when Amy would need this help. Reading these comments after the fact, one might conclude that a costly, five-year battle up to the highest court in the land had been waged over what services to supply a deaf child in public school during only one or two more years of her public education.

If a sign language interpreter for one deaf child were the real issue, and assuming any degree of good faith between the Rowleys and the school district, a number of things might have happened differently—even given the doubts and fears front-line teachers had about a classroom interpreter and the school's general ignorance of the problems of teaching deaf children: more preparation for and a longer kindergarten test of the sign language interpreter concept was one thing; a more comprehensive test of a different interpreter in the first or second grade, another. Surely, fuller exploration by the District Committee on the Handicapped of what had been happening in deaf education over the previous decade would have occurred.

But the good faith that had existed between the Rowleys and the school's personnel eroded soon after Amy's entrance into school. To the school as well as to the board of education, the civil action filed by the Rowleys with the Department of Health, Education and Welfare had been a declaration of war. Years later, reminded of the date of the filing of that suit, April 1977, five months before Amy's entry into kindergarten, Nancy Rowley blinked and murmured quietly, as though to herself, "Too soon." But the Rowleys had been talking to school officials for a full year before taking this action and did so hesitantly and only because they could see no sign that Amy would be getting an interpreter in kindergarten. They had also been told by someone that they had reason to trust that the issue of money would block the hiring of an interpreter. And, even after all this, there had been that harmonious meeting at the beginning of the kindergarten year to discuss the trial of a classroom interpreter. It was the way that trial was staged and the swift pronouncement of its failure that withered any faith the family had in the school district's intentions.

The problem, I became convinced, went far beyond the question of a sign language interpreter for Amy Rowley. From the beginning, the problem was perceived by the Hendrick Hudson Board of Education as one of control or power. Members of the board I had interviewed expressed this feeling with a question: Who has the power to decide what an appropriate education is— the local school board or the National Association of the Deaf? Virtually everybody I had talked with on the school's side of the legal battle was convinced that NAD had chosen this modest-sized, well-to-do school district either because it could afford sign language interpreters or because the Rowleys had volunteered their child as a guinea pig for a national test of the new law. It was this conviction that eventually wrenched the case about Amy out of that context and made of it something akin to a class action in which parents of children with disabilities were challenging school authority nationwide.

I could never get anyone connected with the school district or the state education bureaucracy to give me even a shred of evidence that NAD or any other national disability or advocacy group had provided the Rowleys with financial support or encouragement to initiate their case. Once the case had been approved for review by the Supreme Court, on appeal by the school district, the advocacy groups had little choice but to support the Rowleys. I had found no evidence of the Rowleys' gaining significant financial support for their case in the mountainous heap of TTY tapes and correspondence in their files. A few individuals had donated token support—that was all—but there were letters from various organizations connected with disability politely and usually apologetically, declining support. One of those letters was from the National Association of the Deaf and was signed by the president of the organization at the time, Albert Pimental.

Pimental had set up the legal defense fund for NAD, and the organization's lawyers were heavily involved, at the time of the *Rowley* case, in matters at issue under Section 504 of the Rehabilitation Act and with the new Education for All Handicapped Children Act. "We had a pretty accurate understanding of other disabilities besides deafness as well," Pimental told me. "We were monitoring what was happening and we had a feel for what was a good case to be pushing on behalf of deaf people."

While Pimental was sympathetic to the Rowleys, whom he knew, his lawyers told him in no uncertain terms that this was a poor case to support at that time. They believed, with Seymour "Sy" Dubow, legal director for the National Center for Law and the Deaf at Gallaudet, that Amy's intelligence, communication skills, and abilities made the case atypical. They feared the very thing that the Hendrick Hudson Board of Education had assumed they desired—an eventual test of the case before the Supreme Court in a period of hard-nosed reaction against gains achieved for individuals with disabilities. The real worry was that the result would be a setback for deaf children and, very likely, for children with disabilities in general.

Pimental sat down with Clifford Rowley and passed along that gloomy assessment. At the same time, he tried to make Clifford see that he understood the family's plight. "They had to think of their own child and we respected that," he told me.

Thus, far from encouraging the family to push its case through the courts, NAD regretted that *Rowley* was in the judicial pipeline at all. No financial aid or other help was forthcoming from that source. And NAD attorneys were not surprised when the Supreme Court decided for review. By this time, it was clear that *Rowley* had become a major civil rights battle, imbued with much of the flavor of the old states' rights versus individual rights confrontations. These were clashes advocacy attorneys were used to winning more often than not in the recent past; *Rowley* was one they feared they would lose.

They felt that appearances were against Amy Rowley's case the farther it was removed from the actual facts. As far as appearances were concerned, the Furnace Woods school program for Amy was a model of propriety under New York State's equivalent of the Education for All Handicapped Children Act. Whatever might be said for or against the adequacy of services, Amy was getting what state law said she should get. She had the service of a certified teacher of the deaf for an hour a day—the much-complained of removal from her classes—and sessions with a speech therapist three times a week. This much was required by state law. In his arguments, school district attorney Raymond Kuntz repeatedly asserted that the school did much more. This amounted to the TTY in the principal's office, which Nancy Rowley felt saved the school the trouble of sending messengers to the Rowley house; the FM wireless, which had a history of malfunction and which Amy found less useful than her hearing aids; and the sign language course members of the school's staff took for several weeks, which did not result—and could not have resulted—in the kind of interpretive help in the classroom that Amy needed and eventually got in Mountain Lakes. What the school really did contribute was a good choice of teachers in the early grades, a choice of as much importance to the district's legal case as to Amy's education.

But, still, power as much as education was on the minds of the school district and the commissioner of education for the State of New York. The danger, in their eyes, was substituting the opinions and policies of the courts for the judgment of the state's educators. Repeatedly, attorneys for the school district and the state emphasized that the Education for All Handicapped Children Act had not required the use of sign language interpreters in the classroom and that the New York State plan under the act did not mention them. Judge Broderick's decision was regarded as an invitation to judicial usurpation of the rights of state educators. Furthermore, in their minds, it was considered seriously flawed. Brandishing the Mansfield dissent, the school's attorneys maintained in numerous documents that Broderick had (1) quoted from the wrong regulations in composing his test of what the term "appropriate education" meant; (2) used language from a law review in formulating his definition of appropriate education; and (3) created tests for determining shortfall from a student's potential that were impossible to administer.

Judge Broderick agreed to meet with my wife and me in his Pelham Manor, New York, home in August 1987. He didn't care to comment on his decision or subsequent decisions on the *Rowley* case. He did tell us, however, that he had delivered a speech dedicating, in the name of the Warren Supreme Court, a law library at North Carolina Central University, a predominantly African American school in Durham, North Carolina, where we lived. He spoke of Justice Potter Stewart, "Stewart's great contribution was that he represented the Warren Court on the Burger Court, to see that the Burger Court did not roll back the clock on the Warren Court," the judge recalled. "He was a conservative, but he believed that simply because you have another vote, you do not roll back the clock."

The judge sent me to his law clerk at the time of the district court's *Rowley* decision, Elizabeth Bradford, then an assistant attorney general in Nassau County, New York. She agreed to reread the opinion and refresh herself on the three complaints raised by Judge Mansfield's dissent. She saw nothing inappropriate in Broderick's having cited regulations under Section 504 of the Rehabilitation Act of 1973 for assistance in determining the meaning of a "free and appropriate" education. She referred me to the brief for the United States on petition for certiorari, which had noted that the act's own regulations called for each state plan submitted to the Secretary of Education to include an assurance that the program would be operated in accordance with Section 504 regulations.

She laughed at the reference to the judge's having borrowed the phrase, "each handicapped child must be given an opportunity to achieve his full potential commensurate with the opportunity provided to other children," from a law review. "It was the *Harvard Law Review*, and it seemed to put the case for equal opportunity very well. I could see criticism if we had borrowed from some Podunk law review maybe."

As to the "battery of tests" (Mansfield's phrase) to be administered to schoolchildren that the school's attorneys maintained that Judge Broderick had created, she seemed as baffled as I had been. "The tests at issue, of course," she said, "were standardized tests, which were the only tests introduced into court." She conceded that some of the language in the judge's opinion may have been "a little too clinical" on the matter of testing schoolchildren—"I can criticize the language because it was probably mine"—but she insisted that it was not the intention to create new tests to measure shortfall from this or that child's potential, but merely to rely on tests the schools were giving. "Pretty much what had been done in Amy's case as presented in court," she concluded.

I asked her whether she thought that omitting the words "full potential," thus reducing the operative phrase to "each handicapped child must be given the opportunity to achieve commensurate with the opportunity given other children," might have made a difference in the ultimate outcome. I asked the question fully aware that both Congress and the judge had been referring to the educational goal of helping *all* children reach their full potential, but also with awareness that the media had seized on these words as though they had been intended to apply only to children with disabilities. Bradford paused momentarily before answering. "What the judge called for was equal opportunity, plain and simple," she responded. "To overturn the decision, you had to overturn that."

13

Is It Really Money?

In an effort to understand better the thinking of key media writers about *Rowley* at critical times in the history of the case, I decided to begin by looking up Roger Starr. His article, "Wheels of Misfortune," in *Harper's* magazine in January 1982, had taken the position, just two months before the Supreme Court hearing, that individuals with disabilities had no special "rights" as a result of their condition and would have to compete for "heavy" costs of rehabilitation with other social concerns that might be more pressing. Because Starr was on the editorial board of the *New York Times* during this period, I assumed he had also written the editorials the newspaper had carried on the case.

A friendly, florid, outgoing man, Starr invited me to his office and we shared a lunch in the *Times* cafeteria. He talked about his days as administrator for New York City (upon which experience he had drawn for his book, *The Rise and Fall of New York City*), where his views on disability were rooted.* "I got into it," he told me, "because the organizations advocating rights for the disabled were insisting that the subways be made wheelchair accessible. And we're struggling to keep the subway system going and the cost–benefit analysis that one could do on the back of one's shirt cuff would indicate that trying to make the subways wheelchair accessible might end the subway system entirely. It was a really unreasonable demand and I got into it at that point."

---

* New York: Basic Books, 1985.

Starr's other point of entry into the discussion of disability rights was philosophical. As a student of philosophy at Yale, he became interested in the issue of "natural" as opposed to "political" rights. "Unless one is willing to say as the Founding Fathers did that the Creator endowed us with rights, it's very hard to understand what the meaning of 'rights' is other than a political decision on the part of government which has public support. Absent that, there are no effective rights, then, only 'natural rights' and there surely are no natural rights in regard to the disabled.

"The government makes a statement that rests almost purely on economics, such as you have the right to an individual tutor sitting behind you in a mainstreamed class so that you are not feeling yourself to be different . . . and people cannot object to this strange person in the class, [then] the government ought to say here is the money to pay. The government, in effect, welched on its contract. There is a moral obligation to provide the money, because there is no reason to believe that the local school board has the money or can force taxpayers to assess themselves to pay for this. . . . Personally, I'm compassionate but there is a big difference between being willing to work for something you feel strongly about and imposing the burden on the taxpayers when the Congress is unable or unwilling to put out the money."

Starr said he didn't think his article in *Harper's* or the editorials in the *Times* had any effect on the Supreme Court's decision in *Rowley*, but, he said, he hadn't written the newspaper editorials, having taken the position that it is bad policy to write about a case when it is in the court system for settlement. He told me he could find out who had written them, left the room, and returned some minutes later with a name, Hugh Price, then an executive for WNET, Channel 13, in New York City.

Price proved willing to discuss the matter with me, although he was not willing to say which of the *Times* editorials I had sent him he had written or to discuss any of them in detail. He took the position that the editorials were the product of discussion with other members of the editorial staff and the editor of the editorial page, Max Frankel, and as such were not ascribable to individual authorship.

Price recalled being troubled by the language of "free and appropriate" education in the Education for All Handicapped Children Act. On principle, this concern went to the meaning of the word "appropriate." He said he could look about at the school system of New York City and see many children who did not receive an "appropriate" education. "No other children I could discover had a comparable right. No other comparable group of children could get custom-tailored education and receive services that other children did not have. I had a problem with that. I didn't have a problem with handicapped children, but I had a problem with that. . . . I could see poor children who were not getting service that could be described as 'appropriate.' " His problem with the act also went to fiscal concerns. The amount of money available was finite, he said, and what was given to one group might not be given to another. "If you put dollars here, you do not have dollars to put there."

I had two exchanges of letters with Frankel, who by this time had become executive editor of the *New York Times*. I wrote him in September 1992, describing the book project I had undertaken and asking if he remembered anything that could account for the newspaper's understanding that Amy Rowley's parents or attorney had sought "raising the handicapped child to its full potential." He responded that he "did not remember much about the *Rowley* case," but he did remember discussions of "the broader issue of special education, then and since." He continued, "The reason is that New York City's education budget has escalated beyond our capacities by the Federal mandates for special education without matching Federal aid. And we have been further strained by the (often understandable) tendency of teachers sending difficult pupils out of their mainstream classes into the 'special' education track, thus adding new complexities and costs."

I wrote again thanking him and noting that I was familiar with the cost issue and was not concerned at this time with the point of view expressed by the editorials, but only with what seemed to me to be repeated misstatements of fact. I told him that I was puzzled with the way the major media, particularly in the media power centers of New York and Washington, had managed to miss the "equal opportunity" thrust of the *Rowley* case. Did he have any thoughts on this? His second written response begged off further discussion on the basis of the passage of time and the fact that he no longer had responsibility for the newspaper's editorial page.

My letter to Linda Greenhouse enclosed copies of her stories and the correspondence between her and Chatoff. I asked if she knew why, having heard from the Rowleys' attorney on the subject and having said, in effect, that she had understood his point, she had used the same language in the lead of her story after the Supreme Court decision. When she had not responded in some time, I asked a friend who knew her, an old *Times* hand, to find out if she intended to respond. He reported that she had received my letter and did not intend to respond.

Looking over these comments, I noted again the sense of power and funding lost by ordinary people to a group they considered dominated by, if not entirely represented by, a powerful special interest. I thought it might be difficult for someone with a disability, who honestly felt that she or he faced unequal odds in attaining life goals, to imagine herself or himself as a genuine threat to the welfare of her or his neighbors. Not for the first time, I struggled to plumb the source of this repudiation by people who could describe themselves, with apparent sincerity, as "caring" and "compassionate."

Pushed to explain, they seemed always to settle defensively behind one bulwark that they felt could not be assailed. It was too expensive. Whatever individuals with disabilities felt was essential to right the scales that were weighed against them was beyond the power of the commonweal to fund, or it could be done only by sacrificing others who were equally deserving. These others might be poor children, as Price thought, or they might be well-off children, as in the case of the mother in Westchester who equated Amy Rowley's needs with her son's desire for special training in the arts in secondary school. This attitude invited anyone to fill in the blank with the name of the offended individual child whose interests were subverted by any gains children with disabilities might make.

No matter how vehemently attorneys and school officials protested to the contrary, money was central to the *Rowley* case. Money colors the record of the case from New York State's claim that a victory for the Rowleys could cost the state $100 million a year to the closely related question asked of Chatoff by Judge Mansfield in the appellate court and Justice Stevens in the Supreme Court hearings, "Will your interpretation of the statute require every school board to provide sign language interpreters for every deaf child in the country?" Although Chatoff responded with an emphatic "no" on each occasion and although he explained why his answer was grounded in the realities of the situation with deaf children, it may not be unfair to observe that the judges who asked that question both ultimately came out against the Rowleys.

Whatever the rationale for the question from the bench, it is one that in the asking communicates to the deaf person that the questioner knows nothing about deafness. The National Association of the Deaf, in its friend-of-court brief in *Rowley*, provided a count from the New York State plan of the year in question (1979–80), indicating that there were 3,449 deaf and 1,609 hard-of-hearing children.

"Very few of these deaf and hard of hearing students in New York are in need of interpreter service," NAD noted. "Mildly to moderately hard of hearing students would not be materially aided by such a supplementary aid. Their handicap is not severe enough to require the use of total communication; a properly fitted and maintained hearing aid is sufficient in most cases to give them full access to classroom discussion. Supplementary language and speech instruction would also be needed for some such students but not classroom interpreting. Deaf children who have been brought up utilizing an oral approach and who are enrolled in oral programs do not depend upon sign language interpreting. Many of the severely and profoundly deaf children in New York State are in self-contained classes, whether oral or total communication classes. These children . . . do not require interpretation. . . . Similarly, many profoundly deaf children are in day schools and residential schools and attend classes only with other deaf children."*

NAD noted that New York State educated deaf children in self-contained classes in local schools, in BOCES programs, in one state-operated school, in seven state-supported schools, and in schools supported by special legislative acts. It's interesting that the considerable public cost of educating deaf children in schools or in classes apart from hearing children does not seem to have been an issue. This, despite the fact that the same taxpayers pay the bills for what might be described as this separate-but-unequal education of deaf children. Cost becomes an issue, apparently, only when we are talking about bringing children with disabilities—or, for that matter, adults with disabilities, seeking access to public buildings or transportation—into the mainstream of our life.

And this cost tends to be presented in dramatically disingenuous ways, as, for example, the *Times* editorial's leap from the sign language interpreter for "every" child to a "tutor for every learning-disabled child" in school. The picture Starr had presented to me verbally, of a pupil with an individual tutor situated just behind in the classroom, is vividly reprised in New York State's offhanded multiplication of the somewhat inflated salary of one sign language interpreter by a number supposed to represent all deaf children in the state to arrive at its $100-million-a-year fright figure.

Presentation of the image of a "private tutor" becomes here a code for "too expensive" and spares those who use it the necessity of looking seriously at the issue of disability and cost. Initially, it papers over cost-mitigating practices such as the use of one tutor–assistant for more than one child in the

* Brief amicus curiae of the National Association of the Deaf et al. in the case of Hendrick Hudson Central School District v. Amy Rowley by her parents, United States Supreme Court, October term 1980, pp. 24–25.

same classroom and ignores the fact that children whose disabilities require more expensive services are by far the fewest in number. For instance, deaf children, only some of whom need a sign language interpreter, constitute only 6 percent of all handicapped children, while speech-impaired children, who need the least expensive services, account for 30 percent.

Beyond that, the issue of cost cannot be discussed intelligently without a look at what we spend the money for. Anyone who has studied the subject is aware that we seem willing to pay a great deal to maintain individuals with disabilities outside the labor market, but very little to educate and train them to move inside the labor market, despite studies going back as far as the 1960s. Those cited by the President's Committee on the Employment of Individuals with Disabilities, indicated that the return of tax dollars for dollars invested in rehabilitation ranged from a low ratio of 1:10 to a high of 1:36.

I'm not fully familiar with the studies cited by the President's committee, but I am with a number of programs run by private enterprise in the 1970s and 1980s, in which effort put into hiring and training individuals with disabilities was rewarded with clear economic benefits for the companies involved, as well as for the individual employees. One such program was run in Austin, Texas, in the 1980s, in collaboration with Motorola by Marc Gold and Associates. Gold was a special education teacher in East Los Angeles who formulated a teaching system particularly suited to mentally retarded students. His associates persuaded Motorola to hire full-time, ten mildly and moderately mentally retarded individuals, a group always hard put to find employment of any kind. The ten were picture-perfect unemployables by virtually all standards of that day or this. None had held a full-time job previously; eight had not finished high school; two were in state institutions, and a third in a halfway house; eight were unemployed; and seven were receiving public assistance. I.Q.s ranged from 35 to 75.

I had come to Austin in 1982 in connection with the project that eventually became *Seven Special Kids*. Darryl Townsend was Gold's associate at Motorola, and he started off by telling me that the I.Q.s didn't bother him. "We've found little or no relationship between the I.Q. and what an individual can learn," he said. MG&A's secret, it became obvious as he talked about the program, was a minutely designed reorganization of the training process, breaking down complex tasks into simple units. To do this, the trainers first had to learn the task thoroughly themselves. Then they put the trainees through three months of classroom training, followed by three months of on-the-job-training. Of the ten, five dropped by the wayside in the first nine months of work, Townsend reported. "They had high quality, but they could not get up to the speed needed for production."

The program, supported in part by the Comprehensive Employment Training Act (CETA), cost $150,000. Here are the program's cost-benefit figures:

Prior to training, the group of ten was earning annually only a total of $6,465 while receiving public assistance payments totaling $68,743—in other words, they were receiving in assistance ten times what they earned.

In the year after training, earnings totaled $70,115, a more than tenfold increase.

In the year after training, in place of the heavy bill for public assistance, the group showed an overall payback of $6,111 in federal taxes alone.

In other words, instead of sustaining a public deficit of $68,743, this group of individuals with disabilities paid $6,111 in federal taxes alone.

Interestingly enough, the five who had been "dropped" from the Motorola program, after some training showed dramatic improvement as well, with three of them employed, and the group of five showing an increase in pre- and posttraining annual earnings ranging from $469 to $9,854.

First-year figures such as these generally are thought to overstate economic improvement, and long-term follow-up of such programs is scarce. On a hunch one morning, I put in a call to Motorola in Austin, and got Ginger Byram, human resources services manager. I asked her if she knew anything about this decade-old program. "I guess I do," she said. "I was one of the people who put it in place." She hadn't focused specifically on it recently, but she had an inkling that some of the participants were still on the job. She would look into it and call back.

In a couple of weeks, I heard from her again. She had learned that of the five individuals employed in 1980—thirteen years earlier—four were still employed by Motorola at an average annual salary of $17,700. While two were still at the entry-level, the first of four levels of skills possible to attain on the plant floor, one had moved to the second level and one to the third. Byram wanted me to know that Motorola regularly employed hearing-impaired individuals (approximately twenty at that time) and was working to bring teachers of deaf and blind students into the plant as trainers.

Now this is hardly your classic, academic cost–benefit evaluation, replete with comparison group, but it's worth remembering that few private employers are prepared to give mentally retarded individuals a look, much less a job. If we consider only the support money saved and the earnings of the four who stayed with Motorola, it's entirely possible that these workers have paid back the full cost of their training in federal taxes alone.

But it really should not take much mother wit to grasp what is, after all, fairly obvious—well-run programs that reduce expensive dependence in favor of increased independence and earnings are cost effective to one degree or another. What's not usually understood are the unusually profitable side effects of such programs. Writing in 1981, after the second phase of the program had begun, an assembly manufacturing manager for Motorola had noted, "Our Motorola trainers are working closely with the MG&A trainers . . . they have learned many specialized training techniques used. We have adopted some of these techniques and . . . I am confident that our training methods for all new employees will be improved by this experience." * I asked Byram about that, and she said that Motorola trainers from elsewhere around the country were still learning from this program in 1993.

But in the 1970s and 1980s, when these lessons were striking sparks and often catching fire in our national employment and training programs and in special schools, as a nation we still acted as though the opposite were the case. We continued to move in the direction of massive maintenance and away from rehabilitation. In no single area of our effort was this self-defeating trend more painfully apparent than in our treatment of individuals with disabilities.

Let's look at just one classic, academic evaluation for an example. In their 1988 study, four of the most respected researchers in this field, Monroe Berkowitz, David Dean, Dale Hanks, and Stanley Portny, observed that between 1970 and 1986 disability payments had increased from $19.3 billion to $169.4 billion, an increase swelled by private transfer payments for automobile accidents.† While this was happening, "direct service" (rehabilitation) payments to individuals with disabilities declined from 5 to 2 percent of the total. And only a minuscule 4 percent of that tiny 2 percent, the authors noted, was being spent to assist individuals with disabilities in gaining employment.

"That proportion [money spent on direct services] seems paltry," the report states. "To spend more than $86 billion on cash transfers, more than $79 billion on medical care payments, and less than $4 billion on direct

* Smith, *Seven Special Kids,* p. 141.

† *Enhancing Understanding of the Economics of Disability* (Richmond: Virginia Department of Rehabilitation Services, August 1988).

services designed to . . . rehabilitate seems to be an example of misplaced priorities. How can we account for these distorted allocations? Since the money spent here is aimed directly at getting the people in the labor market once again, . . . the authors conclude that doubts remain whether the direct services programs are effective."

To find out whether the programs actually were effective, the authors tracked fifteen hundred rehabilitation clients in Texas, California, and Virginia over a five-year period, using as a comparison group people who dropped out of the program before receiving substantial services. They looked at preprogram earnings for two years prior to service and postprogram for one year afterward by six measurements—physical, mental, and emotional disability by males and females. In each set, impacts for those treated were positive, with improvements ranging from $400 for the male mentally retarded group to $1,579 for the female physically disabled group. "From the point of view of advocates of the program," the authors concluded, "the empirical results are by and large encouraging. . . . Treatment in the program has its positive effects."

I talked with Dr. David Dean over the phone, and he agreed emphatically that funding for rehabilitation is currently lacking, "What federal–state programs currently do is give a little bit of money to some people." I asked him if he thought results of the University of Virginia study indicated that rehabilitation can be a sound economic proposition, and he sent me three other studies that showed gains more dramatic than the ones cited above. One showed gains of twice the cost of the program in the year after treatment alone, with steadily rising gains over a three-year period.

It is important to remember that these gains were achieved in a system in which the swollen pot of "transfer payments" represents a disincentive to work; the bare level of individual maintenance assumes little or no income and actually penalizes the individual who earns more by reducing or eliminating supports, most critically medical support that the individual has no way of replacing. In such circumstances, work can and does become a high-risk venture. Ordinary prudence would dictate continued idleness.

In blunt economic terms, the system makes tax-eaters out of hundreds of thousands of capable individuals whose disabilities would not otherwise prevent them from attaining a degree of self-sufficiency and the status of taxpayers. The situation is very much as Frank Bowe described it in his debate with Roger Starr in Greensboro: the question is not whether we can afford to help the handicapped get jobs, but whether we can afford not to.

In human terms, a considerable pool of individuals with disabilities who are capable of working and want to work are being bribed not to by a system that feeds them if they stay out of the labor market and starves them for the means—education and training—to enter it. A 1986 Lou Harris poll indicated that two-thirds of all individuals with disabilities of working age were not working at all, although two-thirds of those not working wanted to work. Almost 50 percent of those not working believed that the attitudes of employers prevented them from getting jobs. These are the forgotten unemployed. They are human castoffs. They are also out of sight and out of mind, at a beclouded distance whence we need not observe their discouragement and defeat or look upon their faces.

Perhaps the Virginia researchers' hypothesis is correct, that our disinclination to put money into training individuals with disabilities for work is a result of a lack of confidence in that training. Another explanation is available: we really do not want individuals with disabilities in the workforce. We would rather pay the far greater cost to keep them at home where we will not see them or have to take them into account.

A preacher's daughter, growing up in tight economic times, Elisabeth Hudson had never learned to drive a car. She used the van service that was available on 24-hours' notice for individuals with mobility impairment to get from home to where she wanted to go. One day when I was visiting her, we stopped by the library and she asked the van driver to take us back home via a route that would pass a restaurant she had visited with her son on Mother's Day the year before. She had heard good things about it and wanted to try it out, but she had been distressed to discover that, with shrubbery grown over the sidewalk in front of the ramp, a car blocking two-thirds of the walk directly in front of the ramp, and no handicapped parking places, the restaurant was inaccessible. She and her son went to a second-choice restaurant, and she wrote her usual temperate letter of complaint to the manager of the first, who did not respond.

The driver pulled up at the restaurant and stopped long enough for me to see that nothing had changed from her earlier visit. I remember being mildly puzzled as we sat there, considering that all that was needed to make this building accessible was a ramp or curb cut in the front and a few minutes of work with a set of clippers. Why wouldn't the management incur this minor expense to gain a contented clientele, particularly when word would spread that another "good" restaurant was accessible. I asked Elisabeth and she sat quite still without responding for something like a minute.

"You know," she finally said, "I only landed in this wheelchair a few years ago. I'm a newcomer to all this. I find myself telling my friends now that I had a dear friend in a wheelchair before all this happened to me, and that's true. What I don't always tell them is that I'm ashamed to say that I had not a clue about my friend's real needs and I never said a word to anyone else in a wheelchair or with any other disability. When I try to think back now to what it was like before, it's as though these people who are among my friends now didn't really exist for me. For *me*, understand. I believed in them the way we believe in dinosaurs, without caring much one way or another and knowing, I thought, that I'd never have to deal with them. And not wanting to. Now, I didn't know I didn't want to, understand. I would have denied it, I'm sure. But it was true."

She fell silent and my mind went to the things she had said without saying them. Cost was not the issue with this restaurant: the management did not want people in wheelchairs on the premises. They did not want "cripples" mixed in with their other customers, whom they assumed would be put off by the sight, as they were put off by the idea. I found myself thinking of this incident later on, as I reread Gliedman and Roth's *Unexpected Minority*. In the first chapter of this 1980 book, the authors imagine a visitor from an advanced industrial society, "genuinely respecting the needs of humanity," visiting America. The authors postulate that the visitor would expect to find industry churning out goods for the 10 to 20 million normally intelligent people with disabilities and employing them casually in factories, and a specific wooing of them by political parties—after all, the authors note, one-tenth of all children and one-fifth of all adults have a disability, and at least half of all able-bodied people have a disabled spouse, child, parent, or close friend. Instead, the visitor would find indifference. "Not only are the handicapped generally denied a work identity," the authors observe, "they are also denied an independent identity as consumers." Our visitor would also find that severely disabled individuals were routinely being treated as children. "In many respects, our visitor would find the handicapped as politically weak as blacks were before the legal breakthrough of the 1950s and 1960s."[*]

While individuals with disabilities have unquestionably gained a degree of political strength since 1980, if only through the passage of the Ameri-

[*] Gliedman and Roth, *Unexpected Minority,* pp. 13–16.

cans with Disabilities Act, the situation with regard to their being treated as workers or consumers has changed little. As I reread the Gliedman and Roth chapter, I thought of what my friend Elisabeth had said. It was, for us in the "able" world, as though these people did not exist.

Is it really money that stands in the way of providing equal opportunities for individuals with disabilities in our society? We could save money by reversing gears on our maintenance policy and concentrating efforts on rehabilitation, but we don't. We could do what Americans have always been able to do, make money by marketing to a special group's needs. Why not "designers' " prosthetics and stylish wheelchairs displayed at least as prominently in our malls as clothing stores for the oversized? But we don't do that either. The conclusion is inescapable that we prefer not to see anything that would remind us of the presence of disability among us.

This attitude is well understood in disability circles. "It's as though disability were catching," is the description I have heard many times. It is this awareness that adds heat to reactions against the "it's-too-expensive" complaint that seems to be broached whenever any disability need is demonstrated. In a letter to the *New York Times,* following its editorial on the Supreme Court decision in *Rowley,* Arthur Pepine, assistant to the dean at the Yale School of Drama, noted, "People with disabilities constitute the first minority since the era of slavery upon whose basic rights has been hung a price tag. What is the going price of rights these days, anyway? We properly don't hear the *Times* speak of cost when discussing school integration through busing. Nor do we hear you speak of cost when defending the right of children of aliens to a free, appropriate education. Nor do you speak of cost when discussing the appropriateness of accepting the 'boat people.' Our forefathers long ago made the point that basic rights are neither alienable nor for sale, a position shared by the Court's minority in the *Rowley* case. For the *Times* not to share that position is profoundly shameful, indeed."*

Robert Kleck, a psychologist at Dartmouth University, who has written extensively on issues of disability and social outcomes, recalls a television program from the early 1980s called "How Much for the Handicapped?" in which it was suggested that demands of individuals with disabilities were getting out of hand and somehow had to be resisted on grounds of their outrageous costs. Kleck says that the people who put forth such economic

---

* July 17, 1982.

251

arguments really have a social objective, "What they are saying is 'don't get too close, now . . . get back.'"

He continues: "If we really agreed that individuals needed certain services, we could debate the issue on broader terms, such as would we give up one M-1 tank for improvements that would allow individuals with handicaps to use a staircase to a laboratory in a science building. . . . By the way, nobody ever talks about the cost of access to a building for those of us who *aren't* handicapped. It is only when the question of accessibility falls on those of us who cannot use this rather expensive staircase that the issue of cost comes up," he told me.

Those who raise the cost issue as a reason for opposing gains for children with disabilities in public schools usually assign a heavy burden of blame to Congress for passing the Education for All Handicapped Children Act and then failing to appropriate the money to put it fully into effect. The Congress, Roger Starr said, had "welched" on its promise to the states. Without pursuing the fiscal details of the matter further, most of those who raise this argument simply describe the tax burden this left on the states as intolerable. Coated heavily with a state's-rights flavor, the argument goes like this: if the Congress wants all that fancy stuff for these handicapped kids, let the federal government—not the states—pay for it.

Setting aside the fact that we citizens pay taxes to the federal government as well as to the states, the truth is that Congress can hardly be called irresponsible in this matter. Congress expanded its expenditures for educating children with disabilities from less than $150 million in 1974 to more than $1 billion in 1980 and it has doubled its outlay in the intervening years, an almost twentyfold increase. Much of the impression of Congress' failure comes from the percentage of federal contribution originally specified in the act: "If the federal government actually were paying 40 percent of the cost, as originally planned," Lou Donaldson, chief of the special services branch of the Office of Special Education told me, "it would be paying six times what it is now. Given the inflation that has occurred—and now, of course, the deficit—that's highly unlikely."

But the Education for All Handicapped Children Act was not meant to provide federal funds sufficient to supplant state funds in the first place. Hearings before Congress had demonstrated that the states—which have primary fiscal responsibility for elementary and secondary education—had simply not been serving these children, frequently in disregard of their own laws. Congress, which as Senator Jacob Javits (R–N.Y.) observed on the

Senate floor, itself had been "asleep" at the switch for years now, it was offering funding to assist the states in redressing a social wrong for which there was sufficient blame to go around.

Furthermore, the issue at stake in the legal battles over services in public schools for children with disabilities has not been whether the federal government or the states, or both combined, could wave a wand and make discrimination against these children disappear. After all, efforts to bring African American children fully into the mainstream of public education in this country continue forty years after the Supreme Court spoke to that issue. The real issue under the Education for All Handicapped Children Act is that by saying "equal opportunity," Congress had set forth the proposition that whatever the inadequacies of this or that school system, they could not be brought to bear more heavily on a child with a disability than on a child without one. Stop discriminating against the hundreds of thousands of children whose disabilities never should have kept them out of school in the first place—that was the message. And to the extent that this process of desegregation entailed fiscal discomfort, let that discomfort be borne equally among all.

This was the real cost issue in *Rowley*, and it remains the real cost issue today. Guns and butter priorities ultimately must deal with questions of absolute economic wealth, but before that, they inevitably deal with questions of relative societal values. In passing the Education for All Handicapped Children Act, Congress had pronounced that the cost of continuing to strip a group of American children of the equal opportunity for a good education in our democratic society was too high.

A different issue of cost had stirred the working press, whose representatives had invariably asked members of the board of education and School Superintendent Charles Eible how much defense of *Rowley* at the district court and appeals levels up to the Supreme Court had cost the local taxpayers. After the Supreme Court hearing, the figure given to the press by the school district and the board of education was $100,000. But the question asked by the press went to what the books would show: How much did it actually cost?

I didn't find the question all that interesting. My interviews with school board members who had authorized expenditures on the case had convinced me that, whatever else might be said about them, these were honorable people who believed they were in the right. They felt, as one of them told me, that they had the unfortunate burden of representing the interests of boards and schools all over the country. Given that belief, they were merely doing their duty. In any event, they believed the cost to be far less than the cost of providing the services they imagined would be demanded if Amy Rowley won her case.

Still, I made an effort to learn what the costs had been—for the record. Neither Kuntz nor Eible was returning my phone calls by the time I got around to pursuing this point, so I availed myself of New York's Committee on Open Government, lodged in the Department of State. Director Robert Freeman thought that records of expenses having to do with the case ought to be available under the Freedom of Information Act. He was extremely helpful but we never were able to get anything more useful from the school district than that it did not maintain records containing the information requested. When we reached the point where it appeared that my only recourse was to take this matter to the board of education and possibly to court, I dropped the matter in the interests of my own time and resources.

But there was another strand of inquiry I did feel obliged to follow. It had to do with the so-called impartial hearing system, the method established for adjudicative review below the court level in New York State. I remembered Michael Chatoff's contempt for the way it had operated in *Rowley*, and my own look at it prompted scarcely greater credibility. On the surface, here was an internal hearing process in which the "judge" was chosen by the school board, one of the disputants in the matter. Worse, in practice, choosing the hearing officer often had fallen to the board's attorney, the chief legal arm of its adversarial function. Finally, review of that individual's decision was vested in the office of the chief policymaker for the state school system, the commissioner of education. Here was a system that seemed ripe for the kind of institutional bias that Chatoff had complained of in the treatment Amy Rowley's case had received. His complaints had settled on specific apparent conflicts of interest, and I thought that was something worth looking into.

One day I ran into an item in the Rowleys' files indicating that Inez Janger, one of the two women originally scheduled to testify in the school district's case, had been party to an effort by parents of children with disabilities to force this system to face the need for reform. I asked her about it, and she suggested I call Bruce Goldstein, a professor of law and father of two deaf girls, in Buffalo. Goldstein told me I was on the right track. "If the impartial hearing officer wants to work again in that school district, it behooves him to rule favorably to the district," he said. He told me about a suit currently in process to test the authority of the school district to appoint hearing officers. He also gave me the name of Kate Surgalla in the office of the counsel for the New York State Department of Education.

From Surgalla I got a sheaf of records that enabled me to trace the efforts of parents and advocate groups since the days of the Rowley case to force reform of the review system. Most of these actions were without success, but in 1986 legislation was enacted requiring applicants to take a written examination before being placed on the approved list for impartial hearing officers. The old, established officers, however, had only to present evidence that they had sufficient experience to pass the test, anyway. More progress had been made at the state level, where the commissioner of education, in 1990, had been relieved by the legislature of his duties in reviewing appeals from impartial hearings. He had been replaced, I learned, by a state review officer. Among the doyens of the group that effected this change was Elizabeth "Betsy" Schneider, who worked for the Monroe County Legal Assistance Corporation, an advocacy group for parents who had problems with schools.

Schneider described as typical complaints from parents that the hearing officers were anything but impartial. They were for the most part, she said, school people, often from a school district not far down the road. Their bias was plainly toward the school system. Generally, they knew nothing of special education or the needs of children with disabilities. She told me that New York had been one of the few states whose chief educational officer served as final arbiter of disputes between parents and schools. "It was a matter of school people settling school business themselves," she said. She sent me on to Roger Nellist, protection and advocacy officer for the Western New York Advocacy for the Developmentally Disabled.

Nellist told me that he had been in the field since 1978 and that, apart from the move to a state review officer, little change was observable. He did think that little was a big improvement, however, and that some school districts were doing a better job of finding hearing officers who actually could be impartial. Conflicts of interest on the part of hearing officers continued to be a problem, nevertheless. He told me that one hearing officer had been shown to have had an attorney–client relationship with a nearby school district, and, as a result, a decision he had rendered was overturned. The story rang a bell. Surgalla had sent me an opinion by the Second Circuit federal appeals court, which contained some comment on this, and I pulled out the name of the plaintiff: Edward Joseph Heldman. This was the case mentioned by Bruce Goldstein, challenging the right of school boards to choose impartial hearing officers, and it was still under adjudication.

Before calling Heldman, I went through the appellate court opinion, which I had only glanced at earlier. It concerned a challenge to the Minisink Board of Education by the Heldmans of the placement and classification in high school of their learning-disabled son, Ted. The Heldmans contended that the system of appointment of impartial hearing officers currently in effect was in conflict with the due process guarantees of the Individuals with Disabilities Education Act (IDEA), which is the old Education for All Handicapped Children Act renamed. The Heldman case had been dismissed by the district court for lack of standing and failure to exhaust administrative remedies. That decision had been reversed by the appellate court in the opinion from April 1992 that Surgalla had sent me. It was remanded back to the district court with instructions: allow the Heldmans to amend his complaint. I quote from this court document:

"The Minisink Board of Education selected a hearing officer, who had been recommended by the school district's attorney, to preside over the hearing," wrote the unanimous, three-judge federal appellate court. "During the winter of 1989, prior to the dispute over Ted's IEP, the Heldmans, acting as concerned citizens, became involved in a dispute over the independence of hearing officers. Frank Eckelt, a hearing officer in an unrelated proceeding, was found to have violated the conflict of interest provisions by serving both as a consultant and hearing officer for a school district. The Heldmans actively campaigned for Eckelt's removal from the list of certified hearing officers. As a result of the Eckelt controversy, the Heldmans were made aware of the potential for abuse within the New York system for the selection of hearing officers. This awareness apparently led them to question the impartiality of the hearing officer, one George Kandilakis, assigned to review Ted's IEP. The Heldmans, after being notified of the identity of their hearing officer, requested both a copy of his résumé and a disclosure of past and present relationships with either Minisink or the Karafin [High] School. The hearing officer, however, denied these requests.

"The Heldmans subsequently found a letter in Ted's file from Minisink's attorney—the very attorney they would be arguing against in the upcoming hearing—to the Board of Education recommending that they select Kandilakis as the hearing officer. Furthermore, in the letter, the attorney revealed that 'it was through Dr. Eckelt that I was able to locate Mr. Kandi-lakis.' On the basis of this information, on March 31, 1989, the Heldmans filed a motion of recusal [that the officer withdraw because of bias] and withdrew their hearing request pending a decision on the motion. Officer Kandilakis never responded to the motion and on April 10, 1989, he conducted the hearing without the Heldmans being present."*

I did a classic double take on encountering Eckelt's name in this opinion of the appellate court. Eckelt had been the first officer proposed by Hendrick Hudson attorney Raymond Kuntz for the Rowleys' initial impartial hearing eleven years earlier. When Chatoff had complained that Eckelt had once been associated with Superintendent Charles Eible, Kuntz had withdrawn Eckelt's name, observing that the association complained of had been seven years earlier and that Eckelt was the most experienced of the hearing officers available.

Another link between the *Heldman* case and the *Rowley* case was that the district federal judge who had heard the case initially was Judge Vincent L. Broderick, who had heard Amy's case. When I reached Heldman by phone, I asked him first about Judge Broderick's having found against him. "Yes," Heldman said, "I couldn't get an attorney on a *pro bono* basis and couldn't afford one, so I represented Ted and I made a lot of procedural errors that brought my case down." Heldman added that Judge Broderick had nevertheless issued an advisory opinion indicating that if the case had come to trial in his court, he "would have some very strong things to say about such a one-sided due process hearing."

A scientific photographer who himself had had a learning disability and dropped out of high school, Heldman believes that the experience made him determined to fight for his son Ted. From their home in New Hampton, New York, he and his wife helped organize the Special Education Parents and Advocates Coalition in 1988. "It's definitely nonprofit," he chuckled over the phone, "and not big enough to be called statewide. Just a group of parents who found each other."

Heldman told me that the experience of doing battle for his son's education had seasoned him roughly but thoroughly. Reacting to my having said that I was still working on my own prejudices, he responded: "Me, too,

* United States Court of Appeals for the Second Circuit, Edward Joseph Heldman on behalf of his son, T. H., v. Thomas Sobol, Commissioner of the State Education Department of New York, argued October 31, 1991.

even after all this. Then, there is the pressure. I've talked with many, many parents, and you simply can't imagine the emotional burden it puts on parents to go through this unless you've done it yourself. You see those 70 to 80 percent of kids going through schooling easily and yours has one struggle after another. If you get involved in a legal struggle, it escalates things further. You see punitive things happening to your kid in school, or to some other member of your family. It's unfortunate and a very sad thing to say, but it's a frequent complaint of parents that a sister or a brother is getting punishment for the family's efforts on behalf of a sibling with a disability."

Since Heldman was familiar with the general outlines of the *Rowley* case, I remarked that he might have been talking about John Rowley, and filled him in with the details of what had happened to Amy's older brother in Peekskill schools. "I didn't know about that," he said. "Actually, I'm talking about our Jeffrey, who is two grades behind Ted. We had to take him out of grade school in the eighth grade. This was a kid who had won honors in school, had excellent reports on behavior, and who suddenly found himself in trouble. It was as though he had a target on his back." Jeffrey, he reported, was in private school as a result, another of the many largely invisible costs paid by parents who choose to fight for their children with disabilities.

Heldman, who publishes a monthly, *New York Individuals with Disabilities Education Law Report*, is for drastic reform of the impartial hearing system: abolition, with the function replaced by a separate state agency, such as an administrative court system. He would also replace the state review officer system with a "genuinely impartial tribunal." But he does not hesitate to affirm that things have gotten much better since the state review officer has taken over the old function of the commissioner of education. "Before the state review officer, parents were winning maybe one out of five appeals to the commissioner. Now they are winning two out of three. Of course, that says a lot about the impartial hearing officers." Heldman maintained that while the list of certified impartial review officers numbered around three hundred, only some 20 percent of them were chosen and used. He had calculated that 7 percent were settling 80 percent of the cases.

Later on, he sent me a case-by-case list of all appeals filed in the first two years of the state review officer system. I counted 91 in all (excluding a handful withdrawn or not settled), and, of these, 56 were granted in part or whole. I calculated the overturn rate here at 62 percent, not far off Heldman's estimate. Then I counted the impartial hearing officers to see how many duplications there were. I counted 47 officers for the 91 appeals filed. According to this list, one impartial hearing officer had 10 appeals to his decisions during the two-year period, of which 6 were granted either in part or in whole.

That officer's name especially caught my eye because it was Earle Warren Zaidins, the man who presided over the last two impartial hearings in the *Rowley* case, following the Supreme Court decision. Michael Chatoff and the Rowleys had argued that he was prejudiced against them and should disqualify himself. The hearing officer refused to do that and later ruled for the school and against the Rowleys on both occasions.

On March 30, 1993, the New York State General Assembly approved legislation calling for a training and rotation system for hearing officers, which has spread the work around more equitably. A key element of the legislation is that individuals who are employed by school boards may not serve as impartial hearing officers then or for two years after ending that employment. The act also establishes procedures for dismissal of hearing officers in violation of the regulations.

Heldman agreed to withdraw his motion for summary judgment in Judge Broderick's court, considering that the purposes of his action had been served.

14

Amy Remembering

Early one summer day in 1991, over the TTY, Amy said she had a proposition for me. I should come up to visit her parents in Mountain Lakes, we would all drive up to Croton to visit our mutual friends, Charles and Helen Brooks, and Amy and I would spend a morning walking through Furnace Woods Elementary School slowly, classroom by classroom. Amy would try to slip back into her childhood, as if she were putting on clothing hung away for years unused. She would try to speak again with the voice of a child, but when she had spoken, she would try to tell me how she felt now and what it all meant to her as an adult.

I tried, but I am sure I failed to conceal my delight. Here was an offer to accompany on a voyage of self-discovery someone whose progress through childhood and adolescence I had been tracking for almost seven years. And someone who, while infallibly friendly and fun to be with, had withheld from me for those long, slow, first years any inclination to explore a childhood that burned so hot, so close behind her. I have four children of my own who have passed through the half-dark door of adulthood, but with none of them did I feel quite the shock I felt with Amy, discovering, suddenly, an adult, into whose shadow the child I knew had vanished.

Driving from Mountain Lakes up to Croton, we took both cars, with Nancy and Clifford in one, thoughtfully leaving me with Amy and John in the other. I knew I would have time with Amy the next day, so I concentrated on John, who, at twenty-one, had a different kind of look on his face.

The John I remembered, even as recently as Amy's graduation the summer before, had two significant passions in his life: he loved skateboarding, a sport I had watched him and friends practice on a curved wooden ramp they negotiated at high speed. It seemed suicidal to me, and John did hurt his wrist badly at one point. The other passion was the music of the Grateful Dead. A confirmed Deadhead, John had joined others piling into cars to drive all day to concerts by their heroes, and then all night to get home. John's arrival at a small college campus in Vermont did result in the substitution of snowboarding for skateboarding, but John had hurt himself again that first winter, and I had the impression that he was floundering psychologically as well as academically. Now he was away at the University of Arizona and I wanted a catch-up from him.

"I went out there after a girl," he told me as he drove, with his sister by his side and me in the back seat, "but that didn't work out, but what did was much better for me. I had started to realize that what I was doing wasn't taking me anywhere. You can be an athlete, like doing skateboarding for a little while, and then it's too late for that and by then it's late to be thinking about school. . . . People had ideas and I got some ideas about what I should do, but I started thinking all that wouldn't mean anything to me, wouldn't do anything except for me, and I wanted to do something that would matter to someone else. So I started thinking about working with deaf people like my parents and sister and [with] what had been so much of my life in the past. Well, I was out there, so I looked at the University of Arizona and discovered that they had all these special education courses, and I thought I'd surely be able to put to use what I already knew, American Sign Language. Then, I thought, well it's a good way from snowboarding and maybe it would be good for me to be away from all that. So I decided to sign up at Arizona and give it a try. I didn't tell everyone I had a deaf family. I did tell my professor but he didn't tell the students, and I had a great time whizzing through this course, which I aced. That was summer school. I have a way to go to make up for the bad grades I had before this, but I feel good about where I'm headed now. I'm going back shortly to take more courses and enroll for the fall semester."

I listened and took notes without much comment, but inwardly I was exulting to think that John might have found a relatively early entrance into his own, private way. And again, I remembered a boy, hovering in the background of my first conversation with his parents and sister years before, slipping out of the house without a word to anyone. It hit me that I had arrived in time to see the traumatic effects of the school experience on both Amy and John and had stayed long enough to see them both begin to emerge as adults from the dark, forbidding tunnel of their adolescence—a difficult enough journey for us all, but marked indelibly for children from whom so much is expected by the adult world around them.

I came across another watershed at the Brookses where I discovered that young Charlie, who had a learning disability, had recently graduated from a master's program in special education and was getting ready to teach a class of ten dyslexic third-graders in the Yorktown school system. He was excited. I found myself thinking of the struggle his parents had had with the school system to get him the kind of attention that, now, these youngsters in nearby Yorktown would be getting from him. And, of course, Charlie and John would talk about their goals that now had so much more in common than either of them, growing up in the same neighborhood, could have imagined. As I sat in my room that night thinking, it struck me that, as in so many other cases of societal neglect, significant change in the education of children with disabilities might be fully measurable only generationally.

After breakfast the next morning, Helen Brooks and Amy and I drove over to the school where Amy had spent those turbulent first six years of her education. I had driven past the one-story, brick, and rust-colored wooden building once or twice before but had not been inside. Amy wore a look of almost forbidding intensity, as though struggling back with some effort across a barrier. I looked at her for a moment, realizing that she had withdrawn to where she would not notice. She was wearing jeans and a short-sleeved blouse, tennis shoes, the uniform of the young and uncommitted, yet for all her casual attire she had a kind of inner poise and command that exhibited itself through her stance.

Her smile ignited as she caught me watching her, and she took my arm to guide me down the hall, turning to speak directly to my face as deaf people always do, surely in the hope of reminding hearing people to do the same. "Let's go to the kindergarten first and work up from there." At the end of the hall was the room that had served as the kindergarten. Amy said she remembered the monkey bars. When talking was involved, she sat in front of the monkey bars so that she could see. Did she remember Jack Janik, the nine-day interpreter, I asked. A tall man, she remembered, in dark clothes to make reading signs easier. But no one had told her anything about the complicated situation she was entering. She had been brought up to read signs, but she had read them from the hands of the person speaking to her.

Now her teacher was speaking to her and this man who was not speaking to her was signing. And now she had to look at him. She remembered feeling baffled. "It was something you had to acquire," she reflected.

She looked at me hard as though wondering if I understood fully. "See," she said, "everything was so visual in kindergarten. My teacher would think I was understanding her, but I was really just watching what she was doing. You could get a lot of what was going on in kindergarten just watching what she was doing. It was a very visual experience." Miss Power, her teacher, always encouraged her to think she was doing well, she recalled, but she wanted to be up there with the best students, including her friend Marjorie Augenblick.

We passed by what she indicated was the music room. Looking in, she said, "Supercalifragilisticexpialidocious." She remembered her music teacher fondly. "Still," she said, "I didn't understand anything in music until I had an interpreter. I would hear the beat and that's all. Mr. Cantor said that the interpreter really helped me." By the time she had reached the fourth grade, she was learning to play the trumpet. How, I asked, arms flopping in surprise, could you do that? She just had to learn the notes in the music and where to press down on the keys to the trumpet. She told me, "I didn't really enjoy it that much."

First grade. Mrs. Globerman's room. Amy grinned that grin. "She was a chubby woman with a smile that just about ran off her face. She paid a lot of attention to me and always asked me if it was OK." Odd memories come popping out after all the years. Amy told me a story about a little boy who showed up on his birthday in the classroom with a briefcase and a scarf and put them in the cloakroom, much to the giggling delight of the class. Amy laughed at him and he said, "You're a silly little girl."

Talking, moving along, we encountered some workers repairing ceilings. We missed the second grade and finessed the fourth grade, but I figured it was her highlight show. The third grade was where she received her first interpreter, following Judge Broderick's order: Fran Miller. I asked Amy how it was to have a sign language interpreter in her classroom for the first time. She looked at me evenly, "It was like a glass in front of me that had been dirty a long time, cloudy, hard to see through, and somebody had come in and had cleaned it with Windex. After the Supreme Court decision, without an interpreter, it was like a hurricane had come by and everything was dirty again." Fran, she remembered, had explained things in a way she could understand and sometimes in a way that other, hearing children had understood. "I know because they told me that. Everyone was sad when Fran left."

Out in the hall, as we moved along, Amy talked about Beth Freed, her second and last classroom interpreter at Furnace Woods. Pointing to a classroom, she said, "Beth would take me into an empty classroom when she got me out of class. She was always telling me to be patient. I hated going out of my classroom. I really loved Beth a lot, but she knew that I didn't really want to do this and I thought that she didn't either."

Then Amy identified the special education room. Her eyes widened as we looked inside. "Gee, I almost forgot," she said. . . . "You know, I never would have thought of this unless we were here. But this was the room where they had kids with learning disabilities. I used to come down here when I was in the fourth and fifth grade. These kids never mixed with other kids. They were kept in a group and when they went out of class they wouldn't even *recognize* other kids in the school."

We poked our heads outside. She gestured at the hill that rose up innocently outside the school grounds. "When we were kids, that hill was huge," she said. She remembered at least five field trips in the fifth grade alone. She enjoyed them but felt communication with her classmates virtually impossible under those circumstances. Physical education was the triumphant thing for her. "The long jump," she said in a tone of deep appreciation, "now that was something I was good in."

Inside, we peeked into the big, airy gym, painted in two shades of blue and with windows in the ceiling to let in natural light. This was another place Amy liked, but with a strong reservation, "The FM wireless." In the gym, this bulky contraption connecting her to a teacher directly was a cumbersome burden of little use at best. "Everyone asked me why I wore it and I would always say it was because the school wanted me to, and they would ask why that was and I would say I didn't know."

The library—Amy rushed up to the door as though Brooks and I were not present, a look of holy pleasure on her face. The door was locked but she pressed her face to the window, looking in at the books. She spoke almost as though to herself, without my asking a question, "I was equal here. I loved the library because I could understand the books. I would sit in here and read and understand as well as anyone."

From the peak to the pits: mathematics. The room looked like most of the other classrooms to me but Amy winced visibly as we came to it. "I had a problem managing sums. I wasted a lot of time. Mr. Smelter would talk with the other kids sometimes when he had the FM on and that was confusing. If he had taken the time to teach me, maybe I wouldn't be so bad now. My real teacher is my mother, but Mrs. Conklin [third grade] and Mr. Cousins [fourth grade] taught me a lot, but the truth is that I needed an interpreter most in math. It was my worst class. And now my math is horrible. Maybe I didn't really want to learn it. My mom was worried mostly about my English because most deaf people have trouble with that, but my English is good and my math is horrible."

I remembered occasional references in her school records at Furnace Woods to the difficulties Amy had there with mathematics and more of the same later, at Mountain Lakes. I had had indifferent luck trying to talk with Amy's teachers at Furnace Woods, most of whom were still teaching in the system at the time I got in touch with them. A number declined to be interviewed. Hal Smelter, Amy's math teacher, was one who did agree to speak with me over the telephone. He remembered Amy fondly, he said, and did not find that she had had any particular problems with mathematics, which he said did not get complicated until the sixth and seventh grades, by which time Amy had moved on to Mountain Lakes. "I felt that she was getting what I was putting before her," he said.

Fifth grade: Mr. Brett. Amy and I walked inside the classroom and I took a standing position as Amy paced about for several moments without speaking. She sat down in one of the chairs and looked up at me. I realized that I was standing where Brett would have been. My conversation with William Brett—he was another of those still employed by the school system who agreed to talk although "not in depth"—came back to me. It was the most stressful year in all his twenty-seven years of teaching, he had told me. Whatever anyone said or did could be used in the law suit and it made teaching very difficult. Brett had testified in an impartial hearing in March 1983, after the Supreme Court decision, when the Rowleys were attempting to revive the case on procedural grounds. He had described how he had arranged his class, providing Amy with a seat with a light so that she could read a film script while the other children sat in the dark. He also talked about his extensive use of overhead projections and about putting Amy in the best possible location from which to view the screen. With this treatment, he had testified, Amy had thrived.

Amy looked at me and, as she spoke, I had for an instant the eerie sensation that she was reading my mind. "Mr. Brett did write down a lot of things for me," she said, "but wherever I sat, there were always people in the class with their backs turned to me, and I lost what was said between him and them. I had the worst time in my life reading lips with him. It was that accent, I couldn't make it out. And he really thought that FM auditory trainer was great, and I was telling him and everybody, Dr. Zavarella, everybody, that it was no better than my hearing aids. Worse, lots of times.

"I know he tried to be patient with me, but he lost his patience more than once. Because of his accent, he would have to say things slowly and when I didn't get it he would ask Marjorie to explain, and if I didn't get it then he would be angry with me. Once, I remember, he shook me by the shoulders and said, 'Why don't you understand what I am saying?' When he pulled my pigtails, I started to cry, and he said, 'You're a big girl now.' If I still had had the interpreter, he would have been able to make good speed in the class, and I would have understood and everybody would have been much better off. . . . I didn't think my grades were that good that year."

Brett was at some pains to stress over the phone to me that Amy was "a darn good student, very bright and very intelligent, had a lot going for her" and that he considered her ability to read lips "phenomenal." To his knowledge, he said, she did not have a grade below a C. He said he remembered Marjorie Augenblick, but not the fact that she was coaching Amy in the classroom. He did not remember pulling Amy's hair. His accent, he said, was a combination of British and Australian, a result of his having grown up in both countries.

If it was Mr. Brett's worst year as a teacher, it was Amy's worst as a student. Losing the interpreter was a real blow. "It was much worse than before I had one," she recalled. "It was horrible." Knowing that the family was leaving Peekskill made matters worse. But her parents pulled her out of her unhappy mood. "They were positive about it. They got me through it. I really respect them. People come up to me still and say, 'You're the famous Amy Rowley in the case about the sign language interpreter.' I tell them they should go up to my parents and say, 'You're the famous Nancy and Cliff Rowley in the case about Amy's sign language interpreter.' They deserve the credit for it. I have wondered about how much difference it really made for other deaf children. But people have told me that it did and I feel pride for my mother and father when they say that." She looked at me intently, "Do you think it did? The case, I mean. Do you think it made a difference?"

"I don't know," I said. "But I think your mother and father did a strong thing, the right thing. You have reason to be proud."

As we walked back toward the front of the building, Amy became more ruminative. "You know," she told me, "people look back fondly on their childhood. Some people anyway. You, R.C.?" I nodded. "OK., you, too. I don't think I ever had a childhood and maybe I'm making up for that now with Australia and things like that."

Back in the main lobby, we paused near a school banner proclaiming the years "1965–1990," done in blue and gold, the school colors. Amy looked about as though for the last time. For no reason I could discern, she began talking about Clarisse Miller, whom she had never mentioned to me before. Clarisse had poor handwriting and was considered a problem in school because of that. "There was a bond between us," Amy said.

She fell silent as Helen Brooks began to drive back home. I had forgotten about Amy's last comment, but she apparently had not. "If you turn here," she said to Brooks, "we can go by Clarisse's house." Brooks turned and we drove down one of the tree-lined residential streets, from which comfortable, upper-middle-class houses stretched back to a line of woods. "There," she said, pointing suddenly, "that's it." With a glance at me, Brooks turned the automobile up the driveway, and we found ourselves parking and walking the rest of the way up, around a white brick wall, toward the front door.

I rang the doorbell, and after a good little while the door opened. Then, we experienced one of those rare, beautiful instants like the recognition scenes in plays when two old friends who have not seen each other in years meet again. It was more stunning in this case for Clarisse, for here was someone she could not in her wildest imagination have expected to see on her doorstep after all the years. The two girls fell into each other's arms. After the expressions of mutual delight, Amy was introducing Helen Brooks and me to Clarisse Miller, a most attractive young woman with a broad, welcoming smile, who, among her other attributes, was an African American.

Her mother came up behind her and insisted that we join them in the living room, apologizing for the mid-morning clutter as the two young women chattered along and followed. I followed, too, mentally going through the motion of slapping myself, palm up, on the side of my head— a gesture men like myself, old enough to remember the pop culture of the World War II period, affect to reconnect loose parts rattling around uselessly. Of course, Clarisse Miller was "different" from the rest of her classmates. Bad handwriting would not have been enough to set up bonding between her and a girl who was "different" because she was deaf. Being an African American, though, surely could.

As it turned out, the girls were convinced that Clarisse was the first African American student in Furnace Woods school. Her mother told us that she had taken Clarisse out of a succession of private schools in Manhattan and decided to move to Westchester County in order to provide her daughter with a better education. Since Amy's day, Clarisse had gone on to attend college in Westchester and was planning on transferring to one in Manhattan the next year.

I asked Clarisse what the experience of being the only African American in Furnace Woods had been like. "Well, let's see," she said, with a mock-serious tilt of her head. "The first day nobody in my class spoke to me at all. How's that for a good start? The whole first year was a disaster. I hated it. Amy was the only friend I had. But middle school the next year was a lot better."

"We were natural friends," Amy said later, after we had left the Millers' home. "Minorities," she said. "We were both minorities."

15

Not Quite Human

What I remember most about President Franklin Delano Roosevelt, besides that unforgettable voice over the radio, was the boy's-eye view of him I had in the Fox Movietone News segments with Saturday afternoon movie double-features. I remember the toothy smile and the expansive wave and the businesslike fedora and the glasses glinting in the sun, and I am sure that I placed no significance in the circumstance—if I ever noticed it—that he always seemed to be photographed seated. I was a gangly, teenager before I realized that the president had been paralyzed by polio and was for the most part confined to a wheelchair.

Roosevelt could not have used the word, which hadn't come into historical sight in this specific meaning yet, but he understood that he had a "stigma." In his ground-breaking book, *Stigma: Notes on the Management of a Spoiled Identity* published a quarter-century later, Erving Goffman described stigma as a "deviance" or as "a form of undesired differentness." Goffman wrote that the stigmatized individual goes through phases of learning the "normal" point of view, learning that he is disqualified according to it, learning to cope with the way others treat him, and learning to "pass" if at all possible. "Passing" means presenting oneself in a manner in which the stigma is invisible, a relatively simple achievement for a homosexual, for example, who desires to hide that fact about himself. "Covering" is what an individual does whose stigma is apparent but who is willing to go to great efforts to keep it from looming large to others. This can

269

be done by a wide assortment of individuals with disabilities, but being president of the United States at a time when the press was sympathetic and cooperative might seem the ideal situation for covering. With the inattentive and the young in the 1930s and 1940s before television, Roosevelt was able to "pass."*

Hugh Gregory Gallagher's *FDR's Splendid Deception* makes it clear that Roosevelt was far too politically perceptive to be deluded about how the public would react to daily reminders of his paralysis.† His friends would refer to his courage, but the public at large would see a man at the head of a great government who couldn't "act" at a time when they desperately needed one who could. And his enemies would sneer at that "cripple" in the White House. This was a day, remember, when women were still regarded by many as chattel rather than as private citizens and African Americans were called "niggers" and relegated to the back of the bus. Gallagher describes how individuals with disabilities were viewed: "[They] were kept at home, out of sight, in back bedrooms, by families who felt a mixture of embarrassment and shame about their presence."

Gallagher's research turned up a medical textbook, widely circulated in those years, that gives us a glimpse of the dark netherworld of prejudice that affected public perceptions without people's being aware of it. "A failure in the moral treatment of a cripple," an eminent physician wrote, "means the evolution of an individual detestable in character, a menace, a burden to the community, who is only apt to graduate into the mendicant and criminal classes." Of whom was the doctor who wrote this thinking? Why, of Ahab, of course, and of Long John Silver and Captain Hook. Individuals with disabilities all, and in those years our general models in literature, setting aside a rare Tiny Tim. Roosevelt was far too sharp not to sniff out the fear that lay beneath the veneer of pity for cripples like him (p. 30).

The president accordingly set about to construct for himself a safe identity. Stricken with polio in 1921, he referred to himself privately as "recovered" or "recovering." Publicly, he strove to make his condition totally invisible. As president, he could command the tools of deception. His favorite place to be photographed was in the back seat of an open, seven-passenger touring car. He forbade movies or photographs of him being helped into this seat, and an obliging press kept that confidence proudly. He also had

* New York: Prentice-Hall, 1963.

† New York: Dodd, Mead, 1985.

a brilliant ally in fending off detractors who whispered abroad the canard (all too easily believed) that his condition had adversely affected his brain. Asked in a press conference if she thought her husband's illness had affected his mentality, Eleanor Roosevelt replied: "I'm glad that question was asked. The answer is yes. Anyone who has gone through great suffering himself is bound to have a greater sympathy and understanding of the problems of mankind" (p. 95). Eleanor got a standing ovation for that one, but FDR would battle stigma to the end of his days.

Persons so stigmatized are victims of a mental process on the part of unhandicapped people that transforms the perception of "undesired differentness" into active, virulent prejudice. From observation of the differentness, this process next takes the step described in numerous journals and books as "leveling," in which all other attributes of a person are overridden by the attribute of the particular disability. That is to say, deafness "marks" the victim as disabled, and becomes code for the person's entire being. After that, what remains is the process of "labeling." A person is deaf and by that single-word label known, stigmatized by definition and thus the target of prejudice before he or she has taken action of any kind.

This means of stigmatization has universal application. She is a *woman* can be used in such a way that the deflating adjective "only" is invisibly inserted before the noun in the sentence. In *The Unexpected Minority*, Gliedman and Roth compared the lot of individuals with disabilities with that of African Americans in the United States. "In some ways," they wrote, "the handicapped are better off; they meet no organized brutality, no lynch mob 'justice,' no Ku Klux Klan rallies. But in other ways the handicapped are surprisingly much worse off. . . . Only when he encountered a black who refused to observe the color line did the racist place the black in the sociological no-man's-land known as deviance. The stigma of handicap, on the other hand, hampers its bearer's ability to assume virtually any positive social persona. . . . Perceived only as a blind man, a cripple, or a dwarf, the handicapped person is assumed to be incapable of any normal social functions, even the most humble and demeaning" (p. 23).

I found myself pondering, as I read through these materials, the ways in which prejudice against individuals with disabilities was different from that against other minority groups. I thought, first, of my own reaction to the blind man at my newspaper friend's Christmas parties. It could be described in a single word: avoidance. Robert Kleck of Dartmouth has done an experiment comparing the reaction of "normal" people, first, to a physically intact man in a wheelchair and, second, to a man in a wheelchair who appeared to be an amputee. The amputee received a more marked aversive reaction. "Exposure to a handicapped individual creates in the unhandicapped a detectable, aversive emotional response," noted Dane Archer of the University of California, commenting on Kleck's experiment.*

Kleck and others have observed that while the aversive reaction is common, most of us feel ashamed of it. "People are motivated to avoid the handicapped," Archer notes, "but are unwilling to acknowledge that motive. At the same time, they are aware of the norms calling for compassion and help toward the disadvantaged. Perhaps the handicapped remind the non-handicapped of their own mortality."

The language used by a man with muscular dystrophy who had spent his life in mental institutions, as quoted by Paul Hunt is even more vivid. "We are the symbol of the things they [the able bodied] fear most. . . . Involuntarily we walk—or more often sit—in the valley of the shadow of death. Contact with us throws up in people's face the fact of sickness and death in the world. No one likes to think of such things, which in themselves are an affront to all our aspirations and hopes. A deformed and paralyzed body attacks everyone's sense of well-being and invincibility. People do not want to acknowledge what disability affirms . . . that life is tragic and we all shall soon be dead."†

It seemed to me as I thought about this passage that I understood for the first time what sets prejudice against individuals with disabilities apart from other forms of prejudice in our society and makes it potentially more poisonous than the rest. It is not at all prejudice against "otherness" as, for instance, against a group who are forever different from us in the religion they practice, or the color of their skin, or their gender. It is a prejudice that awakens in the viewer a terrible intimation of mortality and a fear that to look upon the face of disability is to look into a prophetic mirror. We will never be dark-skinned if we are not already, but if we live long enough, we will probably suffer disability that, as we shrink from it, seems to wear the mask of death. We retreat for fear that the face under that mask is our own.

It is from this fear of our own death, then, that we turn from the approach of the halting gait or the extinguished eye or the toneless or garbled

---

* "Social Deviance," in *Handbook of Social Psychology*, vol. 2, edited by Gardner Lindsay and Elliot Aronson (Hillsdale, N.J.: Lawrence Erlbaum Assocs., 1985).

† *Stigma: The Experience of Disability* (London: G. Chapman, 1966), p. 146.

speech. It is this conviction that explains, and at the same time, elaborates on Goffman's oft-quoted sentence: "By definition, we believe that the person with the stigma is not quite human" (p. 5). This is our way of putting that person at a safe distance from ourselves. As we "feel" this we also feel shame, for we are aware at some deeper level that what we call our "compassion" for this individual is false. Real compassion is wholly accepting, embracing—the very opposite of what we are doing. We wish to put this "not quite human" person out of our sight and mind at whatever cost. Frightened, ashamed of our fright, we have only anger left to express.

Chilling phrase, "not quite human." But there is more to the Goffman quote, a sentence which follows: "On this assumption [that the individual is not quite human] we exercise varieties of discrimination through which *we effectively if often unthinkingly reduce his life chances*" (p. 5). The emphasis is mine. I use it to stress the words that struck me as I read them. They seemed to apply to the deaf actors who were never considered for the part in the film *Voices*. And they reminded me again of W. Handy "Dub" Hipps, the telegraph editor of the old *Virginian-Pilot* in Norfolk.

Now, in 1947, the employment of Hipps was in itself a high-minded, democratic, and unusual act, the result in part quite likely of the mood of gratitude over our land toward disabled, returning veterans of World War II. Someone at the *Pilot* had stuck out his neck more than a little in hiring Hipps. We can assume that many others, at least at first, had strong doubts into which were mixed the feelings of fear and aversion described above. In the end, Hipps, who in fact had not served in World War II, profited. But what if he had really been a returning war veteran whose legs had been blown away?

Well, he would have been in a wheelchair for one thing. He would have been confronted with an inaccessible building. He could have been hired only at some real extra cost. He would have confronted as well the invisible barrier that is in the mind. Those in positions of power would have told themselves, in a quiet, deeply inner voice, that they did not want an employee wheeling himself about under their eyes. If this idea were put into the outer voice at all, it would come out as a concern that "others"—visitors to the newsroom, for instance—might be offended. Management probably would have overcome its guilt twinges, expressed regrets to Hipps, and said no. Ever practical, Hipps probably would have understood all too well, lowered his sights, and gone on with his life.

But suppose he had a whiff of the reformer, our veteran, legless Dub Hipps. He might have said to management: Look, it isn't fair. I am qualified, probably more qualified than the person you will eventually hire. The investment you put up to make the building accessible will be for everyone who is mobility-impaired, including lots of customers who can't visit your newspaper now, maybe even one day for you or a loved one. If I agree with you, I will be agreeing that forever, at your discretion, people like you will keep people like me from getting to places of education, training, study, and work, not to mention places of entertainment and pleasure. *Forever,* isn't that right?

Faced with an ever-more obdurate management—"He has about him something of the troublemaker," someone would say—Hipps could not have sued the newspaper, there being no laws on the books to rely upon. He might have begun wheeling his chair back and forth on the sidewalk in front of the newspaper building, holding up a sign proclaiming the newspaper's unwillingness to employ him. In doing so, he would be expressing his anger, and we may be sure that it would be returned in kind, manifold. For in addition to feeling singled out for accusation, the authorities at the newspaper would have to deal with the deep-down realization that their "compassion" had been exposed as false.

What the newspaper would have accomplished in this hypothetical case, as certainly as if it controlled the strings of destiny, was to have reduced Hipps' life chances significantly. Trained for news work, he would have certainly faced the same mental barriers on smaller, more rural newspapers, where accessibility might not be so much of a problem. Driven from one failed interview to the next, he might easily have become bitter and would certainly have shared the anger he felt directed at him for his obstinate efforts to put himself where—I can almost hear it expressed in a whisper finally, in some quiet quarter—he wasn't really wanted.

Kleck refers to this phenomenon of shared anger as the "transactional" nature of prejudiced behavior. He and other psychologists stress that prejudice is not just something that one group or individual does to another, but is an outgrowth of how two groups of individuals interact with each other. This interaction can induce unjustified conclusions based on expected behavior. Kleck has performed a fascinating experiment in which an individual agreed to have a scar makeup applied to his face and was told that he was to be used to measure reactions from people he was about to meet. Then, just before he was to meet with the others, the scar was removed from his face without his knowing it, on the pretext of wiping it dry. What the psychologists actually were preparing to measure was the "scar-faced" man's apprehension that he would be rejected by the people he met.

As expected, despite normal reactions on the part of others, he behaved as if rejected. If our wheelchair-using Hipps had been turned down for enough jobs, he might well have concluded that he was being rejected because of his disability even when that was not true.

The experience of Amy Rowley was, on the surface, different. Attractive, bright, from an upwardly mobile, middle-class family with roots in the area, she was in a far more promising situation than that faced by my old colleague Hipps. The school district had accepted Amy as suitable for mainstreaming. From its perspective, that was a far-sighted accommodation in itself, for which it would not be unreasonable to expect gratitude from her parents.

But, for their part, the Rowleys saw the placement of Amy in a hearing school without interpretive help as a continuation of a position that had been utterly discredited by experience. Because their opinions and the opinions of many hearing and virtually all deaf educators were spurned by these school people, the Rowleys reacted with steadfast insistence, which was read by the school as obduracy. Fully expecting gratitude from the Rowleys, the school people were outraged.

If I had asked any of the individuals I interviewed who had either helped set the school district's position or supported it whether they were prejudiced against individuals with disabilities, deaf people, or the Rowley family, I feel certain I would have received a cold, probably angry stare and a firm denial. And I am convinced now, after ten years of work on this book, that these denials would be genuine. Prejudice's most ardent ally is ignorance—and never so true an axiom as in the prejudice against disability, which hides so deeply, emotionally camouflaged, in our psyches. We are not only ignorant of the true condition of those we speak of as disabled, but we are also unaware of what we really think of them. These decent people I interviewed, it's fair to assume, really thought they were unprejudiced.

Yet what they actually were saying about Amy Rowley—the school board members through their lawyers and, later, judges, some members of the media, and countless others—was that she was doing darn well in school *for a deaf girl*. Into the word "deaf" they were loading the full freight of our negative attitudes toward individuals with disabilities. All of Amy's attributes, skills, and determination were subordinated to their idea of her as someone *dis*-abled. They did not believe Michael Chatoff's statement that Amy could be anyone she wanted to be except a telephone operator. They could not imagine that she might seek, as any child should be free to seek, excellence. Given her handicap, they believed, she should be thrilled to be doing as well as she was, even better than many "able" students. What did she want, what could her parents possibly expect? Did they expect the school to make her "well" so she could be a normal child?

It came to me, then, as I tried to absorb this line of thought, that it might help to explain the mystery of the disappearance of "equal opportunity" in *Rowley* and its replacement by "full potential." It was hard to stand up in court and deny anyone in our democratic society equal opportunity, as the district and the state's attorneys themselves discovered in the appellate court hearing. It was hard to do that in an editorial or even a news story. But if Amy's family had been requiring the school to bring her to her "full potential"—and if these words implied some impossibly expensive feat of education above anything being attempted for the other children—then it could be seen as proper to oppose her on simple grounds of fairness. Thus, "full potential" become code for a palatable way to say "no" to Amy Rowley.

Something like this could explain how this patent misconstruing of the case moved so smoothly in either direction between legal briefs and opinions to the media. Only a confirmed conspiracy theorist could countenance the notion of two news organizations as disparate in terms of social outlook as the *New York Times* and the *Washington Post* teaming up with judicial minds on the appellate and Supreme Court to shape deliberately an identical political position on the case. Far more likely, early versions of the "full potential" code were simply picked up and repeated as accepted fact for the good reason that they helped to explain why a "compassionate" society had to deny Amy Rowley her sign language interpreter. Locate this commentary in the atmosphere of those early Reagan administration years, electrically charged with backlash against the perceived social engineering of the Carter years, and the mistake is less surprising. Ultimately, this misconception of the crux of the case made its way into the majority opinion of the Supreme Court and influenced what is to this day the law of the land on the subject of educating children with disabilities. In an important sense, the Supreme Court's majority opinion codified—and not for the first time in history—a popular prejudice of the day.

———

Elisabeth Hudson and I talked about President Roosevelt once. I can't remember how the subject came up, but it was probably because I had read Gallagher's book and had Roosevelt on my mind. I do remember our sharing admiration for the man and my saying that I thought he was most courageous. I remember that because of the curious way Hudson looked up at me, head cocked slightly, the skin around her eyes wrinkling into a quizzical expression. I told her that when she looked at me that way she reminded me of Ethel Barrymore. She said, smiling, that it was Lionel Barrymore who was in the wheelchair. Nonetheless, I responded, she reminded me of Ethel.

Unfailingly patient with me, Hudson always put her responses in general terms, often with reference to her own ignorance prior to finding herself in a wheelchair. I kept no notes of the conversation, but as I remember, she said something like this: "I've always thought that courage had to be measured by the choices available. You are courageous when you choose a hard path over an easy one out of conviction. We disableds don't have that kind of choice. We do what we have to do. It's very difficult for "normals" to imagine the adjustment we make. I think FDR feared that sympathy we disableds get that's close to pity—you know, the kind that makes people come up to you on the street and pat you on the shoulder, all teary-eyed, and say 'God bless you.' They'd be shocked to learn that that's a put-down but it is. It's part of the whole business of how they categorize us as pitiful."

I wondered aloud whether she approved of Roosevelt's actions in covering his disability. She said she understood and respected what he had done. Given the times, she said, he probably had no political alternative. "Still," she added, "it's too bad he couldn't have showed himself as the great leader he was *with* a disability. That way Americans could have seen that losing your power to walk or being born deaf or whatever didn't mean you were helpless. Instead, he became just another normal as far as the public was concerned. You see what happens there? To achieve, you must be normal. So if you achieve, then you can't be disabled, because being disabled defines you out of achievement: Catch 22 for the disabled."

She felt that the real achievement was to be exactly who you were and cope with what had to be coped with. I told her once I was amazed at how my mother had moved into what seemed to me a state of grace, never complaining, only occasionally asking, always in a patient, inquiring tone, "Why am I still here, why am I living?" I said that my wife and I had begun to respond to this question with, "To inspire us," an answer that made her laugh like a child who has been told she is beautiful and good. Hudson smiled but her comment surprised me. "Your mother's not complaining for a reason. She has learned that if she complains, people will avoid her. She's simply playing the game to her advantage." And then she added, "As for my own cheerfulness cloak—what a title for the book that's running around in my head!—I put it on when people visit or call so I won't drag them down into the Slough of Despond, which I hardly ever visit anymore."

I knew from her daughter, Carol Kinsley, that Hudson was in constant pain. She had described it to Carol as a burning fire spreading from within. Her health problems had begun with cobalt treatment for breast cancer, which gradually caused her to lose the use of her legs. Yet she weaned herself of all medication except an occasional aspirin. She had read Norman Cousin's book about the healing power of laughter and got from it, along with the comfort of its good humor, a way of doing battle with the weight of time's agonizingly slow pace. When she told herself that she did not know whether she could stand a lifetime of the pain she was in, she was able to respond, "One minute at a time."

Without spending too much time thinking about it, I had concluded that she had sources of strength not available to the average person, from her faith perhaps. Here she was telling me that her behavior, and possibly my mother's, was not solitary courageous coping, but perhaps an attitude calculated to maintain their places in their private slipstream of human concourse. In this process, Hudson was capable of advising people in situations similar to hers to toughen their skin. One of her many pen pals had written her that she was disappointed at being dropped by letter-writing friends who had discovered she had a disability.

"We're all just a step or a second away from being handicapped," she wrote to this person. "I am not telling everyone I write to about my disability. I don't tell everyone right off the color of my hair or skin or if I'm bald. I might not think it necessary to mention deafness or poverty or wealth or religion. My disability is not *me*. It makes life harder for me, but I have quite a life going on and plenty to write about and that's what's important about letter-writing. Your correspondents who dropped you probably are insecure in their wellness. . . . I would feel, if I were you, that the correspondents who dropped me because I was disabled were not worth writing to."

She listened to my concerns about my continuing ambivalence toward individuals with disabilities patiently and then tried to help me put it in perspective. "I think you worry that you're still as prejudiced in your way as a lot of people you are writing about in this book," she told me one day. "You non-Christians don't understand sin, R.C., you don't get it. We're all prejudiced in our ways. I can work both sides of the street. I'm prejudiced against Temporarily Able-Bodieds who are judgmental and I still have prejudice left over from when I used it on people like me. We all grew up in this world, and prejudice comes to us through the air we breathe."

I don't remember much more of the conversation in Hudson's kitchen that afternoon, but I do remember that she used one particular word to describe what she felt we all had to do. The word was "grapple." She felt we owed it to the Lord, 100 percent, to grapple for as long as we were around. Then she said that she personally planned to be around at least until she was a hundred because it would take her that long to do what she wanted to do and, as she put it, "to see how all this sorts itself out."

Hudson didn't get her hundred years. She had melanoma and treatments for it at Duke Hospital, but that didn't carry her away. She had developed a bad chest cold and ran a fever in the spring of 1988. She wasn't interested in seeing a doctor and thought she had it licked. Her son talked with her one night and thought she sounded incoherent. He got her to the emergency room, and the next morning, Easter Sunday, a nurse reported that she was fine. Forty-five minutes later she was dead. Her daughter likes the symbolism of her Christian mother's death on Easter morning, and so, I find, do I.

Still thinking of the potential for reducing life chances of children with disabilities, I looked about for more serious studies of the impact of *Rowley* on court cases dealing with the old Education for All Handicapped Children Act (now the Individuals with Disabilities Education Act). I found two substantial studies.

Writing in 1989, Ellen Gallegos, a lawyer and former special education teacher, looked first at the decision's limiting aspect. "Many view the Court's opinion as discouraging parents seeking judicial review," she wrote. "Since a plausible and reasonable argument usually can be made that a child will obtain some benefit from the services offered, parents may feel helpless to challenge their child's IEP."*

After noting that the decision seemed likely to minimize the role of the lower courts as well as that of the parents of children with disabilities, Gallegos also questioned the Supreme Court's apparent reluctance to see the judicial system used as a last resort in disputes. "Does the court's lack of

---

* "Beyond *Board of Education v. Rowley:* Education Benefit for the Handicapped," *American Journal of Education* (May 1989): 241–42.

expertise in the area really interfere with its ability to review and evaluate the evidence presented as the Court in *Rowley* suggests?" she wondered. "When other types of litigation in which courts are continuously called upon to resolve disputes of a highly technical nature are considered, it is difficult to agree that courts should avoid making judgments in education because they lack specialized knowledge and experience. This may not have been Congress' intent when it created a review process allowing courts to make 'independent decisions based on the preponderance of the evidence.' "

Nevertheless, Gallegos noted that seven years after *Rowley* was decided the lower courts had not turned their backs on children with disabilities. Of the approximately one hundred cases ruled on under the act at the time she wrote, Gallegos observed: "The courts have not sacrificed services for the handicapped child through strict application of *Rowley's* minimal standard. Instead, courts continue to support parents in their efforts to obtain expansive services for their handicapped children including summer school services and health services."

Mark C. Weber, associate professor of law at DePaul University, had even more sweeping criticism of the Supreme Court decision on *Rowley* the following year. "The legislative history and social context of the 1975 Act," he wrote, "established that Congress enacted it to achieve major social change. . . . The *Rowley* opinion appeared to blunt the social impact of the Act by saying that it was intended to provide only access to services that would provide 'some benefit' to handicapped children. In doing so, the opinion rejected legislative history, lower court decisions, and regulatory interpretations—all of which called for education that would maximize opportunity for handicapped children's educational achievement to an extent comparable to that afforded nonhandicapped children."*

And while agreeing with Gallegos that lower courts generally had managed to construe *Rowley* favorably from the standpoint of children with disabilities, Weber went significantly further in this regard. "They [the lower courts] have retreated dramatically from *Rowley*," he wrote, "distinguishing it when they could, and minimizing it and finding other sources of guidance when they could not. . . . The Act is a radical statute. The Supreme Court's decision in *Rowley* sought to transform it into something less challenging to the settled way of doing things, but the real transformation of the law has been the lower courts' restoration of the statute's original meaning" (p. 436).

* *University of California at Davis Law Review* 24 (Winter 1990): 353–54.

One of the key ways in which the lower courts have required extensive services to children with disabilities, he noted, is through application of the "least restrictive environment" mandate of the act. The courts in a number of cases have bent the "some benefits" requirement of the *Rowley* majority to the advantage of these children, reasoning that if children with disabilities are to sit in classrooms alongside other children, they ought to have full opportunity to compete. In one case, the court required a school district in Illinois to provide psychotherapy to a highly intelligent student whose academic performance, while enabling him to move from grade to grade, was below expectations. Here the court relied on expert testimony that the child needed the services and on the individualized nature of the determination—in other words, that the services were necessary to meet that child's "unique" needs.

Wouldn't that same reasoning have resulted in Amy Rowley's keeping her sign language interpreter, I asked Weber in a phone conversation. He responded that he thought that it would have, and that this was an example of a lower court's choosing the more permissive features of *Rowley* and combining them with other legal history, including more generous interpretations of the act. "That's why I think that what the lower courts have done amounts to a transformation," he said.

In a sense, then, what the lower courts have ruled—not uniformly and not in so many words, but persistently after as well as before 1982—is that children with disabilities should be educated with other children whenever that is possible, and be given every reasonable chance to compete equally. In his article Weber also made a comparison with African American children: "Forced separation of handicapped children, like forced separation of minority children, fosters inequality," he wrote. "Indeed, handicapped children's history of legal exclusion from school places them in a position of inferiority quite similar to that of black children legally barred from schools by whites" (p. 416). Weber saw the mainstreaming movement as a force for enhanced services and equality of opportunity.

Weber also dealt with the question of why Congress had not taken action to overrule the Court majority in *Rowley*. Pointing to the lack of authoritative impact of the decision already cited, he concluded that a legislator who felt *Rowley* misinterpreted the act probably would investigate the effect of the opinion on the lower courts and decide to leave well enough alone. In fact, Weber observed, an argument could be made that Congress' failure to amend the statute is an endorsement of recent lower court case law imposing increased obligations on states and localities to serve children with disabilities.

16

Struggling *and* Succeeding

Of all the public schools I had seen that had done good work with children with disabilities, one stuck in my mind, because it had received no foundation grants and was included in no nationally touted educational programs. It was Public School 213 in Bayside, New York, which I had visited back in 1982 while working on *Seven Special Kids*.

P.S. 213 was on the surface just another public school in the New York City system. An ordinary school constructed in 1956 in a solidly middle-class Jewish, Irish, and Italian neighborhood, it had not been built to deal with a high proportion of children with disabilities. But young people did not stay in that part of Bayside, and gradually, as the neighborhood aged, it became one of middle-class adults and few young children. Because of this and its architectural adaptability to wheelchairs, in 1964 the school became the site of a unit serving physically handicapped students from a much broader geographical area. Established as a place where children with disabilities were welcome, it naturally attracted more of them in succeeding years.

My interest in the school originally had stemmed from an article I had read by Dr. Odey Raviv, coordinator of the resource program for the school. He had described a kind of vigorous integration of activities involving mainstream students and those with disabilities that took account of every child's real abilities.* I had arrived in time to be briefed by the

* "Mainstreamed Handicapped Children: Challenge to Teachers," *Behavior Today*, January 5, 1981.

school's principal, Malcolm Cooper. I asked him if he could give me a picture of how the school operated. He answered with a detailed description of a recent intramural basketball game in which all students, including those in wheelchairs, participated.

I was still groping with that image—wishing I had been there—when, on my way to Raviv's office, I spotted a boy in a wheelchair being pushed along the hallway by another boy. They were both about twelve years old, I judged. The boy in the wheelchair kept turning around to look up at and speak to the boy who was pushing him. The boy doing the pushing seemed to be paying close attention. Now and then, he spoke briefly and when that happened, the one in the wheelchair turned back to him again, leaning up to speak while his chauffeur nodded.

I forgot about this scene temporarily as Raviv talked with me about the school. As he described it, my impression was that P.S. 213 was using all potential resources to the utmost. Students tutored students. Parents were involved in night programs at the school. A group of older persons—stroke victims undergoing physical rehabilitation—came to the school two afternoons a week to help in the tutoring process. Walking about the school, I saw this happening and absorbed the spirit of the school, which was as easygoing as it was collaborative. Everything I encountered made me feel that learning was a twenty-four-hour-a-day experience here, and that it would include life and value lessons not necessarily on the menu of the average public school.

"They see it all," Raviv told me, when I mentioned this, "dwarfs, kids with speech problems, kids in wheelchairs, everything. . . . There's very little name-calling or laughing at what handicapped kids look like or sound like or what they can't do. . . . If these typical kids went into a store, they wouldn't have any trouble dealing with a handicapped salesperson."

Psychologist Robert Kleck's experiments, which had shown aversion and avoidance on the part of people confronted by individuals with disabilities, also showed a lessening in these tensions with repeated exposure. Studies of the behavior of hearing-impaired and hearing students in the same classroom suggested that physical proximity was not in itself a guarantee of social interaction or social acceptance. More important, it appeared, was the willingness of teachers to develop social communication skills.

Meeting with another staff member, I recalled the boy pushing another boy in a wheelchair and mentioned them. The staff member knew the two boys and what was going on between them. The boy in the wheelchair was tutoring the other boy in mathematics, she told me. The image has lingered in my mind over the years as an example of a perfect mutual assistance pact and also of a principle of education sorely overlooked in the average school—that we all learn through a process that involves passing our new information (or inspiration) along to others. On an imaginary poster, with the images of the two boys moving briskly along the hall, helping each other, I had superimposed, from my own education over the years, the legend: Teach to Learn to Teach. Thinking of that one morning, as I thought of P.S. 213, I put in a phone call, ten years after that first visit.

I was surprised and delighted to find that Raviv and Cooper were still there. Raviv told me first, almost apologetically, that the ranks of the physically disabled students in the school had been thinned by the decision some years before to stop busing students in from outlying areas. But didn't that mean, I asked, that these same students were "integrating" lots of other city schools? He agreed that it did. I told him that I wanted to talk with someone who could comment on the impact that the school's heavy involvement with children with disabilities had had, someone who went back a long way with the school. He suggested Margaret D'Emidio.

D'Emidio had been the occupational therapist at P.S. 213 when I first visited, and I remembered her as a an understanding person who obviously had rapport with her charges. Over the phone, she reflected on the experience of P.S. 213. She agreed that it had changed many people who came in touch with it. "It even changed my daughters," she said, "and all they got out of it was the way I felt about it and a chance to see the school and the kids now and then." I asked what exactly she meant by "changed," and she responded, "Made more aware, sensitive to differences between people and yet their essential sameness."

She also agreed with Raviv that while the changes most often observed were in the confidence and self-image of children with disabilities, the biggest impact probably would be on the other children who were exposed as a matter of course every day to a variety of disabilities. "They simply didn't take disability as something that affected academic performance," she said. "They saw these kids with disabilities struggle or succeed just [as] they were struggling or succeeding. Or struggling *and* succeeding."

D'Emidio thought of Kathy Collins at some point in that first phone conversation. She told me that Kathy Collins was a graduate of P.S. 213 who had gone on to success as a lawyer and was currently working for the

New York Port Authority, specializing in appeals cases. She was scheduled to deliver the graduation address to the school that June 1993, and D'Emidio thought she would be an excellent person to talk with. She was, then, I asked, someone who could speak for the average youngsters in the school? "Not exactly," D'Emidio said, "she's a quadriplegic. She'll speak for herself, but she'll tell you what's on her mind, and she's very observant. Bright as a pin, full of good humor, you'll love her."

One story that has made its way to the school level is about Kathy's parents. When her father came to her mother's bedside after Kathy's birth with rudimentary limbs, her mother asked whether her daughter would be a model. Well, her father is supposed to have said, she doesn't actually have legs. Ah, her mother is reported to have said, then she'll have to model blouses. Well, her father said, she doesn't have arms either. Then, her mother replied, she'll have to model hats. When I told Collins the story over the phone, she laughed. She wasn't sure of its authenticity, but she granted that it *did* suggest the head-on, undismayed way the family met her disability.

During her P.S. 213 days, this matter-of-fact approach made her a great favorite with D'Emidio, who watched her educate the other children. She remembers one child who was fascinated by the screw in Collins' prosthetic arms. "How come you have screws in your arm?" he asked. Collins shrugged, "It's just the way I was made," D'Emidio remembers her saying, and the answer seemed to satisfy the boy.

D'Emidio's lingering tableau is of Collins reading stories to the kindergartners. They sat in a circle around this fourth-grader in a wheelchair while she read. Kathy remembers that period in her schooling vividly, too. Her fourth-grade teacher had suggested it, and Kathy's only concern was whether the younger children would be attentive or up the wall mentally or physically. "They were very attentive," she recounts. "It was good for me to see how they enjoyed it. It was nothing for them to sit there. I was just another somebody reading to them."

"Yes and no," D'Emidio responded, when I read her that Collins quote. "She was very good at it. Clear voice, good delivery, and funny, too. She made them laugh. You just couldn't have found anybody better for the job of a kid reading to kids."

"The school was good for my confidence, too," Collins told me. "I learned that I could compete with the others. I learned that everybody has some kind of disability. And, yes, I do believe they learned from me and the other kids who had disabilities. They didn't look down on us once they saw what we could do." It actually worked the other way around from time to time. D'Emidio and Collins both remember that Collins' handwriting with her prosthetic was so superior to that of the other children that they were occasionally compared unfavorably in this regard to "a kid who has no hands."

I asked Kathy Collins what she planned to say to the graduating eighth-graders and other students. She said she had spoken to a group of eighth-graders in a Catholic school the preceding year and would say much the same thing this time, "leaving out the holy part." She would tell them, she said, to be true to themselves, not to be afraid of making mistakes, and not to worry about what others think.

She did just that. She rolled her wheelchair into the auditorium and up on the stage, which had a ramp as well as a staircase. She got to the podium, picked up the microphone, and spoke directly and plainly to the students, their parents, and staff. When she was finished, she took the warm applause with a smile and moved on down off the stage. D'Emidio, in the audience, thought of the little fourth-grader reading to the kindergarten kids and of how the years tend to get away from one so fast.

Revisiting New York's Public School 213 renewed my interest in the lessons that "special" schools have for public education. MDC's work for the Lilly Endowment in Indiana had put us in touch with the current school reform movement and with educational leadership interested in im-proving kindergarten-through-twelfth-grade performance for all Ameri-can children, with an emphasis on poor and minority children who consti-tute a disproportionate percentage of dropouts and unready graduates. One of these leaders was Phyllis Hart, who had performed something akin to a miracle in Banning High School in Los Angeles in the late 1970s.

In 1975, Banning was a school more renowned for turning out tailbacks for the University of Southern California football team than for producing scholars of any stripe. With a student body 40 percent African-American and 40 percent Hispanic, Banning offered honors courses to only thirty sopho-mores each year and sent only about 5 percent of its graduates to college. Asked about this record, school officials reacted as many school administra-tors still would react around the country today: This was a heavily minority, poor school, and hence the low college-going rates were to be expected.

That was the year that Hart was named college counselor at Banning. She found that she was dealing mainly with three groups of young people. The first group, and by far the largest, was composed of the glum, uninspired refugees from books who had no idea of pursuing further education beyond high school. The second group consisted of students who blithely told her that they were going to college but were not taking the courses necessary for college admission. These were heart-breaking innocents, but no more shaming than the third, much smaller group made up of former graduates who returned to the school like bees in angry clusters to berate anyone who would listen for not preparing them to compete with their college classmates.

Hart took hold. She didn't think her Banning students were inferior either by birth or by upbringing. She, herself, had come from a poor family; neither of her parents had finished high school, and she had been in constant rebellion against their rigid religious style. She happened to have been in a peer group in her native Malvern, New York, that took the PSATs, and she had little confidence either in passing the exam or going on to college, but she did both and then found an inspirational teacher in college as well. Looking about her now, she didn't see that much difference between these minority high school students and herself at their age.

She concluded from long, lacerating interviews that these adolescents had been getting bad advice based on someone's view that they would be lucky to finish high school and were not college "material." Apparently, no one saw that they had the potential Hart could glimpse beneath the everyday-wear attitudes of indifference they assumed to conceal their disappointment and low self-esteem. She told the principal she wanted to sign up a batch of sophomores for college core courses and keep them to their resolve by getting them, their parents, and the school to sign a joint contract, pledging each party to do its best to see that the students succeeded. The principal was dubious, wondering what test Hart would use to screen out applicants who had no chance at all. Hart said she would use no test, ignore all past grades, and sign up anyone who would pledge. The principal balked but was finally worn down by his new counselor's persistence. He decided to let her go ahead and sink, having no notion that she might be able to swim.

Many conversations with students, teachers, parents, and counselors were required, but Hart got a sizable group of pledgees. One day a teacher telephoned to tell her that most of the college-contract students in her class had not bothered to do their homework the night before. Hart walked into the classroom and asked for a show of hands of those who had turned in homework and who had not. Sheepishly, the sizable group of defectors raised their hands. Hart told them that if they wanted to break the contract, they had to get their parents' permission to do so. Otherwise the homework had better be in the next day. To a student, the homework was turned in, and no further problems developed.

Building on modest success her first year, Hart galvanized the school, using various systems of rewards for the academic work similar to those offered for excellence in athletics—a "college-bound" T-shirt for contract-signing honors students among them, for example. She encouraged peer-tutoring and persuaded teachers to teach to the differences as well as the commonality of their students. In the way these things can work with peer-oriented young people, it gradually became "in" to succeed academically at Banning. The thirty sophomores enrolled in honors courses the year before Hart took her assignment grew to two hundred then five hundred and then, astonishingly, eleven hundred in her third year. The college-going rate rose from 5 percent to 68 percent over a seven-year period.

What Hart had done seemed to me to be similar in many ways to what had been done in "alternative" schools I had visited around the country and to what I saw at P.S. 213. The alternative schools were working with students considered to have "failed" in the school system, and P.S. 213 had many students who, because of their disabilities, were thought simply to have no real chance for success. Hart applied the same principles to an ordinary high school in the system. She established academic success as a possibility, showed students that their parents and the school cared about their success, empowered these students with personal responsibility for success, and conferred upon them group or "family" status rewards for sticking to it. She also saw to it that every young person in school had an adult role model providing personal attention. Hart got the students working for each other and eventually won over their teachers to the principles by the sheer force of that success.

The other thing that struck me was that what P.S. 213 and Banning had done could be done by any school with an understanding of the principles of student empowerment, parental involvement, and mutual responsibility. Money was important, particularly the funds needed to provide equity among the poorer and richer school systems, but none of the vital requisites on Hart's list involved major new money.

Clearly, the methods used in schools, like P.S. 213, working with students with disabilities, worked just as well for all students, and perhaps especially well with poor and minority children. The reverse proposition came home to Hart as special education teachers began approaching her with their students' problems. "It opened my eyes," Hart told me. "It extended my range of vision. I realized that I simply hadn't thought of kids with disabilities when I thought of kids who *could* succeed. And there they were, facing the same attitudinal problems in school that minority kids were facing, most of them fully capable of competing once they understood we were behind them." Resource books began to show up at Banning, and students with disabilities began to take advantage of the new opportunities.

Here is a vision of the American public school more in practice today than is commonly thought. I have had the privilege of working with educators around the country who are making these newly collaborative, success-demanding schools work. My own mind's-eye vision is still the boy pushing the wheelchair in P.S. 213 while being tutored by the boy in the wheelchair. A school that prompts this kind of attention to needs and the use of skills teaches more than just the necessary academic skills. It teaches moral values, sharing, and individual responsibility—the very things those who have complained about public education today find too often missing.

In the years since Amy Rowley was admitted to kindergarten at Furnace Woods Elementary School, the operative word for integrating children with disabilities into regular classrooms has changed from "mainstreaming," a word that avoided connotations of degree, to "inclusion," a word more suggestive of full integration.

In an Associated Press column carried by the *Raleigh News and Observer* and many other newspapers, Marcia Reback, chairman of the American Federation of Teachers' Task Force on Special Education, argued that some disabled children should be in special education classrooms, as their learning behavior or emotional disability requires the constant attention of a highly skilled special education teacher.

The viewpoint is one that is shared widely and finds strong support among some parents who believe that their children will suffer as a result of an influx of special education classmates. But Reback's picture of inclusion differed from the inclusion in action I had seen in schools integrating special education students into regular classrooms. While some schools I had observed had featured "full" inclusion, others had made judgments as to which special education students were to be taught separately. And the inclusion classes featured team teaching, using the skills of regular and special education teachers together.

In thinking over these issues and exemplars, at some point I thought of Charlie Brooks, Charles and Helen Brooks' son who had been diagnosed with a learning disability in high school (while Amy Rowley was in Furnace Woods Elementary School) and who had gone on to become a special education teacher. When I telephoned him, I was delighted to learn that not only had he been teaching inclusion classes, but he had also researched and written a paper on the subject.

Sure enough, Charlie Brooks' inclusion involved team teaching. He was paired with a regular education teacher, Debra Cagliostro, in Brookside Elementary School in the Yorktown Heights School District in Westchester County. Together the team recommended which special education children should be included with regular education children in which subject classrooms. The pair pooled their skills to teach in these classrooms. Brooks also had his own adjoining room, where he taught some of the same special education pupils who needed more help in specific subjects.

Young Brooks had been at this task for four years and had made at least one recommendation, which was accepted, that a mentally retarded child be removed from an inclusion classroom because she was not progressing satisfactorily. He was also aware through interviews he had conducted of a child with a traumatic head injury, included in another classroom. This student needed special attention involving up to eight adult attendants at a time, and the highly motivated team teaching her considered her presence detrimental to the class as a whole on that account.

His classroom work combined with research for the paper had given him a broad view of the subject. He pointed out that not all advocacy groups were pushing for full inclusion—among those not doing so were the advocates for the deaf and the learning disabled. In his experience, parents of mentally retarded children and children with physical disabilities have been the most aggressive in seeking inclusion for their children.

For all its difficulties, Brooks is sanguine about inclusion as practiced in Brookside. He and Cagliostro have developed rapport with their twenty-one regular and nine special education pupils and now get positive feedback from both groups. "It's allowed us to demonstrate to some of these learning-disability kids that reading problems don't have to be forever," he says. "The other kids see how the special education kids can excel in some areas. It's not like 'special education' was tattooed on their foreheads." Some parents who did not favor the idea at first seem to be coming around. A survey he made of elementary school educators showed a relatively high degree of acceptance. In fact, he was unable to find any educator who did not believe in some level of inclusion.

At the same time, he picked up concerns that reflected his own. He and others are convinced that criteria must be established by an inclusion committee for appropriate placement of students. In effect, their position is that what Reback described as full inclusion—*all* special education students placed daylong in *all* regular classes—although desirable in principle, may not be in actual practice. Another concern is that school administrators, seeking to save funds, will simply assign all special education students to inclusion classes without supports and—most particularly—without funds for training regular teachers.

What should be done? Brooks presented a plan in his paper calling for selection of a volunteer core of team teachers, assuring them of administration support and extra planning time, providing monthly team meetings to discuss progress and problems, using open houses to explain inclusion to community members and continuing that educational process once classes start, allowing visitors to come into the class at certain times of the year, and encouraging parents of pupils in the class to volunteer to help with projects during the year.

It struck me as a sensible, thoughtful plan, one that has the advantage of coming from the trenches. It also reminded me of Nancy Rowley's plan years before to use the Furnace Woods school for educating educators and the general public about disability. Finally, it stressed the heart's core of the case built up for Amy's education: teach to each child's "unique" learning style and needs in circumstances that provide, insofar as possible, an equal opportunity for that child to learn.

The conflicts over inclusion, however defined, will continue, and at the margins there will be clashes of will that produce unsatisfactory results, but the good schools will find a way and, in the process, develop skills in team teaching that will be productive for all students, not just special education children. If inclusion, however defined, moves us toward fulfilling the promise of an appropriate, free public education for all students in the least restrictive environment, it will be worth the growing pains it produces.

17

If Heaven Isn't Accessible, God Is in Trouble

Two stories in one day's worth of newspapers fixed my mind on the steep, stony road we have had to climb even to be as far along as we are today in our attitudes toward individuals with disabilities. The first news story was about a deaf, ninety-five-year-old African American named Junius Wilson who had had the bad luck to be arrested on an attempted rape charge back in 1925. The State of North Carolina adjudged him insane because he couldn't hear and didn't talk, put him in a segregated hospital, castrated him as a sexual deviant, and forgot about him for sixty-seven years, despite the fact that the criminal charge against him had been dropped. Wilson was in the news because, through efforts of a court-appointed guardian, he was at last being released from the hospital and was receiving sign language services from the state on his outings to malls and restaurants in the city of Goldsboro. On another page in the same paper there was a story about John Hockenberry, a thirty-six-year-old National Public Radio newsman who was joining the new ABC television newsmagazine, "Day One." In an interview, Hockenberry promised that the wheelchair he occupies would be the least interesting thing about the show.

Which was more remarkable, I wondered: that Junius Wilson could have his life stolen from him because he was an African American and deaf or that now, at his age, an effort at restitution was going on? Whether to take heart from that intercession and Hockenberry's move to television? Or to see these events as minor blips on a national-awareness scan that still showed a flat line, indicating no life pulse? I thought of someone who might help me with these questions. I had met Phillip Calkins while working on *Seven Special Kids*. Calkins had grown up in Evanston, Illinois, the son of parents who were Norman Thomas–activists and full-time do-gooders. An academician by training, with graduate work in history at the University of Chicago, he wound up teaching the subject at Duke. A house fire in 1977 cost him his legs and changed his attitude.

"My attitude about people with physical disabilities was typical," he says now. "I had been taught that it was rude to stare. I didn't know any, and I avoided knowing any." Suddenly, one day, there he was, legless, undergoing a long recovery period in the hospital. He saw all about him cheerful, outgoing, persuasive medical people who were devoting themselves wholeheartedly to the program, which for those who had lost use of their legs was to be taught to walk again. He threw himself into this with the abandon that comes from a competitive nature and a seething need to feel whole again. He became a "star," proudly proclaimed by the medics throughout the hospital as "the best" double amputee they ever had. Still, for all the success, he felt uneasy. One day in therapy he was watching a hospital staff person supervising another double amputee who was using the parallel bars in an effort to walk. Tears were pouring down this man's face. "It hurts so bad," he told the staff person. And this bright-eyed, twenty-something woman responded by pointing to Phil, "If Phil can do it, you can do it." A violent light exploded in Calkins' head. "Don't you ever say anything like that again," he told her, his voice rising, "you can't measure this man's pain or anyone else's either."

Later he raked over the residue of his anger for its source. It was, he concluded, that these people were so sure of what their charges needed, so positive that they held the key to recovery, and to whatever happiness might still be in store for patients who had suffered such traumatic injuries. Injuries, he told himself, that the staff members had never experienced and that were not only alien to their comprehension but apparently outside their sphere of real interest. He began reading voraciously about the subject and by degrees turned himself into the ward gadfly, the hospital version of the jailhouse lawyer. He constantly asked awkward questions. Would he need hand controls for his car? Yes, they said. Well, where would he get them? They didn't know.

Finally, on the outside, he would not let matters rest. He came back to the hospital to suggest that he could put them in touch with others who had lost the use of their legs who could come back to help patients understand what they would go through on the outside. The hospital didn't think that was such a good idea. A few more rounds of questions answered or evaded that way convinced him that "they didn't want their patients to have any contact with people like us on the outside. I didn't get it at first, but they didn't want us to be in touch with wheelchair users."

Despite this, he put himself to the task of struggling along on the artificial limbs he had worked so hard with. "You know," he told me, "those legs don't have ankles. If you can imagine it, try thinking of yourself walking up or down a little hill without ankles. It could take you forty minutes to get somewhere you could have gotten to in three minutes in a wheelchair." In search of advice, Calkins went to the wheelchair "jocks," the men who raced and performed athletic events in their chairs. He made a startling discovery: every one of these men had left his hospital walking on artificial limbs or with the aid of braces. The only difference between them now was how long it had taken each to decide to use a wheelchair. In some cases, it was years. Calkins decided it wouldn't take him that long.

"What do you think the people in the hospital were really trying to do?" I asked him, when he took a breath after telling me this story. "Oh," he said, "that's easy. They were trying to make all of us just like them."

Long after we had concluded our talk, I found myself thinking of what Phil Calkins had said. These good, well-intentioned, highly motivated people in the hospital were trying to make amputees and paralytics regain the appearance of normality. To be avoided at all costs was the wheelchair with its visible acceptance of the reality of disability. Walking, even on painful, less practical prosthetics was in this medical way of thinking a far better outcome than being perceived as a cripple. The last thing that would occur to people with such a mind-set would be to ask those who had experienced the injury what they might think about this issue—they were, after all, sick people in need of medical care.

I was struck by the parallels that I detected in the ways Calkins and Amy Rowley had been perceived and treated. Each was seen as a sick person, not really curable but capable of being made more presentable. Amy was to be kept from sign language, which was her "crutch" to this way of thinking, so that she could succeed in a hearing world. For Calkins and his fellow amputees, the wheelchair was the equivalent of sign language. In the medical view, it stamped the word "failure" on the doctors' efforts. From this viewpoint, the object was to produce an individual whose disability would be as nearly invisible as possible. If such an individual could not be made to "pass" she or he could at least be helped to "cover." The school people and the doctors never doubted that this was what an Amy or a Phil would choose to do. They assumed the alternative for each would be disappearance into a world of disability, necessarily separate from those of us who live normal, healthy lives.

It is a hard thing to say because, of course, these are people who believe that they do what they do for the benefit of individuals with disabilities. But that's true only if you accept that they know better than their patients what's good for them. From the point of view of the recovering patients, these medical caregivers are concerned mainly with making them socially acceptable by standards weighed down by a common prejudice. These medical personnel do what they do in the advancement of their idea of what will make their patients acceptable to society, with no heed for the felt needs or the real welfare of the patients themselves.

Phil Calkins tells people that one of the problems individuals with disabilities have is that they lack a written history. As a historian himself, he finds this intriguing, in particular because so much history has been made recently by members of this latest civil rights movement—the various acts of Congress including the historic Americans with Disabilities Act (ADA), the Gallaudet Deaf-President-Now movement, and the protests against the inaccessibility of public transportation led by ADAPT (Americans Disabled for Accessible Public Transit), for a few examples.

In that connection, he agrees that it is too bad that few people in the "able" majority are even aware of the existence of an authentic hero within the disability movement. His name is Wade Blank, and Calkins was not the least surprised that I had never heard of him. Blank attended white, segregated elementary schools, marched to Selma with Martin Luther King, Jr., on a dare from an African American college roommate, and later was ordained a Presbyterian minister. He took his mission and King's message to nursing homes, described in advocacy literature as the "doorstep of the disability ghetto," because they are seen as swallowing up and warehousing working-age individuals with disabilities.

Blank went to work in a nursing home in Denver to change the system from the inside. Everything went well until he suggested that many of those in the nursing home would be better off if they could live, with proper supports, on the outside. He was fired for this lack of fealty to the private nursing home business ethic and decided to pursue his mission from the outside. In 1974, he formed an organization called the Atlantis Community, after the lost continent, a model for consumer-controlled independent living. Then, as now, various state laws made it difficult for individuals with disabilities receiving Medicaid to receive care anywhere except in a nursing home setting, where control of lifestyle goes with the service supplier. Often those so circumscribed were persons of working age who, with minimum care in a home setting, could be productive and regain control over their lives. But to have this chance, they needed an Atlantis to live in, they needed transportation, and they would eventually need fuller integration into society, including education and training.

Blank saw the issues as closely related to those faced by African Americans three decades earlier. "The black movement wanted to ride the buses equally," he said. "The black movement wanted to eat at the Woolworth lunch counters. The black movement wanted the right to vote. The black movement wanted the right to keep their families together. The black movement wanted the right to be integrated into the school system. That's what the disability rights movement wants exactly."

Former nursing home patients "freed" by Blank joined him on July 5 and 6, 1978, in holding an inaccessible bus hostage in downtown Denver. To Blank's surprise, late that night, as the wheelchair siege continued, Colorado Congresswoman Patricia Schroeder handed him coffee and a doughnut. The battle for accessibility of city transit buses spawned ADAPT, the first grassroots, direct action movement of individuals with disabilities, which soon spread to thirty states, Canada, Sweden, and England.

Blank's mild, bespectacled visage peered out at me from the pages of *Incitement,* ADAPT's newsmagazine. In these pictures, he seemed uncomfortable as the target of a camera, shrinking back, turning aside, as though a little unhappy with the attention. Clad in jeans and an ADAPT T-shirt, his sandy hair shoulder length, he was being memorialized in these February 1993 columns. He had drowned the week before in a vain effort to save his son, Lincoln, from an undertow off a Mexican beach where the family was vacationing. On the front page of *Incitement,* the story of his heroism is headlined, "If Heaven Isn't Accessible, God Is in Trouble." I am told it is the kind of humor Wade Blank would have approved.

Calkins points out that Blank lived long enough to see accessible buses mandated by the ADA. At the same time, Calkins feels that a backlash has developed against ADA. "It's too broad, hard to interpret, and it includes a lot of 'nasty' people such as dope addicts and alcoholics," is the way Calkins describes these complaints. He grants some of them are legitimate. "After all, it's harder to define disability than it is race or gender. The 'yeses' and 'nos' are harder to come by." But behind the complaint, he sees the same stonewalling prejudice that has stood fast against gains by individuals with disabilities immemorially. His live-in companion, Sharon Mistler, tells of a wealthy supporter in establishing centers for independent living, in Tulsa, Oklahoma, who objected to her forceful support of the drive for accessible buses. Not one to mince words, he told her that he had supported the center to take care of handicapped people precisely so that they wouldn't be on the same buses normal people took.

Calkins thinks that individuals with disabilities are mistakenly seen by influential people in Washington, including members of Congress and their staffs, as having power. He believes that this is in part the result of the success in passing ADA by a relatively small number of individuals with disabilities who lobbied strenuously and persistently in the halls of Congress, but that it is much more complicated than that. As impressive as it is that a minority could prevail in Congress by saying that what is being done is morally wrong, a closer look shows that this was possible because individuals with disabilities inspire a paternalistic support that springs from the idea that only a mean-spirited person could oppose efforts by such "unfortunate" people to gain a degree of self-respect and self-sufficiency. And, in turn, this paternalistic view—"the 'ain't we nice to you' syndrome," Calkins calls it—rests on the assumption of control by accommodation.

Calkins is pleased with employment gains in Washington for individuals with disabilities in the Clinton administration. But he cites institutional resistance, noting, for example, that it is still very difficult to get an interpreter for a deaf federal employee who could otherwise be sent to computer training to qualify for advancement, but who, without one, is invisibly screened out of the opportunity. This quiet, gray discrimination still extends to the most basic acts of citizenship. Someone in a wheelchair cannot even protest to the polling volunteers that the polling place is inaccessible because, of course, it *is* inaccessible. Mistler once sat in the rain at the bottom of twenty-five steps in a curbside voting situation in Washington, waiting for someone to come out to take her vote—who never came.

Coming face-to-face with this kind of casual disfranchisement can breed either a descent into helplessness or a stiffening of the will that can be seen as unreasonableness. "When we are adamant about something, we're often seen as being mindlessly stubborn," Calkins says. "For instance, I've had criticism for saying that any accommodation that depends upon electricity is unsatisfactory. But the truth is that when a chairlift breaks down somewhere, it falls into the category of the 'Negro' schools in the old racially segregated system needing repair. Remember, in that situation the repairs just never quite got done. It's the same with us now. The money goes where the power is and we don't have the power."

Calkins feels that a fair test of the real power advocates for individuals with disabilities wield is the number of congressional staff people who have disabilities. "When every member of Congress has to have a staff person with a disability just as every member has to have women and minorities now, then I'll say we're developing power," he observes. "At the present time, for all of its effort, the movement for disability rights is far behind similar efforts for every other minority, including Native Americans."

Mary Johnson is one advocate who happens to agree with Calkins' assessment. I came to her for enlightenment on the status of disability rights efforts currently through reading *The Disability Rag*, a potent, hard-hitting, bimonthly journal. She was still editing the *Rag* at the time we talked, in 1993, but was planning to leave it in other hands to look for other challenges.

Johnson describes herself, typically, as growing up not knowing anyone with a disability, not wanting to, and not expecting to. As a college graduate with an English major and a yen for journalism, one day in 1972 she agreed to have lunch with a woman who had cerebral palsy and wanted her to serve on the board of an organization formed to advance civil rights issues for individuals with disabilities. As she listened to a recitation of common problems she felt could easily be solved by a friendly society, Johnson felt that old lightbulb-clicking-on sensation. She took the job, wrote a grant proposed for a center for independent living in 1978, and in 1980 began publication of the *Rag*.

"We have two problems," she told me. "The first is that a lot of individuals with disabilities see themselves as being—I hate this word, but I'll use it—'mainstreamed'. They want so badly to be 'normal' that they do not identify with the problem. They may resent the way they are viewed by the normal majority, but they fear that by expressing this resentment they will lose ground. Do you remember how gays were back in the 1940s?—afraid of being identified—well, that's where lots of people with disabilities now are.

"Secondly, we never seem to be able to deal with the press in a sophisti-cated way." She cited as an example a debate going on in New York City at the time over the issue of public toilets. The issue was whether public toilets, which most observers agreed were badly needed in the city, should be installed with only some of them accessible to individuals with mobility disabilities or whether all the toilets should be accessible. JCDecaux, a prominent European installer of kiosk toilets, had refused to make all the unlocked, coin-operated toilets accessible, arguing that experience showed that the larger kiosks needed for wheelchair accessibility would shelter drug dealers and other undesirables. The company proposed to install a number of locked, accessible toilet kiosks and provide passkeys to individuals with disabilities. "To read the press," Mary Johnson told me, "you would think that it's the fault of individuals with disabilities that the city doesn't have public toilets. The advocacy folks are simply saying that we've got the law on our side instead of explaining our position that the company should manufacture one toilet for all and if it can't do that, bids ought to be con-sidered from others who can."

Reading through a batch of stories and editorials about the situation, I did get the impression that individuals with disabilities were the "bad guys" in most accounts of what was then a stalemate. The *New York Times* had found editorially the case made by JCDecaux "cogent." The editorial con-tinued, "Representatives of the disabled, however, oppose that idea as dis-criminatory. Preventing the misuse of larger units, they say, is a law en-forcement problem. And they wonder if a different company might be able to provide a more workable design, accessible to all. These responses are unrealistic. . . . Compromise, therefore, offers the best answer."* The *Dis-ability Rag* noted that same month acidly that by compromise, the *Times* clearly meant for folks with disabilities to accept that they would have only a fixed percentage of toilets available and that they would be locked.

In the summer of 1992, a four-month trial of the JCDecaux toilets in three Manhattan locations took place. However, for each inaccessible toilet, an accessible one was provided and, while locked, was staffed by an attendant who handed out a magnetic entry card to wheelchair users. The attendant also cleaned the toilet, as the accessible model, unlike the regu-lar one, wasn't self-cleaning. Major media proclaimed the experiment a success. "Some of the disabled consider the separate units discriminatory and vow to resist any city-wide program that includes them," the *Times*

---

* *New York Times*, November 13, 1982, p. A-28.

editorialized. "But that objection ought not to obstruct the service for the whole city. The success of the JCDecaux models puts the burden on the disabled groups either to come up with a plausible alternative or accept the separate units."

But that meant accepting at face value everything the toilet manufacturer had said; the test was set up on ideal grounds not intended for actual use. Clearly, there would be fewer accessible, locked toilets than regular ones (some reports of the JCDecaux kiosks in Europe put the ratio at 1 to 6). When the need arose, someone using a wheelchair would most likely find herself or himself nearer an inaccessible toilet than an accessible one, not a favorable situation for someone whose mode of locomotion is a wheelchair. And who, exactly, would be issued the passkeys and how would that be done? And how would it help wheelchair visitors to the city? How would the accessible toilets be cleaned in actual practice?

Beyond these practical matters, which got little editorial discussion in the major media, lay the principle of equity, which got no serious discussion at all. This was illustrated neatly, if unintentionally, by *New York Newsday* which, on November 14, 1992, opined that demands of equal treatment over the toilet issue created "practical problems" and suggested that City Hall "should install only as many larger toilets as warranted by the needs of the disabled."

Mary Johnson noted in a December 3 letter to *Newsday* that it had only the day before—observing that "sometimes plumbing reflects our values"—complained that two women senators had to "schlepp downstairs to a public loo" when toilets for their male colleagues were just off the Senate floor. "Certainly," *New York Newsday* had summed up, "Equal access to toilets must count among the blessings of liberty."

"Just not for disabled people, eh,?" Johnson noted in her letter to the editor.

Some time after this, I discovered, the saga of public toilets in New York City departed from the level of the curious and soared to new heights of the bizarre. Having earlier declared that fully accessible toilets for every location would be prohibitively expensive and a societal threat, JCDecaux eventually declared itself ready to build and install the most accessible toilets ever seen, across the board. By then, however, advertising and site-selection problems, not to mention politics, had complicated the issue. When requests for proposals were called for, JCDecaux didn't bid. The only bidder was a German company, Wall Design. At this writing, when, how, and where the toilets would be available was up in the air. It did appear, however, that disability advocates won few adherents to their cause while carrying the day on their legal position.

I asked Johnson whether the public relations weakness disability advocates exhibited in this conflict wouldn't make it even more likely that difficult issues, such as the one about supplying attendant services for employees who need them on the job, will be looked on with disfavor. I noted that these were, after all, issues different from those faced by minority and women's groups who don't need physical adjustments or modifications to achieve their measure of equality.

"I think it is a mistake to try to make exact comparisons between other civil rights kinds of organizations and the disability movement," she said. "One comparison that does stand up is that we can easily go back in time to when women simply had no rights and blacks were slaves. Times change, attitudes change, and we believe that the time for disability rights will come, too. But I like to think of the movement more in terms of an environmental one. We are trying to create a society in which everyone has freedom. We are technologically capable of doing that right now. Our problem is that we are still stuck with an 'us' and 'them' viewpoint of disability. Why do we have to do that for 'them,' is the question we ask ourselves. We forget that the ramp we are putting in for 'them' may serve 'us' one day, quite likely will serve someone close and dear to us. The issue is, Do we want a society that takes account of this fact or ignores it? Do we want to continue to turn away from disability because we are afraid of it?"

18

To Be Who We Are

For Michael Pierschalla, there have been two great blessings. The first occurred when he could hear his own voice and the voices of others again; the second, when he could, at last, hear music again. It is not quite what it used to be when he was a nineteen-year-old playing guitar in his garage and listening to Eric Clapton and Aretha Franklin, but music once again moves him and now, in his late thirties, his tastes have broadened and he is even listening to jazz.

The cause of Pierschalla's loss of hearing is still unknown. He awoke one morning to a loud roaring in his ears that left him during succeeding days entrapped in total silence. But there is no mystery about how he regained the hearing he has after many years of deafness. It is a tiny chip, about the size of a shirt button, implanted in the snail-shaped cochlea in his inner ear. Pierschalla, from Cambridge, Massachusetts, spent time in 1993 with doctors and scientists at Duke University and North Carolina's Research Triangle Institute helping them develop a new-generation cochlear implant they believe will significantly improve hearing for those who can profit from implantation. Pierschalla's talent for analyzing and describing what he hears proved useful to the medical science team doing the fine-tuning.

But as local newspapers discovered when they checked with deaf advocacy groups around the area, cochlear implants are not precipitating a long, waiting line of deaf persons. The least interesting reasons for this are physical and technical. The implants do not work for everyone, and there is no way to predict before surgery how much help they will be. Previous generations of implants have been, in many cases, disappointments. For this reason, and because most of us fear sudden change of an unfathomable nature, a number of deaf people would disqualify themselves as candidates for implants.

The more interesting reason deaf people decline the opportunity, however, has to do with a powerful sense of community shared by many, especially those who are prelingually deaf. Properly regarding sign as a real language, and their own, and observing that their situation breeds a personal expressiveness, a deafness-oriented sense of humor, and other commonalities, they have come to see themselves as sharing a deaf culture. They have invested pride in it. At its extreme edge, this view has a strong separatist tilt. In his book, *The Mask of Benevolence*, linguist Harlan Lane quotes British deaf leader Paddy Ladd: "The deaf community regards the birth of each and every deaf child as a precious gift," and picks up a quote from the *Boston Globe* in which a deaf woman from a deaf family said she hoped that her baby would be born deaf.*

Is there such a thing as a deaf culture? Nancy and Clifford Rowley believe that the deaf culture exists inevitably among deaf people with few or no contacts with hearing people, in part because of sign language and in part because of isolation. Amy felt an ideology of deafness all around her at Gallaudet University, as she moved back and forth between that world and the hearing world around it. She told me once that she was teased by deaf friends at Gallaudet because her signing was "slurred," the result, she was sure, of the amount of time she was spending in the hearing world.

One of the most interesting responses I got to the question of whether there is a deaf culture was from a hearing person, Margaret Higgs, Amy's schoolmate from Mountain Lakes who became fascinated with the world of the deaf and was studying, when I last talked with her, education of the deaf at Flagler College in Florida. Her world is populated by a strong mixture of hearing and deaf persons, and she has no doubt that there is a deaf culture, which she described to me in some detail in a letter: "Deaf people have their own culture, shown by their attitudes, art, belief, manners, common experience, and history. Even courtship is different. Deaf people have a general view of what is right and wrong according to their culture. Fast relationships are not looked upon [permissively] as they are in our culture. Views on drugs as well as many current social issues differ from hearing

* New York: Alfred A. Knopf, 1992, p. 20.

people." Although this mentality draws some deaf people together in an "us" versus "them" stance to the hearing world and eventually produces a call for deaf separatism, it's worth remembering that virtually every minority that has borne up against prejudice and discrimination has had at one time or another a strong, vocal separatist minority.

But as Roger D. Freeman, Clifton F. Carbin, and Robert J. Boese point out in *Can't Your Child Hear?*, for most deaf people "it is misleading to talk of choosing *either* the deaf world (or 'ghetto') *or* full integration into the hearing world" (p. 192). The existence of a deaf culture does not change the fact that deaf Americans belong to many 'us' groups based on professional, social, and personal attachments that have little or nothing to do with the fact of their deafness. Deaf people are Chicago Bulls fans, gourmet cooks, fitness freaks, table tennis players, and fashion models. Progress toward breaking down barriers has been swift and now deaf people can communicate with others on the telephone through a national relay system, closed-television captioning is mandatory, interpreting services are significantly improved, and films about deafness no longer are chained to stereotypes. In Marlee Matlin, the deaf even share with hearing people a matinee idol who is one of their own.

Far from prefiguring a powerful movement toward exclusivity, the current fascination with separatism may mask a more general concern deaf people have that the uniqueness of their world—the ease and grace of their mutual signing, their emotional openness, the camaraderie that attaches itself to their public and private meetings—may be threatened with extinction. The arrival of another deaf baby not only presents the deaf parents with the familiar rather than new and potentially problematical communication, it symbolically reassures the deaf community of cultural continuity.

It is only in this context that the promise and the threat of a new generation of vastly improved cochlear implants can be understood. For someone like Michael Pierschalla who heard perfectly until he was nineteen, the question of whether he would like to hear again answers itself. For someone born to silence, nurtured by silent, signing parents and peers, grown to adulthood swathed in the protective culture of the deaf, the question is far less easily answered. To the prelingually deaf person, it may be unanswerable. What would it be like to hear? Would hearing interrupt concourse with one's only friends, one's deaf friends? These are the first questions the lifelong deaf person might have to deal with. The emotional turmoil associated with the assumption of one of the senses at an adult age was described by

Oliver Sacks in a *New Yorker* article about a blind man who suddenly re-gained his sight, lost in childhood forty years earlier.* He found himself physically and psychologically overwhelmed by the task of adjusting to a visual world that he could not imagine as a blind man and could not fully comprehend as a seeing person. "One must die as a blind person to be born again as a seeing person," Sacks wrote. "And here blindness is no more a negative condition, a privation, than seeing. It is a *different* condition, a different form of being, with its own sensibilities, coherence, and feelings" (p. 70).

So it must surely be in the world of the prelingually deaf. It is not difficult to grasp the magnitude of potential conflict. "One friend of mine," writes Margaret Higgs, "who is profoundly deaf, wants a deaf child because she feels she will be more involved in the child's life, and that they will have a better understanding of each other. Another friend, who is hard of hearing, says that she doesn't necessarily want her child to be deaf, however, she would rather have a deaf child than one who is hard of hearing. She has felt that she is not accepted in the deaf or the hearing world and does not want the same for her child. She wants her child to be one or the other, deaf or hearing."

—

Michael Chatoff's law school friend and courtroom helper, Harvey Barri-son, believes to this day that the law firms that supported *Rowley* should later have found work for Chatoff. Barrison is referring to firms representing the numerous advocacy groups that filed friends-of-the-court petitions on the Rowleys' behalf when the case went up to the Supreme Court. "These were large firms," Barrison told me, "who could have made room for him. It was really a low blow that as soon as the case was decided, he never heard again from those law firms he had worked so closely with over months. Often they didn't even want Mike to take the case. They wanted to put their own people in to do the oral argument. They didn't give Mike much support then and they totally abandoned him afterwards."

I asked Barrison if he thought that the failure to help Chatoff might not be, in itself, a form of prejudice. "It seems to be very bad against lawyers who are deaf," he said. "It has to do with perceptions of the dynamics of the courtroom. You will find blind lawyers but not many deaf ones. I

* "A Neurologist's Notebook: To See or Not to See," *New Yorker* 69 (December 27, 1993/January 3, 1994): 59–73. Sacks also wrote a knowing book about deafness, *Seeing Voices: A Journey into the World of the Deaf* (Berkeley: University of California Press, 1989).

thought Michael proved a lawyer who was deaf could do well in courtroom situations, but that negative feeling is still there."

Chatoff rarely talks about this phase of his life, and it is clear, when he does, that it was painful. He had felt himself to be king of the mountain before the first, staggering illness robbed him of his hearing. Temporarily downed by that, he had struggled through law school against considerable odds and had worked his way up, through the *Rowley* case, to a degree of prominence he could not have predicted. But the celebrity came to him at a cost that would prove incalculable. He had worked long, daily hours, week in and week out, between the demands of the case and his job. Then came the frightening and baffling recurrence of the tumors and the second set of operations.

The new illness served to distance him farther from friends, one of whom had written him while he was working on the case. Too busy to respond just then, Chatoff was further delayed by the illness and, when he did write later, he did not hear again from his friend. He blames himself for the lapsing of this friendship, which had not been harmed by his first set of operations. Other friendships simply did not survive his becoming deaf. One college friend of Chatoff's I talked with made it clear that difficulties of communication had something to do with the ending of their friendship. Chatoff attributes being dropped by this man and one other of his old friends to fear: "They knew me as a healthy and vigorous person," he wrote me. "I represented what could happen to them and they didn't want to be reminded of it."

While he still does see old friends and has made others in recent years, he is acutely aware that becoming deaf as an adult has left him dangling between the two worlds of the deaf and the hearing. He has deaf friends and hearing friends but no sense of belonging to either world. For a time, he dated a young woman who was legally blind. Since then, his dates have more often than not been with women who have no disabilities. He has not found a deaf woman he was attracted to. In 1987, he suffered yet a third recurrence of the tumor in the right ear, necessitating another painful and dangerous operation, and other less major procedures have been performed. Nevertheless, he tries to keep an optimistic view of the future and has annual tests to see if more trouble is on the way. Lately, the news has been good. He lifts weights, plays bridge, rows, and in warm weather jogs. He also tries to keep his finger on the pulse of discrimination, often speaking to groups on the 1990 Americans with Disabilities Act.

He likes to use the story of his discovery of the inaccessibility to the deaf of the 911 emergency phone system in New York City in connection with these public discussions of ADA. As a younger, hearing man, he says, he assumed all deaf people could use 911, but he didn't care much because he didn't know any deaf people and didn't want to. Even after he lost his hearing, he assumed that the deaf could use this vital emergency system just as others did.

When a friend told him he was wrong, he reacted at first with shock and, then, as he learned how the system worked, with anger. If a deaf person in New York City wanted to use 911, this individual would have to dial an eleven-digit number on his TTY first, which would put him in touch with a relay station in Goshen, New York. The operator in Goshen then would look up the seven-digit number of the deaf caller's particular precinct and would dial that number. However, even that call would not get the caller to the 911 system but only to the precinct desk that handles routine calls. From there, the caller might be only one more connection away from 911, but, in the event of a real crisis like a fire, and given the time already consumed, quite possibly beyond help even before the call for help had been received.

It angered Chatoff that he and other deaf citizens of New York had been paying taxes and phone surcharges all those years for a system that excluded them as surely as if they had no telephones. It was insulting. To his mind, it was fraud if not downright thievery. Worse, it was an obligation that the city knew it had and one to which a "life or death" responsibility could properly be assigned. Last, he believed it was in direct violation of ADA, which had been passed two years earlier, and which had called for the 911 system to be extended to deaf patrons by January 26, 1992, when the act went into effect. On January 27, 1992, Chatoff filed suit against the City of New York.

The city's position was that it had planned to install TTY capabilities as part of a major, more comprehensive revision of the emergency phone system. The revision was scheduled to be completed no earlier than June 1995, at a cost estimated at around $200 million. But while delays sought by the city's legal staff slowed down the progress of Chatoff's suit, it took a judge only a brief portion of a hearing to tell both parties that he would find for the plaintiff, set a deadline for compliance, and impose a daily fine against the city for each day of delay after that date. He suggested that a wise alternative for the city would be to work out a settlement with the plaintiff.

On December 1, 1992, Mayor David N. Dinkins held a press conference to announce that on that day New York City had begun operation of a system that provided immediate access to 911 for the deaf and hard-of-hearing. This was accomplished by the installation of TTYs at all 74 of the city's 911 stations and the training of operators to use these devices. The total cost was put at $46,300. The mayor's press release referred briefly to Chatoff's suit.

Chatoff might well take up the cudgels again for another deaf cause, as he also believes that individuals with disabilities have to create and pursue crises in order to be heard. Referring to the city's stated original plans to make 911 accessible, he wrote in the house organ of Telecommunications for the Deaf, Inc.: "If you believe that, I have a bridge I'd like to sell you. If I had not brought this suit against New York City, it is a virtual certainty that it [the city] would never have done anything. Many government and private entities will continue to do nothing more than pay lip service to the obligation to provide disabled people with equal opportunities as long as they believe they can get away with it."*

He believes that the *Rowley* battle was more than worth the waging for the educational value it had for the public, but that, while significant progress has been made by the deaf in recent years, they have been maligned for so long and began the race so far behind that they still lag sadly. "The problem is one of attitude on the part of people without disabilities," he wrote to me. "There are loads of laws and regulations on the books, but the laws and regulations mean nothing until you change people's attitudes."

Chatoff is aware that many deaf people would prefer not to be able to hear. "Deaf culture is almost like a sheltered workshop, a security blanket," he wrote me. "I understand it but I want no part of it. I do not need a security blanket. I'm not deaf because I want to be. It was either deaf or dead. I chose the former but I have the wherewithall to stand up for myself with anyone." He has a TTY, light relays, and uses sign language. "The difference between someone who believes in deaf culture and me is that I do them or have them to ameliorate the effects of my deafness so that I can be a part of society at large. People who believe in deaf culture have them and do them to establish a culture separate and apart from everyone else." He does believe that being deaf, however, has made him a better person, more sensitive to the needs of others and more understanding.

While he would like to move into active practice or the teaching of law, the fact that his courtroom fame was fleeting does not seem to bear heavily on his shoulders. He did not comment on this to me, but I noticed that

* "Emergency Services in New York City," *GA-SK* newsletter (Spring 1993): 13.

not once, in the stories I saw written by the New York press about the 911 suit and its settlement, was Michael Chatoff ever identified as the first deaf lawyer in history to argue before the Supreme Court. In one story about the case, in fact, the *New York Times* reporter identified him as "a Queens florist with a hearing impediment."*

His former clients, the Rowleys, have generally fared well in the eighteen years since their battle for Amy's education began. Nancy Rowley was operated on for a tumor near the brain in October 1988—a major operation and not without its risks—yet was able to attend a ceremony on December 8 of that year to receive, from New York attorney Joseph Blum, the Berger Award for Achievement of the New York Society for the Deaf, given for "enhancing the quality of life for all deaf people." She made a gradual but essentially full recovery from the effects of her surgery. Much of her time in recent years has been spent with the New Jersey State Task Force on Educational Interpreting, teaching young students at her church's Bible school, and making speeches to major corporations on their responsibilities in the area of deafness under ADA.

Clifford, too, has been recognized for his work in pushing out the frontier of communication for the deaf. He has been instrumental in establishing a relay system that enables deaf individuals to call any number in the telephone book by TTY, get a relay operator who will convert the message to the proper mode of communication, and pass it on to its intended recipient. In February 1989, Clifford represented the New Jersey Association for the Deaf in a presentation to the state Board of Public Utilities that persuaded the board to try the relay system, already available at that time, to phone customers in California, New York, and Alabama. Clifford and Albert Hlibock, who worked with him on the project, were honored in September 1992 with a testimonial dinner.

Amy and John have done well also. At this writing, Amy was taking premed courses at the University of Wisconsin, and John, now married, was continuing his degree work at the University of Arizona.

Looking back over the years, the Rowleys feel that their battle for Amy's education was worth the fight. They have no regrets. They see the technological progress that is all around us now and still savor the legislative achievement of the ADA. But their store of optimism is not sufficient to make them feel upbeat about attitudinal change. They haven't seen much of that on the part of hearing and nondisabled people up to now. They pin

* *New York Times,* June 28, 1992, p. I-26.

their hopes on ADA to bring individuals with disabilities into the list along with those who cannot be discriminated against by reason of their race, their creed, their gender, or their religion.

Like others in this narrative, their views about the education of deaf children have broadened in the years since litigation for Amy was begun. If anything, they feel more strongly now that the wishes of the parents in this regard must be respected. While they are still convinced that the means of communication chosen for Amy, total communication, remains the best available, they would put even more emphasis now on the surroundings in which the child matured. Clifford recently quoted favorably the principal of the New York School for the Deaf, Dr. David Spidal, that whatever means the family chooses in the education of a deaf child will work so long as there is love in the family and full inclusion of the child.

Writing to me recently for Clifford as well as for herself, Nancy observed that they knew one deaf family who had a stated preference for a deaf child, but that this was a matter of one member of this family's fears for the future of the child outside the protective layering of their deaf culture. "For a family like us," she wrote, "we are happy to have either a hearing or a deaf child. Both of our hearing and deaf children blend well in the love of the family as well as having clear communications."

Would Clifford or Nancy "take the cure" assuming that one were available in the form of a cochlear implant or some other device? They would not. "For a family like us, we have created our life style," she told me. "The psychological impact is something we wouldn't want. Amy feels the same way and Johnny understands that. We are who we are."

And who am I, now? In the years it has taken me to write this book, I have aged ordinarily. Instead of arthritis in one knee, I now have it in both. I am losing hearing, as measured by a further falling away from my wife's acute hearing. My lenses are thicker by the year. I've been blind-sided by a bleeding ulcer, an event that has changed the level and octane of my fluid intake. I know these are common, unspectacular symptoms of aging, and I am grateful. Maybe I am even more grateful for having spent time working with and listening to people far less lucky who have had no time for self-pity.

I have found measuring rods, events that help me to see change in myself. Recently, I have been reading of a dispute over a memorial to FDR under construction in Washington. The plan has included a sculpture of the former president, who will be seated with his cape draped around him and his dog at his feet. Nothing in the sculpture will show a wheelchair or in any other way indicate his disability. Defenders of this decision say that Roosevelt managed it this way during his life and to show him otherwise now would be revisionist history.

I think there is something to that position, but I find myself resonating immediately and deeply to the opposing position, that Roosevelt's disability was a vital part of who he was and hiding it now, long after the fact of its political expediency, fosters the idea that disability continues to display a negative personal value today. I believe that a Roosevelt today would not shrink from showing himself as he really was, that he would feel safe in showing pride in what he had overcome. Believing that gives me a sense of some little progress made in our thinking on the subject over the last half-century.

A different, more contemporary spirit imbues the opening lines of a poem by Wanda Barbara in the issue of *Incitement* dedicated to Wade Blank after his drowning death:

> Wade, what a way to go,
> You could have at least become a crip first,
> after all your work, perseverance, commitment,
> love, and refusal to give up on our behalf.*

"You could have at least become a crip first." The line is one I might not have understood at all a while back. I think I get the message now. Barbara sees Blank as "wise" in the sense Goffman borrowed from usage by homosexuals for someone not one of them but understanding and accepting of their difference. She is deeply admiring of a comrade lost, but will not blind herself to the irony that his death may have robbed him of a central experience of those for whom he fought so hard in life.

In *Disability Rag*, Ed Hooper, a paraplegic, takes that thought a logical step further. He is measuring himself for the "would I take the cure test?" In that connection he makes the point that acceptance of one's disability is a vital part of "disability pride."

Looking at who he is, Hooper observes: "I am happier now than I was before I broke my neck. . . . I love my wife and family more. I have a better rapport with most everyone. . . . I'm a better person now than I was before my disability."† What he is saying goes beyond the pride and self-

---

* Untitled poem, *Incitement,* published by Atlantis/ADAPT (January–February 1993): 6.

† "A Question of Cure," *Disability Rag* (January–February 1989): 19.

esteem gained through dealing with the rough knocks of life applicable in different degrees to us all. It has to do with the attainment of self-knowledge and the truism that the more deeply one digs into one's own reservoir of strength to continue, the more universal one's acceptance by and tolerance of others and one's empathy with the human experience.

Could we "take the cure," lose the disability, and retain the pride and the experience—have the best of both worlds—Hooper asks himself. He admits that it would be wonderful to rise from his chair and "run like hell." It isn't going to happen but, beyond that, he doesn't need to be cured. He has survived, stronger and more sensitive to others than he was before. Confronting that, the question of "cure" becomes anachronistic, a proposition without a first person pronoun in it. The answer is—forget the question.

I wish I could say that I am entirely comfortable with who I am but that would be wishful thinking. I'm still absorbing what I think I've learned, still processing data. But I do know I'm a more open person than I was ten years ago, more willing to listen, working harder to understand. I have come to see how blinding the prejudice of the person who wrote the *Voices* column really was and that the real victim of prejudice is, not just the target whose life chances are reduced, but also the prejudiced person, who locks the gates of understanding against himself.

And it comes to me again that, because there are so many of us who mistakenly buy the idea that we feel kindly toward and protective of individuals with disabilities, this prejudice is more pernicious than others we have dealt with in our society. If you are an anti-Semite, you must choose your company carefully, so as not to put yourself with others who might not only disagree but hate what you think. This cadre of others is a civilizing force because it is capable of inflicting shame. As it grows stronger, it drives the prejudice down by bringing it out in the harsh light of day. This has the effect of making the prejudice unpopular. How could such a force come from those of us who regard ourselves as able? If we can't imagine that we are prejudiced, we may not be so easily shamed. Is it possible nonetheless for us to find our way down the road of self-awareness to the place where we might understand and empathize with an Ed Hooper or a Wanda Barbara?

I think it necessary to believe this can happen—against all odds. The fear that drives us to reject the one minority we may become a part of is, on its very face, self-imprisoning. It holds us at length from ourselves and makes us less than we might be. It stands in our collective way of creating a society that replaces passive, rejecting pity with active, involving acceptance.

Because understanding this is a deeply personal act on each person's part doesn't mean that we don't badly need leadership. A Roosevelt for today, willing to show himself strong in a condition that otherwise might have suggested weakness, could provide public inspiration.

Failing that, I think we have to make do with what we already have, which is far more than we have yet noticed. We are in the second generation of the "coming out" of individuals with disabilities, the dawning of an era of visibility under new laws that place all of us more often together on common grounds in schools, workplaces, and public meeting places. The Amy Rowleys and the Charlie Brookses and the children of the Carol Blumbergs, the Inez Jangers, the Barry Felders—along with the new breed of poised, confident, "able" collaborators like John Rowley and Margaret Higgs—constitute the new wave of the future.

Laws such as the Americans with Disabilities Act are crucial, but just as important is this everyday, everywhere visibility. The experience of African Americans and other ethnic minorities warns us to prepare for bitter setbacks at every point of advance, but it also suggests that an increment of hard-won gains will remain. The children with disabilities born in the age of ADA will have opportunities that their parents never dreamed of and we have reason to hope that their children will look back on narratives like this one with the amazement that tales from slavery inspire in the young today.

If we take seriously the imperative of creating a good society, this has to happen because our democratic ideals tell us that fair is fair. It may happen also, I think, because we will have in our homes, among our friends and family, many more individuals who would suffer the stigma of prejudice if we could not change. We are living longer as a society and, with greater age, comes more of what we call disability as well as what we have not yet learned to recognize as special, invaluable ability.

I feel more ready for what I think is to come. I look harder now than before to discover who this new person is rather that what she or he appears to be. I am more willing to step forward and less likely to hide behind avoidance. In a curious, new way I'm looking forward to seeing how we handle this challenge to understand our common humanity, to join in averring life rather than running in fear. Like my friend Elizabeth Hudson, I'd like to live to be a hundred just to see how much progress we make on the subject of ability–disability in the intervening years. Or, as she put it, to see how all this sorts itself out.

INDEX